THE BUREAU

Also by Ronald Kessler

THE

BUREAU

The Secret History of the

FBI

RONALD KESSLER

ST. MARTIN'S PRESS ❧ NEW YORK

www.stmartins.com

ISBN 0-312-30402-1

First Edition: May 2002

1   3   5   7   9   10   8   6   4   2

For Pam, Rachel, and Greg Kessler

Contents

BOOK THREE

PROLOGUE

When Barry Mawn headed the Boston Field Office, the copilot of EgyptAir Flight 990 purposely plunged his Boeing 767-300 into the Atlantic off Nantucket. When Mawn headed the Newark Field Office, the Unabomer struck in New Jersey, killing public relations executive Thomas Mosser. Federal Bureau of Investigation agents joked that they did not want Mawn, an affable Irishman from Boston, to come to their office. He brought trouble.

Now, as the fifty-six-year-old Mawn was going through his in box at the New York Field Office just before 8:45 A.M. on September 11, 2001, he heard an airplane flying lower than it should have. As the assistant FBI director in charge of the office of 1,100 agents, Mawn had a corner suite on the twenty-eighth floor of the Jacob Javits Federal Building at 26 Federal Plaza. From his north window, he could see the Manhattan skyline. From his west window, he could see part of the World Trade Center.

Just then, Mawn heard an explosion. Kathy MacGowan, his secretary, screamed.

"The World Trade! The World Trade!" she shouted.

Mawn ran to her window, which had a full view of the 110-story Twin Towers. Black smoke was billowing from the North Tower. MacGowan said a commercial jet had crashed into it. Mawn thought it was an accident.

"Call my Evidence Response Team," Mawn told her. "Just in case, call the SWAT and the Joint Terrorism Task Force. Send them to Church and Vesey. I'll head in that direction."[1]

Mawn removed his .40-caliber Glock from his oak desk, the one J. Edgar Hoover once used in New York, and stuffed the pistol in his holster. Behind the desk on the wall was an artist's sketch of Mawn and others at a hearing in federal court in Newark on charges against Unabomer Theodore J. Kaczynski.

As Mawn was about to leave, David N. Kelley called. He was the chief of the U.S. attorney's Terrorism Unit. Mawn agreed to meet him outside the building. Together, they hustled the eight blocks to Vesey and Church streets, at the northeast corner of the World Trade Center. As they got closer, Mawn saw people hanging out of the highest windows. One person jumped.

Police Commissioner Bernard Kerik and other police officials were already there. Like Mawn, they thought the crash was a ghastly accident.

"As we were standing there, we saw another plane come in from the north and turn around," Mawn said. "We lost sight of it for a minute, but the next thing, it hit the South Tower. We were stunned. Everyone instantly recognized it's not an accident. We're under attack."

With both towers in flames, dozens of people were jumping from a hundred stories up. Huge slabs of concrete and hunks of burning metal started raining down. Mawn learned later that an eight-hundred-pound wheel assembly from one of the planes landed three blocks north of where he was.

Everyone started running for their lives. Mawn wedged himself into the space behind the cab of an ambulance van. When the rain of debris began to diminish, he headed back to the corner, where he saw Kelley and the police officials. By now, hundreds of FBI agents had converged on the area. Mawn told agents to set up a command post.

After several tries, Mawn got through on his cell phone to Robert S. Mueller III, the new FBI director. Mawn told him that the phones were down and they needed Air Force jets. A week earlier, Mueller, a prosecutor and former Marine, had taken over from Louis J. Freeh. Under Freeh, the FBI had lurched from one debacle to another, its credibility and morale shattered. Now the bureau faced the greatest chal-

lenge in its ninety-three-year history: tracking down those responsible
for the worst attack ever on America and making sure another attack
did not occur.

After the White House, Congress, and the Supreme Court, no institution was as powerful as the FBI. No institution was as important in
preserving American freedoms. But from the beginning, the bureau had
engaged in abuses, trampling on individual rights. From DNA analysis
to profiling, from confirmation of Supreme Court justices to investigations of plane crashes, Mafia figures, corporate frauds, and spies, the
FBI would become involved in almost every aspect of American life.
Yet the question remained whether having what amounted to a national
police force was consistent with a free society. And now the question
was whether the agency could be trusted with the unprecedented task
before it.

Mawn's mind flashed back to the 1993 hit on the World Trade
Center, when six people were killed. He remembered when the FBI
foiled an attempt to blow up the Holland and Lincoln tunnels, the
United Nations, and the FBI's New York Field Office. Osama bin Laden
and his al-Qaeda were behind the terrorist plot and, as it later turned
out, had connections through Al Kifah Refugee Center in Brooklyn to
some of those convicted in the 1993 attack. Now bin Laden had succeeded beyond his wildest expectations.

As Mawn and Kelley began walking west on Vesey, Mawn looked
down and saw a female leg on the street. It was severed at the knee, a
pink sock and white sneaker still on it.

"Jesus," Mawn whispered.

Mawn heard a rumble. He and Kelley were standing outside 7 World
Trade Center, a smaller building in the shadow of the Twin Towers.
Edmund Hartnett, the police department's chief of intelligence, had just
joined them. The deafening, earthshaking roar was the South Tower
imploding, coming down all around them, along with more people,
some holding hands on their way down.

"I knew I couldn't outrun it," Mawn said. "I have a herniated disk.
A couple of firemen ran by me. I figured they'd know what to do, and
I ran with them. Hartnett and I ran into the lobby and ducked behind
a huge column."

A firefighter inside 7 World Trade Center told them, "Hold on to one another with one hand. Don't let go no matter what! With your other hand, try to cover your nose and mouth."

Even though they were inside the building, a tidal wave of dust, ash, and debris smashed through the windows and engulfed them. Chunks of glass, steel, and concrete were falling all around. It sounded like a freight train whooshing past, and everything seemed to be moving at the velocity of bullets. Then a black cloud, as dense as toner, descended on them.[2]

"It was like getting caught in a wave when you were a little kid," Mawn said. "You just get tossed around, and you can't come up for air. I couldn't see my hand in front of my face. It passed through my mind that I might die there. I was having difficulty breathing." Kelley was nowhere to be seen.

When the roar subsided, it was pitch black. Someone opened a door at the side of the lobby.

"Anybody out there?" the man asked.

Spitting out dust, Mawn yelled back.

"Come here," the man said. He had a camera and began setting off the flash to guide them. Holding on to each other, Mawn and Hartnett followed the light out the building, which collapsed later that day. They walked north on Greenwich Street. After two or three blocks, they saw daylight and happened to run into Mayor Rudolph Giuliani and Police Commissioner Kerik, who had been unable to enter a new $13 million command center at the building Mawn had just left. As CNN zoomed in, Mawn walked with them. Mawn, to the right of Giuliani in the shot, is six feet tall and looks like a trim Daniel Patrick Moynihan. He was covered with gray dust.

Mawn got through on his cell phone to his wife, Carol. They had been married just four years. From this and a previous marriage, Mawn had six children and stepchildren, all grown. Mawn told Carol he was okay. He asked her to put together a change of clothes; an agent would pick them up. Until he called, Carol, who had watched the attacks on TV, was frantic. She knew, without a doubt, that her husband would be at the scene.

Mawn called Mary Jo White, the U.S. attorney. "Mary Jo, it's Barry," Mawn said. "I think we may have lost Dave Kelley. I was with him, and we got separated. I think he's dead."

"Thank God you called!" she said. "I have Dave on the other line. He just told me he thought you had died." It was, she said later, the best phone call she had ever had.

Mawn was almost one of the 3,024 victims. He had a personal stake in getting even.

When Mawn returned to the office, he learned that a third plane had hit the Pentagon and a fourth hijacked plane from Newark had crashed in Pennsylvania. Because the command center at the field office was too small and phone lines were out, agents began setting up one at the field office's garage at Twenty-sixth Street and the West Side Highway.

Agents had open lines to the command center at FBI headquarters in Washington. The Strategic Information Operations Center was a $20 million, twenty-room complex of phones, secure computers, and video screens. Mueller was there. FBI agents and the bureau's top brass began pouring into the center, along with representatives from the Central Intelligence Agency, Secret Service, Defense Intelligence Agency, Customs Service, Bureau of Alcohol, Tobacco and Firearms, Federal Aviation Administration, Justice Department, National Security Council, Department of Energy, and National Security Agency. Attorney General John Aschroft would arrive that afternoon.

America's war on terrorism had begun, and the FBI was at its epicenter.

BOOK ONE

1

SPEED

When Attorney General Charles J. Bonaparte created an unnamed investigative bureau of thirty-four special agents within the Justice Department on June 29, 1908, no one could have guessed that it would grow into an agency that would involve itself in almost every facet of American life.

In that year, Henry Ford introduced the Model T, an $850 car with a steel frame and wooden body that made it "stronger than a horse and easier to maintain." The nation commemorated Mother's Day for the first time. The Boy Scouts were founded. "Take Me Out to the Ball Game" and "It's a Long Way to Tipperary" were the popular songs. Corn was the country's biggest product.

The country was at peace, and the rate of homicides was a sixth of what it would later become.

Crime was considered a local matter. When it needed agents to investigate violations of the few federal statutes that existed, the Office of the Attorney General, created by Congress in 1789, borrowed Secret Service agents from the Treasury Department. They investigated bankruptcy frauds, antitrust crimes, violations of the neutrality laws, and peonage—the use of laborers bound in servitude to pay off debts.

Within two years of its creation, the tiny group—referred to as the "special agent force"—had an additional task. Congress enacted the White Slave Traffic Act, known as the Mann Act, and agents began investigating the transport of women across state borders for immoral purposes.

Already, the force of thirty-four agents had almost doubled to sixty-four. Nine support employees had been hired as well. On March 16, 1909, Bonaparte's successor, George W. Wickersham, named the agency the Bureau of Investigation. No one remembers the force's first chief, Stanley W. Finch, or his successor, A. Bruce Bielaski, who had worked for him. Until J. Edgar Hoover became director in 1924, the bureau was faceless.

Even the date of the founding of the bureau is in dispute. While the first special agents began work on June 29, 1908, the FBI, with some justification, considers July 26 the beginning of the agency. That is when the agents began reporting to a director, Finch, who was called chief examiner. The agents were called "special" because, when Congress appropriated $50,000 back in 1871 for the "Detection and Prosecution of Crimes," the attorney general appointed an agent to investigate "special crimes."

Congress had been leery of creating a national police force in the first place. In considering legislation to authorize the bureau, members of Congress had asked uneasily if the new special agents would become a secret police, carrying out the dictates of whoever was in office. Bonaparte assured Congress that while theoretically there was always that risk, his force would never be used for such purposes. Still, Congress gave the new force no power to carry weapons or even to make arrests. Instead, agents would make "citizen's arrests" or ask the local police or U.S. Marshals to arrest suspects.

Despite the limitations on its power, questions arose very quickly about the extent of the bureau's authority and its methods. Yet whenever a new threat arose, those questions would be set aside, and Congress would entrust the bureau with new powers.

By April 6, 1917, the United States was at war against Germany and Austria-Hungary. Germany had already sunk the *Housatonic*, a U.S. ship, and had announced it would sink every vessel approaching Great Britain, Ireland, and certain Mediterranean ports. GERMANY BEGINS RUTHLESS SEA WARFARE; DRAWS 'BARRED ZONES' AROUND THE ALLIES; CRISIS CONFRONTS THE UNITED STATES, read the *New York Times* headline.

President Woodrow Wilson issued a proclamation authorizing the Justice Department to apprehend and detain "enemy aliens." Two months later, Congress enacted the Espionage Act. The bureau began investigating individuals who opposed military conscription, sowed dissension within the armed forces, or willfully aided foreign adversaries.

Overnight, the bureau had been transformed from an agency that merely investigated violations of criminal laws to one that investigated spying and was responsible for the internal security of the country.

To help fulfill that role, a new attorney general, A. Mitchell Palmer, on August 1, 1919, created within the bureau a Radical Division—later renamed the General Intelligence Division—to collect information on revolutionaries or radicals who might threaten the United States from within. The biggest threats were considered the Communist Labor Party of America and the Communist Party of America, supporters of the Bolsheviks, who had overthrown the czar in Russia, a country that had signed a peace treaty with Germany. Palmer placed the new division under the direction of attorney J. Edgar Hoover.

■　■　■

Born in Washington, D.C., on New Year's Day in 1895, Hoover was a short boy with a heavy torso and spindly legs. He was the youngest of four children born to Dickerson Naylor Hoover Sr. and Anne Marie Scheitlin. Dickerson, chief of the printing division of the U.S. Coast and Geodetic Survey, was of English and German extraction. Hoover's mother's ancestors were Swiss.

The Hoover home was a modest two-story stucco house at 413 Seward Square, a neighborhood of God-fearing government bureaucrats who lived in the shadow of the Capitol. A Methodist church now stands at the site. Annie Hoover dominated the family and imbued her young son—whom she called "Edgar"—with a drive to succeed. Hoover continued to live with his mother in the family home until she died in 1938. This, and the fact that he never dated, would create ceaseless speculation about his sexual orientation.

Hoover was a perfectionist. Margaret Fennell, a niece who lived next door, recalled that each day for breakfast he would have a poached egg on toast prepared by a maid. If the egg was broken, he wouldn't eat it, and it had to be done over. He fed the offending egg to his Airedale,

Spee Dee Bozo. When an egg was perfect, he usually gave the dog a few bites anyway.

Hoover had a stutter, but he found he could overcome it if he spoke rapidly. Gaining confidence, Hoover took up debating. By his junior year at Central High School, Hoover led the team undefeated through eleven straight contests. Among his topics: "Cuba Should be Annexed to the United States" and "The Fallacies of Women's Suffrage," in which he argued that women should not have been given the right to vote.

Hoover made friends easily, but he had no close pals. First a Lutheran, then a Presbyterian, Hoover sang soprano in the church choir and later taught Sunday school. He believed deeply in God, in his country, and in the value of integrity, and he made sure everyone around him knew it. Dominating conversations, he usually got his own way.

By high school, Hoover had acquired the nickname "Speed." Some attributed the name to his staccato delivery, others to the fact that, after school, he would race to deliver groceries from the Eastern Market. For each delivery, he received a tip of a dime. The faster he ran, the more tips he received.

By his freshman year in high school, Hoover had grown to almost his full adult height of five feet ten inches.

As he got older, Hoover became interested in current events. According to Richard Gid Powers's *Secrecy and Power*, he recorded in his diary news of crime and disasters: "Estimated report of loss of life in Sicily 200,000 and loss of property $1,000,000,000," he wrote. "Miss Dalton [his eighth-grade teacher] prophesied that there would be an earthquake in the eastern part of Asia & bordering islands at 11:16 today." He noted that her prediction turned out to be wrong.

Having graduated from Central High as valedictorian, Hoover decided to study law. The 1913 Central High Annual described Hoover as a "gentleman of dauntless courage and stainless honor."

Hoover enrolled in night school at George Washington University. Under an accelerated program, he was able to earn a bachelor of laws degree and a master's in four years. While attending school, he took a job as a junior messenger at the Library of Congress, four blocks from his home. Soon he became a cataloger, then a clerk. His salary rose from $360 a year to $840 when he left four and a half years later.

While at the library, Hoover mastered the Dewey decimal system. Later, he applied the same concept to numbering FBI files: Each would begin with a number denoting a specific federal statute, followed by an abbreviation indicating which field office was in charge of the case, followed by a sequential number assigned to the particular case.

Having passed the District of Columbia bar exam, Hoover, on July 26, 1917, took a $990-a-year job as a clerk on the legal staff of the Justice Department. Three months earlier, the United States had entered World War I. Because he worked for the Justice Department, Hoover was exempt from the draft.

As Curt Gentry noted in *J. Edgar Hoover: The Man and the Secrets*, Hoover could not afford to enlist. While Hoover was a senior in high school, his father suffered a nervous breakdown and was placed in a sanitarium near Laurel, Maryland. Although he was released after several months, Dickerson's condition worsened. On April 5, 1917, the day before war was declared, Hoover's father had to leave his job. He had no pension, and Hoover and his brother Dickerson Jr. became their parents' only source of income.

War hysteria had hit Washington. "I Want You," declared Uncle Sam in a war recruitment poster. The most popular song was "Over There" by George M. Cohan, who wrote the song for the American military embarking for the war in Europe. The second most popular song was "You're in the Army Now."

The Justice Department was at the center of it. From his parents' home, Hoover rode the trolley along Pennsylvania Avenue to Justice Department headquarters, which consisted of leased space in the Denrike Building at 1435 K Street NW. The bureau occupied the third floor and part of the fourth floor.

Hoover was placed in charge of a small unit within the Enemy Alien Registration Section and was allowed to hire a secretary. He chose Helen Gandy, who was from Port Norris, New Jersey, and already worked for the department as a file clerk.[3] Gandy would continue as Hoover's secretary and later executive assistant until he died on May 2, 1972.

"From the day he entered the department, certain things marked Hoover apart from scores of other young law clerks," Jack Alexander wrote in a 1937 *New Yorker* profile. "He dressed better than most, and a bit on the dandyish side. He had an exceptional capacity for detail work, and he handled small chores with enthusiasm and thoroughness. He constantly sought new responsibilities to shoulder and welcomed chances to work overtime. When he was in conference with an official of his department, his manner was that of a young man who confidently expected to rise. His superiors were duly impressed."

■　■　■

As Attorney General Palmer turned out the lights downstairs in his Washington home at 11:15 P.M. on June 2, 1919, he heard a heavy thump on his front door. A blast came immediately afterward, strong enough to shatter windows throughout the neighborhood.

Within an hour, similar explosions occurred in eight other cities. A watchman was killed. A month earlier, explosive devices had been mailed to thirty-six prominent men, including John D. Rockefeller and J. P. Morgan. While the maid of one senator had both her hands blown off during these attacks, none of the bombs hit its intended target.

"The morning after my house was blown up," Palmer later recalled, "I stood in the middle of the wreckage of my library with congressmen and senators, and without a dissenting voice, they called upon me in strong terms to exercise all the power that was possible . . . to run to earth the criminals who were behind that kind of outrage."

The body of an unidentified man was found at the site of the explosion at Palmer's house, apparently the bomber himself. Copies of an anarchist leaflet, *The Anarchist Fighters*, were found in the debris. Newspapers like the *New York Times* assumed that the Bolsheviks or other Communist-related groups were responsible.

Two weeks after the bombings, Palmer met with William J. Flynn, a former Secret Service chief who then headed the bureau, and other department officials. They decided to deal with the violence by rounding up and deporting alien radicals. They would set up a General Intelligence Division to gather information on the aliens, and they appointed Hoover to head it. Even though the division was in the bureau, Hoover was given the title of special assistant to the attorney general.

Using skills acquired at the Library of Congress, Hoover directed his division to record information about radicals on 450,000 index cards. Disregarding the right to freedom of speech, Hoover made no distinction between criminal conduct and beliefs. Thus, when he was with the Enemy Alien Registration Section, Hoover recommended that a twenty-four-year-old man who had "belittled the United States, talked against the war, spread pacifist propaganda, and wrote against conscription" be imprisoned for the duration of the war. He was. Similarly, Hoover recommended that a German who had "engaged in a conversation with a Negro in which he indulged in pro-German utterances and in derogatory remarks regarding the United States government" be jailed. The man, who had been in the United States for thirty years, was imprisoned.

Hoover applied the same standards when compiling index cards on radicals. Within a year, Hoover's division was scanning 625 newspapers for information on the radical movement, indiscriminately entering on each card a mix of hearsay, rumor, and fact.

On January 2, 1920, based on the index cards, the bureau, joined by local police, conducted dragnet arrests of thousands of alien residents and U.S. citizens attending meetings of the Communist Party and the Communist Labor Party in thirty-three cities. Newspapers reported that some suspects were beaten.

Known as the Palmer Raids, after the targeted attorney general, the arrests became notorious. It turned out that most of those arrested were not aliens but U.S. citizens. In the end, only 556 people were deported. Even though the Communist Party espoused the violent overthrow of the U.S. government, it was not a violation of law to be a member. Thus, most of those arrested were released. Finally, the mass arrests were not calculated to solve the problem at hand. No one was ever apprehended for the bombings. In fact, the crimes were never solved.

In later years, the bureau would repeatedly face the same problem: In response to a perceived threat, politicians would demand that *something* be done. Instead of focusing on the problem, the bureau would respond by taking measures that sometimes violated the law and often did not address the issue at hand.

Congress held hearings questioning the propriety of the Palmer Raids. Hoover claimed he had not participated in their planning, but testimony before Federal Judge George W. Anderson in Boston established that Hoover and another Justice Department official had devised them with immigration officials. The spurious information about the suspects came from Hoover's index cards.

When prominent lawyers signed a petition condemning the Justice Department's "continued violation of the Constitution," Hoover opened a file on each of them. Attorney Isaac Schorr of the National Civil Liberties Union merited special distinction. He asked for an investigation of the beatings. Hoover not only opened a file on him, he wrote to an assistant to the attorney general recommending that Schorr be "disbarred from further practice before the immigration authorities."

Thus began a pattern of retribution and intimidation that Hoover would employ throughout his career.

■ ■ ■

Working with Palmer, Hoover had made a number of influential friends, including key members of Congress. Hoover never forgot that Congress controlled the purse strings. Because of that, it could be more powerful than the president and could come in handy as Hoover moved up the ladder.

When Harry M. Daugherty took over as attorney general in 1921, he sent a curt telegram to Flynn, the FBI director, firing him. He replaced him with his boyhood friend William J. Burns, another former Secret Service agent who headed a private detective agency. The influential people Hoover had cultivated recommended him for a top job, and Daugherty gave him a position he had been lobbying for: assistant director.

Burns was happy to be director of the bureau, but he didn't want to give up his private detective business, which consisted mainly of spying on labor organizations. So he not only continued to run his company, he began assigning bureau agents to work on his company's cases. With no hiring standards, Burns and Daugherty recruited political hacks as agents, including Gaston B. Means, who sold bureau protection to some and bureau files to others.

Soon, Daugherty enmeshed the bureau in the Teapot Dome scandal, which began when a Senate committee investigated Interior Secretary Albert Fall's decision to lease to businessmen Edward Doheny and Harry Sinclair oil reserves in Teapot Dome, Wyoming, and Elk Hills, California. The leases had been awarded without competitive bidding.

The committee found that under Daugherty's direction, bureau director Burns had begun an investigation of Burton K. Wheeler and Thomas Walsh, the two Democratic senators who had launched the probe into the award of the leases by the Republican administration of Warren G. Harding. Not only had agents tried to uncover damaging information about the senators, they had wiretapped their phones, opened their mail, and broken into their homes. Agents had conducted surveillance of other critics of the administration as well.

By then, the bureau had become a corrupt force, known as the Bureau of Easy Virtue. When asked where he worked, Hoover would say simply that he worked for the government. There was even talk of transferring the bureau's functions to the Secret Service.

In 1924, a new president, Calvin Coolidge, requested the resignation of Daugherty. To replace him, Coolidge named Harlan Fiske Stone. A former Columbia Law School dean who would later become chief justice of the United States, Stone had a mandate from Coolidge to clean up the Justice Department and the bureau. In his notes, he said the bureau was "filled with men with bad records . . . many convicted of crimes . . . organization lawless . . . many activities without any authority in federal statutes . . . agents engaged in many practices which are brutal and tyrannical in the extreme."

Stone decided to rebuild the bureau in the image of Scotland Yard. By that he meant he wanted a force that was law-abiding itself and staffed by men of intelligence and education who were well trained. He sought a director who was experienced in police work but free of the "more usual police tradition that it takes a crook to catch a crook, and that lawlessness and brutality are to be more relied upon than skill and special training."

In a cabinet meeting, Stone mentioned that he was casting about for a replacement for Burns. Herbert Hoover, the secretary of commerce, told his assistant, Lawrence Richey, of the need for a new director. Richey, who had worked for the Secret Service and knew J. Edgar Hoover from the Masonic lodge where they both belonged, suggested his friend for the job.

Passing the recommendation on to Stone, Herbert Hoover would later claim credit for the appointment of J. Edgar Hoover as director. On May 9, 1924, Stone demanded Burns's resignation. The following day, Stone issued a statement to the press. With the expansion of federal legislation, the bureau had become even more necessary. "But," he said, "it is important that its activities be strictly limited to the performance of those functions for which it was created and that its agents themselves be not above the law or beyond its reach."

Stone then made as precise a statement about the bureau's proper role as has ever been made: "The Bureau of Investigation is not concerned with political or other opinions of individuals. It is concerned only with their conduct and then only with such conduct as is forbidden by the laws of the United States. When a police system passes beyond these limits, it is dangerous to the proper administration of justice and to human liberty, which it should be our first concern to cherish."

That same day, May 10, 1924, Stone asked Hoover, then twenty-nine, to come to his office. Hoover knew that Burns had been fired; he did not know who would replace him.

"Young man," Stone said, "I want you to be the acting director of the Bureau of Investigation."

Hoover displayed the political savvy that would keep him in office nearly forty-eight years.

"I'll take the job, Mr. Stone, on certain conditions," he said.

"What are they?" Stone asked.

"The bureau must be divorced from politics and not be a catch-all for political hacks. Second, promotions will be based on proven ability, and the bureau will be responsible only to the attorney general."

"I wouldn't give it to you under any other conditions," Stone replied. "That's all. Good day."

Three days later, Stone put his expectations for the bureau in writing. He told Hoover that the "activities of the bureau are to be limited strictly to the investigations of violations of law, under my direction or under the direction of an assistant attorney general regularly conducting the work of the Department of Justice." He instructed Hoover to reduce the staff, fire incompetents, and get his approval on each new hire. Preference would be given to men with legal training.

At the time, the agency had 441 agents and 216 support employees. Its budget was $2.3 million.

Three days after his appointment, Hoover reported back that he had issued orders implementing Stone's instructions. All investigations would address violations of federal law. All new employees would have legal training or a background in accounting. Or so he claimed. In fact, exceptions to the rule were made quietly.

A chameleon, Hoover renounced his previous position on radicalism. "There is no federal statute against entertaining radical ideas, and we are wasting no time collecting information that we cannot use," he told his staff.

The first person Hoover fired was Gaston Means, who was in jail for larceny but was listed as a "temporarily suspended" bureau employee. Another agent continued to run errands for a prominent senator while ignoring his bureau work. Seeking to give him another chance, Hoover transferred him to another state. The senator complained to Stone, who met with Hoover and the senator. After listening to the facts, Stone said, "I am not sure, Mr. Hoover, that you haven't made a mistake." After a pause, he added, "I think you should have fired the agent."

With that firm support, Hoover began a restructuring to impose discipline and accountability on the bureau. He had a natural talent for management and a clear sense of how he wanted the bureau to operate. Hoover established six divisions, each with a different function, such as administration or investigations, and each headed by a chief. Before, there had been four divisions with ill-defined responsibilities. Below the divisions were fifty-three field offices, each headed by a special agent in charge (SAC).

Hoover told the SACs (pronounced es-ay-seez), "I look to you as the special agent in charge as my representative, and I consider it your duty and function to see that the special agents and other employees assigned to your office are engaged at all times upon government business."

Hoover insisted that promotions would be based on merit alone. He would personally grade the SACs on their performance. Successes beyond what was required would bring letters of commendation; violations of rules would bring letters of censure. The letters would be considered in determining raises, demotions, and firings. Each SAC would be personally responsible for mistakes made by his subordinates.

To check on compliance, an Inspection Division was established.

Teams of inspectors would descend on offices at irregular intervals to check on conformance with regulations, the number of cases being handled, and the total number of hours worked by agents.

The chiefs of divisions were to report to Hoover and keep him informed on major cases and developments. Each week, they would meet with Hoover and his assistant director, Harold "Pop" Nathan, at the Seat of Government—Hoover's quaint term for headquarters—to discuss issues that needed to be addressed.

Hoover standardized the work of the bureau. Previously, reports of investigations were telephoned in or, if written, prepared sloppily. Often, reports were lost. Hoover introduced a printed form for interview reports. He issued instructions on filling them out. Thus, an agent from any field office could walk into another one and find the same system. Each outgoing letter had to be approved by five to eight people. A special unit checked each one for spelling, punctuation, grammar, and conformance with bureau policy.

Hoover imposed strict rules on the use of bureau files. They could not be taken except by agents working investigations, and then only with the approval of the SAC. A written record was to be kept of the withdrawal. By September 15, 1927, Hoover had created a *Manual of Investigations* containing his instructions and rules.

Like bureau forms, agents were interchangeable. Each agent was expected to be able to work any kind of case within the bureau's jurisdiction. Hoover wanted agents to look like young businessmen, dressing conservatively in dark suits, ties, white shirts, and snap-brimmed hats.

Hoover liked agents to have what he thought of as an all-American look. Anyone who looked like a foreigner—whether from Ireland or Germany—was rejected. In later years, before new FBI agents met Hoover, Simon Tullai, who was in charge of new agent training, gave them a lecture on how to present themselves. They were to have neatly trimmed hair, wear white shirts, have shined shoes, look the director squarely in the eye, and shake his hand with a dry palm. There was nothing the director hated more than a clammy handshake. Tullai recommended that agents pat their hands on their pants legs to make sure their hands were dry before entering Hoover's spartan office, then on the fifth floor of the Justice Department building.

After the meeting, Hoover would question whether certain agents had what it took to be FBI agents. He thought some were too short or too bald. Others, he complained, had protruding ears, bad posture, pear-shaped heads, or eyebrows that were too bushy.

In contrast to the corrupt standards of the previous director, Hoover told his SACs that even the *appearance* of improper conduct was to be avoided. "I do believe that when a man becomes a part of this bureau he must so conduct himself, both officially and unofficially, as to eliminate the slightest possibility of criticism as to his conduct or actions," Hoover declared.

Hoover followed his organizational and discipline changes with a series of farsighted moves to employ technology and other advanced crime-solving techniques. On July 1, 1924, Hoover created a national registry of fingerprints after Congress authorized "the exchange of identification records with officers of the cities, counties, and states." He consolidated the bureau's existing fingerprint files with the records of the International Association of Chiefs of Police.

Hoover had been impressed by scientific evidence presented at a hearing in the controversial Sacco and Vanzetti murder case. When Charles Appel, an accountant and documents examiner, asked to attend a police science course at Northwestern University, Hoover agreed, as long as he helped the Chicago office catch up on its work. When Appel returned to Washington in 1931, he reported to Hoover, "The bureau should be the central clearing house for all information which may be needed in criminological work."[4]

On November 24, 1932, the bureau opened the lab in a converted lounge, chosen because it had a sink. Appel was the only full-time employee. The equipment consisted of a borrowed microscope, ultraviolet lights, a drawing board, and a "helixometer," which supposedly allowed examiners to look into gun barrels. In fact, according to David Fisher's *Hard Evidence*, it was useless and was there to impress visitors. Soon, Appel added a comparison microscope, test tubes, and wax and plaster to make impressions of shoe prints and tire tracks. The lab had a Packard sedan agents called Old Beulah for going to crime scenes. In its first year, the lab conducted a thousand examinations.

In January 1928, Hoover instituted a training course for new agents.

Before being retained by the bureau, agents were assigned to duties for two months in the Washington Field Office, where their performance was evaluated.

On July 29, 1935, Hoover established the FBI National Police Academy, forerunner of the FBI National Academy in Quantico, Virginia. He issued a publication called *Fugitives Wanted by Police*, later changed to *FBI Law Enforcement Bulletin*. And Hoover began collecting national crime statistics. These functions—along with the laboratory, which offered its services to local police—gave the bureau a new role as a national resource for all law enforcement agencies. In turn, that meant the bureau could count on cooperation from local police who had attended the academy, made use of the laboratory, or received other help from the bureau.

Hoover even hired two female special agents. They had been in the accounting section and received their badges and credentials in 1924. For personal reasons, they resigned fewer than four years later. Hoover decided the experiment had been a failure.

"Two ideas were constantly drummed into us: pride at membership in an elite organization, and fear of failure," recalled Robert J. Lamphere, who became an agent in 1941.[5] FBI agents were "expected to be better in every category than ordinary lawmen," Lamphere said. "We knew more about firearms. We knew how to behave in the courtroom— to stand erect to take the oath, to testify impartially as to the facts in simple language cleansed of legalisms that might confuse the jury and in a voice loud enough so that all might be able to hear. It was 'Yes, sir,' and 'No, sir,' to all citizens, regardless of their station." Eventually, Lamphere said, "Our self-esteem became interconnected with the FBI's image, and we took our strength from our membership in the organization."

At the same time, Lamphere said, agents were afraid of earning Hoover's displeasure. Hoover "could fire us at any time for any violation of the multitudinous rules that governed the conduct of an FBI man, on or off the job." FBI agents were not covered by civil service rules that protected the jobs of other federal workers. If something went wrong on a case, "someone had to pay; this was true even when the director had personally approved the course of action that eventually resulted in the error having been made. The rationalization was that if the director had personally approved the course of action, the error must have been made in the way the instructions were transmitted down or in the way they had been carried out," the former agent said.

After seven months as acting director, Hoover had passed his own test. On December 10, 1924, Stone called him into his office. The attorney general had considered other men for the post but decided that Hoover gave "far greater promise than any other man I had heard of." He thought Hoover a man of "exceptional intelligence, alertness, and executive ability." Stone told Hoover he would be dropping "acting" from his title.

Six months later, Hoover presented Stone with statistics showing a marked increase in the number of thefts and frauds investigated by the bureau when Hoover was acting director as compared with the same period in 1923.[6]

Despite the improvements initiated by Hoover, it would be ten years until Congress finally authorized agents to make arrests and carry firearms. In the meantime, the Justice Department allowed agents to carry weapons "for their personal protection" when approved in advance for special situations. Not until 1935 would the bureau be renamed the Federal Bureau of Investigation—after briefly being named the United States Bureau of Investigation.

If the restructuring and modernization demonstrated Hoover's genius at management, they also reflected his personality. As a perfectionist with a passion for order, Hoover saw the world in black and white. If a subordinate made a mistake, he would be censured, no matter how good a job he was doing overall. Nothing was more important to Hoover than preserving his own good name. When a department store denied him a charge card, he found out that another John Edgar Hoover had been bouncing checks. So Hoover began using the name J. Edgar Hoover.

If an agent conducted himself poorly, Hoover felt it reflected on him personally. He codified his philosophy in the phrase, "Don't embarrass the bureau." By that, he also meant, "Don't embarrass me." As far as Hoover was concerned, he and the bureau were one and the same: His agents were his family.

Complex man that he was, Hoover left nothing to chance. Hoover shrewdly recognized that building what became known as the world's greatest law enforcement agency would not necessarily keep him in office. So after Hoover became director, he began to maintain a special Official and Confidential file in his office. The "secret files," as they became widely known, would guarantee that Hoover would remain director as long as he wished.

2

G-MEN

When Hoover's appointment as director was announced, only the *Washington Evening Star* ran a story, under the headline DAYS OF 'OLD SLEUTH' ARE ENDED. Calling Hoover a disciple of Blackstone, the article said, "The old-time detective, the man of 'shadows' and 'frame-ups' and 'get the goods in any way you can' is a thing of the past."

The story in the *Star* ran on the obituary page. Most of the press ignored Hoover's appointment. To Americans, the Bureau of Investigation was just another government agency.

But by 1932, after the son of Charles Lindbergh was kidnapped, everyone had heard about the bureau. Following the stock market crash of 1929, the country was in a depression. Franklin D. Roosevelt was running for president, offering a "new deal." Prominent Americans—including novelist John Dos Passos, journalist Lincoln Steffens, and teacher Sidney Hook—endorsed communism as a solution to the nation's problems. Washington's population was 487,000 but, because of the swelling federal workforce, would grow to 663,000 over the next ten years.

The *Walter Winchell Show* began on radio, featuring the *New York Daily Mirror* columnist with his signature introduction: "Good evening, Mr. and Mrs. America, and all the ships at sea . . ." Campbell's Soup Company introduced its tomato soup, and Rosefield Packing Company of California began shipping Skippy peanut butter. Besides the smooth version, Skippy offered the first peanut butter with chunks of roasted peanuts.

J. Edgar Hoover had taken to eating dinner most evenings at Harvey's, a red-blooded American restaurant on Connecticut Avenue a block from the Mayflower Hotel. Hoover sat just inside the door, underneath the stairway to the second floor. It was the most secure spot in the restaurant, according to Alex Stuart, a former Harvey's owner.[7] When Julius Lulley owned it, Hoover never saw a check. Jesse Brinkman, a new owner, sent Hoover a bill in the mail. The director's visits tapered off, and when a new owner moved the restaurant to 1001 Eighteenth Street NW, Hoover switched his allegiance to the Mayflower, where he ate in the bar or in the Rib Room.

In those days, his companions were usually T. Frank Baughman or Charles Appel. He had one drink—Jack Daniel's Black Label whiskey—and ordered steak or roast beef, along with a Caesar salad. Usually, Hoover took home a briefcase full of work. In case an emergency arose, he had had a direct telephone line installed linking bureau headquarters to his home on Seward Square.

On the evening of March 1, 1932, just after eleven o'clock, the night supervisor called him on the special line. Charles Augustus Lindbergh Jr., the twenty-month-old son of the famous aviator and his wife, Anne Morrow, had disappeared from their home in Hopewell, New Jersey. The supervisor said the local police were sure the baby had been kidnapped. Muddy footprints ran from the baby's crib to an open window. A ladder was found outside; Lindbergh did not think it was his.

By now, several key federal statutes had expanded the bureau's jurisdiction. In particular, the Motor Vehicle Theft Act, known as the Dyer Act, gave the bureau the authority to investigate car thefts. Kidnapping was not yet a federal offense. Nonetheless, Hoover asked the supervisor to keep him informed. Just after 1 A.M., Hoover received a second call. A ransom note, asking for $50,000 in small bills, had been found at the Lindbergh home.

Hoover called his driver and returned to headquarters. Other bureau officials were already there. Hoover chose Thomas Sisk to head a special Lindbergh squad of twenty agents. They would offer their "unofficial" assistance.

The kidnapping immediately captured national attention. Lindbergh was an adored hero who had made the first solo nonstop transatlantic flight in his monoplane *The Spirit of St. Louis*. An estimated one hundred thousand officers and volunteers searched throughout the country for the child. Any police force that could successfully return the Lindbergh child to his parents would gain tremendous recognition. For Hoover, there was a special incentive: Senator Dwight Morrow, who was leery of granting the bureau too much power, was the child's grandfather.

But the state and local police had no interest in obtaining help from the bureau. Nor would they share any evidence with what they called the "federal glory hunters." For weeks, the bureau could not see facsimiles of the ransom note. When Hoover personally showed up in Hopewell to offer his assistance to the parents, they refused to see him.

Undeterred, bureau agents investigated every lead, no matter how bizarre. At one point, based on a tip, agents thought they had found the child, only to discover that the supposed victim was a girl. Leon Turrou, one of the agents, recalled that the bureau took "special pains to keep these blunderings out of the reach of reporters. . . . The [bureau] was struggling for recognition and respect, and it couldn't afford the public horse laughs."

On the morning of April 2, agents learned that the kidnappers had arranged for Lindbergh to pay the ransom that night at St. Raymond's Cemetery in the Bronx. Turrou wanted to stake out the area. But Hoover, afraid that such a plan might backfire, instructed agents not to intervene until the child had been safely recovered.

Dr. John F. Condon, a retired school principal from New York City, had volunteered as a go-between with the kidnappers. At midnight, he handed a package of $50,000 to a tall man with a German accent. The man gave Condon a receipt and slip of paper with the name of a ship— the *Nellie* at Martha's Vineyard, Massachusetts—where the child supposedly could be found.

It turned out there was no such ship. On May 12, a truck driver found the body of the boy in a wooded patch in the Sourland Mountains four and a half miles from the Lindbergh home. The body was facedown, covered with leaves. The child had been brutally murdered, apparently on the night of the kidnapping.

Through the attorney general, Hoover had lobbied President Herbert

Hoover to name the bureau the "coordinator" of the investigation. Instead of doing so, the president now ordered all federal law enforcement agencies to assist. J. Edgar Hoover persisted, writing a letter to the New Jersey governor. The governor ignored it. So Hoover sent out press releases implying that the bureau was coordinating the case. After a while, the public came to believe that the bureau was in charge.

At first, the maneuver backfired. The press criticized the bureau when the case remained unsolved. But Hoover got the expanded jurisdiction he wanted. On June 22, Congress passed what came to be known as the Lindbergh Law, making kidnapping a federal offense if the victim was transported across state lines. Congress later amended the law to create a presumption that the victim had been taken across state lines if he or she were not found within seven days. Another amendment authorized the death penalty. Finally, on October 13, 1933, Roosevelt, who had decisively defeated Herbert Hoover, gave the FBI principal jurisdiction over the case.

■ ■ ■

More than two years after the Lindbergh kidnapping, on September 15, 1934, a gas station attendant in upper Manhattan became suspicious when a customer paid for five gallons of gasoline with a $10 gold certificate. All gold certificates were to have been turned in to banks by May 1, 1933, when the United States went off the gold standard. The attendant made a note of the customer's license number—4U-13-41 NY—on the back of the bill. Three days later, when the gas station attendant turned in the note at the Corn Exchange Bank and Trust Company, the teller identified the note as one of the marked bills paid as ransom in the Lindbergh case.

Elmer Irey, Treasury's chief law enforcement officer, had urged that the ransom be paid in part with gold certificates so they could be traced more easily. The bureau had distributed notices to banks and other businesses asking them to be on the lookout for gold certificates. The notices listed the serial numbers of the bills used to pay the ransom.

The alert teller called the bureau's New York Field Office. Checking back with the gas station attendant, bureau agents verified that the number written on the bill was the license number of the customer's car, a dark blue Dodge sedan. It was registered to Bruno Richard Hauptmann, an unemployed carpenter who lived at 1279 East 222nd Street in the Bronx.

Assisted by the New York City police, the bureau placed Hauptmann under surveillance. But the next day, when Hauptmann ran a red light, officers in one of the police cars pulled Hauptmann over and arrested him. The officers later explained that they thought he was trying to flee.

Agent Turrou obtained copies of Hauptmann's application for a New York driver's license and persuaded him to copy in longhand several newspaper articles. Turrou submitted these handwriting samples to Charles Appel in the bureau's laboratory. Appel worked all night, comparing the samples with the ransom note. The most obvious similarity was spelling errors made by Hauptmann in both the ransom note and the handwriting samples. Turrou had fallen asleep on a cot in the New York Field Office when Appel called him.

"It checks," Appel told him. "Congratulations."

When arrested, Hauptmann had a ransom bill on him. State police searched his house but could not find any more of the bills. Given Hauptmann's dull mind, Hoover was sure he would not have thought of hiding the money anywhere but in his home. Although the state police at first protested, Hoover had his agents search the home themselves. Hidden in the garage, they found $1,830 in $10 gold certificates, all part of the ransom. Later, they found additional ransom money, bringing the total to $14,600.

The agents had not obtained a search warrant, and no one was home at the time to give them permission to search. Therefore, the notes would not have been legally admissible as evidence. No problem. The agents returned the money to the hiding place, obtained Hauptmann's wife's permission to conduct a search, and "found" the money.

Hauptmann, who claimed he had had nothing to do with the kidnapping, insisted he had obtained the money from a man named Isidor Fish, who had since unfortunately died.

During the trial, an expert linked the homemade ladder found at the crime scene to materials and tools in Hauptmann's home. Appel testified that Hauptmann had written the ransom note. And Condon, although initially unable to make a positive identification during a police lineup, testified that Hauptmann had been the man with the German accent who received the ransom in the cemetery.

A jury convicted Hauptmann on February 13, 1935, in state court in Flemington, New Jersey. After he was led away, Hauptmann slumped to the floor. The next day, the *New York Times* ran an eight-column headline at the top of page 1: HAUPTMANN GUILTY, SENTENCED TO DEATH FOR THE MURDER OF THE LINDBERGH BABY. On April 3, 1936, Hauptmann was electrocuted.

As with other famous bureau cases, revisionists would claim that the trial had been unfair and that witnesses had been intimidated, had perjured themselves, or had given conflicting testimony. While witnesses are notoriously unreliable, nothing undercut the fact that Hauptmann's handwriting matched the ransom note's, that the ransom bills were found secreted in his home, and that marks on the homemade ladder matched those made by tools found in Hauptmann's home.

■ ■ ■

Despite this and other successes, Hoover had no assurance he would remain as director in the Roosevelt administration. Typically, new administrations replaced agency heads with their own candidates. Aides had urged on Roosevelt various police chiefs to replace Hoover, who was already receiving some criticism in the press. An August 19, 1933, article in *Collier's* noted that the "director's appetite for publicity is the talk of the capital, although admittedly a peculiar enterprise for the bureau, which, by the nature of its work, is supposed to operate in secrecy."

In an oblique reference, the article raised the issue of Hoover's sexual orientation: "In appearance, Mr. Hoover looks utterly unlike the storybook sleuth," the article said. "He dresses fastidiously, with Eleanor blue as the favorite color for the matched shades of tie, handkerchief, and socks." Moreover, "He is short, fat, businesslike, and walks with mincing step."

Hoover immediately began a campaign to win over Roosevelt, as well as his new boss, Attorney General Homer S. Cummings, a highly regarded Connecticut lawyer. Hoover barraged Cummings with memos showing that he was on top of the biggest cases. He visited Burton K.

Wheeler, a powerful senator, to enlist his support. Harlan Fiske Stone, by now a Supreme Court justice, wrote a letter on Hoover's behalf, passed along by Roosevelt aide Felix Frankfurter.

"I think I can assure our friend [Stone], whose letter I am returning, that it is all right about Edgar Hoover," Roosevelt wrote to Frankfurter. "Homer Cummings agrees with me."

Buoyed by his reappointment, Hoover began focusing on a new threat. On the morning of June 17, 1933, Frank "Jelly" Nash, an escaped federal prisoner, was being transported under police and bureau guard to Leavenworth federal penitentiary. After he arrived at Union Railway Station in Kansas City, Missouri, three gunmen opened fire with machine guns and pistols.

"Let 'em have it!" one of the gunmen yelled.[8]

In the ambush, four of the lawmen—including agent Raymond J. Caffrey—were killed, along with Nash. Two other lawmen were wounded. A bureau investigation determined that the gunmen were Vernon C. Miller, Adam C. Richetti, and Charles "Pretty Boy" Floyd. All had lengthy criminal records.

Floyd had been convicted in a series of bank robberies and was then a fugitive. Portraying himself as a Robin Hood in a time of depression, he hit banks that were foreclosing on thousands of homes, farms, and businesses. Along with cash, "Pretty Boy" took bank loan and mortgage records.

The idea that four lawmen could be shot in broad daylight outraged the nation. The Kansas City Massacre, as it became known, was "a challenge to law and order and civilization itself," Hoover said. He ordered a nationwide manhunt for the three men believed responsible. In a speech to the International Association of Police Chiefs the next month, Hoover asked all police forces to unite in a nationwide crackdown on crime. "Those who participated in this cold-blooded murder will be hunted down," he promised. "Sooner or later, the penalty which is their due will be paid."

Miller turned up choked to death a few months later. He was lying in a drainage ditch near Detroit. For good measure, apparently in retribution for stirring up the feds, his tongue and cheeks had been punctured with ice picks, his body burned with hot irons, and his head bashed in with a blunt object. Police and bureau agents apprehended Richetti and shot Floyd, who died of his wounds.

A month after the massacre, on July 23, two kidnappers armed with a machine gun and a pistol abducted Charles F. Urschel, a wealthy oilman. His wife immediately reported the kidnapping to the bureau on its newly installed kidnapping phone number. The Lindbergh Law having just passed, this would be the bureau's first kidnapping case.[9]

Four days after the kidnapping, E. E. Kirkpatrick, a friend of the oilman, received a ransom note demanding $200,000 in used $20 bills. Kirkpatrick was told to bring the money to Kansas City. When he delivered the money, the man who received it said Urschel would be released within twelve hours. The next night, the kidnappers released him near Norman, Oklahoma.

Urschel proved to be an excellent witness. Although the kidnappers had blindfolded him, he told bureau agents how they traveled and what the kidnappers talked about. He recalled that on the farm where he was held, he heard a plane fly overhead each morning and evening. On one morning when it rained, the plane did not fly. He also said the water he drank tasted as if it had a high mineral content.

Checking weather reports and airline schedules, agents pinpointed the area. On August 10, 1933, they raided a farm near Paradise, Texas, owned by the Shannons, in-laws of notorious gangster George "Machine Gun" Kelly. The Shannons were arrested after they implicated themselves by admitting they had helped guard Urschel. They identified Kelly and Albert Bates as the kidnappers.

Bureau agents tracked Bates to Denver and arrested him. Then, with local police, they raided a house in Memphis on September 26. As Kelly gave up without a fight, he is supposed to have said, "Don't shoot, G-men! Don't shoot!"

Both Kelly and his wife were convicted on October 12 and sentenced to life in prison. Bates and the Shannons also received life sentences.

Previously, bureau agents were known as "the feds." Now, thanks to "Machine Gun" Kelly, they were G-men, for government men. Perhaps it was fitting that, like their targets, they had acquired a colorful nickname.

As agents closed the case, another band of outlaws, headed by Clyde Barrow and Bonnie Parker, roamed the Midwest, robbing banks, engaging in shoot-outs with local police, and even kidnapping local peace officers. In April 1934, bureau agents and local police learned that Bonnie and Clyde were in Louisiana. After Frank Hamer, a former Texas Ranger who had pursued the couple, received a tip that they were driving on a highway outside Sailes, Louisiana, Hamer organized a posse to capture them. On May 23, as the couple was trying to ram through the posse's barricade, the officers opened fire and killed them both.

The previous year, John Dillinger and his gang had begun commanding the attention of the bureau and the media with a crime spree through the Midwest. After a series of ten bank holdups, the murder of a police officer, and a holdup of a police station to obtain guns and ammunition, Dillinger escaped from jail in Crown Point, Indiana. He used a wooden pistol, carved from a washboard, to intimidate his guards. In making his escape, Dillinger made the mistake of stealing the sheriff's car and driving to Illinois. Since he crossed a state line, Dillinger violated the Dyer Act, a federal statute. The bureau had jurisdiction.

Twice, bureau agents almost captured Dillinger, but he slipped away. Then, on April 22, 1934, agents received a tip that Dillinger, Lester Gillis a.k.a. "Baby Face" Nelson, and other members of Dillinger's gang were at Little Bohemia Lodge, a summer resort fifty miles north of Rhinelander, Wisconsin. The two closest field offices were Chicago and St. Paul. Hoover ordered agents from both offices to charter planes and converge on the scene.

The Justice Department had moved to its permanent quarters, a seven-story building covering an entire block between Ninth and Tenth streets and Pennsylvania and Constitution avenues. The FBI occupied the fifth, sixth, and seventh floors of the building, which was dedicated in October 1934. Hoover's domain was a long suite of offices extending down the Ninth Street side of the building on the fifth floor.

Hoover called in reporters and announced that his men had Dillinger surrounded. They were under the command of Melvin H. Purvis, the SAC in Chicago. The son of an aristocratic plantation owner in South Carolina, Purvis, just under five feet tall, had almost been rejected by the bureau because he had failed to meet the minimum height and weight requirements. But Pop Nathan took a liking to him, and in 1932, he was hired.

At nightfall, Purvis led his agents to Little Bohemia Lodge, intending to surround it. But barking dogs gave them away. Purvis told his men to be ready to fire. Alarmed by the commotion, three local residents who had stopped by the lodge for a cocktail ran outside and tried to drive away. In the dark, the men did not see the agents. Nor, with engines running, could they hear the command to surrender. The agents opened fire on them, killing one man and wounding the other two.

Alerted by the gunfire, Dillinger and his gang—"probably the largest aggregation of modern desperadoes ever bottled up in one place," Purvis would later say ruefully—escaped through the back windows.

Shortly thereafter, "Baby Face" Nelson encountered three of the lawmen a few miles away. He immediately began shooting, killing one agent, W. Carter Baum, and wounding a second agent and a local police officer.

Reporters, having been alerted to expect "good news," now descended on the bureau. They asked Cummings if Hoover would be demoted or fired. Cummings claimed that the disaster would have been averted if Congress had given the bureau funds for an armored car. No one bought the explanation.

Everyone in the bureau assumed Purvis to be Hoover's favorite SAC. Now Hoover called Purvis on the carpet, and Purvis submitted his resignation. Hoover did not accept it, but he put Samuel Cowley from headquarters in charge of the Dillinger case. A former Mormon missionary who had been an assistant to Pop Nathan, Cowley had little field experience but was a good administrator.

"Take him alive if you can, but protect yourself," Hoover told Cowley.

Cummings was more blunt. He announced that the bureau's policy would be: "Shoot to kill, then count to ten."

In a stroke of public relations genius, on June 22, 1934, Hoover declared Dillinger "Public Enemy Number One." He borrowed the term "public enemy" from the Chicago Crime Commission. Hoover increased the reward for Dillinger's capture to $10,000.

On July 21, 1934, the madam of a brothel in Gary, Indiana, told

Sergeant Martin Zarkovich, a local police officer, that she would turn in Dillinger, a friend and customer, in exchange for reward money. She also asked for a halt to proceedings to deport her to her native Romania. The officer conveyed this to Purvis, the head of the Chicago Field Office. Purvis and Cowley met with the madam, Anna Sage, whose real name was Anna Campinas, and verified that she indeed knew Dillinger. They then told Hoover, who agreed that if the madam gave the bureau Dillinger, she would receive a substantial amount of the reward money. In addition, the bureau would recommend that the Immigration and Naturalization Service allow her to stay in the United States.

Sage told Purvis that she and Polly Hamilton, a prostitute who took care of Dillinger, were planning to go to a movie the following night. They did not know which one, but Sage said she would call Purvis and let him know as soon as she found out. At 5:30 P.M. on July 22, 1934, Sage called Purvis. They still did not know which movie they were seeing, but it would probably be at the Biograph or the Marbro. Purvis sent agents to both theaters, and Purvis kept an open line to Hoover. This time, the director did not alert the press.

At 7 P.M., Sage called Purvis. Dillinger had arrived, but she still didn't know which movie they were seeing. Finally, parked outside the Biograph, Purvis saw Dillinger enter the theater with Sage and Hamilton. Sage was wearing an orange skirt that looked blood red under the lights of the marquee. To avoid harm to innocent people, Purvis wanted to wait to capture Dillinger until he left the theater. Purvis learned that the movie, *Manhattan Melodrama* starring Clark Gable and William Powell, would run for ninety-four minutes. He told his agents he would light a cigar when he spotted Dillinger coming out.

Seeing a lot of strange men waiting outside, the theater manager thought they were planning to hold up the establishment. He called police. Under orders from Hoover, Purvis had not told the local police of the impending arrest. At 10:20, minutes before the movie was to end, two Chicago police officers jumped out of a patrol car, pointed their guns at two of the agents, and ordered them to identify themselves. The agents showed their credentials and said they were looking for a fugitive. Satisfied, the police drove away.[10]

At 10:30, Dillinger and the two women walked out of the theater.

Purvis, who was standing outside, spotted them immediately. He later said his hands were shaking so badly he could not light the cigar.

Seeing the grim-looking men in ties and white shirts, Dillinger ran into an alley alongside the theater.

"Stick 'em up, Johnny. We have you surrounded," Purvis shouted in his high-pitched voice.

Instead, Dillinger pulled a .380 Colt automatic from his jacket pocket. He wasn't able to get off a shot before three of the agents fired. Agent Herman Hollis missed, but agents Clarence Hurt and Charles Winstead got their man.

While Hoover had continued to claim that his agents all had legal or accounting backgrounds, he had quietly recruited former police officers with practical experience on the street. They included Winstead and Hurt. Most wore cowboy boots and Stetsons and carried their own guns. Winstead had a .357 Magnum revolver. Hurt had a matched pair of Colt .45s.

Purvis called Hoover at home from the theater box office.

"We got him!" Purvis said.

"Dead or alive?" Hoover asked.

"Dead," Purvis said. "He pulled a gun."

"Were any of our boys hurt?" Hoover asked.

"Not one," Purvis replied. "A woman in the crowd was wounded, but it doesn't look bad."

"Thank God," Hoover said.

Hoover rushed to his office to alert the press. Asked later what the biggest thrill of his career had been, he said, "the night we got Dillinger."

Hoover had Dillinger's death mask—an impression of his face taken at the morgue—mounted in an anteroom outside his office.

DILLINGER SHOT DEAD IN CHICAGO; SHOT DEAD BY FEDERAL MEN IN FRONT OF MOVIE THEATRE, read the headline over the lead story in the next day's *New York Times*.

Purvis talked freely with reporters about the well-executed confrontation. The *Times* story quoted him in the third paragraph. While he downplayed his role and never claimed he had killed Dillinger, the press soon attributed the entire success to Purvis. In Hoover's FBI, every agent was not only interchangeable but also part of a team. Only Hoover was allowed to claim personal credit, his name always the first words in any press release. While he promoted both Purvis and Cowley in salary grade, Hoover wrote to Cowley, "To you . . . must go the major portion of the credit."

Later that year, Purvis led agents who confronted and shot "Pretty Boy" Floyd on an Ohio farm. A Hollywood studio announced that it intended to make a movie on the "man-hunting activities of Melvin H. Purvis." Hoover was fuming, and Cummings announced that the Justice Department would not approve such a project. On November 27, 1934, "Baby Face" Nelson killed agents Sam Cowley and Herman Hollis in a gun battle near Barrington, Illinois. After he rushed to the scene, Purvis told reporters he had taken an oath in Cowley's blood to avenge his death. For Hoover, this effort of Purvis's to call attention to himself was the last straw. He yanked him off the case.

Because Purvis had become a hero, Hoover could not demote or fire him. Instead, he decided to make his life miserable. Hoover sent him on back-to-back inspection tours, downplayed his role in the Dillinger case to reporters, and let it be known within the bureau that he blamed Purvis for the deaths at Little Bohemia, including the killing of agent Baum.

That, more than anything, infuriated Purvis. On July 12, 1935, citing "personal" reasons, Purvis announced his resignation from the bureau. The press speculated that he had resigned because the FBI, while giving Sage $5,000 of the reward money for the capture of Dillinger, had not intervened to block her deportation.

Purvis wrote a book, *American Agent*, which did not mention Hoover and became a best-seller. Purvis opened his own detective agency, but when Hoover put out the word that no cooperation should be given to him, law enforcement shunned him. When Hoover learned that the Motion Picture Producers and Distributors of America wanted to hire Purvis, Hoover let the organization know that he would "look with displeasure, as a personal matter" at their hiring the ex-agent. If the organization wanted technical advisers, Hoover said he would supply them "free of charge." Hoover had the head of the Los Angeles office track Purvis's contacts with movie producers. When Purvis was close to landing a job, Hoover would move in with offers of free help.[11]

In FBI personnel records, Hoover changed Purvis's departure from the bureau from a resignation to "termination with prejudice." Hoover deleted references to Purvis from official FBI accounts of the Dillinger shooting and gave credit to Sam Cowley, who was conveniently dead and therefore could not deflect glory from Hoover.

In 1960, after learning that he had cancer, Purvis shot himself to death with the gun agents had given him at his retirement party. After sounding out Hoover, Hoover's lieutenants sent him a memo recommending that he not send Purvis's widow a note. "Right," Hoover wrote on the bottom of the memo.

After the funeral, Purvis's widow telegraphed Hoover. "We are honored," she said, "that you ignored Melvin's death. Your jealousy hurt him very much, but until the end, I think he loved you." In the margin of the telegram, Hoover wrote, "It was well we didn't write as she would no doubt have distorted it."

There would be several more well-publicized cases before what is known in bureau history as the Gangster Era ended. If the press had not given them fanciful names and glamorized their exploits, some of these colorful outlaws might not have been remembered. Compared to later criminals, they seem almost benign. But they were, in fact, vicious killers, and they captured the attention of the nation.

Because of the likes of Dillinger, "Pretty Boy" Floyd, Bonnie and Clyde, and "Machine Gun" Kelly, Congress in May and June of 1934 passed a package of major crime bills drafted by Hoover and Cummings. "The underworld," Cummings said, had "more men under arms than the Army and Navy of the United States." As Sanford Ungar noted in *FBI*, the new laws were "one of the most important, if least recognized," New Deal reforms.

Under the new laws, the robbery of a national bank or a member of the Federal Reserve System was a federal crime. Transportation of stolen property, transmission of threats, racketeering in interstate commerce, the murder of an FBI agent, and flight by a felon or witness across state lines to avoid prosecution or to avoid giving testimony were also brought under the bureau's umbrella. Finally, fulfilling a promise made by Hoover after the October 25, 1925, death of Edwin C. Shanahan, the first bureau agent killed in the line of duty, Congress gave bureau agents the authority to make arrests and carry firearms.

The gangster cases showed Hoover at his best and worst. On the one hand, he had built a cadre of professionals who had the intelligence, courage, and imagination to capture bad guys who had eluded local police. Field offices in every major city could quickly develop leads and respond wherever a fugitive ran. The bureau's laboratory could develop unassailable forensic evidence to be used at trial.

Hoover tightly managed agents and provided direction that brought out the best in them. For example, just before Purvis began developing leads in the Dillinger case, Hoover wrote to him that he was "somewhat concerned" that Purvis did not seem to have underworld informants.[12] Almost twenty years later, Hoover wrote to all SACs to complain that some had a "defeatist attitude." He said those SACs who are "unable to meet the problems in their divisions with the personnel and equipment that they have will be promptly replaced by men of enthusiasm, interest, initiative, and a desire to get the job done." But Hoover's treatment of Purvis, who was most responsible for the capture of Dillinger, showed what a petty, vindictive man he could be. It was a harbinger of things to come.

3

LEPKE

Besides giving the bureau new powers, the gangster cases—along with the Lindbergh kidnapping—had propelled the bureau to national prominence. The G-men were now folk heroes. But the bureau itself still didn't have a catchy name. Hoover asked his lieutenants for recommendations, and Edward A. Tamm, an assistant director who later became a federal judge, suggested Federal Bureau of Investigation.

Hoover was not persuaded; Tamm pointed out that the initials FBI also stood for the qualities that make for a good agent: fidelity, bravery, and integrity, which became the bureau's motto. Finally, Hoover accepted the idea. On July 1, 1935, the bureau changed its name to Federal Bureau of Investigation. FBI became a brand name.

Suddenly, there were G-man radio shows, magazines, comic strips, toys, and bubble gum cards. In 1935 alone, Curt Gentry calculated, there were sixty-five movies glorifying the FBI, the most popular being Warner Brothers' *G-Man* starring James Cagney. In every show, the G-man was a hero.

Hoover fed the craze, giving bureau cooperation only to those producers and reporters who could be counted on to portray the FBI in a glowing light. Hoover wanted to make sure he never had a Melvin Purvis hogging the limelight again. He began to cultivate a small cadre of reporters who would spotlight him in return for access to what the FBI called Interesting Case Memoranda. The Interesting Case Memoranda presented bureau cases in readable fashion, minus anything that might suggest that the bureau was fallible. Based on these, for example, Hoover's friend Rex Collier of the *Washington Evening Star* wrote an article about the Dillinger case that conveniently omitted any mention of the fiasco at Little Bohemia, the fact that Anna Sage had cooperated, or the deal Hoover made with Sage to obtain her cooperation.

As if the FBI were not getting enough publicity, based on a recommendation from columnists Drew Pearson and Robert Allen, Attorney General Cummings hired Henry Suydam, Washington correspondent for the *Brooklyn Eagle*, as a public relations man. He did not have to prod Hoover for colorful quotes. In a talk to the International Association of Police Chiefs in 1935, Hoover attacked the parole system, along with "sob-sister judges," "criminal coddlers," and "shyster lawyers and other legal vermin." These had allowed "human rats" like John Dillinger to flourish, according to Hoover.

While the publicity fed Hoover's ego, it also served the public interest. Hoover recognized that in order to be successful, the bureau needed the public's cooperation. The image of the all-knowing FBI that always got its man not only generated more cooperation in the form of tips or help from witnesses, it also theoretically made criminals think twice before robbing a bank or planning a kidnapping. Other law enforcement agencies might make brilliant arrests; only Hoover knew how to capitalize on those successes.

Hoover always portrayed himself as shy and averse to personal publicity. "Someone had to be the symbol of the crusade, and the director decided that because of his position, it was plainly up to him," Jack Alexander naively wrote in the *New Yorker* after interviewing the director. Hoover had been "reluctant to accept the role," Alexander said, "because it meant sacrificing the personal privacy he had enjoyed before all the G-man excitement began, but he felt he was not justified in refusing it simply because it was distasteful."

There was no better example of Hoover's PR savvy than his creation on March 14, 1950, of a "Ten Most Wanted Fugitives" list. "Give me your ten worst," an International News Service reporter said, the FBI's "ten toughest guys you would like to capture." From that request evolved a program that led to the capture of 140 fugitives based on tips from the public. "Most Wanted" FBI posters with photographs of the suspects were sent to police departments and post offices. Much later, the list would be posted on the Web. With the cooperation of the FBI, shows like *America's Most Wanted* would achieve extraordinary success helping to find fugitives by portraying their stories on the air.

The FBI would select candidates for the Most Wanted list based on how dangerous they were and how much agents thought publicity would help catch them. The first to make the list were bandits like "Tough Tommy" Holden, the most notorious train hijacker since Jesse James, and Willie Sutton, the "Babe Ruth of bank robbers." As antiwar revolutionaries, organized crime figures, serial killers, and terrorists became threats, their names appeared on the list as well.

Occasionally, the FBI would slip in an eleventh or twelfth name. Names would be removed from the list only if fugitives died or were captured, or if charges against them had been dropped. The FBI dropped five from the list because they no longer posed a danger or listing them likely would not help locate them. Of the 467 fugitives who would be placed on the list, 438 would be located, and process would be dropped against 15.

■　■　■

As predictable as gyrations in the stock market, the reputations of government officials go up and down in Washington. A government official who becomes too prominent is likely to be criticized by the press and his peers, either out of jealousy or an unconscious desire to distribute power more evenly within the nation's capital.

So it was with Hoover. While he had successfully cultivated many of Roosevelt's aides, others around the president—including his wife, Eleanor; his chief aide, Harry Hopkins; and his patronage chief, Postmaster General James Farley—mistrusted him as an empire builder. Hoover even put out the word that he would like to take over the Secret Service—an idea he discarded only after the assassination of John F. Kennedy.

Roosevelt himself "dealt with the bullet-headed boss at arm's length," his son Elliot remembered. "He recognized his efficiency . . . though he suspected that on many matters, Hoover was not a member of the administration team. But his competence was unquestionable, so

Father made it a practice never to interfere, this in spite of the fact that he knew there were many rumors of Hoover's homosexuality. These were not grounds for removing him, as Father saw it, so long as his abilities were not impaired."

Hoover's chief critic was Senator Kenneth Douglas McKellar, who headed the subcommittee over Justice Department appropriations. As early as 1933, Hoover had refused to appoint several of McKellar's constituents as special agents. As Francis Biddle, a later attorney general observed, McKellar was "obstinate, vindictive, shrewd—and he never forgot."

In the spring of 1936, Hoover appeared before the Tennessee Democrat's subcommittee to request an annual appropriation of almost $5 million, nearly twice the previous budget. Hoover told the subcommittee that since the FBI had assumed jurisdiction for kidnapping, the crime had been virtually eliminated. Federal bank robbery, he pointed out, had been reduced dramatically. The crime wave in the Midwest was over.

Hoover did not mention another gangster, Alvin "Creepy" Karpis, who was then Public Enemy Number One. Karpis was a member of the Kate "Ma" Barker gang, which committed bank robberies, kidnappings, and murders throughout the Midwest between 1931 and 1935. Karpis would later brag, "My profession was robbing banks, knocking off payrolls, and kidnapping rich men."

Questioning Hoover, McKellar asked if the FBI paid for advertising or hired writers. "Not in the Federal Bureau of Investigation," Hoover replied carefully, failing to note that Cummings had hired a bureau publicist on the Justice Department payroll.

"How many people have been killed by your department since you have been allowed to use guns?" McKellar asked.

"I think there have been eight desperadoes killed by our agents, and we have had four agents in our service killed by them."

"In other words," the senator concluded triumphantly, "the net effect of turning guns over to your department has been the killing of eight desperadoes and four G-men."

Hoover explained that agents fire only if a suspect pulls a gun or fires it.

"I doubt very much whether you ought to have a law that permits you to go around the country armed as an army would, and shoot down all the people you suspect of being criminals or that you suspect of having guns, and having your own men shot down," the senator said.

McKellar asked Hoover about his qualifications for his job. Hoover mentioned his nineteen years in the Justice Department, twelve of them as director of the FBI.

"I mean crime school," McKellar said.

Hoover said he had set up a training school within the bureau.

"So that whatever you know about it you learned there in the department?" McKellar asked.

"I learned firsthand, yes, sir."

"Did you ever make an arrest?"

"No, sir. I have made investigations."

Of course, there was no need for the director to make arrests, any more than a police chief would be expected to make arrests or the chairman of General Electric to design a jet engine. The FBI had only recently been given arrest power in any case.

Still, when Hoover returned to headquarters, he notified his subordinates that when Karpis was found, he wanted personally to arrest him. This would be the first of what the bureau called "the director's cases."

Three weeks after Hoover's testimony on the Hill, the FBI learned that Karpis was staying in an apartment on Canal Street in New Orleans. Hoover was in New York with Clyde Tolson.

Born on May 22, 1900, near Laredo, Missouri, Tolson received a law degree in 1927 from George Washington University.[13] A ruggedly handsome man, Tolson joined the FBI in 1928. Within a year, Hoover had named Tolson SAC in Buffalo. A week later, Hoover made him an inspector. Only two years after Tolson joined the bureau, Hoover named him an assistant director—a remarkably fast ascendancy. On July 1, 1936, Tolson became assistant to the director, and, in 1947, Tolson became associate director. In that position, Tolson was second in the chain of command to Hoover, whose private office was back-to-back with Tolson's.

Both bachelors, Hoover and Tolson were inseparable. They ate lunch together every day and dinner together almost every night. They vacationed together, staying in adjoining rooms, and they took adoring photos of each other. When Hoover died, Tolson briefly became acting FBI director.

Hoover never showed any interest in women and, until she died when he was forty-three, he lived with his mother, Annie. When he was out of town, he called her at least once and sometimes twice a day. When Hoover would return, he would bring her a gift. Annie kept a tight grip on her son, expressing suspicion of women who might be attracted to him and imposing her strict religious principles on him.

After Annie died in 1938, Hoover bought a one-story brick house in the Rock Creek section of Washington at 4936 Thirtieth Place NW, where he lived until he died. After he moved in, he added a second story.

After his mother's death, Hoover loosened up, but only slightly. He began to indulge a fondness for going to the racetrack on Saturdays. For show, Hoover placed $2 bets, but he had agents place his real bets at the hundred dollar window. In addition, each summer, he and Tolson vacationed in La Jolla, California, where they watched the races at the Del Mar track. Each December, they spent two weeks together in Florida, usually with Walter Winchell, always claiming that they never took a vacation.

Hoover and Winchell met after Hoover heard that the columnist was in Washington, attending a reception at the Shoreham Terrace Hotel, where autograph hounds besieged him. The most influential columnist of his day, Winchell had a daily readership of forty-eight million. His Sunday night radio broadcasts reached millions more. Hoover invited Winchell to his office, where he showed him Dillinger's death mask in his outer office.

Soon, Hoover and Tolson were traveling to New York to enjoy themselves with Winchell at the noisy Stork Club, Winchell's favorite hangout, where he usually sat at table 50 in the Cub Room. Along with Hoover's Florida and California trips, the bureau picked up the tab for the New York trips. No matter where he was, Hoover had the bureau send him pouches with memos to go over. During his trips, Hoover made sure to visit the local field office.

At the Stork Club, Hoover mixed with Hollywood magnates, bankers, newspaper and book publishers, and actors and actresses. He en-joyed his image as the nation's number one G-man and would pose for pictures with celebrities of the day, from Milton Berle to Marilyn Mon-roe, but only after someone removed the drinks from the table.

Winchell, who had invested well in real estate, would pick up the tab at the Stork Club. In turn, Hoover supplied Winchell with an FBI driver when he traveled. When Winchell received death threats, Hoover provided him with a bodyguard. When Winchell referred in one of his columns to Hoover's "nightclubbing," Hoover gently reproved him. The virtuous image of the director had to be maintained.

Almost every one of Winchell's columns carried a reference to "G-man Hoover." Hoover always denied that he gave Winchell information from FBI files or investigations. "The truth is that Winchell got no tips from me of a confidential nature," Hoover told the *New York Times* in 1954. "I cannot afford to play favorites."[14] But Herman Klurfeld, Winchell's longtime assistant, said, "We got a lot of stuff from the files from Hoover on plain paper. It arrived in a plain envelope. Walter knew it was from Hoover."[15]

Hoover used Winchell "practically every time he wanted to leak a story," said William C. Sullivan, who would rise to be one of Hoover's top officials.

"Perhaps the greatest affinity between them was that they both traded in secrets: Hoover with his thick investigative files, Winchell with his gossip," Neal Gabler wrote in *Walter Winchell: Gossip, Power, and the Culture of Celebrity.*

The night before Hoover learned that Alvin Karpis had been located in New Orleans, Hoover and Tolson were at the Stork Club, guests as usual of Winchell. When told about Karpis, they chartered a plane to New Orleans on April 30, 1936.[16]

On a blackboard in the New Orleans Field Office, agent E. J. Con-nelley drew a diagram of the apartment building where Karpis was hiding out. He assigned agents to cover the entrance, fire escapes, and nearby streets. Unexpectedly, when the agents descended on the area, Karpis and Fred Hunter, another fugitive, came out of the building and got in a car. Karpis sat in the driver's seat.

As recounted in authorized books and articles, Hoover ran to the driver's side, while Connelley ran to the passenger. Hoover lunged through the open window and grabbed Karpis by the collar before the outlaw could reach for the rifle on the backseat.

"Stammering, stuttering, shaking, as though he had palsy," Hoover would be quoted as saying, "the man upon whom was bestowed the title of Public Enemy Number One folded up like the yellow rat he was." Then, according to the official version, Hoover said, "Put the cuffs on him, men." No one had remembered to bring handcuffs, so agents tied Karpis's hands behind his back with a necktie.

At a press conference to announce that Hoover had made the arrest, a reporter asked the director, "Now that Karpis has been captured, who takes his place as Public Enemy Number One?"

Recognizing a way to get back at Senator McKellar, Hoover declared, "Politics itself is Public Enemy Number One. Political attempts to hamper and interfere with federal and other police and prosecuting agents are the real menace at the moment."

KARPIS CAPTURED IN NEW ORLEANS BY HOOVER HIMSELF, read the headline over the story in the May 1 *New York Times*. Kate Smith told her radio audience to congratulate Hoover, and thousands of letters poured into the bureau.

Now Senator McKellar was on the defensive. On the Senate floor, Arthur H. Vandenberg, a Republican from Michigan, attacked the senator for recommending a $225,000 reduction in Hoover's appropriation request. He portrayed McKellar as a miser whose parsimony could lead to more kidnappings. After one Democrat after another heaped praise on Hoover and his G-men, the Senate gave the director the full amount he had requested. The same week, Congress increased Hoover's salary from $9,000 to $10,000 a year.

McKellar never again caused any problems for Hoover. In 1943, he even attended a graduation ceremony at the FBI's National Academy. There, he praised "this great instrument of law and order that has been built by the grand man who is your director."

Karpis had the last word. In his 1971 autobiography, he said that Clarence Hurt, not Hoover, arrested him. Hurt was one of the former lawmen hired by Hoover and one of the two agents whose bullets killed Dillinger.

As Karpis told it, Hurt ran up to the driver's side of the car. Putting a .351 automatic rifle to Karpis's head, Hurt asked, "Karpis, do you have a gun?"

"No," Karpis said.

In his book, Karpis explained that it was a hot day, and he and Hunter had not worn jackets to hide their .45s. He said he had two rifles wrapped in blankets, but they were in the trunk of the car. As for a rifle on the backseat, "What rifle?" Karpis asked. "What back seat? We were in a 1936 Plymouth coupe that had no back seat."

According to his version, after Hurt got the drop on Karpis, Karpis heard someone shout, "We've got him! We've got him! It's all clear, chief." Then two men emerged from behind an apartment building. "Both were wearing suits and blue shirts and neat ties. One was slight and blond. The other was heavy-set with a dark complexion. I recognized the dark, heavy man," Karpis said. "I'd seen pictures of him. Anyone would have known him . . . I knew at that moment, for sure, that the FBI had finally nailed me."

The Karpis version and the official FBI version agree on only one point: No one remembered to bring handcuffs.

Karpis was charged with kidnapping two businessmen—William Hamm Jr., president of the Hamm Brewing Co., and Edward Bremer, president of a bank, both of St. Paul, Minnesota. Karpis pleaded guilty to one count of kidnapping in the Hamm case and received a sentence of life in prison. Released after serving thirty-three years at Alcatraz and McNeil Island, Karpis died in Spain at the age of seventy-one.

■　■　■

Three years after the arrest of Karpis, Hoover again made headlines by claiming to have arrested another notorious gangster, Louis "Lepke" Buchalter.

At forty-two, Buchalter, short and dimpled, headed a protection racket that largely controlled the garment industry in New York City. He was linked to a nationwide hit squad, Murder Inc., and was said to have been responsible for seventy killings. Hoover called him "the most dangerous criminal in the United States." Buchalter had gone into hiding, leading to law enforcement harassment of the underworld in general.

In August 1939, Walter Winchell, whose friendship with Hoover was widely known, received an anonymous call at the Stork Club. FM radio receivers had just been put on the market for the first time. General Foods Corporation, through its Bird's Eye brand, introduced the first precooked frozen foods, and Pepsi-Cola challenged Coca-Cola with the jingle, "Pepsi-Cola hits the spot!/Twelve full ounces, that's a lot/Twice as much for a nickel, too/Pepsi-Cola is the drink for you."

The caller told Winchell, "Don't ask me who I am. I have something important to tell you. Lepke wants to come in. If he could find someone he can trust, he will give himself up to that person. The talk around town is that Lepke [if captured by state authorities] would be shot while supposedly escaping."[17]

Winchell asked if Lepke trusted him. The caller said he would find out. When the anonymous man called again, he told Winchell solemnly that Lepke did trust him. The columnist offered to phone Hoover to obtain assurance that he would not be killed if he turned himself in to the FBI.

At a time when police departments regularly engaged in brutality or even killings of criminal suspects, Hoover had a strict policy banning such abuse. Long before the Supreme Court's 1966 decision in *Miranda v. Arizona*, Hoover required FBI agents to warn suspects of their rights when they were arrested. If agents treated suspects with respect, they were more likely to obtain cooperation, Hoover reasoned.

While Hoover and Tolson rushed to New York, the mystery man again called Winchell. Buchalter wanted Winchell to broadcast Hoover's assurance that he would guarantee Lepke's safety. The next evening, after explaining that Buchalter was interested in turning himself in, Winchell said breathlessly on his show, "Attention Public Enemy Number One, Louis 'Lepke' Buchalter! I am authorized by John Edgar Hoover of the Federal Bureau of Investigation to guarantee you safe delivery to the FBI if you surrender to me or to any agent of the FBI. I will repeat, Lepke, I am authorized by John Edgar Hoover . . ."

Punctuating his sentences with his trademark long pauses, Winchell added, "He may contact me at the *New York Daily Mirror* or John Edgar Hoover—in charge of the search for several years—in Washington at National 7117 . . ." Winchell added in his clipped style, "No part of the $35,999 reward to be claimed by me."

After Winchell went off the air, he received a call. "Walter?" the caller said. "That was fine. See you."

There were more calls, including a request for an estimate of how much time Buchalter would have to serve in prison. By turning himself in to federal authorities, Buchalter hoped to get less time, because the federal charges against him were less serious than the state charges. Winchell conveyed to the caller Hoover's estimate that he could get up to fourteen years.

Winchell and the go-between agreed that Buchalter would surrender on the corner of Twenty-eighth Street and Fifth Avenue on the night of August 24, 1939. Once again, the FBI issued a phony version of events. According to this account, Hoover met Buchalter alone at the corner and made the arrest himself. In fact, more than two dozen agents had the intersection under surveillance. As Winchell told it, Buchalter, wearing sunglasses, met him at the corner. The two then got in Winchell's car and drove to Hoover's black limousine several blocks away. Winchell gently took Lepke's arm and escorted him to Hoover's vehicle, where he made the introductions.

"Glad to meet you," Buchalter said to Hoover. "Let's go."

Hoover declined to shake Buchalter's hand. "You did the smart thing by coming in," Hoover told him.

On the ride to the federal building at Foley Square, Lepke complained about his celebrity. "Lepke, Lepke, Lepke! Everything is Lepke. All of a sudden, I'm a big shot," he said.

Hoover's penchant for rewriting history was pointless. The fact that Buchalter trusted the bureau and Hoover enough to turn himself in to them spoke volumes about the credibility the bureau had managed to acquire. It would have been foolhardy for the director of the FBI to meet alone with a murderer like Buchalter and take him in. Yet, at a press conference, called minutes after reaching the New York Field Office, Hoover insisted on claiming that he had single-handedly collared the gangster. Without going into the details, he credited Winchell only with having "assisted" in getting Buchalter to surrender.

The director used the occasion to note that neither the New York police nor Thomas E. Dewey, the New York district attorney who had sought Buchalter, played any part in the arrest. Hoover hated Dewey, and it was clear that by claiming he had personally arrested Buchalter, Hoover was getting back at the prosecutor, who nevertheless congratulated Hoover on the arrest.

After being tried and convicted on federal narcotics charges, Buchalter was sentenced to fourteen years in prison. But federal authorities turned him over to state prosecutors, and he was convicted of murder. On March 5, 1944, Buchalter was electrocuted at Sing Sing Prison in New York.

As the power of the FBI grew, Hoover's thirst for glory would become unquenchable.

4

SUBVERSIVES

By 1936, the U.S. population was 127 million, 50 percent greater than when the FBI had its beginnings. New York candy maker Philip Silverstein introduced the Chunky chocolate bar, containing Brazil nuts and raisins. The Waring blender, designed by bandleader Fred M. Waring, began modernizing kitchen chores. As if the gray-haired homemaker actually existed, General Mills began signing the name Betty Crocker to replies to consumers. Dale Carnegie's *How to Win Friends and Influence People* was a best-seller. The in dance was swing, played by Duke Ellington, Count Basie, and Benny Goodman.

Europe once again was heading toward war. Josef Stalin ruled the Soviet Union, and the Communist International announced it intended to infiltrate American labor unions. Adolf Hitler had seized power in Germany, which was sending spies to the United States.

On August 24, 1936, Franklin D. Roosevelt met with Hoover in the White House. According to Hoover's memorandum of the meeting, Roosevelt wanted to discuss "subversive activities in the United States, particularly Fascism and Communism." Two years earlier, Roosevelt had asked Hoover to look into Nazi groups and their anti-American activities.

Ever since his days in the Radical Division, Hoover had been more concerned about the Communist threat than fascism. Hoover told the president at their meeting that the West Coast longshoremen's union, headed by Harry Bridges, was "practically controlled by Communists." The Communists had plans to "get control of" John L. Lewis's United Mine Workers union. The Newspaper Guild had "strong Communist leanings." If the Communists were able to control these unions, Hoover told the president, they would be "able at any time to paralyze the country."

Roosevelt told Hoover he wanted a "broad picture" of the Communist and Fascist movements in the United States and how they might affect "the economic and political activity of the country as a whole."

Faced with such a fuzzy mandate, Hoover responded that the FBI lacked authority to pursue such an investigation. By law, the FBI was supposed to investigate only violations of criminal laws, which included laws against espionage. But Hoover knew of a loophole. The FBI could carry out any investigation requested by the State Department.

The next day, Roosevelt arranged to meet with Hoover and Secretary of State Cordell Hull. "The president pointed out that both of these movements were international in scope and that Communism particularly was directed from Moscow," Hull wrote after the meeting. Therefore, he said, "it was a matter which fell within the scope of foreign affairs over which the State Department would have a right to request an inquiry to be made." Hull told the director, "Go ahead and investigate the hell out of those cocksuckers."

In a memo to an aide, Hoover wrote that the president wanted investigations "for intelligence purposes only, and not the type of investigation required in collecting evidence to be presented in court." In other words, the information gathered could not be used for prosecutions, either because it pointed to no violation of law or because the evidence had been gathered illegally. Thus Roosevelt established a broad new avenue of FBI investigations that had no basis in law.

On September 5, Hoover instructed all field offices to obtain "from all possible sources"—meaning wiretaps and bugs as well as human sources—information concerning "subversive activities" being conducted within the United States by Communists and Fascists.

In theory, Hoover's immediate boss was the attorney general, but Hoover was in no rush to let him know about the FBI's expanded jurisdiction. Five days after he let field offices know, Hoover informed

Frank Murphy, a former Michigan governor who replaced Cummings as attorney general on January 2, 1939, what he was doing.

After enlisting the Army's Military Intelligence Division and the Office of Naval Intelligence, Hoover wrote to Roosevelt that it was imperative to maintain "the utmost degree of secrecy in order to avoid criticism or objections which might be raised to such an expansion." For that reason, he was against any increase in bureau appropriations to pay for the new investigative program.

When Germany invaded Poland on September 1, 1939, Hoover decided that secrecy was no longer warranted. He urged Attorney General Murphy to ask Roosevelt to issue a public statement "to all police officials in the United States" instructing them to turn over to the FBI "any information obtained pertaining to espionage, counterespionage, sabotage, and neutrality regulations."

As released by Murphy, Roosevelt's statement said the FBI would be in charge of investigating "subversive activities," along with espionage, sabotage, and violations of the neutrality laws. Roosevelt asked all law enforcement agencies to report to the FBI any information that would help pinpoint such activities.

Hoover was especially pleased by the last point. The New York City police department had taken it upon itself to look into subversives. Always turf conscious, Hoover wanted to make it clear that when it came to the security of the country, the FBI was in charge.

On November 30, 1939, Hoover appeared before the House appropriations subcommittee. He informed the subcommittee that he had already hired 150 new agents, opened new field offices, and staffed the Seat of Government to work twenty-four hours a day. He said he needed an emergency supplemental appropriation of $1.5 million, on top of the bureau's existing budget of about $7 million.

Without acknowledging previous criticisms of such an approach, Hoover informed the congressmen that two months earlier, he had created a General Intelligence Division. He said the division was compiling and indexing information about individuals and groups engaged in "subversive activities, in espionage activities, or any activities that are possibly detrimental to the internal security of the United States."

Hoover had reverted to the same blunderbuss technique he had used when he headed the Radical Division, which became the General Intelligence Division. That approach had been rejected by Attorney General Harlan Fiske Stone, who asserted that the bureau "is not concerned with political or other opinions of individuals" but rather only with "their conduct, and then only with such conduct as is forbidden by the laws of the United States."

Roosevelt had authorized the bureau to go beyond the existing laws because an aggressive response was needed in a time of war. But the net cast by Hoover's directives was so broad that inevitably it would conflict with constitutional guarantees of free speech while not necessarily focusing on real threats. Moralist that he was, Hoover never understood the difference between criticism of the government and illegal conduct aimed at subverting the government.

Without statutory authority, and without informing Congress or the public, Hoover set up a Custodial Detention List of people to be rounded up and placed in concentration camps if the need arose. Those on the list consisted of "both aliens and citizens of the United States [who were of] German, Italian, and Communist sympathies," along with radical labor leaders, journalists critical of the administration, and some members of Congress.[18]

After Hoover told Congress that he had reestablished the General Intelligence Division abolished by Stone in 1924, Representative Vito Marcantonio of New York charged that Hoover's system of "terror by index cards" smacked of the Gestapo. It was, he said, "a general raid against civil rights . . . very similar to the activities of the Palmer days."

Hoover had a ready answer, one he would use repeatedly. He told friendly politicians and reporters that the controversy was inspired by Communists, who wanted to "smear" the FBI and destroy it.

While Hoover was compiling files on critics of the government, he made sure to create files on those in power, including his new boss, Attorney General Murphy. Even before Murphy was sworn in, Hoover placed information about him in his Official and Confidential file, the one he kept in his suite of offices. The file noted that Murphy was a lifelong bachelor and a "notorious womanizer" who was as likely to bed a married woman as a single one.

If the files were a source of potential blackmail, they could also be used to ingratiate. Despite Germany's invasion of Belgium, the Netherlands, and France and its attacks on Great Britain, by 1940 the United States still had not entered the war. Roosevelt faced tremendous opposition from isolationists, who were promoting Joseph P. Kennedy, the American ambassador in London, for the presidency.

Kennedy had just met at the German embassy in London with Herbert von Dirksen, the German ambassador. Dirksen later reported on the conversation in great detail to Baron Ernst von Weizsäcker, the German state secretary. According to his account, the father of the Kennedy clan told the German ambassador that no European leader spoke well of the Germans because most of them were "afraid of the Jews" and did not "dare to say anything good about Germany."[19] In his view, Hitler's government had done "great things" for the country.

On May 16, 1940, Roosevelt addressed a joint session of Congress. He spoke of the need to help America's allies with war supplies. But the speech drew criticism from isolationists, who, fearing another war, deluged the White House with telegrams. Two days after the speech, Steve Early, the president's press secretary, wrote Hoover, "I am sending you, at the president's direction, a number of telegrams he has received since the delivery of his address . . . These telegrams are all more or less in opposition to national defense. It was the president's idea that you might like to go over these, noting the names and addresses of the senders."

Hoover was only too eager to please. He not only recorded information from the telegrams, he gave Early reports from the files on each writer. On May 21, Roosevelt sent Hoover more telegrams. Eventually, Hoover simply ordered investigations of Roosevelt's critics and sent the results to the president.

Hoover singled out for investigation Charles A. Lindbergh, who not only was an ardent isolationist, but he had also credited the Treasury Department, rather than the FBI, with solving the kidnapping of his son. At Hitler's invitation, Lindbergh had toured Germany and reviewed its air force. Lindbergh concluded that the Luftwaffe was the strongest air force in the world. In Germany, he found "a sense of decency and values which, in many ways, is far ahead of our own." Hitler was a "great man" who had "done much for the German people,"

Lindbergh said. It was American Jews who were "among the principal war agitators."

In a June 12, 1940, letter, Roosevelt thanked Hoover for his reports. "You have done and are doing a wonderful job, and I want you to know of my gratification and appreciation."

Hoover replied that he was "deeply thankful that the head of our government . . . possesses such sterling, sincere, and altogether human qualities." Hoover enclosed more reports on the president's political enemies.

For good measure, according to Oliver Pilat, a son-in-law of columnist Drew Pearson, Hoover leaked some of the more interesting tidbits to Pearson and Walter Winchell. Hoover was, according to Pilat, "harassing isolationists under orders from the White House."

Pleased with the reports from the FBI, Roosevelt stepped up his requests. On July 2, 1940, Interior Secretary Harold Ickes, apparently acting under Roosevelt's orders, asked Hoover to conduct a background check of Wendell Willkie, Roosevelt's Republican opponent. However, heeding the advice of Ed Tamm, by now assistant to the director, Hoover turned down the request. The fact that Hoover drew the line on Willkie is significant. If Willkie won the election and found out that Hoover had investigated him, Hoover would have been out of a job. When Roosevelt was safely reelected, Hoover sent Roosevelt reports on Willkie's remarks and associations.

One could argue that Hoover was a subordinate acting under presidential orders. But Hoover had created vast files of material suitable for blackmail for a reason. Certainly knowing that a politician had an active sex life was not relevant to the FBI's mission of investigating violations of criminal statutes. A man like Harlan Fiske Stone would have simply rejected Roosevelt's requests. A coconspirator with the president, Hoover not only agreed to his requests but enlarged upon them. In all, Hoover sent Roosevelt two hundred reports on his political opponents.

Meanwhile, with Roosevelt's backing, the bureau's agents increased from 353 when Roosevelt took office in 1933 to 4,380 when Roosevelt died in office in 1945. Support employees increased from 422 to 7,422. Appropriations rose from $2.8 million to $44.2 million.

■ ■ ■

When Robert H. Jackson replaced Murphy as attorney general on January 18, 1940, Hoover was faced with a boss who would not knuckle under. When Jackson learned about the Custodial Detention Program, he demanded that it be transferred from the FBI to the Justice Department. Hoover resisted, saying he needed to keep the names of informants confidential. Jackson then asked for the dossiers, but Hoover gave him summaries, carefully choosing what information to include.

After this clash, Hoover on April 11, 1940, secretly began a new filing system. Under this "Do Not File" procedure, sensitive memos for the director were to be prepared on blue paper. They would not bear serial numbers like the rest of the bureau's documents, and no copies were to be made. After reading them, the director would decide whether to retain or destroy them.

There was one problem. "In the file-conscious bureau, agents recognized that any paper potent enough for 'Do Not File' status was important and worth keeping," said Neil J. Welch, a former SAC in New York. Thus, the New York office kept a nearly complete record of surreptitious entries, or black bag jobs, from 1954 to 1973.

Hoover himself retained many of the "Do Not File" memos in the Official and Confidential files, which contained derogatory information about presidents, cabinet officers, and members of Congress. If some of the material in the Official and Confidential file no longer interested him, he returned it to the bureau's general files. Like a squirrel hiding nuts, Hoover stored away other sensitive material in still other files. In his office, he kept a Personal and Confidential file, which he began in 1941 and initially used to retain information about "subversive activities" that Attorney General Stone would have considered outside the bureau's legal purview. As documented by Athan Theoharis in *From the Secret Files of J. Edgar Hoover*, Hoover included in the Personal and Confidential files documents authorizing illegal FBI break-ins beginning in 1942.[20]

Hoover also routed some sensitive material to Clyde Tolson's personal file. Tolson destroyed much of this material. For reasons unknown, the records in Tolson's personal file from January 1965 through

May 1972 survived. They include memos about Richard Nixon's attempts to change the composition of the Supreme Court by having the FBI collect damaging information on liberal Justice William O. Douglas so he would be impeached. They also include Hoover's November 1970 order to provide Nixon, at the request of the White House, with derogatory information about members of the press, including information on gay reporters.

After the secret files, nothing created as much controversy—or gave Hoover as much power—as his use of wiretaps. With or without Hoover's approval, the bureau had engaged in sporadic wiretapping from its beginnings. However, in 1924, Attorney General Stone banned the practice. Hoover himself declared the practice "unethical." By 1932, the bureau was again tapping phones. Hoover claimed that the practice was limited to kidnapping and white slavery investigations, along with cases where the "national security is involved."

However, in 1934, the Federal Communications Act, under Section 605, banned the interception and divulgence of telephone calls. That meant that listening in on calls—except by telephone company personnel who did not divulge their contents—was prohibited.

At first, Hoover ignored the ban. Despite the clear language of the law, he argued that so long as the bureau did not disclose the contents of a call outside the Justice Department, it was not disclosing its contents. When the Supreme Court knocked down that argument, Hoover claimed that the act meant that the bureau could wiretap so long as the information was not used as evidence in court. In December 1939, the Supreme Court rejected that argument as well.

Based on that decision, Attorney General Jackson on March 15, 1940, issued an order prohibiting the bureau from engaging in wiretapping. As he had in the past, Hoover pretended to go along, proclaiming, "I do not want to be the head of an organization of potential blackmailers." But privately, Hoover fought to overturn Jackson's ban.

Rather than going over Jackson's head and appealing directly to Roosevelt, the director waged a campaign through the press and cabinet officers. He told Drew Pearson that FBI agents had heard German agents plotting to blow up the *Queen Mary*, but because of Jackson's order, they had to stop listening. Hoover presented his case to Treasury

Secretary Henry Morgenthau, who sided with him and conveyed his concerns to the White House. When Roosevelt learned of Morgenthau's position, he immediately met with Jackson and followed up with a confidential memo saying that, while he agreed with the Supreme Court decision, he was sure the Court never intended to apply its ruling to "grave matters involving the defense of the nation." Roosevelt ordered Jackson to obtain information through "listening devices" about people "suspected of subversive activities against the government of the United States, including suspected spies."

Appalled that he was being forced to participate in a circumvention of a Supreme Court ruling, Jackson told Hoover he did not want to authorize specific wiretaps and did not even want to know who was being tapped. However, Jackson loyally told the House Judiciary Committee that he interpreted the court's ruling to mean that the FBI could continue to wiretap as long as it did not divulge in court the information obtained. That reasoning—clearly at odds with the plain language of the 1934 FCC statute—would be used to justify FBI wiretapping into the late 1960s.

Jackson, who became a Supreme Court justice, would later write of his misgivings about a "central police" that has "enough on people" so that no one would oppose it. Significantly, he wrote, "Even those who are supposed to supervise it are likely to fear it."

Like so many public officials, Jackson himself had something to hide, implicitly giving Hoover power over him. The married Jackson carried on a lengthy affair with Elsie Douglas, his secretary at the Supreme Court. Walter Trohan, who was chief of the *Chicago Tribune*'s Washington bureau, recalled that Hoover told him about the affair over dinner one night at Harvey's.

Trohan's friendship with Hoover began on a decidedly sour note. When Trohan came to Washington in 1934, his city editor asked him to write a story about Hoover and the fact that he had never made an arrest. "I went to the Secret Service, where he wasn't liked, and to other police units," Trohan told me. "They gave me a lot of stories about Hoover, that he posed in front of a mirror every morning before he shaved. I wrote a highly critical story."[21]

Soon after Trohan's story appeared, Ed Gibbon, a friend from college, came up to him on the street. Gibbon had become an FBI agent. "He said he was assigned to shadow me," Trohan said. Gibbon explained that he was telling him because Trohan might recognize him anyway.

"You don't have to shadow me," Trohan said. "I'll tell you where I'm going and what I'm doing. You'll get a little vacation."

Since both Trohan and his paper were fiercely anticommunist, Hoover eventually cooperated with Trohan, and—like Walter Winchell and Rex Collier of the *Washington Evening Star*—they became friends. "Hoover changed his tune on me because I was anticommie, and he was running against the commies," Trohan said. Regularly, Trohan had dinner at Harvey's with Hoover and Tolson, who said little and always had a dour expression.

When Trohan traveled, Hoover had agents meet him at the airport. "In Paris, London, Rome, and Madrid, he would have agents offer help. They took me to tourist sites or to restaurants, where I bought them dinner. The guy in London introduced me to Scotland Yard people," Trohan said. "Hoover told me his goal was to make the FBI like Interpol and to keep records from throughout the world."

Hoover introduced Trohan to Louis B. Nichols, who since 1935 had been in charge of what Hoover euphemistically called the Crime Records Division, a public relations department that promoted Hoover and the bureau. Born in Decatur, Illinois, Nichols graduated from Kalamazoo College and received a law degree from George Washington University School of Law in 1934.

Besides handling press inquiries and dealing with Congress, the Crime Records Division responded to letters asking for Hoover's favorite recipes, sent out autographed photos of Hoover, and wrote angry letters to newspapers that published anything critical about the director or the FBI. Most important, the division helped create books, movies, television and radio shows, and newspaper and magazine articles lauding Hoover and the FBI.

Despite Hoover's claims that the bureau's files were never improperly disclosed, if Trohan wanted a file, he would simply ask Nichols for it.

"Lou Nichols would do pretty near anything for me," Trohan said.

"If I wanted a file, he would bring it to his home in Alexandria. I wouldn't touch it, but he read it to me. 'You might want this, you might want that.' It was helpful to me. I did that quite a bit."[22]

When Justice Jackson died, Hoover had the last word about his former boss, who had had the temerity to challenge his authority to wiretap and to compile a Custodial Detention List. Hoover had Nichols tell the press that Jackson had died in his secretary's apartment, Trohan said. Announcing the sixty-two-year-old justice's death, a Supreme Court spokesman was forced to mention that Jackson had died in his secretary's apartment, but he claimed Jackson went there for help after suffering an attack in the vicinity.[23]

Over time, the secret files would become even more useful to Hoover.

5

SUBMARINE

Robert L. Shivers, the SAC in Honolulu, called Hoover at 2:30 on December 7, 1941. "Listen!" the SAC said. In the background, Hoover, who was in New York, could hear the sounds of the Japanese attack on Pearl Harbor. The strike, by 360 Japanese warplanes, sank or seriously damaged eight United States battleships, fourteen smaller ships, and two hundred aircraft. The attack killed 2,388 people.

JAPS BOMBING HAWAII; WAR DECLARED ON U.S., the headline in the *Washington Post* read the next day.

With one dissenting vote, Congress immediately declared war. Roosevelt remarked that December 7 would be a "date which will live in infamy."

Hoover had been preparing for something like this. Agents had compiled a list of Japanese, Italian, and German aliens living in America who might pose a threat in time of war. Within seventy-two hours, the FBI had rounded up 3,846 of them. They were turned over to the Immigration and Naturalization Service until hearings could be held on their status.

When Francis Biddle, a friend of Jackson who replaced him as attorney general, discovered that Hoover had compiled such a Custodial Detention List, he called it both illegal and unwise.

A former solicitor general, Biddle got along with Hoover, who regaled him with intimate details of the personal lives of Washington figures. "Edgar was not above relishing a story derogatory to an occupant of one of the seats of the mighty, particularly if the little great man was pompous or stuffy," Biddle later recalled. "And I must confess that, within limits, I enjoyed hearing it. His reading of human nature was shrewd, if perhaps colored by the eye of an observer to whom the less admirable aspects of behavior were being constantly revealed."

But Biddle ordered Hoover to discard the detention list. Cunning as always, Hoover merely changed the name of the list to the Security Index and retained it. Later, Biddle approved the forced internment of 110,000 Japanese Americans, most of them born in the United States, in barbed-wire camps. Because Hoover felt the bureau had already arrested any likely spies in the first seventy-two hours after the attack, he viewed the Japanese internment as an affront to the bureau, and he opposed it.

A day after the bombing, Roosevelt asked Hoover to take charge of "all censorship arrangements." In the roughly two weeks that he had this duty, Hoover managed to squelch a *New York Times* headline calling the attack the worst naval defeat in U.S. history. Threatening them with jail, he also persuaded Drew Pearson and Robert Allen to kill a "Washington Merry-Go-Round" column detailing American losses.

Without legal authorization, in early December 1941, Hoover asked the telegraph and cable companies to delay transmissions to a half dozen countries, giving the FBI a chance to copy the messages before they were sent. Eventually, Western Union, RCA, and ITT simply gave the FBI copies of messages. The FBI also began opening and reading mail to and from diplomatic establishments of Germany, Japan, and their allies. This was called Z-coverage. During the Cold War, the program was aimed at the embassies of Russia and its allies. The program came to include mail to anyone who might be in league with enemies of America.

Hoover had already established an FBI language school, which turned out translators who could read Japanese and German dispatches. He had also set up a "plant protection system," so that informants would report anything suspicious at defense plants and other key industrial sites. At war's end, Hoover could boast that American industry had been free of sabotage.

■ ■ ■

Just before midnight on June 13, 1942, a young coast guardsman named John Cullen, who was patrolling a beach near Amagansett, Long Island, encountered four men struggling in the surf with a large raft. When Cullen questioned them, the men claimed to be fishermen. But Cullen noted that they were armed, and one of the men said something in German. About 150 feet offshore, Cullen noticed a long, thin object that looked suspiciously like a glistening black submarine. It was beached.

When Cullen continued to question them, the men offered him $260 as a bribe for his silence. Since he was alone, Cullen decided to play along and accept the money. After returning to his headquarters, Cullen reported them. He was convinced that the men were German spies or saboteurs, but his superiors were skeptical. They did not want to be ridiculed if they turned out to be wrong. The German intruders, meanwhile, took a 6 A.M. train at the Amagansett station of the Long Island Railroad.

At dawn, Cullen and an armed patrol returned to the beach. Buried in the sand they found explosives, fuses, blasting caps, timers, and incendiary devices, along with German uniforms, brandy, and cigarettes. The submarine had disappeared.

Not until noon did the FBI learn of the incident, and then from a Long Island police chief. Hoover informed Biddle, who recalled, "All of Edgar Hoover's imaginative and restless energy was stirred into prompt and effective action. He was determined to catch them all before any sabotage took place. He had steadily insisted that this war could be fought without sabotage. But he was, of course, worried."

Rather than alert the public, possibly causing panic and enabling the saboteurs to get away, Hoover recommended a news blackout. It was a calculated risk. If more invasions were in the offing, the public should have been on the lookout. Hoover would have been blamed for not sounding the alarm. But Hoover was confident that his men could catch the invaders and detect any future intrusions on American soil.

In short order, the FBI had a lucky break. The day after the landing, George John Dasch, the leader of the saboteurs and one of those confronted by Cullen, confided to his partner, Ernst Peter Burger, that he sympathized with the United States and was thinking of calling the FBI. So that they would fit in, the Nazis had recruited Germans who had lived in Germany but had also lived for decades in the United States. Indeed, Dasch had lived in the United States for twenty years. Burger was a naturalized U.S. citizen. They had grown attached to the country.

Dasch later said he was prepared to push his partner out a window if he stopped him from calling the FBI. But Burger admitted that he also had no intention of carrying out their sabotage plan. Instead, he had planned to disappear with the $84,000 in cash that the Abwehr, the German army's intelligence service, had given them. On hearing this, Dasch promptly placed himself in charge of the funds.

Dasch did, in fact, call the New York Field Office of the FBI in the middle of the night. He said he wanted to meet with Hoover. The agent's supervisor read the report of the call the next day and dismissed Dasch as a nutcase. Dasch decided to travel to Washington and try to see Hoover himself. He checked in to the Mayflower Hotel and tried to call the director. After being passed around, he wound up talking with D. M. "Mickey" Ladd, who headed the Domestic Intelligence Division. Ladd, who was over the investigation of the landing on Long Island, had Dasch talk with Duane L. Traynor, who headed the Sabotage Unit. Traynor told me that he had the Washington Field Office send agents to pick up Dasch at his hotel.

"We knew from the Coast Guard that one of the saboteurs had a white streak in his hair. When Dasch came in, he had a white streak in his hair. I knew he was the real thing," Traynor said.[24]

Dasch later claimed that no one took him seriously until he dumped the contents of his suitcase on Ladd's desk. Packets of bills cascaded over the desk and onto the floor. Even then, Ladd was skeptical. "Is this stuff real?" he asked. A few minutes later, Ladd brought Dasch in to see Hoover, according to Dasch's account.

But Traynor said Dasch's version was "a lot of malarkey." According to Traynor, agents searched Dasch's room at the Mayflower after they picked him up. They found $50 bills in a suitcase.

"Dasch's idea was he was going to turn himself in and then go free. He was first enamored of Hitler but became disenchanted. He was going to use the money to broadcast anti-Hitler propaganda to Germany," Traynor said.

During eight days of interrogation, Dasch gave Traynor information about the training he had received at the Abwehr's school for sabotage in Berlin. He listed his contacts in the United States and his intended targets, which included the Niagara Falls hydroelectric plant, locks on the Ohio River, and the Aluminum Corporation of America. Dasch told the FBI as well about German war production, secret codes, and submarine capabilities. He said German submarines could dive to six hundred feet, a far greater depth than American submarines. He also informed the bureau of the location of a German submarine base at Lorient, France, the origin of the sub that had transported the Germans to Long Island.

Dasch told the FBI that a second submarine with more saboteurs had just landed on Ponte Vedra Beach near Jacksonville, Florida. Additional groups were scheduled to land every six weeks. By detonating bombs in public places like railway stations, and by sabotaging key industries, the Nazis planned to unleash a "wave of terror" on the United States.

Two days after Dasch met with Traynor, the FBI arrested Burger and the other two saboteurs in New York City. To find them, the bureau's lab had to read secret writing on a handkerchief Dasch gave Traynor. Burger was cooperative as well, and with the information he provided, agents were able to track down and apprehend the saboteurs already in Florida.

It was a great victory for Hoover and the bureau, but one that might have seemed less impressive if the public knew that Dasch had turned himself in.

FBI CAPTURES 8 GERMAN AGENTS LANDED BY SUBS read the headline in the *New York Times*. Hoover, the article said, "gave no details of how the FBI broke the case. That will have to wait, FBI officials insist, until after the war."

While it could be argued that keeping the details secret in time of war was warranted to make the Germans think the FBI had a more impressive way of finding out about their plans, Hoover concealed even from Roosevelt the real story of how the FBI broke the case. In a June 22 memo to the president, Hoover proudly informed him that the FBI had apprehended "all members of the group which landed on Long Island." Hoover said he expected to have in custody all members of the second group as well. There was no mention of Dasch's turning himself in. The implication was that the FBI, through outstanding investigative and scientific work, had tracked down the saboteurs all by itself.

By order of Roosevelt, because they were an arm of Germany's war effort, Dasch and his fellow saboteurs were tried by a special military tribunal, a procedure that the Supreme Court later upheld. Both the press and the public were excluded, and, to prevent leaks, censorship was imposed. The tribunal consisted of seven generals, but the prosecutor, Attorney General Francis Biddle, was a civilian. It took a month to try the eight men and find them guilty. They were all sentenced to death, and six were electrocuted. The public did not learn about the trial and the deaths until a few hours after the execution. The records were sealed until after the war.

In light of their cooperation, President Roosevelt commuted the sentences of Dasch and Peter Burger. Dasch wound up with thirty years at hard labor, while Burger got life at hard labor. At the end of the war, President Truman commuted their sentences, and they were deported to Germany.

It was the most sensational case of World War II, and congratulations poured in to Hoover. Lou Nichols secretly organized a campaign to bestow upon the director the Congressional Medal of Honor. While that never materialized, Roosevelt and the attorney general released statements extolling the FBI director, who was about to celebrate his twenty-fifth anniversary with the Justice Department.

Even after the war was over, Hoover objected when he learned that Tom C. Clark, President Truman's first attorney general, had let *Newsweek* look at the Nazi saboteurs case files. In the fall of 1945, Hoover persuaded Clark to call the magazine to ask them to delay publication, but the magazine went ahead. Hoover then ordered Lou Nichols to beat *Newsweek* with a press release revealing new details about the case. The release minimized Dasch's role and omitted the fact that the FBI initially had turned him away.

In nearly all spy cases to come, the FBI would benefit from inside information from a defector. But, contrary to Hoover's desire to appear invincible, the fact that a case began with a tip did not detract from the reputation of the bureau. Solving almost any case—or, for that matter, discovering anything new—usually involves some luck. In the Lindbergh kidnapping case, for example, the fact that a gas station attendant wrote down the license plate number of Hauptmann's car led to his eventual apprehension, but that would not have happened if the FBI had not distributed to banks a list of the ransom bills.

The fact that a defector chooses to trust the FBI in the first place is a reflection on its credibility and the way the bureau handles informants. Regardless of how a case is broken, what counts in the end is whether the FBI is successful, properly following up on leads and apprehending suspects so they may be tried in a court of law.

As Hoover unremittingly pointed out, never again did the Nazis attempt to land saboteurs on American shores. When the Germans landed two spies—as opposed to saboteurs—by U-boat on November 29, 1944, at Point Hancock, Maine, the FBI quickly picked them up.

■ ■ ■

On April 12, 1945, Hoover and Tolson were leaving headquarters for dinner at Harvey's when Ed Tamm, an assistant director, stopped them on their way down from their offices. Roosevelt, Tamm told them, had just died of a massive cerebral hemorrhage in Warm Springs, Georgia. Eight minutes later, at 5:48 P.M., the White House announced the president's death.

Hoover was then in a battle with William J. "Wild Bill" Donovan, who formerly headed the Office of Strategic Services, a predecessor of the CIA. Donovan wanted Roosevelt to establish a worldwide intelligence service, which would become the CIA. Hoover was opposed. The two men had clashed before. Two days after Pearl Harbor, Donovan had persuaded Roosevelt to give him authority for coordinating all agencies dealing with intelligence. When Hoover heard of the plan, he protested that the FBI already had responsibility for intelligence in the Western Hemisphere. Since July 1940, the FBI had collected intelligence in Central and South America through its Special Intelligence Service (SIS), focusing mainly on German agents. At its peak, the FBI had 360 agents operating in the SIS. Roosevelt had sided with Hoover, allowing the FBI to continue its SIS operations. At the end of the war, the SIS was disbanded.

Upon learning of Roosevelt's death, Hoover returned to his office and called Lou Nichols. He wanted all the files on Harry S. Truman, Roosevelt's vice president, who was sworn in as president at 7:09 P.M. in the Cabinet Room of the White House. The oath was administered by Harlan F. Stone, who by now was chief justice of the United States.

As he had when other presidents took office, Hoover ordered a search within the bureau for anyone who had a personal connection to Truman. The quest turned up Morton Chiles Jr., the son of one of Truman's childhood friends from Independence, Missouri. At Hoover's request, Chiles asked to see the new president, who had known him since Chiles was born. After exchanging pleasantries, Chiles, as instructed, told Truman he had come as the personal emissary of J. Edgar Hoover, who stood ready to assist the new president in any way he could.

Truman thanked Chiles and asked him to relay a message to Hoover: "Anytime I need the services of the FBI, I will ask for it through my attorney general."

From that time on, said William C. Sullivan, who was then in the Domestic Intelligence Division, Hoover hated Truman. Two years later, Truman wrote to his wife, Bess, that he was sure "Edgar Hoover would give his right eye to take over [the Secret Service], and all congressmen and senators are afraid of him. I'm not, and he knows it. If I can prevent [it], there'll be no NKVD [a predecessor of the KGB] or Gestapo in this country. Edgar Hoover's organization would make a good start toward a citizen spy organization. Not for me."

Despite his bravado, Truman fell for Hoover's adroit manipulation. On April 23, 1945, Hoover met with Truman to brief him on current investigations. Truman made a point of having Brigadier General Harry Vaughan, his military aide, sit in on the meeting. After introducing them, Truman told Hoover that in the future, he should route such reports through Vaughan.

Later that day, Hoover sent Vaughan partisan political intelligence concerning key liberals who feared that Truman would reject Roosevelt's political agenda. Truman found the material irresistible. He wanted more. Within a month, the White House was asking for specific information about political opponents, and the FBI was conducting secret investigations for Truman. The following month, the FBI began wiretapping on behalf of the White House. Among the targets was Thomas "Tommy the Cork" Corcoran. A former aide to Roosevelt, Corcoran was known as a political fixer and influence peddler.

The wiretaps were installed on June 8 on Corcoran's office and home telephone lines. They would remain in place for three years until Corcoran, having figured out that his conversations were being intercepted, became guarded on the phone. Ostensibly, the taps were to uncover the source of leaks of classified information. Nothing was ever uncovered. But because Corcoran talked with everyone from Supreme Court justices and cabinet officers to columnists like Drew Pearson, the 6,250 pages of transcripts provided Hoover with enough gossip and juicy stories to guarantee his job throughout the Truman administration.

■ ■ ■

On July 1, 1945, Truman replaced Attorney General Biddle with Tom Clark, who had been a lobbyist for Texas oil interests before joining the Justice Department. Biddle considered Clark inept and had tried to fire him without success. Clark had little interest in supervising the FBI. He turned over wiretap requests to an assistant because, as Clark later said, he "didn't want to know who was tapped and who wasn't tapped."

The consummate bureaucrat, Hoover invariably got authorization for any controversial action. There was one exception: Despite Roosevelt's May 1940 directive that the attorney general approve each wiretap, Hoover initially authorized the Corcoran wiretaps himself. However, in November 1945, Truman dutifully asked Clark to authorize continuation of the wiretaps, and Clark did so.[25]

Since the underlying authority for wiretapping had been signed by Roosevelt, now that Truman was president, Hoover informed Clark that he would need to obtain from Truman an extension of the bureau's authority to wiretap without a warrant or court order. Hoover drafted a letter for Clark to send to Truman for his signature. It recited the language in Roosevelt's 1940 authorization, but it omitted a key sentence, one that instructed Hoover to keep the wiretaps to "a minimum" and to "limit them insofar as possible to aliens."

Thinking he was merely ratifying an existing policy, Truman approved the letter. Neither he nor Clark was aware that, because of Hoover's sleight of hand, they had just expanded the bureau's wiretap authority.[26]

Just how many wiretaps the bureau was operating at any given time was always a mystery. Each year, Hoover would appear before John J. Rooney, chairman of the House appropriations subcommittee with jurisdiction over the FBI's budget. "What is the average number of daily telephone taps used by the bureau throughout its entire jurisdiction at the present time?" Rooney would ask.

"The number of telephone taps maintained by the bureau as of today totals ninety," Hoover would say. "They are utilized in cases involving the internal security of the United States."

The number was always between fifty and a hundred. While Hoover never specified, when he referred to one wiretap, he apparently included the dozens of wiretaps that might be required to intercept multiple lines going to an establishment like the Soviet embassy in Washington.

Upon being presented with a letter from the Justice Department, the telephone company would tell the FBI where it could find particular phone lines between the central office and the targeted location. The appearances, as they are called, could be on a telephone pole, on an apartment or office telephone circuit board, or in a utility vault under the street. FBI soundmen, as they were called, would place a wiretap on the line and connect it to a second line leased by the FBI from the telephone company for the purpose of wiretapping. The leased line ran to the FBI's field office, where agents listened to the calls and recorded them. To make sure there was no drop in current, the FBI used a loop extender, which picked up electronic emanations from a line being tapped without penetrating the wire. Thus, a tap could not be detected.[27]

The key to understanding Hoover's testimony was his use of the phrase "as of today." Before his congressional testimony, said James E. Nolan Jr., a key former FBI counterintelligence official, "You were supposed to reduce the wiretaps."[28]

In a deposition given in connection with a lawsuit against the FBI, Horace R. Hampton, who for twenty-three years handled FBI requests for wiretaps for Chesapeake and Potomac Telephone Company, said the number of wiretaps in Washington alone was a hundred.

Eventually, on Hoover's instruction, Helen Gandy would destroy documents that apparently showed the true number of bureau wiretaps. Hoover left nothing to chance.

6

VENONA

As Soviet troops converged on Berlin, Adolf Hitler committed suicide in the Reich chancellery on April 30, 1945, at the age of fifty-six. Truman declared May 8 Victory in Europe Day. THE WAR IN EUROPE IS ENDED! SURRENDER IS UNCONDITIONAL; V-E WILL BE PROCLAIMED TO-DAY, read the eight-column headline in the *New York Times*. Devastated by two atomic bombs dropped by the United States on Hiroshima and Nagasaki, Japan surrendered on August 10.

As two superpowers emerged and the rest of the world took sides, George Orwell's *Animal Farm* was a best-seller, warning in metaphor against totalitarian regimes. "Coke," symbol of capitalism, was registered for the first time as a trademark of Coca-Cola.

While the Soviet Union had allied itself with the United States during World War II, Josef Stalin was seen as a threat to the West. In a speech in Fulton, Missouri, Winston Churchill, Great Britain's wartime prime minister, would declare that the Soviet Union desired "indefinite expansion" and that Stalin had imposed an "iron curtain" across Europe.

Not until the fall of 1945 did the FBI realize how great a threat the Soviets were. On September 5, Igor Gouzenko, a cipher clerk in the Soviet embassy in Ottawa, defected to Canada. He reported that the Soviets had organized a network of agents to obtain secret information from the Canadian military about Canada and particularly the United Stares. Two months later, on November 7, the FBI got its own break when Elizabeth Bentley walked into the New Haven Field Office of the FBI. For years, she told the agents, she had been a courier for the KGB, the Soviet intelligence service. Bentley had carried classified documents to the KGB from U.S. government employees in the OSS, the War Department, the War Production Board, the Air Force, and the departments of Treasury, Agriculture, and Commerce.

A Vassar graduate, Bentley joined the Communist Party when she began working on her master's degree in Italian at Columbia University in the early 1930s. She fell in love with Jacob Golos, a Russian-born KGB officer and member of the Communist Party's inner circle. He tasked Bentley to pick up documents from Mary Price, a secretary to columnist Walter Lippmann, and from Abraham Brothman, a chemical engineer.

After Germany attacked the Soviet Union in 1941, Russian-born Nathan Gregory Silvermaster of the Farm Security Administration volunteered to help Golos. With his wife, Helen, he formed a network that gave material to the Soviet operative through Bentley. The Silvermasters boasted that their sources included Laughlin Currie, a White House counselor; Harry Dexter White, assistant secretary of the treasury; and Alger Hiss, who worked in the State Department and headed the department's postwar planning staff. Eventually, Bentley said, she acted as a courier for more than eighty individuals, known in counterintelligence parlance as agents.[29]

Twice a month, Bentley picked up copies of documents at the Silvermasters' home near Chevy Chase Circle in suburban Maryland. She later picked up microfilm of documents. As the volume increased, she would take as many as forty undeveloped rolls of microfilm in her knitting bag on a train to New York. After Golos died of a heart attack, Bentley became disillusioned with communism, seeing it as a tool of the KGB. However, according to John J. Danahy, an FBI supervisor on the case, she did not decide to talk until one night she picked up a man at a bar at the St. George Hotel in Brooklyn. After they had sex in her room at the hotel, she searched his pockets and found a badge that said, "U.S. Probation Department."

"Thinking the FBI was on to her, she turned herself in and cooperated," Danahy said.[30]

While Hoover had been targeting the Communist Party, the success of the KGB at committing espionage came as a total shock. Without naming her, Hoover sent a complete rundown on Bentley's disclosures to the White House on November 8, 1945. Truman mistrusted Hoover and suspected he exaggerated the extent of Communist influence. Hearing nothing from Truman, Hoover circulated reports of the debriefings to other government officials. Soon, the information began to leak. When Hoover assigned hundreds of FBI agents to follow some of the suspects, they realized they were being tailed.

In those days, recalled Robert J. Lamphere, an FBI agent who worked many of the major spy cases, the bureau's program to detect spies—known as counterintelligence—was in its infancy. The bureau had no idea how to deal with the KGB. "One example was surveillance," Lamphere said. "If you put physical surveillance on a Soviet agent, he's going to find out that you're following him very soon."[31]

Hoover expected agents to dress in the traditional white shirts and dark suits. Agents could easily be spotted. There were occasional exceptions to the dress code, and no one was quite sure whether Hoover's aides, always eager to please, had exaggerated Hoover's instructions. According to legend, when Hoover wrote on one memo "watch the borders" because the writer of the memo had not left enough room for Hoover's comments, the bureau deployed agents to watch the Mexican and Canadian borders.

Walter R. Walsh, who became an agent in 1934, recalled that no one insisted he wear a white shirt when he posed as a meter reader while working the Edward Bremer kidnapping case. After Alvin "Creepy" Karpis and the Ma Barker Gang released him, Bremer recalled that a meter reader had come to the house where he had been held.[32] So Walsh tried unsuccessfully to locate the house by retracing the steps that a meter reader would take.

In later years, said Leonard M. "Bucky" Walters, who became an assistant director under Hoover, "I wore colored shirts—blue or tan. Hoover saw me in them and said nothing."[33] Walters said he always made sure to wear a colored shirt when he gave a talk to the new agents' class on their last day of training. Joseph J. Casper and Simon Tullai, who were in charge of the program, had indoctrinated the agents on what they thought was Hoover's dress policy. "They would get all upset," Walters said.

Aside from the dress issue, Hoover and the Justice Department were spinning their wheels when it came to pursuing spies. Rather than developing evidence for prosecutions, they tended to amass information for its own sake, as in an academic exercise, while making sure that questionable government employees were quietly fired. After all, the FBI was using wiretaps—which could not be admitted as evidence in court—along with surreptitious entries or black bag jobs that were clearly illegal. Another reason spies were not prosecuted was that the agencies that were penetrated were embarrassed and did not want public attention drawn to them. Finally, the FBI did not really know how to develop evidence against spies.

While assigned to the Albany Field Office, agent C. Edward Nicholson worked a case involving a young woman who slept with army officers in order to obtain defense information from them for the Germans. The FBI had intercepted some of her reports, sent through Spain to Berlin. When the Justice Department decided the FBI had not developed enough evidence to prosecute, Nicholson—who later headed espionage prosecutions in the Justice Department—persuaded the janitor at the woman's apartment house to let agents into her apartment when she was out.

"We found the woman's diary containing names and dates of all the men she had slept with, but no mention of the information she may have obtained from them," Nicholson recalled. Undeterred, Nicholson said, "While searching the apartment, we opened the medicine cabinet in the bathroom," where agents discovered a diaphragm. The agents "borrowed a needle from her sewing drawer and, ever so carefully, we punched a dozen minuscule holes in the diaphragm," he said. The agents put it back on the shelf in the medicine cabinet. "The woman indeed became pregnant within the next few months, and we then placed our investigation in an inactive status," Nicholson said.[34]

In Philadelphia, Nicholson was assigned to monitor wiretapped conversations of members of the Communist Party. Often, party functionaries remarked that they were probably being tapped. They would go to a bank of pay phones on the first floor of the office building where party headquarters was. "Unfortunately for the Communists, we had taps on the pay telephones," Nicholson said. One of the top party officials, a married man, constantly boasted about his conquests. When he told a friend on the phone that he was taking a gorgeous blonde to the Royal Motel in Camden, New Jersey, one of the other agents decided he had had enough.

The agent looked up the man's home number and anonymously called his wife. He told her that her husband would be with a blonde that night at the Royal Motel. The next afternoon, the agents heard the man call the friend. He said that shortly after midnight, his wife and her two brothers forced their way into his motel room. The two men then proceeded to beat him up. Now his head was bandaged, and his arm was broken.

The friend asked the Communist official how his wife could have found out about the assignation. There was only one way, the Communist said, because the friend was the only person who knew he would be at the motel. With that, the Communist announced that their friendship was over.

"Needless to say, J. Edgar Hoover was never told about this," Nicholson said.

In the Bentley case, rather than turning her into a double agent and using her to help corroborate her story, the FBI conducted surveillance of the people she named in government. They quickly caught on, and when it came time to verify her allegations, the bureau had little to go on. Part of the problem was that Hoover viewed Communist rhetoric as being just as threatening as espionage itself. While the Soviets contributed to the finances of the party and recruited key party members to conduct espionage, most party members were gullible Americans who thought socialism was the solution to poverty. They considered debating such issues at party meetings fashionable.

In Hoover's black-and-white view of the world, any questioning of the government and of authority was seen as a threat. Confusing talk with espionage, Hoover often failed to focus on the criminal conduct that must be proven to bring a spy case.

In the Bentley case, agent Robert Lamphere recalled in *The FBI-KGB War,* "very early the FBI could have forced things by moving in aggressively and interviewing everyone connected with her; in this way we might have gotten some of them to break, or to contradict one another's stories. We also could have obtained warrants and searched the Silvermasters' home . . . for evidence. No such actions were taken. In addition," Lamphere said, "a number of leads were not pursued to their logical end."

Ultimately, only one prosecution arose from the Bentley case. While Bentley herself was not prosecuted, she eventually testified before the House Committee on Un-American Activities (HUAC), courtesy of Hoover. For her testimony, Bentley wore a slinky black silk dress and pinned two artificial red roses in her light brown hair. She became known as the "Red Spy Queen."

The Bentley case, along with other information the FBI developed, led to a more promising suspect, Álger Hiss. In testimony before HUAC in early August 1948, Whittaker Chambers, an ex-Communist who was then an editor at *Time*, accused Hiss, a former State Department official, of having been a member of a Communist cell in Washington, along with eight other government employees. Initially, Chambers did not accuse Hiss of espionage. However, after Hiss appeared before the committee and denied Chambers's allegations under oath, Hiss dared Chambers to repeat the accusations in public. When Chambers did, Hiss sued him for slander.

During the ensuing litigation, Chambers produced Hiss's handwritten summaries of classified State Department documents, along with copies of other State Department reports typed by Hiss's wife, Priscilla. Chambers claimed that Hiss had given the material to him in the 1930s. On December 2, 1948, Chambers brought HUAC investigators to a garden on his farm near Westminster, Maryland, where he retrieved five rolls of microfilm from a hollowed-out pumpkin. These copies of documents that Chambers said Hiss had given him became known as the Pumpkin Papers. Chambers then admitted that, contrary to his earlier testimony, both he and Hiss had been involved in Soviet espionage.

Because a three-year statute of limitations had expired on espionage, the Justice Department prosecuted Hiss for perjury. During the trial, FBI experts testified that the documents had been typed on a machine once owned by Hiss. The first trial ended in a hung jury, but, after a second trial, Hiss was convicted on January 21, 1950. He spent forty-four months in a penitentiary.

As the Hiss case was proceeding, the FBI obtained even more shocking intelligence: A KGB agent was working in the Justice Department. The information came from a top-secret program called VENONA run by the Army Signal Security Agency, a predecessor of the National Security Agency (NSA) then commonly called Arlington Hall, after the location of its Virginia headquarters. In 1939, when the Soviet Union was an ally of Nazi Germany, the Army had begun collecting copies of encrypted cables sent by commercial carrier to Moscow by the Soviet diplomatic and trade missions in the United States. Because the cables were thought to be diplomatic in nature, no significant effort was made to decrypt them. However, in 1943, the United States learned that the Soviets, who were by then American allies, were negotiating a separate peace treaty with Germany. The effort to decipher the cables became more urgent.[35]

Because the code entailed use of a one-time pad, meaning that a new code was created for each message, the cables proved nearly impossible to decipher. However, by 1946, Meredith Gardner, an Arlington Hall analyst, was able to decipher the first messages. Eventually, 2,900 messages were decrypted.

By then, the war was over, but Gardner and his colleagues made a startling discovery: A large portion of the messages were not diplomatic in nature but rather concerned espionage activities of the KGB and GRU, the Soviet military intelligence. The messages revealed that during the 1930s and 1940s, hundreds of Americans were working with the Soviet intelligence services. By 1948, Arlington Hall was able to begin passing the old decrypted messages along to the FBI.[36]

Lamphere, the bureau's liaison with VENONA, was able to determine from the deciphered material that the spy referred to as working at the Justice Department was a woman. She had been employed in the Justice Department's New York office and, in January 1945, she had been transferred to Washington. That information fit Judith Coplon, a twenty-eight-year-old Brooklyn-born graduate of Barnard College. As an analyst in the Foreign Agents Registration Section, she had access to many FBI reports on known or suspected Soviet agents.

After making sure she was given no more access to sensitive documents, agents placed her under surveillance. After obtaining authorization from Attorney General Tom Clark, they wiretapped her office and home telephones, along with the phones of her parents in Brooklyn and the phones of Harold Shapiro, a Justice Department attorney with whom Coplon was having an affair.

The surveillance soon paid off. Coplon visited her parents once or twice a month. On January 14, 1949, instead of taking the subway to Brooklyn, she headed toward Washington Heights. There, on the corner of Broadway and 193rd Street, she met Valentin Gubitchev, a Soviet who was an employee of the United National Secretariat.

Agents followed them to an Italian restaurant, where they had dinner. The agents did not see Coplon pass any documents to Gubitchev, but Lamphere hoped to arrest Coplon in the act on another trip. Instead, while Lamphere was working one Saturday at headquarters, his boss, Harold Fletcher, informed him that Hoover wanted the case closed. Embarrassed that the Justice Department had been penetrated, Attorney General Clark had been pressing to have Coplon quietly fired. Hoover was now inclined to go along.

"You can't let this happen," Lamphere told Fletcher. "You've got to do something about it."

Fletcher said he would try, and later that afternoon, he told Lamphere that Hoover had given them some extra time.

Recognizing that Hoover might close down the case at any moment, Lamphere tried to increase the frequency of Coplon's trips to New York. He drafted a bogus document suggesting that the FBI had informants in Amtorg Trading Company, which the Soviets controlled. Then he made sure Coplon had access to the phony document. Sure enough, on February 18, she hopped on the train to New York. This time, Coplon and Gubitchev took more precautions than usual to avoid surveillance. As they passed each other, Coplon had her hand in her purse, but agents could not tell if she had passed along any documents.

Back in Washington, Lamphere again baited a trap. This time, he used a real document from the Atomic Energy Commission revealing sensitive information that would not damage the national defense. In addition, he created another phony document with more information about supposed bureau informants at Amtorg.

On March 4, Coplon headed for New York, where the FBI deployed thirty agents and a fleet of cars equipped with two-way radios. Coplon got off the train at Pennsylvania Station and took a subway to 190th Street. Three agents were on the train watching her. Coplon reached the meeting place at 7 P.M., but Gubitchev was not there. From the previous surveillance, the agents knew that if one of them was late, they would automatically meet an hour later at the same place. Sure enough, at 8 P.M., Gubitchev showed up. They came together briefly but then parted, apparently suspecting they were being watched.

Because the agents did not want to give themselves away, they lost Gubitchev. However, an agent got on the subway train with Coplon. At Forty-second Street, Coplon got off and boarded a bus going downtown. At the last second, Gubitchev appeared and got on the same bus.

The agent who was tailing Coplon saw the two board the bus. He called the radio room at the New York Field Office. Soon, FBI cars were racing down the West Side Highway. One Bu-car, as they are called, managed to catch up with the bus at Fourteenth Street. At that moment, Coplon and Gubitchev were just getting off the bus and racing down subway stairs to take a train crosstown. An agent ran out of his car and caught the same train. Because there were few people in the car where Coplon and Gubitchev were sitting, the agent did not get off when the two left the train. Instead, the agent rode to the next stop and called the radio room.

Agents swarmed the area, and when they saw Coplon and Gubitchev on the street, they arrested them on the spot, on the grounds a felony was about to be committed. Gubitchev was carrying a plain white envelope with $125 in small bills, a possible payoff. Coplon's purse contained the bogus FBI document and thirty FBI data slips, which summarized information from FBI documents. Agents also found a typewritten note that began, "I have not been able (and I don't think I will) to get the top-secret FBI report which I described to Michael on Soviet and Communist activities in the U.S. . . . ."

Normally, for purposes of spying, the Soviets were careful to use KGB officers attached to the Soviet embassy or consulate or Soviet representatives to the United Nations. Because these KGB officers ostensibly were diplomats, they were protected by diplomatic immunity. They could not be prosecuted, only expelled. Even though Gubitchev had entered the United States in 1946 as a diplomat, his post at the United Nations gave him no immunity from prosecution. The FBI therefore incarcerated him pending a trial.

Judith Coplon's trial in Washington made sensational copy, not only because it focused attention on the KGB's success at penetrating the U.S. government, but also because it exposed Coplon's sex life. Coplon never drew her curtains, giving agents a show as they watched her liaisons. At her trial, Coplon claimed that her meetings with Gubitchev were innocent, that she had had an unrequited love affair with him. But during the trial, the prosecutor asked Coplon, "If Gubitchev was the only man in your life, how is it that on January 7, 1949, you registered in a hotel in Baltimore as the wife of Mr. Harold Shapiro, and the following night in another hotel, in Philadelphia?"

Demure up to that point, Coplon lashed out at her lawyer.

"You son of a bitch!" she screamed. "I told you this would happen. How could you let it happen with my mother in the courtroom?"

As reporters ran to telephones, Coplon's mother, who attended each day of the trial, began to wail.

The Coplon case established the FBI as the preeminent agency for protecting the nation's security. But the trial highlighted two problems with FBI counterintelligence investigations: First, while Attorney General Clark had authorized the wiretaps, they were not legal. Like his predecessors, Clark had relied on Roosevelt's memo—reiterated by Truman—saying that the Supreme Court surely had not meant to prohibit wiretapping when the national security was at stake.

Second, Hoover had not foreseen that the judge in the Washington case would require the prosecution to introduce as evidence the FBI documents summarized on the slips Coplon had in her purse. The Justice Department was faced with either producing the complete documents in court or dropping the case. A furious Hoover turned over the documents, compromising some sources and making public a number of unsubstantiated allegations. In later years, Congress would pass a law known as the greymail statute, allowing the Justice Department to keep such sensitive material from the public by showing it only to the judge and jury at trial.

Although Coplon was convicted at both her trials in Washington and New York, Judge Learned Hand of the Circuit Court of Appeals overturned her convictions because the FBI had arrested her without a warrant. In addition, in the Washington case, the judge had not let the defense see records of the FBI's wiretapping. It was "extremely unlikely," Hand wrote, that the denial of the wiretap records had affected Coplon's defense. However, he went on, ". . . we cannot dispense with constitutional privilege." While Hand let the indictment of Coplon stand, the Justice Department ultimately decided against trying her again. Gubitchev eventually was expelled.

This was not the first time the FBI's illegal surveillance had impaired a prosecution. When *Amerasia*, a journal on Far Eastern affairs, published a report based on a classified OSS document in January 1945, the FBI broke into the publication's New York offices and conducted illegal wiretapping. As a result, the Justice Department had to make do with lenient plea bargains.

In the Coplon case, Hoover was outraged that the FBI had been compelled to turn over bureau reports, yet Coplon went free. At his urging, Congress quickly gave the FBI power to make arrests without a warrant in espionage cases. Hoover also took steps to ensure that no judge would ever be able to rummage through the bureau's files again. On June 29, 1949, he ordered a special procedure called JUNE MAIL for handling especially sensitive reports or "highly confidential or unusual investigative techniques." As examples of sensitive reports, Hoover cited those that came from sources such as governors or secretaries to high officials who may disclose information about these officials, including "what they were thinking." Confidential investigative techniques included wiretaps, microphone surveillance or bugs, break-ins or surreptitious entries, and interception of mail.

Such material was to be sent to headquarters in a sealed envelope marked "JUNE MAIL." The envelope was to be placed in a second envelope addressed to the director and marked "PERSONAL AND CONFIDENTIAL." These records were to be kept separate from the FBI's central records system in a special file room at FBI headquarters.

Not content with this concealment system, on July 8, 1949, Hoover created a procedure for separating routine investigative reports from more sensitive material reporting "facts and information which are considered of a nature not expedient to disseminate, or which could cause embarrassment to the bureau if distributed." These sensitive matters were to be reported only in "administrative pages," a category later called "cover letters." Thus, when a judge ordered the bureau to turn over reports on a case, or when the attorney general requested a file, Hoover could produce the investigative reports, not the administrative pages or the JUNE MAIL files.

Hoover later went a step further. He ordered senior FBI officials to destroy regularly the contents of their office files, which often had particularly sensitive information. Assistant directors were to destroy their files every six months; supervisors were to destroy them every ninety days.

■　■　■

Just after President Truman announced that the Soviets had exploded an atomic bomb on September 23, 1949, Special Agent Lamphere pored over newly deciphered VENONA dispatches indicating that the KGB had had an agent inside the Manhattan Project, the earlier American program to develop the atomic bomb. The FBI quickly identified him as Klaus Fuchs, a British scientist.

The FBI passed along the information about Fuchs to the British counterintelligence service, MI-5, which already had its suspicions about him. William Skardon of MI-5 interviewed Fuchs, gaining his confidence over the course of several weeks. Eventually, Fuchs confessed to providing the Soviets with information on the design of the atomic bomb. He identified his Soviet contact as "Raymond."

In time, Lamphere figured out that Raymond was Harry Gold, a Communist Party member employed as a chemist in Philadelphia. In May 1950, Gold confessed to having acted as a courier. In addition to Fuchs, Gold identified a second source of information at the Los Alamos laboratory, a soldier whom the FBI identified as David Greenglass. When agents questioned him, Greenglass implicated his sister Ethel Rosenberg and her husband, Julius. Greenglass said Julius Rosenberg had recruited him into the espionage ring. Ethel was present and transcribed her husband's notes on classified information to be passed to the Soviets.

On July 17, 1950, the FBI arrested Julius Rosenberg. A month later, agents arrested Ethel. Her round face and tiny mouth and his mustache and protruding ears became burned into the American consciousness. Morton Sobell, believed to be part of Rosenberg's spy network, was also arrested.

At the trial, Greenglass gave detailed testimony about the data he gave the Rosenbergs. He sketched the mold design for a spherical lens and described a series of plutonium experiments, all related to development of the bomb and turned over to Rosenberg. Gold, already sentenced to thirty years, identified Anatoli Yakovlev, a Soviet officer, as Rosenberg's KGB contact.

On March 29, 1951, a jury found the Rosenbergs and Sobell guilty. In a report to U.S. District Court Judge Irving Kaufman, Hoover opposed the death penalty for Ethel. He was concerned about how the public might react to the execution of the mother of two small children. But Kaufman sentenced both Rosenbergs to death and Sobell to thirty years in prison. Greenglass had previously pled guilty and was sentenced to fifteen years. ROSENBERGS EXECUTED AS ATOM SPIES AFTER SUPREME COURT VACATES STAY; LAST-MINUTE PLEA TO PRESIDENT FAILS read the eight-column headline over the lead story in the *New York Times* reporting their executions.

Over the decades, the Rosenbergs' sons and others would question their guilt, but in March 1997, Alexander Feklisov, who said he was the Rosenbergs' Soviet handler, would describe in interviews with the *Washington Post* and the Discovery Channel some fifty meetings in New York from 1943 to 1946 with Julius Rosenberg. He said Rosenberg had passed secrets involving military electronics, including the development of radar systems, but not the secrets of the atom bomb, which he claimed the Soviets obtained from other unnamed Americans.

As for Ethel Rosenberg, Feklisov said she had not been directly involved but was aware of her husband's activities.[37] That conformed with a VENONA intercept of a November 27, 1944, KGB message from New York to Moscow. It said Ethel "knows about her husband's work" but was in "delicate health" and "does not work." It also conformed with a recent admission by Greenglass in Sam Roberts's *The Brother* that he lied under oath by implicating his sister to save himself. Greenglass admitted that he relied on his wife's recollection that Ethel typed her husband's notes. "I had no memory of that at all—none whatsoever," he said in December 2001.

■ ■ ■

The VENONA intercepts pointed to the existence in the United States of several Soviet illegals who could not be identified. Illegals are officers of an intelligence service sent to spy on another country without diplomatic cover or any overt connection to their government. In May 1957, the FBI learned from a defector that such an illegal may have been in New York, and this led to one of the FBI's biggest cases.

Called back to Moscow because of his drinking, Reino Hayhanen decided instead to defect to the United States at the American embassy in Paris. Demanding vodka after being flown back to New York, Hayhanen told the FBI that he worked for a KGB officer whom he knew only as "Mark."

Counterintelligence terminology is very specific: An intelligence *officer* is an employee of an intelligence agency like the KGB or CIA and is considered a patriot in his own country. An intelligence officer recruits *agents* who work for the governments of opposing countries and provide the officer with secrets of those countries. Agents are considered traitors by their own countries and are subject to prosecution.

Mark's job as a KGB intelligence officer was to uncover U.S. military and atomic secrets and to recruit new agents. He had entered the United States from Canada in 1949.[38] Hayhanen said Mark had left secret documents for his Soviet handler in unobtrusive dead drops in parks. Dead drops are nooks and crannies in trees, walls, or bridges where spies leave documents for their handlers. Because handlers pick up the documents days or even weeks later, no one can spot them meeting together.

Hayhanen said Mark posed as a photographer and had a studio in Brooklyn. Hayhanen had been there only once, but he was able to give FBI agents enough details so they could narrow the area where it might be located. He also gave agents a description of Mark. He was fifty-five to fifty-seven years old, five feet ten inches tall, and weighed 175 pounds. He had thinning gray hair and a large thin nose with a slight hook. He wore glasses with gold frames.

Having learned that his assistant had defected, Mark, whose real name was Rudolf Abel, fled to Florida to await further instructions. When none came, he made the mistake of returning to his studio. On May 28, 1957, agents noticed a man who fit the description of Abel sitting on a bench across from 252 Fulton Street in Brooklyn. Checking with the building's janitor, they discovered that Emil R. Goldfus—one of Abel's aliases—rented Apartment 505 as a photo studio.

The FBI agents followed Abel to the Hotel Latham at 4 East Twenty-eighth Street in Manhattan, where he lived. They took clandestine photographs of Abel and showed them to Hayhanen, who identified him as the man he knew as Mark.

At 7:02 A.M. on June 21, two FBI agents knocked on Abel's door at the hotel. Sleepily, he opened the door slightly, and the two agents pushed their way in. Abel was naked, and the agents told him to put on his shorts and sit on the bed. Abel gave a false name and refused to answer further questions. Agents called in the Immigration and Naturalization Service, which arrested him as an illegal alien.

Searching Abel's apartment, agents found cipher pads used for sending messages in code, a hollow shaving brush and hollow pencils for concealing microfilm, and cameras and film used for producing microdots—photographic copies of documents one to two millimeters in diameter. A newsboy later turned in to the FBI a hollow nickel that contained one of Abel's microdots. In an old wallet, agents found microfilm instructing Hayhanen to make a payment to Helen Sobell, the wife of Morton Sobell, who had been convicted of espionage with the Rosenbergs.

In interviews over the next month at an INS detention center in San Antonio, the spy admitted that his real name was Abel. He confirmed that he had visited many of the dead drop locations pinpointed by Hayhanen—an iron picket fence at the end of Seventh Avenue, the base of a lamppost in Fort Tryon Park. But he claimed he had been in the area for pleasure. When asked if he was an intelligence officer, Abel refused to answer.

"What would you do if you were in a position such as mine?" Abel asked. He said he could not live with himself if he were a "rat."

John J. Danahy, a supervisor on the case, said agents had to hide from Robert Simon, the SAC in New York, the fact that in return for his cooperation, they had kept Hayhanen supplied with liquor. On the morning he was to testify against Abel, Hayhanen demanded a drink. The agents took him to the bar of a nearby restaurant, where he downed two double vodkas.

"He testified brilliantly," Danahy said.[39]

Because the FBI never learned exactly what secrets he had obtained, Abel was charged with conspiracy to obtain defense information. On October 25, 1957, a jury found Abel guilty. He was sentenced to thirty years in prison.

Abel's lawyer, James B. Donovan, appealed the conviction, arguing that the FBI's initial use of an INS detention procedure was illegal. The FBI had used the procedure because the bureau thought Abel would be more likely to cooperate if he were detained secretly. In a five-to-four decision in March 1960, the Supreme Court upheld Abel's conviction.

In February 1962, the United States returned Abel to the Soviet Union, trading him for Francis Gary Powers, who had been shot down over Russia in a U-2 spy plane.

■ ■ ■

Still having trouble penetrating KGB networks of illegals, Hoover approved a plan in 1961 to kidnap suspected illegals and hold them until they talked. John Danahy, a supervisor on the Abel case in New York, was transferred to headquarters to identify potential targets.

"We kidnapped Soviet illegals," Danahy said. "We did four or five of them. I participated in one of them. We took them to a retreat in the woods in New York, where they couldn't leave without starving to death. They feigned cooperation, then flunked polygraphs." And there was a nagging problem about the whole operation: "We violated their civil rights," Danahy said.[40]

After two years, the program was stopped. Soon, Hoover would approve other illegal activities.

7

RED MENACE

On February 9, 1950, Joseph R. McCarthy, an obscure Republican senator from Wisconsin, gave a speech to 275 members of the local Republican women's club at the McClure Hotel in Wheeling, West Virginia. The spy cases had heightened concerns about Communist penetration of the government. Republicans were using the issue to attack the Truman administration, which they said was "soft on Communism." With Lincoln's birthday coming up, Republican politicians had fanned out across the country.

"While I cannot take the time to name all the men in the State Department who have been named as members of the Communist Party and members of a spy ring, I have here in my hand a list of 205—a list of names that were known to the secretary of state and who, nevertheless, are still working and shaping policy of the State Department," McCarthy said, holding up a scrap of paper.

By the time he got to Salt Lake City, the next stop on his speech itinerary, McCarthy—an alcoholic—could not remember the number he had cited. He told his audience there that the number of Communists was fifty-seven.

The conservative *Chicago Tribune* had been running a series on the Communist threat. The day after McCarthy's speech in West Virginia, Willard Edwards, the author of the articles, urgently asked to talk with Walter Trohan, the Washington bureau chief, in Edwards's office at the

Albee Building at Fifteenth and G streets NW. Edwards confided to Trohan that just before he gave his speech, McCarthy had asked Edwards about the number of Communists in the State Department. Edwards said he gave McCarthy the figure of 205. Now he realized his mistake.

"Edwards said it was more or less a rumor. It was just a piece of gossip," Trohan said. "He probably got it from some ultra-rightist, someone who probably didn't know what he was talking about. Edwards was a drinker, among other problems. He got fired, and I got him back. Then he got into trouble again, and they were going to fire him again. When Edwards gave the figure to McCarthy, he was probably drinking."[41]

Trohan was "furious" at Edwards. "Edwards was afraid that McCarthy was going to blame him for it. I will say that McCarthy never revealed his source," Trohan said.

As for McCarthy, besides being an alcoholic, the senator was "crazy about girls about eighteen," Trohan said. "I always thought if the Commies wanted to get him, all they had to do was supply him with a girl."

Bogus figures or not, McCarthy soon became a national figure. Without Hoover's help, it might never have happened. The FBI, through Hoover's speeches and contacts with the media and Congress, had been highlighting the Communist menace since 1946. McCarthy and Hoover had been friends since 1947, when McCarthy met with the director to convey his respects. Soon, the junior senator was dining with Hoover and Tolson at Harvey's.

McCarthy knew how susceptible Hoover was to flattery. "No one need erect a monument to you," the senator wrote to Hoover in one letter. "You have built your own monument in the form of the FBI—for the FBI is J. Edgar Hoover, and I think we can rest assured that it always will be."

Upon returning from his tour, McCarthy called Hoover and told him his speech was getting a lot of attention, according to a memo Hoover wrote after the call. There was only one problem: McCarthy said he had "made up the numbers as he talked." In the future, Hoover advised him, he should not give specific numbers. McCarthy asked if the FBI would give him information to back up his charges.

"Review the files and get anything you can for him," Hoover ordered.

"We didn't have enough evidence to show there was a single Communist in the State Department, let alone fifty-seven cases," said William Sullivan, who became the number-three man in the bureau. Nevertheless, FBI agents spent hundreds of hours reading files and making abstracts for McCarthy. As time went on, the FBI supplied speechwriters for McCarthy and for two of his aides, Roy Cohn and G. David Schine. Lou Nichols provided public relations counsel. Nichols cautioned McCarthy not to use the phrase "card-carrying Communists," because that could not be proved. Instead, he should refer to "Communist sympathizers" or "loyalty risks."

The phrases were as fuzzy as Hoover's files, which were a repository of any rumor, thirdhand account, or gossip agents happened to hear. Soon, McCarthy began using the files as the basis for hearings he held on Communist penetration of the government, instilling fear in anyone who might have looked at a Communist. Because of the pressure, the Hollywood studios blacklisted playwright Lillian Hellman because her lover, mystery writer Dashiell Hammett, was one. John Melby, a State Department officer who had impeccable anti-Communist credentials, was fired for having had an affair with Hellman.[42]

Washington Post cartoonist Herbert L. Block (Herblock) dubbed McCarthy's tactics "McCarthyism," a witch-hunt that created as much fear among loyal Americans as terrorism. One of his cartoons portrayed McCarthy with a three-day growth of beard holding up a "doctored photo" and a "faked letter."

FBI agents like Robert Lamphere who worked counterintelligence were aghast at Hoover's support of McCarthy. "McCarthyism did all kinds of harm because he was pushing something that wasn't so," Lamphere said. To be sure, the VENONA intercepts showed that over several decades, "There were a lot of spies in the government, but not all in the State Department," Lamphere said. "The problem was that McCarthy lied about his information and figures. He made charges against people that weren't true. McCarthyism harmed the counterintelligence effort against the Soviet threat because of the revulsion it caused. All along, Hoover was helping him."[43]

■ ■ ■

When Truman ran for his first full term in 1948, Hoover, still seething over the fact that Truman had ignored his warning about Harry Dexter White being a Communist, decided to take matters into his own hands. The supposedly apolitical FBI director would support Thomas E. Dewey, the former Manhattan district attorney, to run against Truman. Toward that end, during the primary battle, Hoover supplied Dewey with derogatory material about his primary Republican opponent, Harold Stassen. If the plan worked, Hoover would be attorney general and later a Supreme Court justice, while Tolson would be assistant attorney general. Lou Nichols would be FBI director, keeping the bureau under Hoover's control.[44]

"Many agents—I was one—worked for days culling FBI files for any fact which could be of use to Dewey," William Sullivan said. "I remember that there was such a rush to get material to him that after it was collected it was sent in a private plane to Albany."

Armed with the material, Dewey demolished Stassen in a key debate. However, after a close election, Truman won his first full term. Even though Hoover's plan ultimately did not work, he decided that influencing presidential elections was good for him and good for the bureau.

During Dwight D. Eisenhower's campaign, Hoover provided Eisenhower's running mate, Richard M. Nixon, with material indicating that Eisenhower's opponent, Adlai E. Stevenson, the governor of Illinois, had been arrested in Illinois and Maryland for homosexual offenses. According to the story, Stevenson had been able to get the records expunged. The allegations came from a college basketball player under indictment for fixing a game. While there was no truth to the rumors, fueled by the FBI, they quickly spread.

After Eisenhower was elected, Hoover gave him derogatory information about a range of public figures, from Supreme Court justices William O. Douglas and Felix Frankfurter to scientist Linus Pauling and philosopher Bertrand Russell. When Eleanor Roosevelt was being considered for reappointment as U.S. delegate to the United Nations, Hoover had Lou Nichols brief White House aides on her supposed affair with Roosevelt aide Joseph Lash. She was not reappointed.

Hoover always claimed that he did not want the FBI to become a national police force, yet by now, the bureau had become a national thought police. Hoover kept files on the comments and activities of movie and television stars, poets, writers, scientists, and playwrights ranging from Thomas Mann, Henry Miller, John Steinbeck, and Ernest Hemingway to Albert Einstein, Lewis Mumford, T. S. Eliot, William Faulkner, John Gunther, Thomas Wolfe, John Dos Passos, and Charlie Chaplin. Hoover even went so far as to put such subversives as Einstein, Steinbeck, Hemingway, and Douglas on a "watch list" so he would be informed if they traveled overseas.

"Unlike Truman, who was skeptical of anything Hoover offered," Sullivan recalled, "Eisenhower blindly believed everything the director told him, never questioned a word . . . He may have been a great general but he was a very gullible man, and Hoover soon had him wrapped right around his finger."

Eisenhower's attorney general, Herbert Brownell Jr., gave Hoover the authorization to conduct the microphone surveillance and bugging he had long been engaging in anyway. Even though such bugging usually involved criminal trespass and was therefore illegal, Brownell said it could be used in cases of espionage or when the FBI was performing an "intelligence function in connection with internal security matters."

As when he used the term "radical" to define who should be arrested during the Palmer Raids, Hoover used the vague terms "intelligence" and "security" to allow the bureau to supersede existing laws in conducting investigations. Now, by legitimizing the bureau's conduct, Brownell gave Hoover the authority to define "internal security matters" at a time when children in public schools were being taught to duck under their desks in case of a Soviet atomic bomb attack.

Even more to Hoover's liking, on November 6, 1953, Brownell spoke to a group of Chicago businessmen and charged that President Truman had named Harry Dexter White to be an executive director of the International Monetary Fund even though Truman knew, from FBI reports based on Helen Bentley's allegations, that White was a "Communist spy." Having made his charge against Truman, Hoover was asked to testify before a Senate subcommittee on internal security. Until that point, Hoover had confined his congressional appearances to testimony before a House appropriations subcommittee, but this time he was only too happy to appear.

It was not the only score Hoover had to settle with Truman. Bowing to Hoover and others, Truman had abolished the OSS and fired William Donovan. But Truman had refused to go along with Hoover when the FBI director insisted that the new Central Intelligence Group, which later became the CIA, should be part of the FBI.

It was payback time. At the Senate hearing, Hoover produced his memos, which he had conveniently declassified, stating that White had been funneling information to the Soviets. Asked why he had not protested Truman's decision to appoint White to the IMF, Hoover said, "I would have been presumptuous to make a public protest. I am merely a subordinate official of the attorney general. I do not make policy. I am advised of the policy to be followed."

It was Hoover's standard disingenuous line. But James Reston of the *New York Times* said that Hoover emerged as "probably the most powerful man on Capitol Hill."

"Hoover has been waiting for a long time for this moment," Drew Pearson wrote in his diary. "He hated Truman and almost everyone around him."

In turn, Truman accused Brownell of McCarthyism, and McCarthy now arrogantly turned his sights on Eisenhower. A former Army general who had led Allied Forces to victory during World War II, Eisenhower was as American as apple pie. As McCarthy began his attacks on Eisenhower, Hoover realized he would have to distance himself from the senator. Just before what became known as the Army-McCarthy hearings started on March 16, 1954, Hoover ordered the bureau to cease helping McCarthy. That would contribute to the senator's downfall.

During the hearings, McCarthy failed to substantiate his claims that the Communists had penetrated the Army, which had hired a shrewd Boston lawyer, Joseph Welch, to represent it. McCarthy noted that Fred Fischer, a young lawyer in Welch's firm, had once been a member of a left-wing organization.

Upon hearing this, Welch responded, "Until this moment, Senator, I think I never really gauged your cruelty or recklessness." When

McCarthy continued to hound Fischer, Welch said, "Have you no sense of decency, sir, at long last? Have you left no sense of decency?"

After two months, the hearings were over, and so was McCarthy's career. Millions of Americans had seen how he bullied witnesses and what an unsavory character he was. On December 2, 1954, the Senate voted sixty-two to twenty-two to censure him. After that, when he rose to speak, senators left the Senate chamber, and reporters no longer attended his press conferences. On May 2, 1957, McCarthy died at the age of forty-seven of the effects of alcoholism.

■ ■ ■

By 1956, the membership of the Communist Party USA had dropped from eighty thousand to about five thousand, and at least fifteen hundred of those were FBI informants, according to William Sullivan. Yet Hoover mounted a new campaign against the almost dormant party, a program called COINTELPRO for Counter Intelligence Program.

Over the next dozen years, the FBI would launch eleven similar programs against such targets as the Socialist Workers Party, the Black Panthers, and the Ku Klux Klan. Each was more foolish than the last. Instead of using the existing laws to prosecute violators, the FBI engaged in a range of improper or illegal acts to harass targets. Although these COINTELPRO programs launched against Americans have often been compared to the counterintelligence programs aimed at the Soviets, true counterintelligence efforts are legal and are far more focused and effective.

In the COINTELPRO against the Communists, Hoover authorized planting newspaper stories, whether true or not, about misuse of party funds by Communist officials; placing anonymous calls or sending anonymous letters to start rumors that party officials were homosexuals or sexual deviants; and assigning agents to conduct lockstep surveillance, intrusive photography, or make hang-up calls to telegraph to associates of Communists that they were under investigation. Agents questioned party officials at their places of employment to intimidate their employers and get them to fire them, planted evidence so that local police would arrest party members, and left what appeared to be FBI informant reports on the cars of party officials so that the party would drop them as suspected snitches.

The bureau informed the parents of one woman that she was living with a Communist out of wedlock. When the FBI found out that a partner in a law firm was having an affair with another partner's wife, the bureau informed all the members of the firm.

The tactics were no different from those used by the KGB in Russia and the Stasi in East Germany. George Kennan, the author of the policy of containment used against the Soviets during the Cold War, had warned that fear of communism could turn Americans "intolerant, secretive, suspicious, cruel, and terrified of internal dissension." He said, "The worst thing the Communists could do to us and the thing we have most to fear from their activities is that we should become like them."

There was no better example than the FBI's COINTELPRO programs. Hoover approved each COINTELPRO plan, writing on memos in his distinctive blue ink, "I concur" or "OK. H." Not until 1958 did Hoover give the House appropriations subcommittee a vague, brief description of the program, saying it was a plan to "disorganize and disrupt" the Communist Party. In addition to informing the subcommittee, Hoover provided the president with an innocuous-sounding description of the program.

Looking back, Courtland J. Jones, who was in charge of counterintelligence in the Washington Field Office, called COINTELPRO "wrong and childish." By the time Hoover initiated COINTELPRO, "The Communist party was basically a bunch of discussion groups," he said. Moreover, "I can't think of any of the COINTELPRO initiatives that were effective."

■　■　■

While Hoover was harassing Communists, he was also harassing the press and the book publishing industry. In August 1950, Hoover learned from an advance review in *Publishers Weekly* that Max Lowenthal, a lawyer who had clerked for Felix Frankfurter and was a friend of Truman, had written *The Federal Bureau of Investigation,* the first critical book about Hoover and the FBI. Hoover blamed Crime Records for not knowing about the book in advance. Reduced to tears, Nichols sobbed, "Mr. Hoover, if I had known this book was going to be published, I'd have thrown my body between the presses and stopped it."

Hoover did his best to discredit the book. His friends in Congress,

Iowa's Senator Bourke B. Hickenlooper and Michigan's Senator Homer Ferguson, attacked it as "an utterly biased piece of propaganda" and a "vile, monstrous libel." Hoover's friends in the press, Walter Winchell, Rex Collier of the *Washington Evening Star,* and Walter Trohan of the *Chicago Tribune,* all unleashed tirades. Agents were instructed to discourage booksellers from selling the book. One SAC suggested that agents steal the book from libraries, but headquarters rejected the idea on the grounds the libraries would only order more.

After all the commotion, only 7,500 copies of the book—which read like a dull lawyer's brief—were sold. However, Hoover determined that the bureau would never again be caught unaware when the FBI was about to be lambasted. "After this," William Sullivan said, "we developed informants in the publishing houses."

In addition, Crime Records developed informants at major magazines such as *Time, Life, Newsweek, Business Week,* and *U.S. News & World Report* so that the bureau would be informed of any forthcoming articles that might be critical and could try to counter them. Publications like *Reader's Digest* and *Look,* which ran glowing pieces on the director, were treated to inside information on cases. Newspapers like the *New York Times* and *Washington Post,* which did not play along, were placed on a "Do Not Contact" list.

■ ■ ■

Besides harassing journalistic critics, Hoover used the bureau to crack down on rumors that he was a homosexual. A female FBI employee, while having her hair done in a Washington beauty shop, heard the owner tell a customer that Hoover was "a queer." Two agents were dispatched to interview the owner. The agents told her "in no uncertain terms that such statements . . . would not be countenanced," according to a 1951 memo from Lou Nichols. As a result of the visit by the agents, the beauty parlor's owner "fully realizes the seriousness of her accusations, and it is not believed that she will ever be guilty of such statements," Nichols assured Tolson.

E. E. Conroy, the New York SAC, wrote to Hoover in January 1944 that he learned that one of his agents had heard someone refer to Hoover as a "fairy." When Conroy heard about this, he looked into the matter and found that the agent had indeed heard such a remark and had done nothing about it because he thought it would be "ridiculous" to pursue it.

Conroy called in the agent and told him he had "displayed extremely poor judgment." The SAC considered the remark "a direct attack on the character of the director." The agent should have brought the matter to Conroy's "immediate attention" Following this, agents interviewed the individual who had made the remark. A supervisor was reprimanded over the incident.[45]

Hoover decided that the best way to counter criticism of him and the bureau would be to issue an authorized book. Don Whitehead, chief of the *New York Herald Tribune*'s Washington bureau and winner of two Pulitzer Prizes, had interviewed Hoover in April 1954 and had written a series of pieces praising the bureau and its director. According to Whitehead, he asked for bureau cooperation in writing a book on the FBI. Nichols claimed that the book was his idea. In any case, Hoover approved the project and wrote a foreword that ironically stated, "In the United States, the subversive is a lawbreaker when he violates the law of the land, not because he disagrees with the party in power." Nichols reviewed the manuscript before it was published, and Hoover's friend Bennett Cerf at Random House agreed to publish it in 1956.

Whitehead's *The FBI Story* recited much of the misinformation that Crime Records had been peddling in its Interesting Case Memoranda. For example, in describing how Louis "Lepke" Buchalter turned himself in, the book said, "On the night of August 24, 1939, Director Hoover walked alone through New York City's streets to the corner of Twenty-eighth Street and Fifth Avenue. And there the hunted man, Buchalter, surrendered to him."[46] In fact, Buchalter turned himself in to Walter Winchell, who drove him to Hoover's car a few blocks away.

True or not, Whitehead's book sold 200,000 copies, and Hoover became jealous. Since the FBI had done all the work, Hoover complained to Nichols, why had he let Whitehead keep all the royalties?

The solution was to bring out his own book, *Masters of Deceit,* about the Communist menace. Published by Henry Holt, the book was written entirely by FBI employees. It sold 250,000 copies in hardcover. ABC bought the rights for *The FBI,* a television series that started in

1965 and starred Efrem Zimbalist Jr. Completely controlled by the bureau, the series was watched by forty million people each week. The show never included Hoover as a character, but Zimbalist's office was next door to an office marked "The Director."

Royalties from the book went to the FBI Recreational Fund. As a later investigation determined, part of the money from the fund secretly went to Hoover, Tolson, and Lou Nichols. It was only the beginning of Hoover's practice of using his position to enrich himself.

8

THE RED DRESS

Ever since the Eighteenth Amendment mandated Prohibition in January 1920, the Mafia had been expanding its grip on American society. Originating in Sicily, La Cosa Nostra migrated to the United States in the 1880s.

Before Prohibition, the country had fifteen thousand legal bars. After Prohibition, it had twenty-three thousand speakeasies, where liquor was served illegally.[47] Prohibition spawned an entire illegal industry to import or make booze, guard it, and distribute it. Hoodlums paid off police, and when drinking illegal hootch became fashionable, the lines between criminals and ordinary law-abiding citizens were blurred. Mafia figures became celebrities. The profits from one Mafia enterprise alone—illegal off-track betting—were estimated at $20 billion a year.

By 1957, by instilling fear through gangland killings, the Mafia controlled labor unions like the Teamsters and major industries, from construction and garbage collecting to garment making and trucking, in most major cities. Through that control, organized crime penetrated politics. The Mafia was able to dictate who should be appointed as judges and police chiefs. Because of those alliances, organized crime was considered untouchable. Yet as the Mafia expanded its grip on the country, Hoover consistently denied what everyone else knew: that organized crime was the single greatest criminal threat to the United States.

"No single individual or coalition of racketeers dominates organized crime across the country," Hoover insisted. There was no such thing as "organized crime" or a "Mafia," he said. The claim that there was a national crime syndicate was "baloney."

To be sure, the FBI had arrested Louis "Lepke" Buchalter, who ran Murder Inc., part of organized crime, but that was only because Buchalter had chosen to turn himself in to Walter Winchell. The bureau had also arrested Al "Scarface" Capone, the chief of the Chicago crime syndicate, but that was because the Treasury Department was pursuing him for tax evasion. Capone failed to comply with a subpoena ordering his appearance before a federal grand jury in Chicago on March 12, 1929, and he was sentenced to six months in the Cook County jail.[48]

Hoover called such figures as Buchalter or Capone "gangsters" or "just a bunch of hoodlums." He insisted they were not connected to each other and that, because the FBI had no jurisdiction, local authorities should prosecute them. Thus, Hoover ignored Capone's involvement in murder, gambling, prostitution, racketeering, and extortion.

All that changed on November 14, 1957, when New York State Police Sergeant Edgar L. Croswell noticed a retinue of long black limousines approach the secluded estate of Joseph Barbara Sr. in the hills outside the village of Appalachin, New York. In this area just north of the Pennsylvania state line, one such limousine was unusual. In the course of an hour, Croswell counted five whiz past, all with out-of-state license plates.

When Barbara purchased the home, Croswell checked his background because he carried a gun. While Barbara claimed to be a Canada Dry distributor, he had a Pennsylvania rap sheet with more than a dozen arrests, including two for murder. However, he had been convicted of only minor offenses.

Under New York State law, Croswell could stop any car and require the occupants to produce identification. So Croswell decided to set up a roadblock on the way to the estate. He radioed for three additional deputies. Just then, dozens of limousines descended on the property.

When those already in the house heard from a delivery man about the roadblock, more than fifty men ran to their cars or fled through the woods. With the help of more troopers, Croswell was able to obtain the identities of sixty-three of the guests, who turned out to be leaders of the Mafia.

Hoover was aghast. The fact that the Mafia leaders came from every part of the country clearly established that organized crime was not just a local problem. "The FBI didn't know anything, really, about these people who were major gangsters in the United States," recalled Robert F. Kennedy, chief counsel of the Permanent Subcommittee on Investigations of the Senate Government Operations Committee.

With newspapers expressing outrage and William P. Rogers, Eisenhower's attorney general, calling for federal action, Hoover asked his men for ideas. William Sullivan proposed to study the question of whether organized crime existed. When Sullivan concluded that there was indeed a Mafia, Hoover privately agreed. Someone had to take the blame, so Hoover censured Al Belmont. Belmont, one of the most admired men in the bureau, headed the General Investigative Division. In ignoring the Mafia, he had only been following Hoover's orders.

The study took a year to complete, but meanwhile Hoover established the Top Ten Hoodlums Program, requiring each field office to identify the ten major mob figures in its area and monitor them. The program was primarily to gather intelligence rather than to target Mafia figures for prosecution. Because it used illegal break-ins and wiretaps that could not be introduced as evidence in court, the program generally could not be used to prosecute Mafia figures. As in the counterintelligence area, Hoover seemed to think that learning about the enemy was equivalent to eradicating the threat.

However, by conducting surveillance, the FBI not only confirmed the existence of the Mafia but also—through a bug in a meeting place in a tailor shop in Chicago—learned of dozens of murders, payoffs to politicians and judges, and voting frauds. The bug turned up evidence that at least two members of Congress—Senators Edward V. Long of Missouri and Representative Cornelius Gallagher of New Jersey—had had unsavory financial dealings with mob figures.

Senator Long, for example, had received $48,000 over a two-year period from the personal lawyer of Jimmy Hoffa, president of the mob-dominated Teamsters Union, even as the senator publicly praised Hoffa and announced hearings into FBI "snooping." Hoover let Long know what the bureau had on him, and Long backed off on his plan to conduct an investigation of FBI wiretapping. But when Long's subcommittee proposed legislation to limit FBI wiretapping and bugging to cases involving national security, the FBI leaked to *Life* the story of Long's Teamsters Union payments. After the magazine ran the story in its May 1967 issue, Long lost a Democratic primary battle to Thomas Eagleton.[49]

"The mob owned almost everybody—police, prosecutors, local politicians," said Neil J. Welch, a former SAC in Buffalo and New York City. Before Appalachin, "Every agent knew about organized crime unless they were on an Indian reservation. Every citizen knew. Hoover's denial that organized crime existed was a total abdication of responsibility."[50]

Contrary to Hoover's claim that the FBI had no jurisdiction, a number of existing laws, such as those barring interstate transportation of stolen goods, could have been used against Mafia figures.

"As long as he lived, Hoover never adopted a comprehensive, realistic battle plan," Welch said.

William G. Hundley, who headed organized crime prosecutions at the Justice Department, had previously prosecuted Communists under the Smith Act. He recalled that even after the Appalachin meeting, Hoover provided far more cooperation on investigations into Communists.

"All the Communists were doing at that point was distributing pamphlets, but Hoover was into investigating them," Hundley said. "If you were hunting Communists, you would have a team of agents assigned to you. If you wanted someone interviewed in Canada, Hoover would do it. While the FBI couldn't do enough for you chasing domestic Communists, they would do nothing in organized crime. They would clip newspapers. They were absolutely useless. Hoover had said there wasn't a Mafia."[51]

While Hoover stepped up the pressure on the Mafia after Robert Kennedy became attorney general, the bureau still adopted a haphazard, piecemeal approach, charging Mafia figures if they submitted a false loan application to the government, for example. Having been allowed to grow, the Mafia was now difficult to eradicate. Even after Kennedy forced the FBI to work organized crime, Hundley said, "They were slow. Hoover discovered the Communist Party, and he wasn't going to give it up."

With the exception of Kennedy, no attorney general was willing to take on Hoover. "All of the attorneys general were afraid of him," Hundley told me. "They never knew what he had on them. Attorney General Bill Rogers said, 'You can pick a fight with anybody, and I'll back you. Pick a fight with Hoover, and you're on your own.' "

In contrast to the FBI, the Federal Bureau of Narcotics, headed by Harry Anslinger, had long recognized the existence of organized crime. After Appalachin, while the FBI had little beyond newspaper clippings on the Mafia, Anslinger quickly shared with members of Congress extensive dossiers on each one of the Mafia members. Based on evidence developed by Anslinger's agents, prosecutors convicted Mafia soldier Joseph Valachi of federal narcotics charges in 1959. Incarcerated at the federal penitentiary in Atlanta, Valachi learned that Vito Genovese, the head of one of the Mafia families, suspected that Valachi had become a federal informer and had targeted him for execution.

"Valachi thought he spotted the fellow in the prison yard who was supposed to kill him," recalled Hundley, who became involved in the case. "Valachi took a shovel and beat this guy to death in the prison yard. They threw him in the hole."

The Bureau of Narcotics told Valachi that he had killed the wrong man. Agents said his executioner was in the prison, and Valachi would be tossed back in the general population unless he cooperated. Valachi agreed to become an informer, first for the Bureau of Narcotics and then for the FBI.

In 1963, the Senate Permanent Subcommittee on Investigations began holding hearings that dramatically exposed the full extent of Mafia control of the country. The hearings included televised testimony by Valachi, who said that Mafia members called their organization La Cosa Nostra, meaning "our thing" or "our family." Valachi described the structure of organized crime, which consisted of "families," each headed by a crime boss such as Genovese, Joseph Bonanno, Joseph Profaci, Carmine Galante, and Thomas Lucchese in New York City, Santo Trafficante Jr. in Miami, Stefano Magaddino in Buffalo, and Joseph Zerilli in Detroit, all of whom had attended the Appalachin meeting. A twelve-man commission coordinated the families. While members had to be Italian, the Mafia worked in tandem with Jewish, Polish, and Irish mobsters. Mafia figures usually had colorful names—Anthony "Big

Tuna" Accardo, Legs Diamond, Al "Scarface" Capone, George "Bugs" Moran, Thomas "Three Finger" Lucchese, and Lucky Luciano.

Aware that Valachi was poised to testify, Hoover had Crime Records prepare an article under his byline for *Parade*. Twelve days before Valachi testified, the article revealed "The Inside Story of Organized Crime and How You Can Help Smash It." For the first time, Hoover referred to La Cosa Nostra. In the September 1963 issue of the *FBI Law Enforcement Bulletin*, Hoover wrote that Valachi's testimony "corroborated and embellished the facts developed by the FBI as early as 1961." Meanwhile, Robert Kennedy called the Valachi revelations "the biggest intelligence breakthrough we have ever had."

Because of his friendship with Robert Kennedy, author Peter Maas was able to interview Valachi for his book *The Valachi Papers*. Initially rejected by thirty publishers who said the Mafia would not sell, the book became a huge best-seller. With the help of the Justice Department, Maas preceded the book with an article in the *Saturday Evening Post*. Recognizing that Kennedy had helped Maas, Hoover, in blue ink, remarked, "I never saw so much skulduggery; the sanctity of department files, including bureau reports, is a thing of the past."

"If it weren't for the trooper in New York and Valachi, we would never have gotten into organized crime," said Wayne P. Comer, former associate SAC of the Philadelphia Field Office and an instructor on organized crime at the FBI Academy at Quantico. "Once Valachi started talking, Hoover had no choice but to go after organized crime."[52]

■ ■ ■

Many theories have been advanced to explain Hoover's aversion to attacking organized crime. One is that building Mafia cases would have been too time-consuming and might corrupt agents. There is no question that Hoover was obsessed with building arrest statistics from quick hits. Without regard to the importance or difficulty of the cases, he criticized SACs if the number of cases per agent fell below certain levels. In Hoover's FBI, all crimes were equal. The theft of a typewriter from an army base was just as important as a bombing or kidnapping.

Hoover loved to present Congress with statistics showing how many cases had been closed by arrests and how much money had been recovered as a result. "Statistical accomplishment," rather than quality of cases, was the measure of success in the FBI. In Hoover's FBI, agents would claim credit for recovering vehicles found by local police. Hoover would then include these recoveries in the figures he gave Congress, claiming that the recoveries exceeded the government's appropriations for the FBI's annual budget.

"When I came into the bureau [under Hoover], we used to go to the Metropolitan Police Department [in Washington] every day and check the stolen car list," said James V. De Sarno Jr., a former FBI assistant director. "If the car was recovered, we took credit. If it was stolen in Washington and recovered in Maryland, we would claim that as a stat—interstate theft."[53]

But there was more to Hoover's policy of ignoring organized crime than statistics. In 1993, Anthony Summers, in *Official and Confidential: The Secret Life of J. Edgar Hoover*, claimed that Hoover did not pursue organized crime because the Mafia had blackmail material on him. In support of that, Summers quoted Susan L. Rosenstiel, a former wife of Lewis S. Rosenstiel, chairman of Schenley Industries Inc., as saying that in 1958, she was at a party at the Plaza Hotel where Hoover engaged in cross-dressing in front of her then husband and Roy Cohn, former counsel to Senator Joe McCarthy.

"He [Hoover] was wearing a fluffy black dress, very fluffy, with flounces and lace stockings and high heels, and a black curly wig," Summers quoted Susan Rosenstiel as saying. "He had makeup on and false eyelashes."[54]

She claimed that Cohn introduced Hoover to her as "Mary." Hoover allegedly responded, "Good evening." She said she saw Hoover go into a bedroom and take off his skirt. There, "young blond boys" worked on him in bed. Later, as Hoover and Cohn watched, Lewis Rosenstiel had sex with the young boys.

A year later, Susan Rosenstiel claimed, she again saw Hoover at the Plaza. This time, the director was wearing a red dress. Around his neck was a black feather boa. He was holding a Bible, and he asked one of the blond boys to read a passage as another boy played with him.

It was episodes such as these, Summers declared, that the Mafia held over Hoover's head. "Mafia bosses obtained information about Hoover's sex life and used it for decades to keep the FBI at bay," the jacket of the book says. "Without this, the Mafia as we know it might never have gained its hold on America."

Lewis Rosenstiel, a former bootlegger during Prohibition, was well acquainted with Mafia figures such as Frank Costello, originally Francesco Castiglia. He was also friends with Hoover, having endowed the J. Edgar Hoover Foundation in 1965 with $1 million. But Susan Rosenstiel was Summers's primary source for the cross-dressing story, and she was not exactly a credible witness. In fact, she served time at Rikers Island for perjuring herself in a 1971 case.

Convinced that Hoover had somehow stacked the cards against her during the divorce proceedings, Rosenstiel had long tried to interest anyone who would listen that Hoover was a cross-dresser. She had taken her allegations to Robert M. Morgenthau, the U.S. attorney in New York, who himself had no use for Hoover.

"She used to call me after 5:30 P.M. when my secretary had left, so I wound up having to listen to her," Morgenthau said. He said he found her claims baseless. But Morgenthau shared her allegations with William Hundley, who had a Justice Department attorney look into them.[55]

"Susie Rosenstiel had a total ax to grind," Hundley said. "Somebody who worked for me talked to her. It was made up out of whole cloth. She hated Hoover for some alleged wrong he had done. Plus the story was beyond belief. I told Summers this. Then he goes ahead and uses it."[56]

Now seventy-seven and living in a single room in a Manhattan hotel where rooms rent for $98.85 a night, Rosenstiel said Summers paid her for the interviews she gave him, and she wanted to be paid for an interview for this book. Like most journalists and news organizations, I believe that paying for information calls into question its credibility. When I told Rosenstiel this and suggested she could generate publicity for herself by telling the truth and admitting she made up the cross-dressing story, she insisted, "It did happen."[57]

Summers said that after Rosenstiel told her the cross-dressing story, she told him that she intended to give the story to another journalist. Summers said he paid her a fee to hold the story until his book came out. The producer of a documentary made for *Frontline* and the BBC also paid Rosenstiel for her appearance with Summers, he said.

In addition to Susan Rosenstiel's outlandish charge, buttressed by a similar claim from two anonymous sources, Summers claimed that organized crime figure Meyer Lansky and others had photos of Hoover and Tolson having sex. Summers wrote that John Weitz, a former OSS officer, was at a dinner party in the fifties, where the host, who had intelligence agency connections, showed Weitz a photograph of Tolson and Hoover engaging in sex. Finally, Summers quoted Gordon Novel, described as "a former CIA counterintelligence chief," as saying that James Angleton, the paranoid former head of CIA counterintelligence, showed him a photo of a man giving Hoover oral sex. While Novel could not make out who the second man was, Angleton told him he was Tolson.

In an article for *Esquire*, Peter Maas said he asked Weitz, now a clothes designer, about the incident reported by Summers. Weitz said the host who showed him the photo was James Angleton. "The photograph, as I recall, was very, very blurry," Maas quoted Weitz as saying. "It seemed to show two men humping on a beach. Perhaps it was Hoover, perhaps not. I didn't give it much import."[58]

Thus Weitz could not tell who was in the photo. As for Novel, his claim to have seen a photo of Hoover having sex with a man has to be evaluated alongside his claim that, at Angleton's bidding, he then walked up to Hoover and Tolson at the Mayflower and said that Angleton had sent him to tell them he had seen photos of them having sex. Only Susan Rosenstiel's story that Hoover engaged in crossdressing at the Plaza was less worthy of belief.

A quick check of clips and the Internet would have revealed to Summers, a prodigious researcher, that an April 27, 1967, FBI memo said that Novel, a conspiracy theorist, had long claimed to be a CIA operative but never had a connection to the agency. After Summers's book came out, another FBI document revealed that when working as an investigator for New Orleans District Attorney Jim Garrison, Novel tried to doctor a photo to make it appear that Lee Harvey Oswald had met with Fidel Castro. When Novel had trouble making Oswald fit into the original photo, he tried to place Jack Ruby in the photo. Novel has since admitted to the press that he has never had any connection to the CIA.[59]

Based on one account from an admitted dissembler and a second account from a man who says he could not tell who was in the photos, Summers concluded that the photos showed Tolson and Hoover having sex. Summers then connected the photos to Lansky with more hot air: "There is no knowing, today, whether the OSS obtained sex photographs of Edgar from Lansky, or vice versa, or whether the mobster obtained them on his own initiative."

Beyond this, Summers said Irving "Ash" Resnick, a mob courier, told writer Pete Hamill in 1971 in the Galeria Bar at Caesars Palace that Lansky had incriminating photos of Tolson and Hoover. Resnick did not say how he knew this. Certainly it was not from Lansky, who was notoriously close-mouthed. Hamill told me he considered Resnick's claim "mob gossip," which he has come to distrust. "It's part of the need for these guys to be big shots, to know more than ordinary people know," Hamill said.[60]

In the *Esquire* piece, Maas, a world-class journalist who died in 2001, pointed out that Summers's rendition of events has a fatal flaw: After the alleged incident at the Plaza, Hoover assigned agents to investigate Lansky, who supposedly had the goods on him. When the Miami Field Office complained that the investigation of Lansky was not producing enough information to justify the manpower, Hoover wrote back, "Lansky has been designated for 'crash' investigation. The importance of this case cannot be overemphasized. . . . The bureau expects this investigation to be vigorous and detailed."

Still presumably cowering because Lansky had incriminating photos of him, Hoover followed up with an order to install bugs in Lansky's apartment. Having been ordered by Robert Kennedy to attack the Mafia as the FBI had attacked communism, Hoover wrote in the January 1962 *FBI Law Enforcement Bulletin*, "The battle is joined. We have taken up the gauntlet flung down by organized crime. Let us unite in a devastating assault to annihilate this mortal enemy." Yet even before Kennedy took over, Hoover, stung by the disclosure of the 1957 Appalachin meeting, had been aggressively pursuing the mob. Doesn't that torpedo Summers's theory? No, Summers told me. Summers said that by that time it didn't matter to Hoover. But, of course, if there were such photos, they would have been just as embarrassing in the 1950s and 1960s as in earlier years. Summers pointed out that he wrote a lengthy rebuttal to *Esquire,* and he called the Maas article "inaccurate and abhorrent."

Despite the clear implication in the book that her story was true and the declaration on the book's jacket that the Mafia knew that Hoover was a "closet homosexual and transvestite" and held that over his head, Summers told me that he merely reported what Rosenstiel said, along with what others claimed. He said he holds "no firm view one way or the other" as to whether she told the truth.[61]

While there was always speculation about Hoover and Tolson, there were never any rumors about Hoover cross-dressing. Oliver "Buck" Revell, a former associate director of the FBI, noted that if the Mafia had had anything on Hoover, it would have been picked up in wiretaps mounted against organized crime after Appalachin. There was never a hint of such a claim, Revell said.

Hoover was more familiar to Americans than were most presidents. The director of the FBI simply could not have engaged in such activity at the Plaza, with a number of witnesses present, without having it leak out. The cross-dressing allegations were as credible as McCarthy's claim that there were 205 known Communists in the State Department, yet the press widely circulated the claim without further investigation. That Hoover was a cross-dresser is now largely presumed to be fact even by sophisticated people.

While no one except Hoover and Tolson knew for sure the nature of their relationship, extensive evidence points to its simply being an unusually close friendship. Beginning in the 1950s, the FBI regularly assigned agents from the Washington Field Office to discreetly follow Hoover and Tolson as a security precaution. R. Jean Gray, one of the agents assigned to what was called HOOWATCH, said the surveillance consisted of agents in two bureau cars who would follow Hoover and Tolson as they left the Justice Department at the end of the day. While the two pals knew that agents watched over them, they usually did not spot them.

"We followed them to Harvey's or to the Mayflower, where they had dinner," Gray said. "Then we took them to Tolson's apartment on Cathedral Avenue, where Tolson got out. Then we went to Hoover's home. We stayed overnight. The next morning, agents would follow Hoover as he picked up Tolson and went through Rock Creek Park and down Constitution Avenue to the Justice Department," Gray said.

"We speculated about Edgar and Clyde," Gray said. "But if anything scandalous had happened with the director, it would have gone coast to coast within the bureau in thirty minutes."

Other agents assigned to HOOWATCH who would have loved to gossip about Hoover said they also saw nothing untoward.

"When Hoover buzzed Tolson, he jumped like everyone else," said Joseph D. Purvis, who headed the Washington Field Office from 1964 to 1970. "It would have been impossible for Hoover and Tolson to carry on a gay relationship without agents knowing."[62]

While Hoover never dated, he liked women. Bucky Walters, an assistant director under Hoover, recalled that when in the presence of attractive women at parties and other social functions, he became energized and was apt to blurt out statements that were not always discreet. "In those days, it was not uncommon for bachelors or spinsters to live together," Walters said. "It was a different culture."

Common or not, the fact that Hoover spent most of his leisure time with a man and that they took adoring photos of each other leaves open the question of whether Hoover was a closet homosexual who was either unaware of his orientation or suppressed it.

Asked by a Washington woman's page editor in 1939 why he had never married, Hoover for once let down his guard. "Well, there are a number of contributing factors," he said. "Of course, there has been my job, which has been confining from a romantic standpoint. It has to be done thoroughly, and by thoroughly, I mean that I have to be ready to leave here for any part of the United States any time. What wife would stand for that? Then," Hoover went on, "there was my mother. Not that she did not want me to marry. It was not that. I made a home for her and took care of her until she died two years ago."

Hoover distinguished between "the girls men take out to make whoopee with" and "the girls they want as the mother of their children." Hoover said he was "not criticizing the so-called glamour girls. They are attractive in their way, but they do not appear to me to be real or sincere, and they do not measure up to my idea of what a girl should be. I have always held girls on a pedestal. They are something men should look up to, honor and worship. . . . And there is something I will confess," Hoover said. "If I ever marry and the girl fails me, ceases to love me, and our marriage is dissolved, it would ruin me. I couldn't take it, and I would not be responsible for my actions."

In that synopsis, Hoover revealed not only the degree of influence his mother had on him and his own puritanical nature but also his need for perfection and control. A wife, like the bureau, had to be without blemish and totally under his domination.

"I liken him to the apostle Paul," said Fred G. "Gary" Robinette III, a former FBI agent whose mother, Lillian House Robinette, was Hoover's sister. "He was celibate and dedicated. He was a perfectionist. He knew he could not be a good husband and father and also run the bureau the way he wanted."[63]

"Everyone's sexuality manifests itself in some way," said Bertram S. Brown, M.D., a psychiatrist who is a former director of the National Institute of Mental Health. "Hoover's sexual energy came out in dedication to work, in his obsessive need to control, and in his ritualistic behavior."[64]

The latter point was illustrated by the arrangements Hoover demanded when he traveled on vacation. When he flew to La Jolla, California, "Hoover insisted on the same seats in the plane, the same rooms in the same hotels, the same restaurants, the same haberdasher, and the same pleasure ride," remembered W. Mark Felt, who became acting associate director after Hoover died. The field office had to schedule each aspect of the trip precisely: The luggage had to arrive in the hotel rooms exactly three minutes after Hoover and Tolson arrived.

By the same token, when it came to keeping his position as director, Hoover wanted to be in complete control. The secret was the files. Defenders of Hoover—a dwindling number of older former agents— have claimed that his Official and Confidential files were not used to blackmail members of Congress or presidents. According to their argument, Hoover kept the files with sensitive information about political leaders in his suite so that young file clerks would not peruse them and circulate stories from them. The files were not secret any more than any other bureau files were secret, Hoover supporters say.

While the files may well have been kept in Hoover's office to protect them from curious clerks, it was also true that far more sensitive files containing top-secret information on pending espionage cases were kept in the central files. If Hoover truly were concerned about information getting out, he should have been more worried about the highly classified information in those files. Moreover, the Official and Confidential files were secret in the sense that Hoover never referred to them publicly, as he did with the rest of the bureau's files. He distinguished them from other bureau files by calling them "confidential," denoting secrecy. But whether they were secret or not and where they were kept was irrelevant. What was important was how Hoover used the information from those files and from other bureau files.

"The moment [Hoover] would get something on a senator," said William Sullivan, "he'd send one of the errand boys up and advise the senator that 'we're in the course of an investigation, and we by chance happened to come up with this data on your daughter. But we wanted you to know this. We realize you'd want to know it.' Well, Jesus, what does that tell the senator? From that time on, the senator's right in his pocket."

William Hundley said that when he headed organized crime prosecutions at the Justice Department, he learned that the FBI had begun an investigation of two members of Congress who had taken Cadillacs and other extravagant gifts from organized crime figures. "Hoover went and told them," Hundley said. "So naturally, they gave the gifts back. He owned them after that. He did not believe in prosecuting corrupt senators and congressmen. He just liked to get something on them and use them."

Lawrence J. Heim, who was in the Crime Records Division, confirmed that the bureau sent agents to tell members of Congress that Hoover had picked up derogatory information on them. Hoover "would send someone over on a very confidential basis," Heim said. As an example, if the Metropolitan police in Washington had picked up evidence of homosexuality, "He would have him say 'this activity is known by the Metropolitan police department and some of our informants, and it is in your best interests to know this.' But nobody has ever claimed to have been blackmailed. You can deduce what you want from that."[65]

Of course, the reason no one publicly claimed to have been blackmailed is that, by definition, blackmail entails collecting embarrassing information that people do not want public. But not everyone was intimidated. When Lou Nichols was head of Crime Records and later assistant to the director, he was usually the FBI official who let congressmen know that the bureau had something on them. Nichols resigned from the FBI in 1957 to become executive vice president of Rosenstiel's Schenley Industries, prompting Hoover—in a fit of pique—to conduct surveillance of him and wiretap him.

In 1959, Cartha D. "Deke" DeLoach, who began with the FBI in 1942 as a clerk in the Identification Division, replaced Nichols. In his 1995 book *Hoover's FBI*, DeLoach wrote, "The popular myth, fostered of late by would-be historians and sensationalists with their eyes on the bestseller list, has it that in his day J. Edgar Hoover all but ran Washington, using dirty tricks to intimidate congressmen and presidents, and phone taps, bugs, and informants to build secret files with which to blackmail lawmakers."

That, DeLoach wrote, was not the FBI he knew.

"As assistant to the director, I sometimes took the O&C [Official and Confidential] files from the Hoover suite to my office, where I could examine them at my leisure. The point is important. Hoover did not keep these files secret, as he would have, had they contained information for blackmail purposes."[66]

Of course, the fact that Hoover let one of his most trusted aides look at the files does not mean they were not secret. Hoover did not call the files confidential for nothing. Secret or not, Roy L. Elson, the administrative assistant to Senator Carl T. Hayden, will never forget an encounter he had with DeLoach. For twenty years, Hayden headed the Senate Rules and Administration Committee and later the Senate Appropriations Committee, which had jurisdiction over the FBI's budget. He was one of the most powerful members of Congress. As Hayden, an Arizona Democrat, suffered hearing loss and some dementia in his later years, Elson became known as the 101st senator because he made so many of the senator's decisions on his own.

As the bureau's liaison with Congress, DeLoach routinely met with Elson in Elson's office next to Hayden's. In the early 1960s, DeLoach wanted an additional appropriation for a new FBI building, which Congress approved in April 1962. Originally, the building was supposed to cost $60 million. By 1972, the estimated cost had escalated, mainly because of changes Hoover made to the design, to $102 million.

"The senator supported the building," Elson said. "He always gave the bureau more money than they needed. This was a request for an additional appropriation. I had reservations about it. DeLoach was persistent."

DeLoach "hinted" that he had "information that was unflattering and detrimental to my marital situation and that the senator might be disturbed," said Elson, who was then married to his second wife. "I was certainly vulnerable that way," Elson said. "There was more than one girl . . . The implication was there was information about my sex life. There was no doubt in my mind what he was talking about."[67]

Elson said to DeLoach, "Let's talk to him [the senator] about it. I think he's heard about everything there is to hear about me. Bring the photos if you have them." At that point, Elson said, "He started backing off. . . . He said, 'I'm only joking.' Bullshit," Elson said. "I interpreted it as attempted blackmail."

In 1975 testimony before the House Select Committee on Intelligence, retired FBI Special Agent Arthur Murtagh testified about a comment DeLoach made to agents receiving in-service training at the FBI Academy. Asked what headquarters did with memos bearing information that might be of possible interest to Hoover, DeLoach said, "The other night, we picked up a situation where this senator was seen drunk, in a hit-and-run accident, and some good-looking broad was with him. We got the information, reported it in a memorandum, and by noon the next day, the senator was aware that we had the information, and we never had trouble with him on appropriations since."[68]

"That is absolutely false," DeLoach commented. "No such thing ever happened. I would not have made any statement lecturing to agents like that." As for Elson's allegation, DeLoach said, "It never happened."

"Hoover's great ambition in life was to have an FBI building," said Hoover's journalist friend Walter Trohan. "He did it with a bit of blackmail. He would find out a congressman had a girl in town. Hoover would go in to the congressman and say, 'This is the kind of thing we get.' He would lay it out. He did that with the idea of having the congressman's vote for his building. I know it was done because a congressman told me it happened to him."[69]

Reading the Official and Confidential files that survived makes it clear they could have been gathered for no other purpose than blackmail. For example, on June 13, 1958, the head of the Washington Field

Office informed Hoover that, prior to marrying a member of Congress, the member's wife had been "having an affair with a Negro . . . [and] also at one time carried on an affair with a House Post Office employee." More recently, the report said, the congressman's wife "endeavored to have an affair with [an] Indonesian, who declined."

In response to this tidbit, Hoover wrote back on June 25 that it was "certainly thoughtful of you to advise me of matters of current interest, and I am glad to have the benefit of this information."[70]

On August 8, 1958, the head of the Washington office advised Hoover that a senator "prepares a personal check each month in the amount of $500, payable to [name withheld]. [The FBI's source] stated that he had heard that [name withheld] is a 'party girl' and that she may be living with Senator [name withheld] at the Shoreham Hotel, Washington, D.C."

A memo on October 21, 1958, told Hoover that a married senator "has been frequently in the company of [name withheld] of the public relations staff of the Sheraton-Park Hotel. The relationship between the senator and [this woman] appears to be much more than casual."

On June 9, 1959, the head of the Washington office informed Hoover that a prostitute said she had had sexual intercourse with a senator in the afternoon "on the couch in the senator's office."

"I have received your note of June 9, 1959, and I want to thank you for bringing this data to my attention," Hoover wrote back.

On April 15, 1970, the head of the Washington Field Office wrote Hoover that, incident to a car theft, an aide to Congressman Charles C. Diggs Jr. of Michigan "advised she has intimate relations with the congressman with some frequency." The memo noted that the aide is a white woman, and Congressman Diggs, who was chairman of the House District Committee, was black.

"Your letter of April 15 has been received," Hoover responded, "and it is indeed thoughtful of you to bring this information to my attention."

"This was a way of putting congressmen on notice that we have something on them and therefore they would be more disposed to meeting the bureau's needs and keeping Hoover in power," said John J. McDermott, who headed the Washington Field Office and eventually became deputy associate FBI director.[71]

While there is ample evidence that Hoover used the information in his files for blackmail, there was usually no need for it. Simply the perception that he had such information was usually enough to keep politicians in line.

"Congress was afraid of Hoover. They had good reason to be," said Joseph Purvis, another former head of the Washington Field Office, who wrote many of the memos to Hoover describing congressmen's activities.

In other cases, Hoover used information from the files to help members of Congress like John J. Rooney, who for decades headed the House appropriations subcommittee that was over the FBI's budget. Hoover gave Rooney derogatory information about his opponent, Allard Lowenstein, who was defeated.

In the end, the answer to why Hoover did not go after organized crime until he was forced into it is the same reason he kept files on members of Congress. Above all, Hoover wanted to keep his job. Many members of Congress—not to mention powerful local politicians—had ties to organized crime and might try to unseat him. The Mafia was as powerful as the president. Moreover, as a perfectionist, Hoover did not want to risk losing a case against a powerful figure.

"We are bigger than General Motors," Lansky boasted, and according to Hundley, that was true.

For the same reasons, for purposes of prosecution, Hoover would not investigate corrupt politicians. The only exception—a bribery prosecution of Representative John Dowdy, a Democrat from Texas—occurred because Stephen H. Sachs, the U.S. attorney in Baltimore, forced the issue. When Sachs asked Attorney General John Mitchell if he could get Hoover to cooperate on wiring a witness to obtain evidence, Mitchell said, "Hoover will not deny me this," Sachs recalled, meaning it would be a struggle.[72]

As FBI director, Hoover had an obligation to go after both Mafia figures and corrupt politicians. Yet, until he was forced into investigating organized crime, those two targets were sacrosanct.

9

INGA

Blond, blue-eyed, and beautiful, Inga Arvad won the title "Beauty Queen of Denmark" at the age of seventeen. After she attended Columbia University's School of Journalism, the *Washington Times-Herald* hired her to write a gossip column. At twenty-eight, she met John F. Kennedy through his sister Kathleen, who also worked at the paper. Soon, Kennedy and Arvad, who was married, were having a torrid affair. Kennedy called Arvad "Bingo" or "Inga Binga."

Kennedy knew nothing of her past. But the FBI already had begun investigating her. Born on October 6, 1913, in Copenhagen, Inga Marie Arvad married Kemal Abdel Nabi, an Egyptian diplomat, when she was seventeen. In 1935, she was having lunch at the Danish embassy when someone said Hermann Göring was going to marry a well-known Berlin actress. A social climber, Arvad called the actress and pretended to represent a Danish paper. The actress agreed to an interview and liked her so much that she invited Arvad to their wedding, where Adolf Hitler was best man. At the wedding, Göring struck up a conversation with Arvad. He asked if he could do anything for her, and she said he could arrange an interview with Hitler.[73]

Although nothing appeared in print, Arvad interviewed Hitler twice and had lunch with him. Hitler called her the "perfect Nordic beauty." Much later she told her son Ronald T. McCoy that she had rejected efforts by the SS to get her to report what she heard at parties in Paris.

She took a part in a Danish movie and, divorcing her first husband before she was twenty, married Paul Fejos, the movie's Hungarian director. Having moved to the United States in September 1940, she entered Columbia Journalism School, which she attended until June 1941.

If Kennedy did not know about Arvad's background, he did know that she was anti-Semitic and pro-Hitler. "She made no secret of her views. She was very pro-Nazi," said Pat Munroe, a classmate at Columbia. "She used to object to the fact that we had several Jewish members in the class. She called them 'Chews.' Those goddamned 'Chews.' That was her accent."[74]

Indeed, Arvad's expressed admiration of Hitler prompted someone from the journalism school to write to the FBI about her, touching off the bureau's investigation. By then in Germany, Hitler was requiring all Jews to wear a yellow star, and the first killing of Jews by poison gas had occurred at Auschwitz.

When the bureau learned from the Office of Naval Intelligence on January 17, 1942, that Arvad was carrying on an affair with Kennedy, it became more concerned. An ensign, Kennedy had access to information classified top secret about American war plans. Moreover, Arvad's husband, Paul Fejos, participated in scientific expeditions funded by Axel Wenner-Gren. The founder and chief stockholder of a Swedish gun manufacturing company, Wenner-Gren was close to various Nazis. Hoover concluded that the expeditions were probably a Nazi "front for an ulterior purpose." Could Arvad be picking up information vital to the Germans through pillow talk with Kennedy?

Several times as they watched Arvad's apartment, Suite 505 at 1600 Sixteenth Street NW, FBI agents saw Kennedy leave the building early in the morning. When he reported to the Sixth Naval District to work on defense plans at the District Security Office in Charleston, South Carolina, Arvad met him there at the Francis Marion Hotel.

The FBI planted bugging devices in the hotel and in Arvad's apartment. The bureau also intercepted Arvad's telephone calls and conducted a search of her apartment. There, agents found evidence that she had received $5,000 from Wenner-Gren in the fall of 1941 and other smaller payments prior to that.

The transcripts of the FBI's bugs usually noted that the two engaged in intercourse on "numerous occasions." But not once did Arvad and Kennedy discuss his work for naval intelligence. She later told the FBI that the payments received from Wenner-Gren were advances on her husband's salary. If Arvad was a spy, she was not very good at it.

Without naming her or Kennedy, Walter Winchell alluded to their affair on January 12, 1942. "One of Ex-Ambassador Kennedy's eligible sons is the target of a Washington gal columnist's affections," the column said. "So much so she has consulted her barrister about divorcing her exploring groom. Pa Kennedy no like."

Almost immediately, Hoover was on the phone to Joseph P. Kennedy. The two men used each other: Kennedy relentlessly praised Hoover as the finest public servant in the land, while Hoover helped Kennedy with information about his enemies.

Hoover urged Kennedy to tell his son to break up with Arvad, according to what Jack Kennedy later told William Sutton, one of his campaign workers and aides. As far as Joe Kennedy was concerned, Arvad posed a threat to his son's political future. For the same reason that he checked the backgrounds of his children's dates and hired private detectives to watch them, Joe did not want John's reputation sullied by a possible German spy. Anyone who married John Kennedy would need to be a political asset, not a liability.[75]

Within days of his father's call to him, Kennedy told Arvad that they were through. On January 19, Arvad wrote to him, "I am not going to try to make you change. It would be without result anyway because Big Joe has a stronger hand than I."

To make sure his son did not see Arvad, Joe Kennedy asked his friend James V. Forrestal, then undersecretary of the Navy, to reassign him. John Kennedy told Arvad that his father had called Forrestal personally and had him transferred to the South Pacific. The rest is history: The Japanese destroyer *Amagiri* rammed *PT-109,* Kennedy emerged a war hero, and, in July 1960, he became the Democratic nominee for president.

If Hoover ever connected his call to Joe Kennedy with his son's ascendancy to the White House in 1961, he never mentioned it. But once Kennedy appointed his brother Robert attorney general, Hoover made it clear how he felt.

Hoover was sixty-six when John Kennedy announced that "the torch has been passed to a new generation of Americans, born in this century." Hoover was neither. Robert Kennedy had already publicly criticized the director over his refusal to acknowledge the existence of organized crime. With Robert's brother in the White House, Hoover had a real boss to contend with.

Immediately, Robert Kennedy raised Hoover's hackles by requiring him to submit his speeches and FBI press releases in advance for approval and revisions. He had a direct telephone line installed between his desk and Hoover's, bypassing Helen Gandy. Most troubling, Kennedy had a habit of calling agents directly, rather than going through Hoover. Hoover and Kennedy made no secret of their enmity.

"I was in Kennedy's office arguing that Hoover was not hiring minorities," William Hundley said. "Besides Hoover's drivers, the FBI was lily white. Kennedy said, 'Do you want me to get Hoover here?' I said, 'Sure.' He pushed a buzzer. Hoover came in, and he and Robert went at it."

Meanwhile, Hoover was forging a relationship with the president, who already knew from his father that Hoover had a juicy file on him, documenting his relationship with Inga Arvad. Now Hoover plied Kennedy with tidbits about senators who opposed him. He told him of the activities of Robert G. "Bobby" Baker, a former page who became secretary to Senate Majority Leader Lyndon B. Johnson. Baker provided call girls to politicians and businessmen at the Carousel Motel in Ocean City, Maryland. Hoover passed along a report of an ambassador caught fleeing the bedroom of a Washington hostess. When Hoover repeatedly asked through his liaison, Courtney Evans, what the president was going to do about it, Kenneth O'Donnell, Kennedy's appointments secretary, finally relayed the president's exasperated response: "From now on I'm going to hire faster ambassadors."

Almost every month, Hoover sent one of the Kennedy brothers some new, embarrassing revelation about his personal life. One report described Frank Sinatra's ties to organized crime and his and the president's double-date with call girls. The report included affidavits from two "mulatto prostitutes" in New York. On November 22, 1961, Hoover informed Robert Kennedy of rumors that before his brother's marriage to Jacqueline, he had been secretly married to another woman.

"The attorney general expressed appreciation for my concern . . . ," Hoover wrote in a memo. "I stated I just wanted him to be alert to this."

The following year, Hoover's White House liaison Courtney Evans told Robert Kennedy that the bureau had received information that he was having an affair with a girl in El Paso, Texas. "He said he had never been to El Paso, Texas, and there was no basis in fact whatsoever for the allegation," Evans reported to Hoover.

On March 22, 1962, Hoover had lunch with the president. Through bugs and wiretaps, Hoover told him, the FBI had learned that he was having an affair with Judith Campbell Exner, a twenty-five-year-old divorcée. Hoover informed him that Exner was also having an affair with Chicago mob boss Sam Giancana. A month later, Hoover told Robert Kennedy that the CIA had enlisted Giancana's help in trying to knock off Fidel Castro by giving him a poison pill. The plan was foiled when the Mafia leader's contact in Castro's entourage lost his position.

Kennedy canceled a trip to Sinatra's Palm Springs estate and stopped calling Exner. He told his brother-in-law Peter Lawford, "I can't stay there. You know as much as I that I like Frank, but I can't go there." Sinatra was miffed that Kennedy never told him why he ended their friendship.

By 1963, Robert Kennedy was telling associates that he looked forward to Hoover's mandatory retirement when the director turned seventy on January 1, 1965. By then, his brother would be safely reelected and could withstand Hoover's pressure to waive the retirement date, Robert Kennedy figured. Word got back to Hoover, who was "very, very unhappy about it," according to Sullivan.

■　■　■

On November 22, 1963, Robert Kennedy was having a luncheon meeting at Hickory Hill, his home in McLean, Virginia, when Hoover called him. Kennedy would never forget how cold Hoover was.

"I have news for you," Hoover said.

"What?" Kennedy asked.

"The president has been shot."

"What? Oh. I—Is it serious? I . . ."

"I think it's serious," Hoover said. "I am endeavoring to get details. I'll call you back when I find out more."

Thirty minutes later, Hoover called back.

"The president is dead," he said matter-of-factly.

Hoover had learned of the shooting from Gordon L. Shanklin, the SAC in Dallas, who had two men monitoring police radio reports from the president's motorcade. By 3 P.M. eastern time, Shanklin told Hoover that Dallas police had arrested Lee Harvey Oswald, a twenty-four-year-old Marine Corps veteran. Oswald was believed to have assassinated the president and J. D. Tippit, a Dallas police officer. Shanklin told Hoover that the Dallas office had an open security file on Oswald because he had defected to the Soviet Union in 1959. Disillusioned, Oswald had returned to the United States in June 1962.

At 3:15 A.M. on November 24, Shanklin woke Hoover to tell him an anonymous caller had told the Dallas Field Office that Oswald would be shot when he was moved that day to a jail from the Dallas Police Department. Concerned, Hoover told Shanklin to call Jesse Curry, the Dallas police chief, and tell him the police should not announce when Oswald would be moved. But when Shanklin spoke with Curry, the police chief said there was nothing to worry about. Oswald would be transferred in an armored car, and the police would deploy a decoy. As for announcing the time of the transfer, the chief said he had to accommodate the press.

At 12:21 P.M. Jack Ruby, a Dallas nightclub owner, shot Oswald to death with a .38-caliber pistol in the basement of the police department. NBC caught it live. PRESIDENT'S ASSASSIN SHOT TO DEATH IN JAIL CORRIDOR BY A DALLAS CITIZEN; GRIEVING THRONGS VIEW KENNEDY BIER, read the *New York Times* headline.

Assassination of the president was not then a federal crime. However, Lyndon Johnson, sworn in as president on *Air Force One* on Love Field in Dallas, ordered the FBI to investigate.

Like a caricature, the bureau by this time reflected all of Hoover's personality traits. On the one hand, it was staffed for the most part by smart, capable, resourceful agents who were highly disciplined. SACs were held responsible for the conduct of agents, and key decisions were made by the executive committee, which consisted of assistant directors and assistants to the directors, chaired by Tolson. Their decisions could be overruled by Hoover.

Month after month, heroic agents made good cases. In February

1960, for example, the bureau solved the kidnapping and murder of Adolf Coors III, head of Coors Brewery. In December 1968, Barbara Jane Mackle was kidnapped in Decatur, Georgia, and buried alive in a specially equipped box. Agents found the victim five days later, recovered almost all of the ransom of $500,000, and arrested the kidnappers.

On the other hand, as Hoover aged, he imposed even more of his quirks on the bureau. Besides the inflexible dress standards, Hoover outlawed drinking coffee on the job. Apparently, drinking coffee conflicted with the image of hardworking supermen who never took a break. As a result, agents took more time off from work in search of a coffee shop than they would have drinking coffee at their desks.

In 1967, members of the FBI's inspection staff saw Phillip M. King, an agent in the Washington Field Office, drinking coffee on the job at what was then the Holloway House cafeteria on Fourteenth Street NW. The inspectors demanded to know the identities of the other two agents drinking coffee with him. When King refused, the inspectors said they would review photos of the several hundred agents in the field office to identify the perpetrators. King finally agreed to ask the other two offenders to get in touch with the inspectors, and they did.

"In my signed statement, I admitted drinking coffee. I said I had done it before, and I would do it again," King recalled.

All three agents were transferred, put on probation for six months, and given a letter of censure.[76]

Hoover's dictum against embarrassing the bureau left no room for agent misconduct, so the bureau simply denied it existed. If an agent got into trouble or cheated on his expense vouchers, he was quietly fired or told to resign. About fifteen to twenty agents were fired each year. In most cases, no one ever knew that misconduct had occurred. If an agent committed a crime in connection with bureau work, he would be severed but—because of the embarrassment it would bring to the FBI—not prosecuted. If he committed a crime outside work, he would be fired, then prosecuted.

"The bureau used to brag that no agent was ever convicted of a crime while in the bureau," said David G. Binney, who later became deputy FBI director. "The reason was he resigned, and the next day he got arrested."

Besides banning coffee, Hoover insisted that agents work "voluntary" overtime even when there was no need to do so. Hoover then boasted of the overtime hours to Congress.

"You had to do something on a case every thirty days," said James D. McKenzie, a former assistant director over training. "Sometimes you couldn't get to an investigation every thirty days, but you were in trouble if you didn't. So an agent put a memo in the file. A waste of time, a waste of taxpayers' money."

Although Hoover's tight control prevented major corruption, the petty rules led to widespread lying and flouting of minor regulations, which had a corrosive effect.

"Under Hoover, there was well-defined hypocrisy," said John L. Martin, who became an agent in 1962 and later headed espionage prosecutions in the Justice Department. "You got paid for unscheduled overtime by signing in earlier or signing out later than was the case. To show that you wrote up reports of interviews on time, you backdated the forms, called 302s. Instead of arresting draft dodgers, you took them into their draft board and made sure they registered. You drank coffee. Everyone knew this was verboten but no one reported it."[77]

William Sullivan recounted receiving a call at 2 A.M. from the Baltimore Field Office. It seemed that Hoover's driver had been arrested for drinking and for hitting the arresting police officer. Sullivan assumed that the driver was reacting to the shabby way Hoover usually treated him. A few hours later, an agent reported to Sullivan that he had seen the driver in his cell.

"He's still drunk and cursing Hoover like I've never heard anyone speak about the old man," the agent reported.

To try to save the driver's job, Sullivan and other headquarters officials told the Baltimore office to submit a memo stating that when Baltimore agents saw the driver in his cell, he was on his knees praying. So the office prepared a memo quoting Hoover's wayward driver as saying, "Good Lord, I'll always condemn myself as long as I live for embarrassing Mr. Hoover. I don't care what happens to me, it's Mr. Hoover I'm concerned about."

The ruse worked. Hoover agreed to overlook the infraction that one time. "That's how we protected ourselves, playing on his ego," Sullivan said. "The bureau system made liars of us all."[78]

The greatest hypocrisy revolved around the inspection process. No matter what they found, the inspectors were expected to finger a respectable number of agents as an example to others. It was a way to control agents.

"The inspection staff used to walk in and say, 'Who can take a hit?' " said Binney, who later headed the FBI's Office of Professional Responsibility (OPR). " 'Who can take a letter of censure, and it won't affect his pay for the year?' They would come every year, and it was very haphazard. If you had just received your promotion to GS-13, and you were not due for another increase for two years, they would say, 'Dave Binney can take a hit this year. But don't get Joe Jones because he is coming up next month for his promotion.' They would go through your files and say, 'On this case, you didn't put something in the files for forty-five days.' 'OK. You got me.' "

Hoover could also be compassionate. He granted transfers to agents who needed to be with ill parents, for example. But he also arbitrarily transferred agents simply because a case, through no direct fault of their own, had not gone well. Because the bureau did not fully pay for moving costs, agents who were transferred were penalized by thousands of dollars.

"Hoover's discipline often was unfair," said "Bucky" Walters, who was a deputy assistant director over inspections under Hoover and later became assistant director for inspections.

Many capable agents left the bureau rather than subject themselves to Hoover's tyranny. In fact, according to Fred Robinette, the nephew of Hoover, Robinette's father left the bureau in a tiff with Hoover over what he considered unfair discipline meted out to other agents in the Washington Field Office.

"People were afraid to tell Hoover things they thought he didn't want to hear. My father told him about the unfair discipline," Robinette said. "Hoover said he appreciated hearing it. Then my father said he can't work for an organization that allows this to go on. Hoover said, 'Then on your way out, leave your badge, credentials, and gun on Miss Gandy's desk.' My father did. Although they eventually reconciled, they did not speak for years."[79]

Other agents responded to the unfair discipline by covering up. When Gordon Shanklin told Hoover that the Dallas office already had a file on Lee Harvey Oswald, the SAC knew he could be in serious trouble. On Oswald's return from the Soviet Union, agents in the Fort Worth office had interviewed him and found him uncooperative. After he was arrested following a fracas while handing out "Fair Play for Cuba" leaflets in New Orleans, Oswald asked to see the FBI. He told the agents he was a Marxist, not a Communist.

When Oswald moved to Dallas, his file was assigned to James P. Hosty Jr. On November 1, 1963, Hosty visited Ruth Payne in Irving, Texas, where Oswald lived. She informed him that Oswald was working at the Texas School Book Depository in Dallas and was staying temporarily in a rooming house there. Hosty briefly met Marina Oswald, his Russian-born wife, who appeared frightened. Hosty assured her the FBI would not harm her.

Payne promised to find Oswald's address in Dallas, and Hosty dropped in on her a second time, but she still did not know where Oswald was. Shortly after that visit—sometime between November 6 and 8—Oswald appeared at the Dallas Field Office and demanded to see Hosty. When told by Nanny Lee Fenner, a receptionist, that he wasn't in, Oswald threw down an envelope, and Fenner read the note inside. She later recalled that it said if the FBI didn't stop bothering him, Oswald would "blow up" the FBI field office or the Dallas police department.

Fenner had worked for the FBI since 1942. People had come in with knives and pistols, and that hadn't bothered her. But she considered Oswald's note a serious threat and brought it to the attention of the assistant special agent in charge. He said to give the note to Hosty, who read the note and tossed it in his in box.

"The note merely threatened unspecified action against the FBI," Hosty told me. "Why would Oswald threaten to blow up the police department?"[80]

After Oswald had been identified as the assassin, Shanklin retrieved the note from Hosty's desk and called him in. Shanklin was "quite agitated and upset," Hosty recalled. Because Oswald was mad at the FBI, the SAC felt the bureau could be blamed for the assassination. Having received the note, Hosty should have followed up and apprised Oswald of the possible consequences of his threat. The FBI should have warned the Secret Service, which would have put Oswald on its threat list. The list includes people who might assassinate the president. Agents would have interviewed and evaluated him, possibly diminishing his aggressiveness. Instead, Hosty ignored Oswald's note.

Shanklin asked Hosty to write a memo recounting his dealings with Oswald and explaining why he did not take action on his note. After reading Hosty's memo, Shanklin became even more apprehensive. He summoned Hosty again. According to Hosty, Shanklin handed him Oswald's note and Hosty's new memo.

"Oswald's dead now," Shanklin said. "There can be no trial. Here, get rid of it."

In front of Shanklin, Hosty tore up the documents, but that was not enough. Shanklin told him to take the scraps out of his office. "I don't want to see this again," he said. Hosty flushed them down a toilet.

There is no evidence that Hoover was informed of Oswald's note or of the cover-up. Given the arbitrary discipline Hoover meted out, it is likely Shanklin acted on his own to protect himself from punitive action. Hoover later testified before the Warren Commission, which President Johnson charged with investigating the assassination along with the FBI, that there was "nothing up to the time of the assassination that gave any indication that this man was a dangerous character who might do harm to the president or to the vice president." The fact that Oswald had dropped off a note to Hosty did not come out until 1975 after a reporter from the *Dallas Times Herald* overheard an agent talking about it at a party. When Shanklin learned that the paper was planning a story, he suddenly retired.

The commission based its conclusion that Oswald killed the president largely on the FBI's investigation. On the day of the assassination, Hoover had made up his mind that Oswald was the killer—"a Communist," Hoover told Richard Nixon when the former vice president called him. Despite the rush to judgment, the FBI conducted a thorough and objective investigation, interviewing more than twenty-five thousand people.

All over the country, the investigation of the Kennedy assassination brought out unstable people. A Cleveland man told the FBI that Jacqueline Kennedy was a Communist, and that the president had been shot with her permission. A Newark woman said Kennedy had made her "chief" so she could investigate a master spy ring. She said Hoover had agreed that she was "chief." Deadpan, the agents who interviewed her wrote in their report: "Although with difficulty, she was admonished, and told never again to refer to herself as being associated with the FBI in any manner. As the agents departed, she said, 'It is always good to see my men.' "[81]

The key piece of evidence linking Lee Harvey Oswald to the assassination was his Mannlicher-Carcano 6.5-millimeter Italian rifle, found on the sixth floor of the book depository at Dealey Plaza, where he had been seen. FBI ballistics examinations concluded that bullets from his rifle killed Kennedy and wounded Texas Governor John B. Connally Jr., who was seated on a jumpseat of the president's limousine.[82]

Theories that Oswald was acting on behalf of the Mafia, the Soviets, or Cuba have not panned out. Given the number of years that have elapsed, those who might have known about such conspiracies would most likely have come forth by now. The greatest fear at the time was that Oswald was part of a Soviet plot. In view of that, it is understandable that Hoover, on November 25, 1963, let the Associated Press know that "all available information" indicated that Oswald "acted alone." The FBI polygraphed Jack Ruby, who passed when he said he was not part of a conspiracy.[83]

Meanwhile, Hoover had scores to settle. "Hoover's main thought was always how to cover, how to protect himself, so he began issuing letters of censure to men in the bureau," Sullivan said. "His theory was that if he was scored for having mishandled the investigation, he could say: 'The moment the assassination occurred, I looked into the matter and fixed responsibility.' "

Hoover gave James Gale, assistant director over inspections, the job of investigating the bureau's actions before the assassination. As a result, Hoover censured seventeen agents for their "failures" and "deficiencies" in the handling of the Oswald case prior to the assassination. Some of the agents, including eight at headquarters, were transferred or received suspension without pay.[84]

Without even knowing about Oswald's note, Hoover placed Hosty on ninety days' probation and ordered him transferred to Kansas City,

Missouri. Then he suspended him for thirty days without pay. Shanklin was censured.

In reality, said a former Secret Service agent, even if the bureau had dealt openly with Oswald's note, it never would have passed Oswald's name along to the Secret Service.

"Hoover didn't share anything with other agencies," he said.

Not until February 1965 did the FBI and Secret Service agree that the FBI would share information needed to protect the president.

10

TAPES

Federal civil rights laws had existed since 1870, yet, as the civil rights movement gathered momentum, Hoover continued to insist that civil rights violations were not a federal matter, and the FBI would not get involved. When Herbert Brownell and Eisenhower wanted to push for a new statute to safeguard civil rights, Hoover told a cabinet meeting on March 9, 1956, "The South is in a state of explosive resentment over what they consider an unfair portrayal of their way of life, and what they consider intermeddling." School desegregation decisions by the Supreme Court were creating tension over what Hoover called "mixed education," which he said could lead to "the specter of racial intermarriage." The Communists were moving to take advantage of the civil rights movement, the director warned.

Almost ten years later, Hoover's views had not changed. In off-the-record remarks, Hoover told an audience of newspaper editors in 1965 that the "colored people are quite ignorant, mostly uneducated, and I doubt if they would seek an education if they had an opportunity. Many who have the right to register [to vote] very seldom do register." Only in "due time" can they "gain the acceptance which is necessary and rights equal to those of the white citizens of their community."[85]

Hoover complained to the editors that the Supreme Court had mandated that blacks, when questioned by police, must be treated with respect. The court had "gone into the field where police officers must address them in courteous language, particularly in the case of Negroes, and instead of saying, 'Boy, come here,' they want to be addressed as 'Mr.' "

Hoover's racist attitudes were rooted in his upbringing in a southern town with segregated schools. Even during World War II, few restaurants in D.C. served black customers. In this area, as most others, Hoover's views were immutable. Hoover made his black drivers agents so they would not be drafted. The only other black in his service was his housekeeper, Annie Fields. In Hoover's mind, the civil rights movement was a threat to the establishment and fraught with potential for Communist influence.

Beyond his personal prejudices, Hoover was aware that southern juries rarely convicted those charged with civil rights violations, and that conservative southern members of Congress, who often controlled the bureau's purse strings, wanted things left just as they were.

Thus, when Hoover received a startling teletype from the Birmingham, Alabama, Field Office on May 12, 1961, he did nothing. According to the teletype, an informant had reported that Eugene "Bull" Connor, the public safety director of the city, was preparing a special reception for the Freedom Riders, blacks and whites who were participating in the Congress of Racial Equality's sit-ins throughout the south. The civil rights activists were expected in Birmingham on May 14.

Connor, according to the memo, had told the Ku Klux Klan that he would turn a blind eye if the Klan engaged in violence. No police officer would appear on the scene for fifteen or twenty minutes after the CORE bus arrived. If any Freedom Riders entered a segregated bathroom, Connor instructed, the Klan should follow them, strip them naked, and beat them to "look like a bulldog got hold of them." At Connor's urging, the Klan agreed to have sixty men show up to assault the Freedom Riders.

As promised, the Klan savagely beat the Freedom Riders. For good measure, one Klan member beat a newspaper photographer unconscious. The police arrested the civil rights activists for violating an injunction against such protests.

Robert Kennedy did not know that Hoover had been aware of the plans to engage in violence and had done nothing. But after the Freedom

Riders arrived in Montgomery, Alabama, the attorney general realized that federal intervention was required to protect blacks meeting at a church to hear Dr. Martin Luther King Jr. speak. To restore order, Kennedy ordered U.S. marshals to the city. After that, Hoover, under Kennedy's prodding, would be forced to tackle civil rights violations. When Lyndon Johnson became president after Kennedy's assassination, protecting the rights of blacks became an even higher priority for the FBI.

Hoover and Johnson had known each other since 1945, when Johnson moved to a house diagonally across the street from Hoover's. Just as he attacked organized crime after Robert Kennedy became attorney general, Hoover complied with Johnson's wishes, even opening an office in Jackson, Mississippi.

On September 2, 1964, Hoover decided to conduct a COINTELPRO aimed at disrupting and harassing the Ku Klux Klan. Under the program, the FBI sent Klan leaders or their wives anonymous letters aimed at breaking up their marriages. The letters, as usual, were pathetic. One, from a "God-fearing Klans woman" to the wife of a Klan leader, said, "Yes . . . he has been committing adultery. . . . My menfolk say they don't believe this but I think they do. I feel like crying. I watched her with my own eyes. They call her Ruby. . . . I saw her strut around at a rally with her lust-filled eyes and smart aleck figure."

Foolish as the effort was, it allowed Hoover to brag to Johnson that he was doing something about the Klan. Meanwhile, as with previous presidents, Hoover baited a trap, feeding Johnson reports on his foes for his bedtime reading. As soon as Johnson took the bait, Hoover sprang the trap by making sure he had documentation verifying that Johnson had requested more reports and investigations. The president then was under Hoover's control.

Cartha DeLoach, Hoover's aide over congressional and public affairs, became a dinner companion of Johnson. When Tolson asked DeLoach to request that Johnson waive Hoover's mandatory retirement date, the president was only too happy to oblige.

On May 8, 1964, Johnson summoned reporters to the Rose Garden. "J. Edgar Hoover is a hero to millions of decent citizens, and an anathema to evil men," the president said. For that reason, Johnson would exempt the FBI director from "compulsory retirement for an indefinite period of time."

As far as Johnson was concerned, "I would rather have him inside the tent pissing out than outside the tent pissing in."

When Johnson asked Hoover if he would monitor dissident factions at the 1964 Democratic convention in Atlantic City, Hoover eagerly complied. Johnson was concerned that civil rights activists might demonstrate and force the seating of the Mississippi Freedom Democratic Party, which challenged the regular delegation. Under the guise of keeping an eye on security, DeLoach sent a team of thirty agents to the convention and sent back forty-four pages of reports to Johnson informing him of any plans to try to deny him the nomination for president.

On August 29, 1964, DeLoach reported that he had successfully completed the assignment, using informants, wiretaps, bugs, and FBI agents posing as reporters. "Through our counterintelligence efforts," DeLoach wrote, "the FBI was able to advise the president in advance regarding major plans of the MFDP delegates. The White House considered this of prime importance."

Once again, Hoover had allowed the FBI to be used to help elect a president.

■　■　■

When three young civil rights workers disappeared near Philadelphia, Mississippi, on the evening of June 21, 1964, the local authorities showed as much interest in investigating the case as Hoover had shown in looking into the planned violence against the Freedom Riders. Robert Kennedy—who continued as attorney general under Johnson—declared the case a kidnapping, bringing in the FBI.

This time, Hoover aggressively pursued the case, code-named MIBURN, for Mississippi Burning. This was a reference to the fact that, just prior to their disappearance, the three civil rights workers—two white and one black—had visited a church that had been burned.

Earlier on the evening of their disappearance, a Neshoba County deputy sheriff had arrested the three civil rights workers—James E. Chaney, Andrew Goodman, and Michael Schwerner—for speeding and placed them in jail. After their release around 10 P.M., they disappeared.

By now, the FBI had developed informants who told agents that Ku Klux Klan members had talked at meetings about a need to eliminate "Goatee," the name they used for Schwerner, a New Yorker. Schwerner and the other two victims had come down to Mississippi for Freedom Summer, an effort to register black voters before the 1964 presidential election.

John L. Martin, one of the agents assigned to the case under Joseph A. Sullivan, began interviewing the Klansmen. "Some of them wouldn't talk to us," Martin said. "Others would and they would lie. They were a sorry bunch—stupid, racist, hypocritical. They were lowlife who felt a need to elevate themselves. They did it through hatred."[86]

Eventually, the agents met with Delmar Dennis. "I could tell from the files that Dennis knew something about the incident," Martin said. "A backwoods preacher, he was smarter than most of his fellow Klansmen. So we went to his church and interviewed him in his office. It was a great lesson in intellectual combat. We struck some chords. He conceded the murders were wrong."

Since Hoover was known as a fervent anticommunist patriot, Martin invoked his name. "As a representative of J. Edgar Hoover, I can tell you that the civil rights movement is not a Communist plot," Martin told Dennis. "I can also assure you that we are not going to leave Mississippi until we solve the crime. There are two ways for you to go. You can be a defendant or you can be a witness. Which is it?"

Martin let him think about it. At their next meeting, Martin pulled out a $100 bill (the bureau later reimbursed him). Dennis went for it. Martin and Tom Van Riper, another agent, would drive to Jackson, Mississippi, and meet with Dennis in hotel rooms. Emergency meets were in a cemetery on the edge of Meridian.

While Dennis was not present at the murders, the FBI could direct him, just as spy handlers operate their agents. "We would sit down with him and say, 'We know Alton Wayne Roberts was the triggerman at the murders. But our evidence isn't that strong. Wayne broke his leg the other day and is in the hospital. Go by and see him. Wayne is alone and in pain. The ominous FBI is all around. His Klan friends are not visiting him. Things are not well in his life.' "

Dennis would visit Roberts in the hospital, and Roberts would pour out his heart to Delmar: "I shouldn't have gone there that night." Later, Dennis testified to what Roberts said.

The agents sent Dennis to talk with Sam H. Bowers Jr., the imperial wizard. In response to their talk, Bowers sent Dennis a coded letter. "Millwork" referred to the murder. At the later trial, Delmar decoded it and read it to the jury. It expressed Bowers's support for the plan to eliminate "Goatee." In two days of testimony, Dennis gave an inside view of the killings.

To try to intimidate the agents working the case, Klansmen would race pickup trucks or cars with loud mufflers in front of their motel at 3 or 4 A.M. The Klan put out the word that some agents might be killed. In particular, Lee Roberts, a brother of Wayne, had been talking about killing an FBI agent. A former Klansman, Lee was a Meridian police officer who was six feet five inches tall and weighed more than three hundred pounds. When Martin and Van Riper saw Lee walking patrol in Meridian, they invited him into their FBI car.

"Lee, we know you've been talking about killing an agent," Martin said. "We don't think you're that stupid. But we're concerned that your brother who isn't as smart as you are might get the wrong idea. I want the talk to stop. If you think you want to kill an FBI agent, why don't you just step out of the car and we'll have it out now."

Roberts was in the rear seat of the car with Martin, and Van Riper was in the front seat. As Martin looked at Roberts, he started to cry.

"He was a coward," Martin said. "The Klan could not face anyone. Wearing hoods and white sheets, its members worked in the shadows behind trees in the middle of the night, attacking poor helpless people."

Eventually, the FBI assigned 258 agents to the investigation and interviewed more than a thousand people, including 480 Klansmen. The bureau found that nineteen Klansmen had abducted and killed the three civil rights workers. Agents found their bodies covered by tons of earth in a dam construction project.

On October 20, 1967, eight Ku Klux Klan members, including Bowers, Roberts, and Cecil R. Price, the chief deputy sheriff of Neshoba County, were convicted on federal conspiracy charges of the murders of the three civil rights workers. Bowers and Roberts were sentenced to ten years in jail.

By March 26, 1965, when the Klan killed Viola Liuzzo, a white Detroit housewife who was transporting civil rights marchers to Selma, Alabama, the FBI had become so effective that the bureau was able to announce arrests of those responsible the day after her murder. In fact, riding in the car with the three Klansmen who were charged was an FBI informant, Gary Thomas Rowe, creating controversy about whether he should have been prosecuted as well.

By September 1965, Hoover was able to boast to the White House that the FBI had developed two thousand informants within the Klan and had penetrated all fourteen of the Klan groups. In contrast to his earlier lack of interest, Hoover noted that the informants had alerted the FBI to plots before the Klan had carried them out.

■ ■ ■

In 1954, the FBI began running a top-secret operation codenamed SOLO, which entailed operating as an informant Morris Childs, the principal deputy to Gus Hall, the head of the American Communist Party. In effect, Childs—referred to by the FBI as Agent 58—was the second-ranking official of the party.

Carl N. Freyman, an FBI agent in Chicago, recruited Childs, a Ukrainian-born Jew and a former editor of the party newspaper the *Daily Worker*, after visiting him in his Chicago apartment. Since Childs was in ill health, the agent arranged for him to be treated at the Mayo Clinic in Rochester, Minnesota. Freyman managed to convince Childs that Josef Stalin had betrayed Marxist ideals.

As related by John Barron in *Operation SOLO*, Childs reported for twenty-seven years on party activities and strategy. In addition, he made fifty-two clandestine trips to the Soviet Union, China, Eastern Europe, and Cuba. The Soviets so trusted him that on his seventy-fifth birthday, the Soviet leader, Leonid Brezhnev, gave Childs a birthday party at the Kremlin. Meanwhile, on behalf of the Soviets, Childs and his brother Jack Childs distributed $28 million in cash for Communist activities in the United States.[87]

The FBI held the secret of SOLO so tightly that officials of the CIA, National Security Agency (NSA), Defense Department, State Department, and National Security Council could only read reports of the operation while agents waited to return them to bureau headquarters. Not until 1975 did the FBI inform the president and secretary of state of the true source of the information.

Morris Childs reported on such items as the Sino-Soviet split, Nikita Khrushchev's speech documenting Josef Stalin's mass murders, and the Soviet invasion of Czechoslovakia. He also reported that Stanley Levison, a close friend and adviser to Martin Luther King Jr., and Jack O'Dell, a staff member of King's Southern Christian Leadership Conference, were key members of the Communist Party.

King had first come to national attention in February 1956 as a leader of the Montgomery, Alabama, bus boycott following the arrest of Rosa Parks for refusing to give up her seat to a white rider. King was arrested for orchestrating the boycott, but he vowed to continue his protests using "passive resistance and the weapon of love." By April 1956, the Supreme Court had ruled that segregation in public transportation was unconstitutional.

The FBI began conducting surveillance of Levison in 1961. On January 8, 1962, Hoover informed Robert Kennedy of the presence of Levison in King's entourage, and Kennedy had Justice Department officials pass along to King vague warnings about Levison. In February, the FBI learned that O'Dell had been hired by King's SCLC. The bureau began surveillance of him as well.

Despite installation of wiretaps and bugs, the bureau never discovered any evidence that either Levison or O'Dell had any undue influence on King. That did not deter Hoover from pursuing King, who had committed a far greater sin than associating with Communists: On November 18, 1962, King was quoted in the press as agreeing with a report of the Southern Regional Council that "there is a considerable amount of distrust between Albany [Georgia] Negroes and local members of the Federal Bureau of Investigation." A major part of the problem, King said, was that the FBI staffed its offices in the South with southerners who sympathized with segregationist views. Even when there was clear evidence of police brutality against blacks, FBI agents often did nothing, the civil rights leader said.

King was wrong about FBI offices in the South being staffed by southerners, but he was right about the bureau's lack of interest in offenses against blacks. For years, Hoover had tended to equate critics of the FBI with Communists. Now he was sure King was a menace.

Hoover asked DeLoach to call King with the idea of "straightening him out." DeLoach was to point out that four of the five agents in the Albany office were not from the South. Notoriously disorganized, King did not return the calls. When DeLoach told John P. Mohr, assistant to the director, that King had ignored DeLoach's call, Mohr said King "obviously does not desire to be given the truth."

Based on Hoover's warnings, John Kennedy on June 22, 1963, personally told King in the Rose Garden that if he did not break with Levison, his movement could be destroyed. King dismissed O'Dell but held on to Levison as a friend. When told that King would not break with Levison, Robert Kennedy suggested on July 16 that King should be wiretapped. Courtney Evans, Hoover's liaison to the Justice Department, informed him that since King traveled much of the time, it was doubtful that wiretaps on King's home or office phones would be productive. Evans urged Kennedy to consider the "repercussions if it should ever become known that such a surveillance had been put on King."

There was no law enforcement justification for wiretapping King. Aside from the fact that interception and disclosure of telephone calls was illegal, after wiretapping Levison and O'Dell and obtaining inside information from Morris Childs, the FBI had developed nothing to indicate that King was engaging in espionage. Nor was Levison influencing King. Even if he had been, that was not against the law. As usual, Hoover had failed to distinguish between free speech and illegal conduct. He thus had no probable cause that would justify wiretapping the civil rights leader without violating the Fourth Amendment.

Underscoring how confused Hoover was about the distinction between criminal conduct and free expression, *PTA* magazine quoted the FBI director as saying in 1966 that the United States was then being confronted by "a new style in conspiracy—conspiracy that is extremely subtle and devious and hence difficult to understand . . . a conspiracy reflected by questionable moods and attitudes, by unrestrained individualism, by nonconformism in dress and speech, even by obscene language, rather than by formal membership in specific organizations."[88]

Confirming that King was not a threat, Sullivan on August 23 gave

Hoover a sixty-seven-page memo that concluded there had been an "obvious failure of the Communist Party of the United States to appreciably infiltrate, influence, or control large numbers of American Negroes in this country."

Hoover was outraged. His entire career had been based on running against the Communists. Recognizing that his job was in jeopardy, Sullivan quickly retreated. "The director is correct," Sullivan told him meekly in a subsequent memo. "Personally, I believe, in the light of King's powerful demagogic speech yesterday, he stands head and shoulders above all other Negro leaders put together when it comes to influencing great masses of Negroes. We must mark him now, if we have not done so before, as the most dangerous Negro of the future . . . from the standpoint of Communism, the Negro, and national security."

The threatening speech Sullivan referred to was King's oration at the Lincoln Memorial. "I have a dream," King told 200,000 peaceful demonstrators on August 28, 1963. "I have a dream that one day this nation will rise up and live out the true meaning of the creed: 'We hold these truths to be self-evident, that all men are created equal.' " Joan Baez sang "We Shall Overcome" at the rally that day, and Peter, Paul, and Mary wondered, "How many times must a man look up before he can see the sky?"

Sullivan even suggested that the FBI promote Samuel R. Pierce Jr., a black New York attorney, as a replacement for King as a leader of the civil rights movement. What concerned Hoover, Sullivan later commented, was not that King might be influenced by Communists. Rather, Hoover "was concerned about King's repeated criticism of the FBI and its alleged lack of interest in the civil rights movement."[89] In addition, by the end of 1963, *Time* had named Martin Luther King Man of the Year. In 1964, King won the Nobel Peace Prize. It was too much for Hoover. "Hoover was jealous of King's national prominence and the international awards that were offered to him," Sullivan said.

Hoover supporters would later claim that Robert Kennedy, rather than Hoover, pushed for a wiretap on King. Kennedy supporters say he wanted to wiretap King to show Hoover that King was not under the influence of Communists. What is clear is that by July 25, 1964, Kennedy had decided that such surveillance of King would be "ill advised." But Sullivan had checked out King's home and office and determined that wiretaps would be productive. When told this, Hoover wrote to Sullivan, "I hope you don't change your minds on this."[90] Hoover then asked Evans to obtain Kennedy's approval for installation of wiretaps.

Still expressing concerns, Kennedy on October 10 said he might authorize the wiretaps on a "trial" basis. Finally, on October 21, Evans persuaded Kennedy to approve the wiretaps, but for only thirty days. At the end of that period, the results would be evaluated. If the FBI wanted an extension, it would have to ask Kennedy for reauthorization. But Hoover never returned for an extension. The FBI continued the wiretaps until Kennedy's successor and former deputy, Nicholas deB. Katzenbach, discovered them in 1965.

At that point, Katzenbach ordered them discontinued. Dismayed at the bureau's failure to return for reauthorization of the wiretaps on King, Katzenbach ordered Hoover to obtain from him authorization to conduct not only wiretapping of telephones but also bugging of homes and offices. He said he would approve microphone surveillance only in select national security cases. He also required the bureau to resubmit to him every six months any requests for electronic surveillance.[91]

When the Justice Department had to submit a brief to the Supreme Court in the tax evasion case of Fred Black, a Washington influence peddler, about the use of a microphone surveillance to obtain evidence, Katzenbach refused to bow to Hoover's wish that the brief state that the Justice Department had authorized such bugging. While the department never authorized bugging, department attorneys were well aware that the bureau conducted bugging illegally, according to former Justice Department official William Hundley.

When Katzenbach told Hoover about the new restrictions on electronic surveillance, "Hoover said he often thought that was what we should do. He pretended not to resent it," Katzenbach said.[92] At that point, according to Katzenbach, "Hoover was getting senile. I would go to his office so I could leave. I didn't want to sit for two hours to hear him talk."

In addition to the wiretaps of King, in January 1964, the FBI installed the first of fifteen microphone surveillances in hotel rooms where King stayed. These did not require Robert Kennedy's approval and could have been aimed only at picking up King's sexual activities in order to embarrass him. Underscoring that point, DeLoach suggested delaying making full transcripts of the goings-on—as opposed to synopses—because "the controversy [between King and the FBI] has quieted down considerably." Hoover disagreed, and DeLoach reported that the bureau had prepared 321 pages of transcripts.

Just after Joseph Purvis took over as SAC of the Washington Field Office in 1964, DeLoach asked for the tape of an orgy King held at the Willard Hotel in Washington. Purvis received a synopsis from an agent who made a transcript.

"It was blacks and whites having a lot of intercourse," Purvis said. "One of the girls said to King, 'You ought not to be doing this; you're a preacher.' King said, 'Tonight, I'm just a nigger.' "[93] At another point, King reportedly said to one of the girls, "Lick me down there."

Sullivan suggested to Hoover that bugging King's hotel room in Milwaukee would be pointless because the local police had taken an adjoining suite to provide security. Therefore, King would not engage in dalliances. Hoover demonstrated that his real interest was in recording King's sexual activities. "I don't share the conjecture," he wrote on Sullivan's memo. "King is a 'tom cat' with obsessive degenerate sexual urges."[94]

Hoover had agents play the King tapes or provide transcripts to Johnson, to select congressmen, and even to Justice Department officials. "Hoover had agents play me the Martin Luther King tapes," William Hundley said. "They thought it was so terrible."

Hoover listened to all the tapes. "Hoover had always been fascinated by pornography, and if any that came to the bureau during the course of an investigation was kept from him, he'd raise hell," Sullivan said.

In the FBI laboratory, two FBI agents were assigned to do nothing but examine pornography in a locked room. "No one went in there," said Jay Cochran, a former assistant FBI director in charge of the laboratory. "It was on the tour route on the seventh floor of the Justice Department. Even the night supervisor did not have a key."[95] The agents compared movies and magazines to see if the images came from the same source for possible prosecution for interstate transportation of obscene material.

"It was something that had to be done," said Clarence W. Brittain, one of the agents who worked in the room.[96]

In November 1964, the FBI drafted a letter to send to King at his office enclosing a selection from the tapes of the orgies. Because Coretta King was known to open her husband's mail when he was out of town, the bureau hoped to have her see the material.

"King, look into your heart," the letter said. "You know you are a complete fraud and a great liability to all of us Negroes . . . King, there is only one thing left for you to do. You know what it is. You have just thirty-four days in which to do this . . . There is but one way out for you. You better take it before your filthy, abnormal fraudulent self is bared to the nation."

Although Sullivan later denied drafting the letter or having any knowledge of it, the only copy of the letter found at the bureau was in Sullivan's personal files.[97] Asked by Curt Gentry why anyone would draft such a letter, Sullivan said, "Because King had broken his marriage vows."

Hoover could just as well have directed his moral outrage at two other married men—John F. Kennedy, who had threesomes in the White House with two secretaries known as Fiddle and Faddle, and Lyndon Johnson, who routinely had sex with his secretaries on a couch in the Oval Office.[98]

On November 18, Hoover invited eighteen women reporters to his office for coffee. A reporter asked about King's old allegation that FBI offices in the South were staffed by southerners. Hoover blurted out that King was "the most notorious liar in the country."

When the story hit the papers the next day, Nicholas Katzenbach, Johnson's acting attorney general, went to see Hoover in his office.

"I know why you're here," Hoover said. "I never should have done that."

The story created a sensation, and by late November, Johnson had ordered Hoover to meet with King and "patch things up." On December 1, 1964, they held a summit meeting in Hoover's office.

To get to Hoover's office—Room 5633 in the Justice Department—a visitor walked down a fifty-foot oak-paneled corridor into a conference room with a glass-top conference table. Beneath the table was an enormous oriental rug. Hoover's inner sanctum was off the conference room. It was furnished with a large desk and overstuffed chairs and sofas. When a visitor entered, Hoover would leap up from behind his desk and meet the person at the center of the room. He would offer a seat to the right and return to his desk.

"The desk stood on a dais, and when you sat in your chair, he stared down at you like Louis XIV on the throne of France," DeLoach recalled. "With a tall window behind him, the sunlight would often slant through the blinds and dazzle you as you stared up at his solemn, bulldog face."[99]

Hoover congratulated King on winning the Nobel Prize. He then gave a fifty-five-minute monologue on the bureau's accomplishments. A wiretap later picked up King complaining that the "old man" did not know when to stop talking. Told about this latest outrage, Hoover became even more obsessed with smearing King. Whenever Hoover learned that a university was considering bestowing an honorary degree on King, he would send it derogatory reports about the civil rights leader.

On April 4, 1968, a sniper assassinated King. Hoover did not want the bureau to become involved. Ramsey Clark, who succeeded Katzenbach as attorney general, ordered the FBI into the case as a civil rights investigation. After spending two days comparing fingerprints one by one, the FBI's Identification Division matched a fingerprint from the rifle that killed King to James Earl Ray, a forty-year-old escaped convict with an arrest record going back twenty years. Two months later, agents flew to London, where Scotland Yard had arrested Ray after the Royal Canadian Mounted Police tracked him from Canada. They brought him back.

Ray pleaded guilty and was sentenced to ninety-nine years in prison. He subsequently claimed that a man called Raoul had directed his activities, leading to speculation that Hoover himself had ordered King's assassination. But Ray kept changing his story and never produced a credible account to support his claim. If indeed there had been a conspiracy, Ray would never have pled guilty without making a deal to expose his coconspirators. He died in prison from kidney failure on April 23, 1998.

King may have been dead, but Hoover had not forgotten their feud. On May 18, 1970, Hoover wrote a memo to DeLoach and his assistant directors informing them that he had told Vice President Spiro Agnew that he had "briefed the [House] Appropriations Committee about his [Martin Luther King's] background, and it had been effective recently because they had been trying to make a national holiday of his birthday, and many of the congressmen who know the facts are opposing it."

Hoover always maintained that the FBI was a "fact-finding agency" that "never makes recommendations or draws conclusions." That claim—along with Attorney General Harlan Fiske Stone's limitation of the bureau's activities to investigations of "violations of law"—had long been forgotten.

11

"WHOREMONGER"

In *The Twilight* *of the Presidency*, George E. Reedy, press secretary to President Johnson, said the "splendid isolation" of the president within the White House had turned the presidency into a monarchy.

"The atmosphere of the White House is a heady one," he wrote. "By the twentieth century, the presidency had taken on all the regalia of monarchy except robes, a scepter, and a crown."

Both Johnson and his successor Richard Nixon were particularly susceptible to the dizzying combination of power and perquisites. Personally insecure and surrounded by sycophants, they became paranoid as they came under attack for pursuing the Vietnam War.

Hoover catered to their paranoia, feeding them reports claiming that Communists were behind the war protests sweeping the nation. When Students for a Democratic Society announced plans in April 1965 to stage demonstrations in eighty-five cities, Hoover told Johnson he had "no doubt" that Communists were "behind the disturbances." He later told Nixon that the bureau suspected but "can't yet prove" that SDS gets "millions of dollars from the Soviet Union via the Communist Party of the United States."

Nixon and Hoover's relationship went back to the days when Nixon, as a member of the House Committee on Un-American Activities, investigated Alger Hiss. During the closing days of Nixon's campaign, Hoover informed the candidate that Johnson had ordered him to investigate Spiro Agnew, Nixon's running mate, by obtaining his long-distance phone records. H. R. Haldeman, Nixon's chief of staff, realized that Hoover was merely "covering his ass." Haldeman added, "And no one was more adept at sheltering that broad expanse than he."

After being elected on November 6, 1968, Nixon summoned Hoover to his transition office at the Hotel Pierre in New York City. Referring to John N. Mitchell, who would become his attorney general, Nixon said, "Edgar, you are one of the few people who is to have direct access to me at all times. I've talked to Mitchell about it, and he understands."

But Nixon actually had no intention of including Hoover in his inner circle. Once he took office, he placed John Ehrlichman, his White House counsel, in charge of dealing with the FBI director. After visiting Hoover in his office, Ehrlichman remarked, "When he stood, it became obvious that he and his desk were on a dais about six inches high." Then, he said, Hoover "looked down at me and began to talk. An hour later, he was still talking."

How did it go? Nixon wanted to know.

"Great," Ehrlichman said. "He did all the talking."

"I know, but it's necessary, John. It's necessary."

Hoover had met his match.

■　■　■

The antiwar protests spawned the term "flower power" to describe their nonviolent approach. But some antiwar groups, frustrated by the failure of mass protests to end the war in Vietnam, adopted more militant positions and were willing to employ violence. As the country was wracked by a series of bombings of buildings on Wall Street and elsewhere, the FBI began to focus on the Weathermen—later called the Weather Underground—as well as on black nationalist groups like the Black Panther Party. In 1970, three members of the Weather Underground were killed in an explosion in a Manhattan townhouse while manufacturing bombs. After an explosion in the U.S. Capitol on March 1, 1971, the Weather Underground claimed responsibility.

While the Black Panthers rejected the civil rights movement's policy of nonviolence, they tended to be more talk than action. However, Hoover decided to use the usual COINTELPRO tactics on them. The St.

Louis Field Office sent an anonymous letter to the wife of a black leader, saying that her husband "been maken it here with Sister Marva Bas & Sister Tony and then he gives us this jive bout their better in bed than you."

On one Black Panther tap, the FBI learned that actress Jean Seberg was pregnant. The father was not her estranged husband, the French author Romain Gary, but rather Raymond "Masai" Hewitt, the Panthers' minister of information, or so an agent thought. As part of COINTELPRO, agent Richard W. Held proposed publicizing the "pregnancy of Jean Seberg, well-known white actress, by [Hewitt] by advising Hollywood gossip columnists. . . . It is felt that the possible publication of Seberg's plight could cause her embarrassment and serve to cheapen her image with the general public."

Hoover responded, "Jean Seberg has been a financial supporter of the BPP and should be neutralized."

As it turned out, Seberg and her former husband had reconciled. When the FBI's leaks hit the press, Seberg went into labor. The child, born two months prematurely, lived only two days. Seberg insisted on an open coffin so everyone could see that the baby was a Caucasian girl.

After the funeral, Seberg attempted suicide by taking an overdose of sleeping pills. She became "psychotic," Gary said. "She went from one psychiatric clinic to another, from one suicide attempt to another. She tried to kill herself seven times, usually on the anniversary of her little girl's birth." Finally, on August 20, 1979, Seberg succeeded in killing herself. Hoover had indeed neutralized her.

■　■　■

On May 9, 1969, the *New York Times* ran a story by William Beecher reporting that the United States was conducting bombing raids of suspected North Vietnamese supply bases in Cambodia. While the Cambodians were aware of the raids, the American people were not. At the direction of the White House, the U.S. Air Force had been falsifying its reports to cover up this latest escalation of the unpopular war.

By 10:35 A.M., Henry Kissinger, Nixon's national security adviser, was on the phone to Hoover asking if he would make a "major effort" to trace the leak. In subsequent calls, Kissinger mentioned Morton Halperin, an aide to Kissinger, as the possible source. Unknown to Kissinger, Hoover asked William Sullivan to wiretap Halperin's home phone. Sullivan called Courtland Jones, who headed counterintelligence in the Washington Field Office. Jones, in turn, assigned Ernest Belter, who headed a technical squad, to make the arrangements.

Jones told Belter that the wiretap was to be installed without generating any paper beyond a daily log to be hand-carried to Sullivan's office each morning. Agents were to listen to the calls and make notes, which were incorporated in the log.

The next morning, Colonel Alexander M. Haig Jr., another Kissinger aide, met with Sullivan in his office and asked for wiretaps of four people, three on the National Security Council staff and one in the Defense Department. One of the targets was Halperin, who was already being wiretapped. Sullivan relayed the request to Hoover, who told him to follow Haig's instructions but "make sure everything is on paper." Hoover instructed Sullivan to obtain John Mitchell's approval.

Jones did not trust Sullivan. A feisty man who read voraciously and wore rumpled clothes, Sullivan was born in Bolton, Massachusetts, where his parents were farmers. After receiving a bachelor's degree in history from American University, he taught English in Bolton. Sullivan became an agent in 1941.

Sullivan's colleagues called him "Crazy Bill" because he was so unpredictable. Jones recalled that during the riots in Washington in April 1968 following the assassination of Martin Luther King, Sullivan called him and said he wanted to take a look. With Jones driving, they stopped at a red light.

"People were standing on the corner," Jones said. "He reached into his pocket and pulled out Mace. He sprayed it at one younger person who probably was involved. I don't know if it hit him."[100]

Joseph Purvis, who headed the Washington Field Office, recalled that when a demonstration was planned in the courtyard of the Justice Department, "Sullivan came up with the silliest idea. He said we should let loose a greased pig. We would arrest the demonstrators for cruelty to animals as they tried to catch the pig."[101]

Jones wondered if Sullivan was "freelancing," ordering the wiretaps without the attorney general's approval, as he had done when asking French authorities to wiretap the Paris home of columnist Joseph Kraft in search of a leak. But both Hoover and Mitchell eventually signed off on the installations requested by Kissinger and Haig.

In all, there would be seventeen wiretaps, including ones on a brigadier general, four newsmen, and two White House advisers. At one point, Kissinger personally reviewed logs of the wiretaps in Sullivan's office. Despite Sullivan's protests to the White House that, while using up valuable manpower, the taps were producing nothing of value, they remained in place for up to twenty-one months. In Halperin's case, they were continued even after he had left the NSC.[102]

Eventually, the original purpose of the wiretaps was forgotten. Instead, they produced political intelligence to be passed along to Nixon. For example, based on information gleaned from the wiretaps, Hoover in December 1969 informed Nixon that Clark Clifford, a former secretary of defense, was planning to write a magazine article criticizing Nixon's Vietnam policy. At the time, this was considered a major development.

The wiretap of reporter Henry Brandon intercepted Joan Kennedy "pouring out her heart to Muffie Brandon about Ted's infidelity," Jones said. "Ernie Belter gave it to me." Recognizing that the Nixon White House would have loved to get its hands on the conversation, Jones told Belter to "tear it up."

To further enhance his importance to the president, Hoover, on November 26, 1969, established a new program called INLET, for Intelligence Letter. This was a mix of reports on demonstrations and "items with an unusual twist or concerning prominent personalities which may be of special interest to the president and attorney general" and were to be sent to the White House.

On June 5, 1970, as the antiwar protests intensified, Nixon called a meeting in the Oval Office with Hoover; Richard Helms, director of the CIA; Vice Admiral Noel Gayler, head of NSA, and Donald V. Bennett, director of the Defense Intelligence Agency. Nixon railed about the demonstrations and said he needed "hard intelligence" in order to "curtail the illegal activities of those who are determined to destroy our society."

It seems Hoover was refusing to conduct FBI break-ins in so-called domestic security investigations. Such break-ins were usually necessary to obtain documents and to plant listening devices or bugs. Hoover's concern went back to Katzenbach's order requiring him to obtain approval for microphone surveillance as well as wiretaps. Hoover knew that no attorney general would authorize the illegal entries that are usually required to plant a bug or obtain documents. As he grew older, Hoover became more averse to taking risks. Now that Katzenbach had specifically said he would not authorize illegal break-ins, Hoover was not about to take the chance of being caught. So on July 19, 1966, Hoover banned FBI break-ins except in foreign counterintelligence cases.

Not until June 1968 did Congress enact the Omnibus Crime Control and Safe Streets Act, which finally authorized the FBI and other law enforcement agencies to conduct wiretapping and bugging with a court order during criminal investigations. Since even this law did not address so-called domestic security cases, Hoover's ban on break-ins still restricted the kind of surveillance Nixon desired.

At the meeting with the four agency heads, Nixon announced that there was a need for "clearly illegal" surveillance. He said he was appointing an ad hoc committee consisting of the four agency heads to work on carrying out his instructions. The liaison to the White House would be Tom Charles Huston. Huston, twenty-nine, was a former chairman of the archconservative Young Americans for Freedom. His only relevant experience was a brief stint with Army intelligence.

Three days later, the committee met in Hoover's office. Immediately, the agency heads ran into problems. Hoover had understood that Nixon wanted a historical summary of unrest in the country. Huston—whom Hoover referred to as a "snot-nosed kid"—said Nixon wanted a current assessment of threats and existing gaps in intelligence. The other three agency heads sided with Huston.

Sullivan had the task of drawing up the report, which became known as the Huston Plan. Sullivan saw an opportunity to return to practices that Hoover had forbidden, including wholesale wiretaps, break-ins, and mail openings. In effect, Sullivan complained, Hoover's strictures had put the Domestic Intelligence Division out of business. But Hoover refused to go along with the Huston Plan. Sullivan suggested that he include his objections in a footnote, and Hoover agreed.

Meanwhile, having previously severed liaison with the CIA in a fit of pique, Hoover ordered ties cut with the Secret Service, DIA, IRS, and Army, Navy, and Air Force intelligence. Apparently, Hoover feared that any improper actions authorized by the White House at those agencies might contaminate the FBI. Despite Hoover's orders, agents continued to cooperate with personnel from the CIA and other agencies.

After the other agency heads had signed off on the Huston Plan, Hoover informed John Mitchell about it. Incensed that he had not been kept informed, Mitchell agreed with Hoover's objections. He said that when the president returned from his home in San Clemente, California, he would talk with Nixon about it.

"I knew that if Hoover had decided not to cooperate, it would matter little what I had decided or approved," Nixon wrote later. "Even if I issued a direct order to him, which he would undoubtedly carry out, he would soon see to it that I had cause to reverse myself."

That was the end of the Huston Plan. In its stead, the Nixon White House would create the "Plumbers."

■ ■ ■

On October 12, 1970, Sullivan gave a speech to United Press International editors at Williamsburg, Virginia. An editor asked if it was true that the Communist Party was responsible for the racial riots and academic violence and upheaval.

"No, it's absolutely untrue," Sullivan said. There was no evidence that any group was behind the disorders on the campuses or in the ghettoes. As for the Communists, Sullivan said the party was not nearly as effective as it once was. He said it was not behind the demonstrations against the war. In fact, the party was now down to twenty-eight hundred members, only half of them active, compared with eighty thousand in the mid-1940s.

Hoover viewed Sullivan's speech as a betrayal, and it was only the beginning. The following month, Ramsey Clark came out with *Crime in America*. The book said the FBI suffered from the "excessive domination of a single person, J. Edgar Hoover, and his self-centered concern for his reputation and that of the FBI."

At the urging of Mitchell, even though the paper was on the FBI's "Do Not Contact" list, Hoover had just agreed to give an interview to Ken Clawson of the *Washington Post*. Clawson's first question was about the book. Calling Clark "a jellyfish," Hoover said he was the worst attorney general in his forty-five years as director—even worse than Robert Kennedy. "At least Kennedy stuck to his guns," Hoover said, "even when he was wrong."

Then Hoover lit into Kennedy. He said Kennedy had wanted to lower standards by recruiting more black agents. At that point, of the bureau's seventy-six hundred agents, only fifty-one were black.

"I didn't speak to Robert Kennedy the last six months he was in office," Hoover boasted.

Clawson later said that Hoover not only was not senile but that he had "one of the most vigorous and active minds I've ever dealt with." But Dean Fischer, who interviewed Hoover shortly thereafter for *Time*, came away with the opposite impression. Fischer said Hoover rambled on about Walter Winchell and Herbert Hoover, but he had "difficulty in responding to a question about repression without losing himself in a forest of recollections." Fischer had prepared a list of twenty-five questions but managed to squeeze in only four in the three-hour meeting. The rest of the time was devoted to "an almost unbroken monologue."

Like his comments about Martin Luther King, Hoover's attacks on political appointees who were his former superiors raised the question of whether he had stayed in office too long. But no one had the guts to fire him.

"Every attorney general, Democrat or Republican, knew Hoover was bad but was afraid to get rid of him," said William Hundley. "I represented John Mitchell. He said he's a problem, and he tried to get rid of him, but he was unsuccessful."

On November 27, 1970, Hoover told a Senate subcommittee in closed session that militant Catholic priests and nuns, including Fathers Philip and Daniel Berrigan, were plotting to "blow up underground electrical conduits and stand pipes serving the Washington, D.C., area in order to disrupt federal government operations." The plotters, he said, were also planning to kidnap a highly placed government official who was later identified as Kissinger.

The FBI's information was fragmentary, based on letters to Father Philip Berrigan from Sister Elizabeth McAlister, who had presented the scenarios as possible options. The letters had been smuggled into Danbury prison, where Berrigan was serving time for destroying draft board records. In a memo to Hoover, Sullivan had warned Hoover not to mention the case because it was still being investigated and could be jeopardized. The Justice Department had already decided there was not enough evidence to present the case to a grand jury. Nonetheless, the FBI handed out copies of Hoover's remarks.

Representative William Anderson of Tennessee, a retired Navy captain and World War II hero, denounced Hoover on the floor of the House. Instead of making the charges in a court of law, Hoover had chosen to air them in the Senate, displaying "tactics reminiscent of McCarthyism," the congressman said.

Hoover immediately ordered an investigation of Anderson. Agents showed photos of the four-term congressman to call girls and asked them if he had used their services. A madam in Nashville thought Anderson had been a customer. On the memo reporting this, Hoover scribbled "whoremonger."[103] He then forwarded the allegations about Representative Anderson to H. R. Haldeman, President Nixon's assistant.

"The information concerning Congressman Anderson's alleged extracurricular activities has also been furnished to the Attorney General [John Mitchell] and to the vice president [Spiro Agnew]," Hoover assured Haldeman. Hoover then leaked the story of Anderson's alleged use of prostitutes to the press in Anderson's home state. In 1972, Anderson was defeated.

After Jack Nelson of the *Los Angeles Times* began writing stories pointing out the flimsiness of the evidence in the Berrigan case and raising questions about other FBI cases, Hoover took the unusual step of meeting with executives of the paper. He told them Nelson was a drunk who was spreading lies that he was a homosexual.[104]

Hoover never thought his files would become public. However, in 1974, Congress included FBI documents in the material that could be obtained under the provisions of the 1966 Freedom of Information Act. Upon obtaining his file under the act, Nelson was appalled to see that informants had, in fact, erroneously told the FBI that he was a drunk, that he had said Hoover was a homosexual, and that he had said he was out to "get" the FBI and its director.

■ ■ ■

On the night of March 8, 1971, more than a thousand FBI documents were stolen from the FBI's resident agency in Media, Pennsylvania. Resident agencies are satellite offices of field offices. In this case, only two agents were assigned to the office. They occupied a single suite on the second floor of the Delaware County Building. The burglars had used crowbars to break the lock on every filing cabinet.

After two weeks, the burglars began sending batches of copies of the documents to selected members of Congress and newspeople. The burglars, who were never caught, called themselves the Citizens' Commission to Investigate the FBI. On April 24, the *Washington Post* published the first story based on the documents, revealing that the FBI had informants on college campuses and monitored left-wing groups.

NBC newsman Carl Stern noticed that one of the documents was labeled COINTELPRO. What did that mean? A lawyer, Stern wrote a request under the Freedom of Information Act for access to the rest of the COINTELPRO documents. When the Justice Department denied his request, he brought suit and eventually won, producing a treasure trove of stories about the bureau's illegal or simply witless activities. For the first time, the public could see how widespread the FBI's abuses were. Now that the program had become public, Hoover ended COINTELPRO.

The disclosures brought calls in Congress for Hoover's resignation. "Hoover's FBI: Time for a Change?" read *Newsweek*'s cover. On the floor of the House, Majority Leader Hale Boggs claimed, without substantiation, that Hoover was wiretapping members of Congress.

"What I am going to say I say in sorrow because it is always tragic when a great man who has given his life to his country comes to the twilight of his life and fails to understand it is time to leave the service and enjoy retirement," Boggs said, adding that he was talking about Hoover, who should resign.

Hoover had never thought of providing alarm systems for resident agencies, but he was not about to blame himself. So he blamed the resident agent in Media, suspending him for one month without pay and transferring him to Atlanta. In a typical overreaction, he ordered all 538 resident agencies closed, but John Mohr, who held the number-three position in the FBI as assistant to the director for administration, persuaded him to close only 103 of them.

Over the years, Hoover had become even more set in his ways, more egocentric, and more unwilling to try new approaches.

"We never challenged Hoover," said Bucky Walters, who was an assistant director under Hoover. "Only Mohr or DeLoach could try to persuade him to change his mind."

When DeLoach, who was just below Tolson, retired on July 31, 1970, to become vice president for corporate affairs of PepsiCo, Hoover became even more detached from reality. Fred G. Robinette III, the agent who was Hoover's nephew, said he spent hours talking with Hoover in his office. "People were filtering information to him," he said.

Bureau officials spent more and more time writing syrupy letters of praise to Hoover. "He liked to be flattered, which I did," said Joseph Purvis, former head of the Washington Field Office. On Hoover's birthday and anniversary as director, he expected presents from SACs and other bureau officials. Hoover forgot about lecturing one SAC whose statistics were below par when the agent gave him a "cocktail hour" wristwatch that substituted fives for the normal numbers on its face. Another agent avoided censure over his statistics when he brought Hoover a coconut cake. Upon being presented with the cake, Hoover forgot about dressing down the agent and buzzed Helen Gandy to bring him two cake plates, two forks, and two cups of coffee.[105]

Ramsey Clark liked to tell the story of his encounter with a Justice Department security guard when he did not yet have a Justice Department ID. He told the guard he was the attorney general. "I don't care if you're J. Edgar Hoover," the guard said, as he barred him from the building.

"I realized from that where I stood in the hierarchy," Clark said.

As he became more rigid, Hoover resisted adopting the sort of innovations that had marked his earlier years. The only new departure was the establishment in January 1967 of the National Crime Information Center (NCIC), a computerized data bank of criminal records, names of fugitives, and listings of stolen vehicles, guns, securities, and other property that could be identified by serial number and checked by law enforcement agencies.

When the bureau did take a novel approach, individual agents usually took it upon themselves to implement the changes without Hoover's knowledge. In doing so, they risked their careers. For example, when he was in charge of the Philadelphia Field Office in 1966, Joe D. Jameson asked Buck Revell, a former Marine pilot who was then a field agent, if he thought the bureau might use planes to conduct surveillance of suspected Soviet spies. Revell said it could be done, and he spent many weekends successfully tracking several spies. Because they knew Hoover would oppose the idea, Revell and Jameson kept the program to themselves.

"Hoover had said he would never have an air force, so they never told him," Revell said.[106]

"Hoover did a good job for many years," said John J. McDermott, a former SAC in Washington who became deputy associate FBI director. "He went wrong along the way. He became a martinet. In seeking to prevent embarrassment to the bureau, he equated the bureau with him. Everyone told him how good he was. He came to believe the exorbitant praise he was receiving. Anybody who can be conned by a flatterer has a character weakness."

If Hoover had no intention of losing his job, he also had no intention of dying. "The biggest enemy," he told a reporter, "is time."

Every morning, Valerie B. Stewart, the chief nurse of the FBI Health Service, gave him an injection of multiple vitamins.[107] Because of his fear of germs, Hoover compulsively washed his hands and equipped his home with an air filtration system that was supposed to electrocute germs. Because they might carry disease, Hoover had an aversion to flies. When a fly appeared in his office, Hoover would call in W. Samuel Noisette, his driver, who would execute the offender.

Occasionally, Hoover cracked a smile or played a prank. James H. Geer, who would later head the Intelligence Division, recalled that when a new agent went to shake Hoover's hand after graduating from training, he mistakenly introduced himself as "Mr. Hoover."

"Very nice to meet you, Mr. Hoover," Hoover responded, as he smiled.

But as happened with Martin Luther King, William Anderson, and Ramsey Clark, any criticism of Hoover was met with a scathing attack, an investigation, or both. E. Barrett Prettyman Jr., a partner with Hogan & Hartson in Washington and a former clerk to three Supreme Court justices, would never forget his court appointment to represent a woman arrested while flagging down cars at 2 A.M. on Fourteenth Street, then Washington's prostitution strip.

For reasons unknown, instead of being charged with soliciting, the woman had been charged with vagrancy. Determined to bring all his legal prowess to bear, Prettyman decided in February 1967 to challenge the law on eleven constitutional grounds. One of the definitions of vagrancy under the law was "leading a profligate life." As one of his points, Prettyman argued that an ordinary person would have difficulty understanding just what "leading a profligate life" meant and that therefore the law itself was unconstitutionally vague. The lawyer sought to prove it by asking each witness what the phrase meant. The arresting officer said that it was someone who doesn't lead "too productive a life."

"Well, let's suppose someone goes to the racetrack on a fairly regular basis and bets on the horses. Is he leading a profligate life?" Prettyman asked.

"Yes," the officer said.

"As an example, what about J. Edgar Hoover? I understand he makes numerous visits to the racetrack and bets on the horses."

Recognizing he was cornered, the officer reluctantly agreed that Hoover led a profligate life.

By chance, a *Washington Post* court reporter had wandered into the courtroom and heard the exchange. The next morning, the paper ran a story quoting the testimony. The following morning, two FBI agents appeared at Hogan & Hartson, one of Washington's most prominent law firms. The agents presented Prettyman—whose father's name would later grace the U.S. District Court building in Washington—with a letter from Hoover.

"Sir," it began. "I note from an article in the *Washington Post* yesterday that you gratuitously injected my name in a case you are representing [and that you referred] to my 'numerous' visits to the race track. This certainly was an unwarranted use of my name to obtain some cheap publicity. The facts are that I only attend the races—an entirely legal pastime—on Saturdays and then infrequently. I am usually one of 20,000 persons present, which include officials—Federal and State—and of all branches of the Government. Why you should single me out of this large number can only be that you are vindictively inclined or hard pressed to make a point completely irrelevant to the true merits of your case. In any event, I do not appreciate such despicable use of my name."[108]

At first, Prettyman thought the letter was a prank. He could not believe that anyone would take himself so seriously and would so completely miss the point he was trying to make—that because the law was vague, even an upstanding citizen such as the FBI director could be considered to be in violation of it.

"Yet," Prettyman recalled, "the letter was on FBI letterhead with his signature."

The appeals court reversed the woman's conviction, but not for the reason argued by Prettyman. Instead, sidestepping the question of constitutionality, the court said the prosecution had not shown that the woman had committed a crime.

12

SHREDDED FILES

On Sunday, October 13, 1971, the *New York Times* began running the first installment of what became known as the "Pentagon Papers." The series started with more than six pages of news stories and documents based on a forty-seven-volume, top-secret study of the Vietnam War and its origins commissioned by Robert S. McNamara, secretary of defense. The stories showed that for years, the American government, and particularly the administration of Lyndon B. Johnson, had been lying to the American people about the progress of the war, its goals, and its rationale.

The *Times* softened the impact of the story by using a low-key lead and by calling the series "Vietnam Archive." In part because of that, the press was slow to jump on the story. The Associated Press did not move a piece until Monday afternoon. NBC featured the *Times* scoop as its lead story on Sunday evening, but the other networks ignored it. Even though Sunday morning shows featured such administration guests as Secretary of Defense Melvin Laird, no one asked them about the Pentagon Papers.

But as he did over the story of the secret bombing of Cambodia, Kissinger became apoplectic. Even though the "Vietnam Archive" stories focused on Johnson's actions, Kissinger convinced Nixon that it was part of a plot to undermine his administration.

"Henry got Nixon cranked up, and then they started cranking each other up until they were both in a frenzy," Haldeman said.

Two days after the first story ran, Attorney General Mitchell ordered the FBI to investigate the leak of classified documents.

The *Times* had taken extraordinary steps to keep its scoop, and its source, confidential. The paper rented a suite on the eleventh floor of the New York Hilton, where four reporters, three copy editors, and support personnel worked on the stories under the eye of a security guard. But Sidney Zion, a former *Times* reporter, appeared on a New York radio talk show and revealed that Dr. Daniel Ellsberg, who had worked on the study while with the Defense Department, provided the *Times* with the documents. As later revealed in the White House tapes, after Kissinger got him pumped up, Nixon said he wanted Ellsberg "destroyed."

During the course of the investigation, Charles "Chick" Brennan wanted to have FBI agents interview Louis Marx, Ellsberg's father-in-law. Since Marx was an acquaintance of Hoover, Brennan had asked Hoover for his approval. Hoover scribbled "no" on the bottom of Brennan's memo, but Brennan mistook it for "ok." Agents interviewed Marx, but Sullivan, who was openly vying for Hoover's job, made sure Robert Mardian, assistant attorney general in charge of the Justice Department's Internal Security Section, knew about Hoover's veto.

Nixon was livid. In his memoirs, he wrote that Hoover was "dragging his feet and treating the case on a medium priority basis. . . . if a conspiracy existed, I wanted to know. . . . If the FBI was not going to pursue the case, then we would have to do it ourselves."

"To me, it was an overreaction," said John L. Martin, the former FBI agent who later headed espionage investigations at the Justice Department and was in charge of the Ellsberg case at Justice. "Leak investigations are invariably politically inspired attempts by one faction of government to keep another faction from disclosing what it believes to be the truth."

On July 17, 1971, Ehrlichman assigned Egil "Bud" Krogh, a lawyer on the Domestic Council staff, to head a leak project. He was joined by former Kissinger aide David Young, former CIA officer E. Howard Hunt, and former FBI agent G. Gordon Liddy. Inflamed by Nixon's paranoia about leaks and his determination to circumvent Hoover, the group became known as the White House Plumbers. Since they were supposed to stop leaks, Young had put up a sign in his office saying "Plumbers."

As if to ratify the need for the unit, William Beecher of the *New York Times* again enraged Nixon when he wrote a story reporting on American strategy during planned Strategic Arms Limitation Treaty (SALT) talks with the Soviet Union. In that case, after administering widespread polygraph tests, the FBI was able to pinpoint the leak behind the July 23, 1971, story to a Defense Department official. The official acknowledged giving Beecher information on the U.S. negotiating position but claimed it had not impaired the negotiations. He was disciplined. Beecher said recently he was unaware of this.[109]

Hoover knew that Sullivan was going around him by dealing with Mardian, whom Hoover called that "Armenian Jew." Besides calling into question the threat of Communism, Sullivan had been opposing Hoover's decision to increase the number of overseas offices, known as legats. Many thought that Hoover considered Sullivan a son, but the director decided that Sullivan was out of control. On July 1, 1971, Hoover summoned W. Mark Felt.

Felt, who had a trademark pompadour, grew up in Twin Falls, Idaho, and attended the University of Idaho. He attended George Washington University Law School in the evening and received his law degree in 1940. He joined the FBI in 1942 and quickly moved up the ladder.

As assistant FBI director for inspections, Felt managed to please Hoover by being tactful with him and tough on agents. One day, Hoover, prompted by a slipup over a piece of mail marked "Personal," asked Felt to conduct an inspection of his own office. As required, Helen Gandy had sent the letter to Crime Records for a response. But she had failed to notify Edna Holmes, the office manager, who would have placed it on her "Special List" so that the handling of the response would be tracked. The response was delayed, and because she did not know about the letter, Holmes had not followed up. When Hoover demanded an explanation from Gandy, she blamed Holmes, who denied any responsibility.

"This put me in a 'no win' position," Felt recalled. "If I sided with Miss Holmes, who was not at fault, I would antagonize Miss Gandy," who was extremely powerful. "To have sided with Miss Gandy would have been dishonest."[110]

Felt did a complete study of the operations of the office, analyzing the mail flow, personnel management, and communications. He made two major recommendations. The clerks who answered the telephones should get a raise, and the Exhibits Section in the laboratory should build a massive console so that the clerks answering the phones would have easy access to calendars and records.

"Everyone, including Hoover, was extremely pleased," Felt said. "Hoover made no further mention of the error which had triggered the inspection, and I am convinced that all he wanted was to stir things up a bit."

When Hoover called in Felt, he told him he was naming him to the newly created position of deputy associate director, just below Tolson. By May 12, 1970, Tolson had reached mandatory retirement age, but to satisfy Hoover, Mitchell had rehired him as an annuitant. Between 1951 and 1970, Tolson had been hospitalized eleven times. He had had a duodenal ulcer, an abdominal aneurysm, and heart disease. He also had suffered a stroke. He was gaunt and had a gray pallor. Unable to write or even to shave himself, he was blind in one eye and walked very slowly, dragging his right leg.

"Tolson said, 'I've had almost everything,' " Joseph Purvis, the former head of the Washington Field Office, recalled.

Beyond the need for someone to take over Tolson's duties, Hoover told Felt he wanted to "contain" Sullivan. In his new position, Felt would be over Sullivan, who was assistant to the director over the investigative divisions. In Hoover's bureau, an assistant to the director for investigations and an assistant to the director for administration supervised the assistant directors over each division.

While Sullivan had a good grasp of Hoover's failings and genuinely wanted to improve the FBI, he had also been part of the problem, having concocted such abusive programs as COINTELPRO and pushed for even more illegal surveillance. Fiercely ambitious, Sullivan told Mardian that Hoover was getting ready to fire him and that he wanted to give Mardian the records of the Halperin wiretaps. He claimed that if the records remained at the bureau, Hoover would use the material to blackmail Nixon so Hoover could keep his job. Mardian accepted the documents and gave them to the White House, along with a fill-in on Hoover's failings as recounted by Sullivan. Mardian assured Sullivan that Nixon would be firing the director later that day. Hours later, Mardian called Sullivan. "Goddamn. Nixon lost his guts," he said. "He had Hoover there in his office. He knew what he was supposed to tell him, but he got cold feet. He couldn't go through with it."

If there was any doubt about the effectiveness of the Official and Confidential files that Hoover began compiling when he became director, it was dispelled by the tapes of President Nixon's conversations in the Oval Office. On them, Nixon stated bluntly in November 1971 that he was afraid to remove Hoover as FBI director because Hoover would "pull down the temple" by releasing damaging information about him. For one thing, Hoover had made sure Nixon knew that when he was in private practice and married to Pat, he had spent time in Hong Kong with Marianna Liu, a pretty married woman.

"Hoover's got files on everybody, God damn it," Nixon would later complain.

On August 28, 1971, Sullivan typed out a letter to Hoover announcing his retirement. "What I have set forth below is for your own good and for the FBI as a whole of which I am very fond," he wrote. Still hoping that Hoover would elevate him, Sullivan outlined his position on their recent disagreements. Three days later, Hoover summoned Sullivan to his office. For two and a half hours, they argued. On September 30, Hoover wrote to "Mr. Sullivan." The letter asked Sullivan to submit his application for retirement effective immediately. Sullivan did not comply, and they met again that day for the last time.

"I never thought that you'd betray me—that you'd be a Judas, too," Hoover said.

"I'm not a Judas, Mr. Hoover," Sullivan said. "And you certainly are not Jesus Christ."

Hoover told Sullivan that both Mitchell and Nixon had agreed he should be forced out. The following morning, October 1, Sullivan returned to his office to find that his name had been removed from the door and the locks changed.

"The greatest mistake I ever made was to promote Sullivan," Hoover told Felt.

On October 6, 1971, Sullivan sent a final letter to Hoover at his home. An indictment of Hoover's tenure, the letter dealt with such topics as "Senator McCarthy and Yourself," "The FBI and the Negro," "Free Services at Your Home," "FBI and CIA," "FBI and Organized Crime," "Our Statistics," "Leaks of Sensitive Materials," and "The Hoover Legend and Mythology."[111]

Soon, items from the letter began to leak to the press as Sullivan met with trusted reporters and treated them to tips about the FBI's abuses over the years. While most of the stories did not name Sullivan as the source, a piece by Jack Nelson of the *Los Angeles Times* quoted Sullivan as criticizing the "fossilized" bureaucracy of the FBI.

Under attack from all sides, Hoover began destroying files from his Personal and Confidential file or transferring them to his Official and Confidential file. He also ordered Felt to collect all sensitive files from senior FBI executives' offices.

On May 1, 1972, Helen Gandy brought Hoover the first in a series of exposés by Jack Anderson, whose column appeared in the *Washington Post*. Previously, Anderson had enraged Hoover by assigning a reporter to rummage through his trash at home. The subsequent column revealed that on Sundays, Hoover had a hearty breakfast of poached eggs and hotcakes and that he brushed his teeth with Ultra Brite, washed with Palmolive, and shaved with Noxzema shaving cream. This latest Anderson column revealed that the FBI had conducted surveillance of Martin Luther King's sex life. It also disclosed that FBI files contained titillating information on the private lives of Marlon Brando and Harry Belafonte, football heroes Joe Namath and Lance Rentzel, and ex–boxing champions Joe Louis and Muhammad Ali.

Referring to Hoover's long-standing opposition to allowing the FBI to enforce drug laws, the column said, "FBI chief J. Edgar Hoover, the old curmudgeon of law enforcement, fiercely resisted a White House suggestion that he spare a few hundred agents to crack down on drug abuses. But he can spare agents to snoop into the sex habits, business affairs, and political pursuits of individuals who aren't even remotely involved in illegal activity."

While Anderson, who inherited the column from Drew Pearson, had written about Hoover's abuses before, this series of columns was based on FBI documents. For a man whose lifelong mantra had been, "Don't embarrass the bureau," the continuing stream of unfavorable disclosures, combined with what he saw as Sullivan's betrayal, had to be unnerving. Yet if Hoover ever had any fears or personal doubts, he never revealed them. Sphinxlike, he projected the same persona on his friends and family as he did to the general public. The only difference was that in person he revealed a sense of humor.

That evening shortly before 6 P.M., Tom Moton, who had replaced James Crawford as Hoover's chauffeur, drove Hoover to Tolson's apartment, where the two had dinner. Moton drove Hoover home at 10:15.

The next morning at 8:15, Crawford came by to plant some rose-bushes Hoover had ordered. About fifteen or twenty minutes later, Annie Fields, Hoover's housekeeper, came outside. She told Crawford she was "concerned." By now, she should have heard the sound of the shower. Hoover's toast, soft-boiled eggs, and coffee were getting cold. Crawford knocked on the bedroom door. There was no answer. He tried a second time and still no answer. Crawford opened the door. Hoover's body was sprawled on the oriental rug next to his bed. Crawford touched one of his hands. It was cold.

Annie Fields called Dr. Robert Choisser, Hoover's physician. Crawford called Tolson. Because of his ill health, Tolson no longer rode to work with Hoover. Instead, his own bureau driver took him to the doctor, then to his office. Tolson, now acting director, called Helen Gandy, who told John Mohr. Mohr, in turn, told Mark Felt.

"He's dead," Mohr said to Felt in a whisper.

Assuming he was referring to Tolson, Felt asked, "Did he have another stroke?"

"No, you don't understand," Mohr said. "The director is dead."

At 11:45 A.M., Richard G. Kleindienst, the acting attorney general, stood before reporters in the White House briefing room and announced Hoover's death. Nixon unexpectedly entered the room and told the press that Hoover had been one of his "closest friends and advisers."

After examining Hoover's nude body and consulting with Dr. Choisser, Dr. James L. Luke, the District of Columbia medical examiner, attributed the director's death to "hypertensive cardiovascular disease."[112] A rumor that Hoover had an underdeveloped sex organ was not true, Dr. Luke told me.

Hoover, seventy-seven, had headed the FBI for nearly forty-eight years.

That afternoon, L. Patrick Gray III, then an assistant attorney general, showed up in Mohr's office and asked about the secret files. Mohr said there were no secret files.

This was a continuation of the semantic game the FBI had long played. As documented earlier, Hoover used information from his Official and Confidential files, from his Personal and Confidential files, and from other FBI files to blackmail members of Congress and other public figures. In addition, in 1954, Hoover ordered that field offices prepare memos on each member of Congress summarizing any existing information about them.[113] But bureau officials did not refer to any of the files as "secret."

"Old Gray was all spooked off," Mohr later told me, proud of himself for having stonewalled an intruder from the Justice Department. Mohr explained that Gray had asked the wrong question. The files were secret to the public, not to select FBI personnel. If Gray had asked if there were "dossiers" on congressmen, "I'd obviously have said yes."[114]

Ruefully, Gray later told a Senate subcommittee, "It now appears, in retrospect, that I did not know how to ask the right questions."

The White House informed Mohr that Hoover would be given a state funeral, with full military honors. Congressmen rushed to place eulogies in the *Congressional Record*. After the funeral, Nixon announced that the new FBI headquarters building still under construction on Pennsylvania Avenue between Ninth and Tenth streets NW would be named the J. Edgar Hoover FBI Building.

Notoriously squeamish about hiring and firing, Nixon told Kleindienst to pick the next director. Kleindienst chose Gray, who became acting director on May 3, 1972. Tolson retired the same day.

When Hoover's will was probated, it turned out that Tolson received the bulk of his estate, estimated at $560,000, including his home. (It was the equivalent of $2.4 million today.) Helen Gandy received $5,000, Annie Fields $3,000, and James Crawford $2,000. Hoover requested that Tolson "keep, or arrange for a good home, or homes, for my two dogs." The dogs, G-Boy and Cindy, died a few months later. Three years later, Tolson died at the age of seventy-four.

Hoover was buried in Congressional Cemetery, thirteen blocks from where he grew up. Tolson was buried nearby.

■　■　■

On May 4, 1972, Gandy turned over to Felt enough files from Hoover's office suite to fill twelve cardboard boxes, blackmail material on everyone from the Kennedys and Mickey Mantle to Supreme Court justices, twelve of whom had been overheard on FBI wiretaps. All the files were stamped "OC" for Official and Confidential.

As Hoover had instructed, Gandy transferred the contents of another thirty-two file drawers to cardboard boxes. They were moved to Hoover's house, which Tolson now occupied. Additional boxes were later moved. Gandy later said these were Hoover's Personal and Confidential files, which included such items as personal correspondence and personal tax returns. However, over the years, Hoover had also kept some of his most potentially embarrassing material in this set of files. After examining each item to make sure it was not an official record, Gandy said she tore up each record and gave the pieces to the Washington Field Office to be shredded.[115]

In June 1968, Congress had enacted a law requiring that future FBI directors be nominated by the president and confirmed by the Senate. Their terms were limited to ten years. Never again would one man so dominate the FBI. Yet it would not be the last time an FBI director abused his position.

BOOK TWO

13

WATERGATE

Ten days after Hoover's death, L. Patrick Gray III, a balding man with a cleft chin, moved into his office. FBI officials had been hoping that one of their own—John Mohr or W. Mark Felt—would be selected as director. Instead, they got a man with no connection to law enforcement at all.

Born in St. Louis on June 18, 1916, Gray attended Rice University in Houston and graduated from the U.S. Naval Academy at Annapolis as a commissioned officer. In World War II and the Korean War, Gray served as a submarine commander and the commander of a submarine flotilla. While in the service, he attended George Washington University School of Law, receiving his degree in 1949. He became an assistant to the Joint Chiefs of Staff. After retiring from the Navy in 1960, Gray joined the personal campaign staff of Richard Nixon.

After Nixon's defeat, Gray practiced law in New London, Connecticut. After working again for Nixon during the 1968 presidential campaign, he was named executive secretary to Robert H. Finch, Nixon's first secretary of Health, Education, and Welfare. After leaving the government briefly to practice law, he was appointed assistant attorney general in charge of the Justice Department's Civil Division in 1970. Among other things, he defended the FBI against litigation brought by women whom Hoover had barred from becoming agents.

While John Mohr had dissembled to Gray about Hoover's secret files, Gray soon developed his own reputation for deviousness. At a meeting of the FBI's executive conference, Gray raised the possibility of removing restrictions on hiring female agents. No action was taken. However, the next day, the papers quoted Gray—who made a point of wearing colored shirts—as saying that female agents would be allowed into the bureau after the executive conference "unanimously" approved the move.

"In fact, no vote had been taken, and if it had been placed before us, there would have been fifteen votes opposed, with Gray and possibly one other official voting for the hiring of female agents," Felt said.

"Gray would lie regularly," said Leonard M. "Bucky" Walters, an assistant director at the time.[116]

In contrast to Hoover, who responded decisively to memos almost immediately, it took Gray weeks to get to his mail.

"Hoover was in at 9 A.M., and he wanted memos on his desk," said Edward S. Miller, who was an assistant director. "By 11 A.M., you got your answer. With Gray, it took up to three months for him to get back to you. Gray would sign a memo and write the date and '1:20 A.M.' " Miller doubted Gray was in at those hours.[117]

"We called him three-day Gray," Walters said. "He worked Tuesday through Thursday. Then he went to his home in Stonington, Connecticut. Gray used chartered planes from the Air Force to visit all but one field office, billed to us at more than $100,000. FBI executives were concerned."

When the press revealed that the FBI had a program for supplying Nixon with information from bureau files for his speeches across the country, Gray ordered a massive leak investigation.

"Gray wanted everyone interviewed, every clerk who handled the teletype to Nixon," said Walters, who was in charge of the investigation because he was over inspections. "It was hundreds of people. Our report was 150 pages." In the meantime, Walters found out that members of Gray's personal staff were themselves leaking stories about FBI investigations.

■　■　■

Six weeks after Hoover's death and a month after Gray moved into his office, a supervisor in the Washington Field Office called Angelo J.

Lano at his Hyattsville, Maryland, home at 8 A.M. The supervisor told the agent that international jewel thieves had broken into the Watergate office building around 2:30 that morning, June 17, 1972.

A man of average height with black hair and a mustache, Lano was assigned to a miscellaneous crimes squad. Among other things, he was supposed to keep track of thefts from the Watergate complex, which included a hotel and condominiums where some of Washington's wealthiest residents lived. It was Lano's day off, and he was about to leave for his son's Little League practice. On weekends, the field office rotated agents so that both a criminal and a counterintelligence agent were on duty.

"I'm not going down there," Lano said to the supervisor. "You already have a criminal guy working. I have Little League practice."[118]

Lano then got a call from Robert G. Kunkel, the special agent in charge.

"What's the problem?" Kunkel asked.

"There is a criminal guy working down there," Lano said. "I have Little League practice."

"You're the only person who knows the place," Kunkel said. "You won't be there long. Just check it out and come right back."

And so, for the next three years, Lano would work nothing but the Watergate break-in, the FBI's biggest case since the assassination of John F. Kennedy. As the case agent, he was the individual most responsible for breaking the case and bringing to justice those who attempted to cover up the involvement of the White House and Committee for the Re-Election of the President.

After receiving the call from Kunkel, Lano called Peter Paul, another agent on his squad, and asked him to ride with him to the Metropolitan police department's second district headquarters, then at Twenty-third and L streets NW. As the police described it, the burglars had been caught in the sixth-floor offices of the Democratic National Committee. They had two Minolta 35-millimeter cameras, rolls of high-speed film, walkie-talkies, Mace, and Playtex rubber surgical gloves. When questioned, two of the suspects had used the same phony name. The police were checking their identities through fingerprints. Eventually, the burglars were identified as Bernard L. Barker, Virgilio R. Gonzalez, Eugenio Martinez, Frank A. Sturgis, and James W. McCord Jr. All had some connection to the CIA. McCord, for example, had retired from the CIA's Office of Security two years earlier.

At the station house, Lano emptied a carry-on bag containing the articles the police had seized from the suspects. He found bugging devices concealed in rolls of toilet paper. The police had not yet noticed the devices. Lano called in a technical agent who confirmed that they were indeed for bugging and wiretapping. Instead of jewel theft, the agents were looking at an interception of communications case.

After searching two of the burglars' rooms at the Watergate Hotel, the police found four packets of hundred-dollar bills and two address books, one listing an E. Howard Hunt with a notation that he worked at "WH"—the White House. It later turned out he had also been involved in the break-in.

Back at the field office, then at the old Post Office Building on Pennsylvania Avenue at Twelfth Street NW, Lano phoned an agent he knew at the Secret Service. As the bills were new, they could be traced. He asked the agent to find out through the Federal Reserve System what bank had received them. He then sent a teletype to Miami, where four of the suspects lived, asking for assistance on the case: "At approximately 2:30 A.M., security guard, Watergate complex, 2600 Virginia Avenue NW, notified Metropolitan Police Department (MPD) that he discovered tape around two doors on offices located at above address on sixth floor. Guard reported that on earlier security check, he had removed the tape not knowing that an apparent burglary was in progress."[119]

By Monday, the Secret Service and Miami FBI agents had traced the bills to a Miami bank account maintained by Barker. In turn, the agents tracked the money through Barker's account to Kenneth H. Dahlberg, who had used funds collected for Nixon's reelection campaign.[120]

Later that morning, Kunkel asked Lano what he thought about the case. "If you want my honest opinion, the agency [CIA] is involved in it somehow," Lano said. "Look at all these guys. McCord had worked for us and then for them. Then the other four guys. They had been contract people."

Lano asked for help. Within two days, two dozen agents from his squad—known as C-2, for criminal squad number two—had been assigned to work the case. Agents from the rest of the office were assigned to work the squad's other cases.

Usually the bureau gives a major case a code name like VANPAC or UNIRAC. That way, agents can refer to it easily, and the subject line on reports is short. But Lano, who often worked on the case from 7:30 A.M. to 11 P.M., never slowed down long enough to come up with a code name.

Agents soon developed suspects in the White House, and they found themselves stymied because the Hoover bureau had a rule that no one in the White House could be interviewed without permission from headquarters. It would take four or five days for headquarters to approve. So Lano told headquarters he needed to conduct interviews at the White House without prior approval, and he received permission to do so.

Almost every field office in the FBI became involved in checking leads. Lano wanted agents familiar with the case to conduct important interviews anywhere in the country. Again, the Hoover bureau required headquarters approval to travel into the jurisdiction of another field office. Lano got permission for agents on his squad to interview key subjects in other cities without obtaining approval from headquarters.

Not only had the FBI never taken on a president before, it had rarely investigated any branch of the government. In Hoover's FBI, if local sheriffs and members of Congress were off-limits, current presidents, cabinet officers, and White House aides certainly were. The break-in began as an effort by Nixon's Plumbers to obtain political intelligence. It ended as a massive attempted cover-up.

Only once did FBI headquarters try to put the brakes on the agents. That was when Gray, as acting director, deferred to the Nixon White House to avoid delving into money funneled through Mexico for the break-in. Nixon claimed he was trying to protect CIA operations in Mexico. In fact, he had invented the excuse to help cover up the involvement of his own reelection committee. The delay lasted only a week.

"They didn't try to suppress what I did," said Daniel C. Mahan, another agent on the Watergate case. "It was one of the FBI's finest hours."

In a public relations ploy, Nixon said he wanted the FBI to seal the

White House so no evidence would be disturbed. Since the Secret Service was perfectly capable of performing that duty, this was an unpleasant task for the FBI. But John J. McDermott, who took over as head of the Washington Field Office in October 1972, was not about to let anyone interfere with his assignment. Along with a dozen other agents, Roger L. Depue recalled standing in front of McDermott's desk as he talked on the phone with a high-ranking Secret Service official. The official was clearly telling McDermott that, before entering the White House, FBI agents would have to check their weapons at the Old Executive Office Building.

"No, you don't understand," McDermott responded. "These FBI agents will be on duty. When an FBI agent is on duty, he is armed."

They went back and forth. Finally, McDermott said, "I don't care if it's unprecedented. FBI agents don't carry out their duties without being armed. At 7:30 P.M., twenty-two special agents of the FBI will be at the west gate of the White House. They will be armed, and they will enter."

McDermott slammed down the phone and looked at the agents.

"What the hell are you waiting for?" he asked.

■ ■ ■

As the leaks from the FBI's investigation of Watergate continued, on June 24, 1973, Gray called in twenty-six agents on the squad and accused them of "suffering from flap jaw." Because a story that had just appeared in the *Washington Post* had come from Mahan's report, Gray singled him out for censure. Later, when Gray was subpoenaed to appear before the grand jury investigating Watergate, Lano selected Mahan to help him serve Gray with the subpoena.

In addition to seven Watergate burglars and accomplices, forty government officials were eventually indicted on conspiracy, obstruction of justice, and perjury charges. Among those ultimately convicted were Attorney General John N. Mitchell, presidential counsel John W. Dean III, White House chief of staff H. R. Haldeman, and domestic policy adviser John Ehrlichman. Nixon himself was named as an unindicted coconspirator and eventually was pardoned by his successor, Gerald R. Ford.

The fact that Bob Woodward and Carl Bernstein of the *Washington Post* were breaking stories on the investigation helped to ensure that it would not be suppressed. The agents were amazed to see material in Woodward and Bernstein's stories lifted almost verbatim from their reports of interviews a few days or weeks earlier.

"The media served a significant purpose," Edward R. Leary, an agent on the case, said. "On the one hand, it was a pain in the neck to us because what would be published in the paper was generally one day to two months behind where we were. We would have to go up the chain with information to explain or critique what was on the street. Why should we be bothered telling whoever wanted to know whether an article was accurate? On the other hand, through media involvement, clearly public focus was placed on the incident, and the glare of the public spotlight eventually opened some doors that would have been closed to us. Did the media solve Watergate? No. Their contribution was focusing a spotlight and causing things to be done in the light of day."[121]

As for the identity of Deep Throat, some FBI agents like McDermott thought Deep Throat was a composite meant to fuzz up the identities of Woodward's and Bernstein's sources. That was a misunderstanding of how the name evolved. From Bernstein and Woodward's *All the President's Men* and from the editors who handled their stories, it is clear that the reporters had a number of sources. With little fanfare, two of the sources have since come out—Hugh W. Sloan Jr., the treasurer of the Finance Committee to Re-Elect the President, and Judy Hoback, a bookkeeper for the Committee for the Re-Election of the President.[122]

In discussing the stories with his editors, Woodward would refer to one of his sources, who was knowledgeable but not always forthcoming, as "my friend." Possessed of a wry sense of humor, Howard Simons, then the managing editor of the *Washington Post*, dubbed the source "Deep Throat" after an X-rated movie then in the news. Because of the notoriety attached to the name, this source acquired a status well beyond others who were also important and to this day remain anonymous.

Other agents were convinced that Mark Felt was Deep Throat. Lending some credence to that, in the summer of 1999, Woodward showed up unexpectedly at the home of Felt's daughter Joan in Santa Rosa, California, north of San Francisco and took Felt to lunch. Joan Felt recalled that Woodward made his appearance just after a minicontroversy broke in the press in late July about whether Bernstein had told his then wife Nora Ephron that Felt was Deep Throat. A friend of their son Jacob made the claim, but Bernstein said Jacob was "repeating his mother's guesswork."

Woodward had been interviewing former FBI officials for a book he was writing on Watergate. However, now confused because of the effects of a stroke, Felt was in no shape to provide credible information. Joan Felt said her father greeted Woodward like an old friend, and their mysterious meeting appeared to be more of a celebration than an interview, lending support to the notion that Felt was, in fact, Deep Throat.

"Woodward just showed up at the door and said he was in the area," Joan Felt said. "He came in a white limousine, which parked at a schoolyard about ten blocks away. He walked to the house. He asked if it was okay to have a martini with my father at lunch, and I said it would be fine."

After Woodward left the house to get the limousine, which was parked almost three-quarters of a mile east at Comstock Junior High School, Joan Felt caught up with him to give him further instructions about what her father could eat for lunch. They walked together to the limo, and Joan Felt rode back with Woodward to pick up her father.

As he has in the past, Felt denied to me that he was Deep Throat. While he could not remember having lunch with Woodward and confused Woodward with a government attorney, Felt insisted firmly, "I was definitely not Deep Throat."

■   ■   ■

Immersed in the Watergate scandal, Nixon did not get around to nominating Gray as FBI director until nine months after he had named him acting director. By the time nomination hearings began on February 28, 1973, Gray had become a part of the cover-up. In his testimony, Gray kept volunteering information that the Senate Judiciary Committee otherwise might not have uncovered. He admitted to having shared with

John Dean copies of FBI reports on the Watergate case. He also admitted burning in his home fireplace two files of Watergate-related documents that Dean and John Ehrlichman gave him, documents that had been in E. Howard Hunt's safe at the White House. It was later disclosed that they included State Department cables Hunt had doctored in an effort to implicate President John F. Kennedy in the 1963 murder of South Vietnam's president, Ngo Dinh Diem.

By March 7, Nixon had decided to throw Gray overboard. Besides making himself look bad, Gray had further implicated the White House in a cover-up. Ehrlichman told Dean, "Well, I think we ought to let him hang there. Let him twist slowly, slowly in the wind." On March 13, Nixon said on the White House tapes, "Gray, in my opinion, should not be the head of the FBI." On March 22, he said, "The problem with him is he is a little bit stupid."

For Bucky Walters, the last straw was Gray's destruction of evidence. Carpooling to work as usual from northern Virginia with William Soyars, another assistant director, Walters told him on Monday, April 23, 1973, that he planned to resign that day. Soyars pledged to do the same. At 9 A.M., Walters met with Felt, the top FBI official under Gray.

"I told Felt that I would not work for a director who had destroyed evidence in a case the FBI was investigating," Walters told me. "I told him I would retire by the end of the day. I also told him I would ask the other assistant directors to do the same."

In the next half hour, Walters called each of the other assistant directors. To a man, they all agreed to resign. Walters passed the news on to Felt, who said he would tell Gray. An hour later, at 10:30, Gray called a meeting of the executive conference and announced he would leave that day.[123]

Walters did not ask Felt to join the palace coup: He knew Felt wanted to be director and likely would not want to hurt his own chances.

Three days after Gray resigned, Nixon accepted the resignations of Ehrlichman, Haldeman, Dean, and Attorney General Richard Kleindienst, all of whom had become enmeshed in Watergate. On May 10, a grand jury indicted former Attorney General John Mitchell on obstruction of justice charges in the scandal. The entire investigation had been done by 330 FBI agents in fifty-one field offices.

■ ■ ■

Nixon appointed William Ruckelshaus, the former head of the Environmental Protection Agency, acting FBI director. He reported to work on April 30, 1973. Ruckelshaus showed little interest in the bureau. During his two and a half months in office, Felt continued to make most of the decisions. Finally, on June 6, Nixon nominated Clarence M. Kelley as director. Three weeks later, the Senate confirmed his nomination, and on July 9, Kelley was sworn in.

Kindly and phlegmatic, Kelley seemed more like someone's grandfather than an FBI director, but his impact on the bureau would be profound. Born on October 24, 1911, Kelley grew up in Fairmount, Missouri. He graduated from the University of Kansas and obtained a law degree from the University of Kansas City School of Law. Kelley became an FBI agent in 1940 and resigned in 1961 to become chief of police in Kansas City, Missouri. As police chief, Kelley was an innovator. Under his direction, the department was the first police force in the United States to have its own helicopters and the first to use computers extensively.

As a former agent, Kelley, a burly, square-jawed man who wore glasses, was well aware of the bureau's failings. Kelley quickly stopped the fixation with statistics and emphasized quality over quantity in pursuing cases. He instituted career boards composed of respected FBI officials who recommended promotions, making personnel selection more objective and fair. He demanded that investigations be opened only when there was reason to believe a violation of law had occurred. And he began a push to hire females and minorities.

"They [the Nixon White House] thought old Clarence, who had been an FBI agent for twenty years and retired and became Kansas City police chief, would be malleable," said Buck Revell, who was in Kelley's office of planning and evaluation. "He was entirely different from that. He was very amiable but also very straight. He brought with him the concept of reorganizing the bureau that today is largely responsible for what we are doing and how we are doing it."

Having been an agent, Kelley knew that Hoover had been virtually unapproachable except through top bureau officials and carefully rehearsed meetings with individual agents. "Almost everyone in the organization was usually afraid to tell Hoover the truth for fear of upsetting him—and for fear of the inevitable punishment," Kelley said in his memoirs. So Kelley made sure agents knew that they could call him if necessary to tell him about problems they were having.

In 1974, Wilbur K. DeBruler, the special agent in charge of the Oklahoma City Field Office, took the risk of insisting on talking with Kelley about a tip he had received. DeBruler told the FBI director that the state's governor, David Hall, was taking kickbacks on construction jobs.

In the old bureau, unsolicited tips about public corruption were ignored. Kelley had already instructed all offices to investigate crime wherever the FBI found it, but headquarters did not take his instruction seriously. An assistant director had ordered DeBruler to drop the investigation. "Mr. Director, they tell me I shouldn't be doing this, but I think it's what you would want me to do," DeBruler said in explaining why he had called. After DeBruler outlined the case, Kelley told him to proceed. The investigation resulted in a prison term for the governor.[124]

Instead of merely reacting to crime, the bureau began to take an aggressive, proactive approach. From informants and wiretaps, agents learned who the important targets were and then went after them using imaginative undercover operations, a concept that did not exist under Hoover.

As one example, when Kenneth A. Giel started in the FBI in 1970, when Hoover was still in charge, he was assigned to a resident agency of the Birmingham, Alabama, Field Office. Giel was told there were "statistics that we have to uphold." The senior resident agent said, "We will always have more stolen cars each year so that each year we will look better and better." Giel had thirty to fifty cases.

In contrast, after Kelley took over, Giel spent three years in New York working just one labor racketeering case. The case started when a wiretap picked up information showing that an air conditioning contractor was dealing with organized crime. When Giel and another agent confronted him, the contractor agreed to cooperate. "So we came up with the idea of setting up a consultant business that would act as a go-between for general contractors who wanted labor peace and wanted to pick up nonunion jobs," Giel said. The FBI whimsically named the phony company James Rico Construction Consultants, after the Racketeer-Influenced and Corrupt Organizations Act (RICO), the powerful federal law that Congress passed in October 1970 to help the FBI combat the Mafia.

Meanwhile, James M. Abbott, another New York agent, wore a body recorder for each meeting with labor officials and organized crime leaders. In one poignant tape-recorded conversation, the FBI heard a contractor plead to be allowed to do a job for $1 million less than the next highest bidder. It seems that the Mafia and the carpenters' union had already decided who would do the job, and Vincent Molinari, the contractor who had submitted the lowest bid, was not the right one. So Molinari was told to see Theodore Maritas, then president of the District Council of Carpenters. In the conversation recorded by the FBI, Maritas explained that the project was "being set up" by "very, very heavy people, including myself. . . . We steer these things. You have no idea what goes on in this town. You think things just happen out of the sky?"[125]

Initially, in undercover operations, the FBI arrested suspects the first time they took a bribe. That changed with a Miami-based case called UNIRAC, which resulted in the conviction of Anthony M. Scotto, a longshoremen's union leader and reputed organized crime figure. Frank Storey, who was over the case at headquarters, had to convince his bosses that the FBI would get more out of a case by playing a waiting game.

"The assistant director [at headquarters] had to approve the payment," Storey said. "He said, 'We're not going to arrest this fellow?' I said, 'No. We're going to let the money walk.' We wanted to develop initial evidence and find out who he was working for and carry this forward. . . . We changed our whole approach on how we addressed organized crime, both from an investigative and management standpoint," Storey said. "That's when it all started. The long-term approach to the problem was new to the FBI."

Along with the change in emphasis came a relaxation of some of

Hoover's rules. "When I came in, agents always wore white shirts and hats," said Mildred C. "Millie" Parsons, who began with the FBI as a clerk-typist in 1939, became a secretary, and still works for the assistant director in charge of the Washington Field Office. "You could tell an agent the minute you saw him," she said. "The female employees wore dresses. No slacks or shorts. There were no female agents. The dress code changed when Clarence Kelley became director. We could wear pant suits."

14

ILLEGAL BREAK-INS

FBI Had Files ON CONGRESS, EX-AIDES SAY, read the headline over the lead story in the *Washington Post* of January 19, 1975. The article quoted Deke DeLoach and Lou Nichols, who was assistant to the director until DeLoach replaced him, as saying that under Hoover the FBI "compiled files containing information on the personal lives of senators and congressmen."

The article, which I wrote, said that the two former FBI officials confirmed that the files contained data on the girlfriends and drinking problems of members of Congress as well as other personal information about them.

"Both men said the information, which was kept in the FBI's general file, was not gathered for purposes of political blackmail and did not result from direct surveillance of members of Congress unless they were targets of criminal investigations," the article said. DeLoach was quoted as saying, "People would volunteer information during a regular investigation on other matters. . . . There was never any investigation by the FBI to find out this junk. We never made any follow-up or disseminated it in any way. There was no federal violation of law involved, and consequently it was none of our business."

However, a "senior agent" said, "If I find a congressman has a girl stashed (in some city), I'd report it to the SAC." Another source said he had seen information of a personal nature gathered by the FBI on members of Congress ranging from Senators Mike Mansfield and Edward M. Kennedy to Representatives Carl Albert and Hale Boggs. After Representative William R. Anderson criticized Hoover for his statements about the Berrigan brothers, Hoover ordered derogatory information gathered about his personal life. Kennedy said that Gray had specifically denied to Congress that such files existed.

Coming a month after Seymour Hersh revealed in the *New York Times* that the CIA, in violation of its charter, had spied on Americans who were against the war in Vietnam, the *Washington Post* story created a furor. The following day, the paper ran an article that quoted Representative Robert W. Kastenmeier, a Wisconsin Democrat who was chairman of the House Judiciary Committee's Administration of Justice Subcommittee, as saying that the practice of keeping files on members of Congress was as "insidious as Watergate." The congressman said that he would call current and former FBI officials to testify.

"Apparently, the purpose was to get something on congressmen and senators so they could be bent to the director's way of thinking," said Senator John V. Tunney, a member of the Senate Judiciary Committee. Senator John O. Pastore, chairman of the Senate Appropriations Committee's Judiciary Subcommittee, said he would call for an investigation of the FBI files by a select committee expected to be established to probe domestic spying by the CIA.

While DeLoach and Nichols had claimed that the files on congressmen were kept in the FBI's general files, both knew that Hoover really kept the material in his suite of offices in his Official and Confidential and Personal and Confidential files. Kelley knew, too. Referring to the articles, the new director on January 21 ordered the Inspection Division to review "the material previously maintained in Mr. Hoover's office, which is now kept in the office of the associate director," Nicholas P. Callahan. Kelley wanted "special emphasis" put on reviewing "any congressional files which might be maintained in these safes." He wanted to know whether there was a "misuse of office by former Director Hoover." The Inspection Division was to "call it exactly as it sees it . . . irrespective of what the consequences might be."[126]

By January 28, FBI agents conducting the review reported to James B. Adams, assistant to the director for investigative operations, that the

material consisted of three hundred items. About 135 files represented
Hoover's Official and Confidential files. The remainder were files maintained by Tolson and DeLoach. Unknown to the inspectors, Helen
Gandy had already destroyed what was left of Hoover's Personal and
Confidential files. Index cards that remained and some material that
had been shifted to the Official and Confidential files showed that even
more damaging information had been kept in some of them.

Included in the material that remained in the Official and Confidential files, the inspectors found, were folders on seventeen present or
former members of Congress, including John F. Kennedy, Harry S. Truman, Edward M. Kennedy, George S. McGovern, Richard M. Nixon,
and William R. Anderson.

Contrary to what DeLoach had said in the *Post* articles, material
from files on at least eleven of the members of Congress had been disseminated to individuals outside the FBI, including members of the
Nixon White House. The disclosure of such material "may have been
improper," the inspectors told Adams. "There was also a folder which
contained considerable derogatory information furnished by our Washington Field Office on a variety of matters and individuals including
members of Congress," the inspectors reported.

The Inspection Division made two recommendations: Undercutting
the rationale that Hoover kept the secret files in his office because young
clerks might read them, the inspectors said the general files of the FBI
were secure, and the material in question should be placed in the general
files. In addition, Kelley should assure the public that no such files
would be compiled in the future. Kelley agreed.

DeLoach, retired from the FBI and working as a vice president of
PepsiCo, wrote a letter to Kelley. While not denying the quotes attributed to him in the original *Post* article, DeLoach referred to me as a
"journalistic prostitute" who had "greatly twisted and distorted truthful
and factual statements." He assured the new director, "Kessler and the
Washington Post will undoubtedly continue to carry on their campaign
of vituperation, distortion, and muckraking."[127]

As a result of the disclosures, when the Senate established the Select
Committee to Study Government Operations with Respect to Intelli-
gence Activities on January 27, 1975, it included the activities of the
FBI along with the CIA. The following month, the House established a

Select Committee on Intelligence, which also included an investigation of FBI activities in its charter. The Church Committee and the Pike Committee, as they became known after their chairmen, Senator Frank Church and Representative Otis Pike, probed a range of FBI abuses, from COINTELPRO and the surveillance of Martin Luther King to illegal wiretapping, mail openings, and surreptitious entries or black bag jobs.

In testimony before the Church Committee on February 27, 1975, Edward H. Levi, President Ford's attorney general, confirmed for the first time that Hoover had maintained an Official and Confidential file in his office and that these files contained derogatory information on prominent Americans, including members of Congress, presidents, and cabinet officers. At a news conference on April 3, Levi said he learned about the files just before he took office on February 7. He said his predecessor, William Saxbe, had told him that no such files existed.[128]

Kelley made Adams, a lawyer who was a Texas state legislator before joining the FBI in 1951, point man on the investigations. Adams reviewed files covering past practices, interviewed other FBI officials who knew about the activities, and testified about the abuses.

"I made it clear that I had to be fully and honestly informed," Adams told me. "I told them we could live with what had happened in the last fifty years. What we couldn't tolerate would be lying about it or obstructing a congressional inquiry. We would be bringing the mistakes of the past into the present. I told them if I testified falsely because of what they told me, they would be out of a job."

Every time Adams learned about a new abuse, he would show up in Levi's office and let him know. "Levi would rush over and say, 'What's the matter? What's the matter?' I got to think that was my name," Adams said.[129]

Under Hoover, oversight by Congress consisted of well-rehearsed colloquy between the director and John J. Rooney, chairman of the House appropriations subcommittee over the FBI's budget. For example, on March 2, 1972, in Hoover's last appearance in Congress, Rooney asked him, "You don't allow gay activists in the FBI, do you?"

"We don't allow any type of activists in the FBI, gay or otherwise," Hoover responded.

As a result of the Church and Pike investigations, that changed. Congress established the House and Senate intelligence committees as permanent bodies with oversight authority. After the exposure of the FBI's abuses in the domestic security area, Attorney General Edward Levi developed guidelines for opening investigations. As part of the new policy of focusing on real threats, Kelley shut down Communist and domestic security cases that had gone stale.

"We had people still in the files who might have been Communists twenty years before or were crippled in a wheelchair," Adams said. A 1974 review by the General Accounting Office, the audit arm of Congress, found that only 2 percent of FBI domestic security cases resulted in prosecutions.

Kelley transferred investigations of domestic radical and terrorist organizations from the FBI's Intelligence Division to the General Investigative Division, where they would be treated like other criminal cases. FBI domestic security investigations dropped from twenty-one thousand to fewer than three hundred.

■　■　■

In the fall of 1975, the House's Pike Committee informed Justice that some FBI officials were profiting from an arrangement to buy electronic equipment—especially devices used for bugging and wiretapping—from the U.S. Recording Company, a private company in Washington. Levi asked Kelley to have the FBI conduct an investigation, but the investigation turned out to be a whitewash, so Levi gave the job to Michael E. Shaheen Jr., head of Justice's Office of Professional Responsibility. To conduct a more aggressive investigation, Shaheen appointed John M. Dowd and Craig A. Starr special counsels.

Dowd, who would become the lead lawyer on the case, had joined Justice in 1969 in the tax division. It fell to him to prosecute Meyer Lansky for allegedly skimming taxes from a London casino. Lansky ultimately was acquitted. Now, for the FBI probe, Dowd assembled a team of thirty FBI agents chosen for their investigative skills. In six months, they conducted more than six hundred interviews.

"They were totally professional," Dowd said. "They never blinked."

By November 1976, the investigation found that, although FBI officials were not profiting from the FBI's arrangement with U.S. Recording, the bureau was improperly buying all its electronic equipment from the company without competitive bidding. Sixty percent of the company's sales were to the FBI, with markups of 40 to 70 percent.

The owner of the company, Joseph Tait, was friends with John Mohr, assistant to the director under Hoover, and Nicholas P. Callahan, associate director under Kelley, along with other FBI officials. They had a regular Friday night poker game at the Blue Ridge Road and Gun Club in Virginia. But FBI officials claimed they used the company as the bureau's exclusive supplier to maintain secrecy about the sensitive equipment they were buying.

Inexorably, the investigation into U.S. Recording led to far more serious allegations involving wholesale misuse by FBI officials of bureau employees and material. The big break came when a carpenter in the exhibits section of the laboratory called Dowd.

"He said he would talk to me if he received protection from the attorney general. He said he had been keeping an insurance policy for forty years," Dowd told me.[130]

After Levi signed a letter guaranteeing that there would be no retribution against the man, he turned over logs, records, and photographs documenting work he had performed at the homes of FBI officials. With the carpenter's leads, FBI agents established that John Mohr, one of Hoover's most powerful lieutenants, had had the bureau perform body work and painting on his son's MG. Mohr had had the FBI laboratory construct an elaborate exhibit for the son's dental practice. At Mohr's home, employees from the Exhibits Section shaved doors to accommodate new carpeting. Radio Engineering Section employees repaired his television set and installed telephones, stereo speakers, and a security alarm system. From finest walnut, Exhibits Section employees built him a cigar box, a tape cartridge rack, wine rack, and two gun cases with glass doors. Mohr had FBI employees mount snow tires and wash his car and bring it to commercial garages for repair. Even after Mohr retired in June 1972, FBI employees repaired electrical switches, television sets, and the alarm system at his home. They also built a birdhouse designed by Mohr.

Ivan W. Conrad, assistant director over the Laboratory Division, had taken home a large quantity of FBI electronic equipment. Callahan,

Kelley's associate director, had had employees assemble a fence to prevent erosion at his beach home. They also built a picket fence and shelves at his Washington home.

DeLoach had FBI employees perform a range of services for his home, including construction of a bar, a bathroom cabinet, and lawn chairs. At least in his case, DeLoach had FBI employees complete these items on their own time, and he paid for materials.[131]

Even Helen Gandy, who was liaison for the improvements to Hoover's home, got some of the goodies. Exhibits Section employees made her a teakwood jewelry box, bookcases, a teakwood TV stand, and a silver chest. They also kept her car washed and filled with gasoline and changed the snow tires.

By far the biggest offender was Hoover himself. Hoover preached that even the appearance of impropriety must be avoided. He disciplined agents for losing their handcuffs or drinking coffee. Yet over the years, Hoover had FBI employees build a front portico and a rear deck on his home at 4936 Thirtieth Place NW in Washington. They installed a fish pond, equipped with water pump and lights, and they constructed shelves and other conveniences for him. They painted his house, maintained his yard, replaced the sod, installed artificial turf, planted and moved shrubbery, and built a redwood garden fence, flagstone court, and sidewalks. FBI employees reset Hoover's clocks, retouched his wallpaper, and prepared his tax returns. Many of the gifts Hoover received from employees, such as cabinets and bars, were built by FBI employees on government time.[132] Meanwhile, Hoover had FBI employees write *Masters of Deceit* for him under his name. He pocketed part of the proceeds.[133]

"Hoover never paid for anything," Dowd said. "He never paid for a meal. He had beef flown in free by suppliers. It was the greatest shakedown in United States history going on behind the badge."

"Hoover [and some of his aides] would be prosecuted under today's standards. No question of it. And should have been," said Buck Revell, formerly the bureau's associate deputy director over investigations. "Hoover for the money he kept from the books he supposedly wrote but didn't write. Using government funds and resources for personal gain. And use of government employees to maintain his residence.

Again, that is fraud against the government. Taking vacations and putting in vouchers for expenses. Agents have been prosecuted for that. Those things that were somewhat taken for granted back then would be prosecuted today."[134]

Based on Dowd's findings, the Justice Department considered prosecuting Mohr, but a five-year statute of limitations had expired. In return for his cooperation, John P. Dunphy, the chief of the Exhibits Section, agreed to plead guilty to a misdemeanor.

The most sensitive aspect of the investigation concerned allegations that Kelley, since becoming director, had accepted services from the Exhibits Section. It turned out that Callahan had arranged, without Kelley's knowledge, to have a set of curtain valances installed in Kelley's Washington apartment. When they were not to Kelley's liking, another set was installed. The Radio Engineering Section also purchased and installed two television sets for him. After the investigation began, Kelley paid for the valances and returned the TV sets.

Dowd thought Kelley should have been fired, but Levi, in the final version of the Justice Department report issued in January 1978, noted that Kelley was not initially aware of installation of the valances. While Kelley had received "limited" goods and services, the report said he had reimbursed the bureau, and his cooperation had made the investigation possible. Kelley also instituted reforms to ensure that the abuses would not recur.

"Kelley did not ask for valances. His wife was dying of cancer. Kelley was unaware of who picked up the costs," Michael Shaheen, who was over OPR, told me.[135]

■ ■ ■

Back in 1971, when the break-in at the FBI's resident agency in Media, Pennsylvania, revealed the bureau's COINTELPRO programs, the Socialist Workers Party, a target of a COINTELPRO, sued the FBI. In the course of discovery proceedings, the Justice Department learned that the FBI had continued to engage in illegal surreptitious entries or black bag jobs even after Hoover had banned them in 1966. Under the direction of Assistant Attorney General J. Stanley Pottinger, FBI agents on March 17, 1976, discovered files in the New York Field Office documenting break-ins from 1954 through 1973, when Gray was director. The documents—twenty-five volumes in all—were in the office safe of SAC John Malone. Under Hoover's "Do Not File" procedure of 1942, they should have been destroyed within six months of their creation.

Appointed SAC by Hoover, Malone was known as "Cement Head." He fit Hoover's image of an FBI agent—square-jawed, confident looking, and conservatively dressed. Judging by appearance alone, anyone could have mistaken Malone for the chief executive officer of a Fortune 500 company. But every agent had his own favorite story about him. According to a former New York agent, Malone introduced a black FBI agent in the elevator to a cabinet officer who was visiting the field office.

"This is one of our black agents," Malone said.

"They didn't call him 'Cement Head' for nothing," said Edward H. Joyce, who worked for him.

Recognizing the need to demonstrate that the FBI must be responsive to the rule of law, Griffin Bell, President Carter's attorney general, decided to prosecute those responsible for the break-ins. The question was, who had been responsible? Between 1970 and 1974, a New York squad under John Kearney had broken into homes and opened the mail of friends of Weather Underground fugitives. Initially, Bell decided to indict Kearney, who had resigned from the FBI in 1972. That provoked a storm of protests from FBI agents, who said higher-ups had approved the break-ins.

Bell expanded the Justice Department inquiry and found that the break-ins had apparently been authorized by Gray, acting associate director W. Mark Felt, and Edward S. Miller, who was assistant director for domestic intelligence. Bell dropped the charges against Kearney and, in April 1978, a federal grand jury indicted Gray, Felt, and Miller.

When the three defendants appeared in U.S. District Court in Washington, more than five hundred agents, clerks, and friends came to show their support.

"All I can say is, God bless everyone," Felt said from the top of the courthouse steps.

"I was shocked that I was indicted," Felt told me recently. "You would be, too, if you did what you thought was in the best interests of the country and someone on technical grounds indicted you."[136]

During an eight-week trial, Felt and Miller admitted they had authorized the break-ins but said the FBI was entitled to engage in such conduct in cases involving the national security. Five former attorneys general testified that they had never approved such illegal activities. Felt and Miller said Gray had approved the break-ins. Gray denied it.

"I talked to Gray with Felt present about the entries," Miller told me. "He was hesitant. There was pressure from the field. Finally, he authorized it. He authorized me to tell the agents. He said he would deny doing it. Just the three of us knew."

Regardless of whether the FBI director had authorized the break-ins, they were still illegal. In a July 19, 1966, memo, Sullivan explained to DeLoach, "We do not obtain authorization for black bag jobs from outside the bureau. Such a technique involves trespass and is clearly illegal; therefore, it would be impossible to obtain any legal sanction for it. Despite this, black bag jobs have been used because they represent an invaluable technique in combating subversive activities of a clandestine nature aimed at undermining and destroying our nation."

After deliberating for two days, a jury convicted Felt and Miller on November 6, 1980. A month later, a judge fined Felt $5,000 and Miller $3,500. In part because of insufficient evidence that he had approved the entries, the case against Gray was dropped.

Miller, a gentle man, had known Ronald Reagan when he was governor of California. After Reagan became president, Attorney General Edwin Meese called Miller and asked if he would accept a pardon. Miller said he would. On April 15, 1981, Reagan announced he was pardoning both Felt and Miller. Reagan said they had served the country with "great distinction" and had approved the break-ins in good faith in pursuing radical fugitives.

Despite the pardons, the case demonstrated that, with Hoover no longer around to protect them, FBI agents who broke the law, regardless of the authorization, would be held accountable.

"I had no problem with the pardons," Bell told me. "The fact that they were convicted meant the point was made."

■ ■ ■

In May 1976, Kelley gave a speech at Westminster College in Fulton, Missouri, the same place where Winston Churchill had given his "iron curtain" speech thirty years earlier. Noting that he had spent much of his time investigating and explaining activities that had occurred before he took over, Kelley said that some of them were "clearly wrong and quite indefensible. We most certainly must never allow them to be repeated." Never again, he said, should the FBI occupy the "unique position that permitted improper activity without accountability."[137]

Kelley's statement came as a shock to agents. In every field office, Hoover had posted a plaque titled "Loyalty" with inspirational writer Elbert Hubbard's exhortation: "If you work for a man, in heaven's name work for him; speak well of him and stand by the institution he represents . . . if you [criticize the institution], the first high wind that comes along will blow you away, and probably you will never know why."

While he was in office, Kelley never directly criticized Hoover, but the import of his remarks at Westminster was clear. The Society of Former Agents of the FBI, taking Elbert Hubbard literally, attacked Kelley for daring to suggest that the FBI had done anything wrong under Hoover. For the benefit of the retired agents, Kelley issued a clarification.

Because of opposition from Hoover holdovers, Kelley never was able to put into effect all the reforms he had in mind. "Too many people liked things the way they were," Kelley said in his memoirs. Nor was Kelley able to devote the energy needed to fully transform the bureau. Every Thursday to Sunday, Kelley returned to Kansas City to see his wife, Ruby, who had cancer.

After Jimmy Carter became president, Kelley retired on February 22, 1978. By that time, 185 of the FBI's 7,931 agents were black, 173 were Hispanic, and 147 were women. Thanks to prodding by Robert F. Kennedy, when Hoover died, the bureau had had 61 black agents, and 59 Hispanics, but still no females among its 8,548 agents.

Despite his achievements, Kelley's public image was that of an honest plodder, a square-jawed traditionalist afraid to make changes. This misperception arose because he had no feel for dealing with the media or Congress and never projected his program outside the bureau.

"Kelley never knew how to handle Washington," said James D. McKenzie, an assistant director under William Webster.

15

THE JUDGE

With confidence in the FBI severely shaken by the continuing revelations of abuses, Jimmy Carter decided that replacing Clarence Kelley with a judge would assure Congress and the American people that the FBI could be trusted. On the recommendation of Griffin B. Bell, his attorney general, Carter chose William H. Webster.

Born on March 6, 1924, in St. Louis, Missouri, Webster received a bachelor of arts degree from Amherst College and a J.D. degree two years later from Washington University Law School. He served in the Navy as a lieutenant during both World War II and the Korean War. He was U.S. attorney for the Eastern District of Missouri from 1960 to 1961, then practiced law in St. Louis. Nixon appointed him a U.S. District Court judge for the Eastern District of Missouri in 1970. Three years later, Nixon appointed him to the U.S. Court of Appeals for the Eighth Circuit, where he remained until he became FBI director on February 23, 1978.

Webster had an ageless face, thin lips, and a high forehead. His slightly graying black hair was always immaculately combed. He wore Brooks Brothers suits, monogrammed button-down shirts, and gold tie clips.

As a former federal judge, Webster came into the job with built-in credibility. "I knew Webster from judicial seminars," said Bell, also a former federal judge. "I gave President Carter a list of three judges, including Webster. One dropped out. The second one was Frank McGarr of the Northern District of Illinois. Carter said, 'I can tell you prefer Webster.' After interviewing him, he chose him. He later told me Webster was the best appointment he made as president."

Webster, who liked to be called "Judge," not only brought probity to the job, he turned out to be a skilled administrator. He chose exceptionally smart, talented, experienced agents as managers and let them run the bureau, always subject to his sharp questioning. He made it clear that agents would be in trouble if they kept problems from him. If Webster thought an agent was not giving him the full story or had not done his homework, his voice became taut and his eyes steely.

"If you briefed Webster, you better know every detail of the case," said Anthony E. Daniels, an official in the Criminal Investigative Division.

"At one of the first executive conferences, they started to give Webster the dance," said William A. Gavin, who became an assistant director under Webster. "He didn't let them dance more than seventeen seconds before he was all over them. He would let you know with a crisp, terse statement with the blue sparks coming out of his eyes. I wouldn't want that happening to me more than once. It was like your dad when he took you to task. You didn't want to upset him again. He saw through the bureaucratic horse manure. All of a sudden, people realized, 'If we don't know the answer, say we don't know the answer.' "[138]

Webster brought in assistants with law degrees from Harvard and Yale to help evaluate proposals. Webster wanted his assistants to make sure bureau initiatives conformed with statutes and guidelines. But he also wanted them to see the FBI as outsiders.

"He wanted us to look at it like Joe Q. Public," said Nancy D. McGregor, one of his assistants. " 'Does this make sense?' "

Webster's assistants were careful to maintain their role as advisers, not managers. "There is a natural aversion by the agents to any outsider," said Howard Gutman, another special assistant to Webster. "No matter how good the director's background, if he didn't go to Quantico and carry a gun, there is at least initially mistrust and an 'us versus them' perception."

Under Webster, the bureau mounted major offensives aimed at the biggest targets, all sacrosanct under Hoover. In one undercover operation, Joseph Pistone, using the alias Donnie Brasco, for the first time infiltrated the Mafia. In another case, called the Pizza Connection, the FBI took on international drug trafficking. Webster, unlike Hoover, thought that the FBI should work major drug cases.

As a result of an FBI investigation that intercepted more than a hundred conversations, eight members of the Mafia's ruling commission were indicted, including the leadership of three of New York City's crime families. All eight were convicted. Agents arrested John Gotti, the boss of the Gambino Mafia family in New York, and Raymond L. S. Patriarca, the head of the New England Mafia.

The FBI took on the Bandidos, a motorcycle gang that dealt in drugs, stolen weapons, and other stolen property. The Bandidos lived primarily off the earnings of young women whom gang members induced to be prostitutes or topless dancers. Each Bandido had four or five women who were considered his girlfriends. Generous to a fault, the Bandidos passed around the women to their friends as sexual gifts.

The Bandidos were terrorizing residents of Lubbock, Texas, and the FBI sent in an undercover agent to pose as the new owner of a bar called the Sidebuster, where the Bandidos hung out.

In choosing an agent to work a particular undercover operation, FBI headquarters consulted a computer data bank listing every conceivable characteristic of FBI agents who wanted to work undercover—hobbies, work experience, foreign languages, and details of their appearance such as tattoos. Dennis Dufour, who was six feet two inches tall and weighed 235 pounds, was perfect for the Bandidos job. As a teenager, Dufour owned a Triumph motorcycle and later raced dragsters in California, where he learned to fix engines. Before joining the FBI in 1978, Dufour had owned and operated several bars in New Orleans. He then became a New Orleans police officer working drugs. Dufour knew about motorcycles, drugs, and bars. But more than that, he was quick-thinking and had the gift of gab—attributes that would save his life on more than one occasion.

Using the name Dennis Donovan, Dufour posed as a drug dealer and murderer who was associated with organized crime figures in New

York. The FBI established a phony history with credit bureaus for Dufour and entered an arrest record for him in police data banks. The Lubbock police department participated in the operation, and some police officials knew about Dufour. To protect Dufour, the FBI programmed the department's computers so if anyone inquired into Dufour's background, the FBI would know who had made the request. The bureau could then investigate the individual to see if he or she was working with the gang members.

After the bar had been wired for sound and video, Dufour allowed gang members to park their motorcycles in the bar overnight. Soon, gang members from other parts of Texas and as far away as Louisiana began flocking to the Sidebuster.

To establish Dufour's credentials as a drug dealer, the FBI had Joe Pistone, the legendary undercover agent from New York, fly in one day with $250,000 in cash in a briefcase.

In front of the video cameras, the gang members discussed business, including thefts of explosives and a murder that one member said he had committed. After closing at 2 A.M., Dufour would take a roundabout route to his apartment to make sure he was not being followed. Then he would meet with Rick Harris, the case agent, and dictate his 302s. Dufour matched and verified the information the FBI was obtaining from the electronic and video surveillance.

"It was tense all the time because you were constantly being tested," Dufour told me. "A guy would take out a gun and lay it on the bar and look at you. One of the big things was to always look them in the eye. You never look away from a person. You are talking to a guy, and he takes out a gun or sticks a Crocodile Dundee or Rambo knife in the bar, you look right back at him."

Another hazard was the women the gang members constantly offered Dufour as a token of friendship. "The bikers thought it was a great honor to offer a female to you for sexual services. You had to figure a way to refuse and not insult them and still maintain you were a bad guy," Dufour said.

The FBI decided to bring the operation to a close when it got word that, for reasons unknown, some gang members in Canada were plotting to kill Dufour. Dufour announced he was going on vacation, and he closed the bar. In the early morning hours of February 21, 1985, Dufour met with some two hundred law enforcement officers from agencies that had participated in the operation, including the Texas Rangers, DEA, and IRS. The FBI arrested more than eighty members of the gang on narcotics, firearms, and racketeering charges in eight states. Nearly all pleaded guilty. The Sidebuster never reopened. But it rang up a profit for the bureau of $60,000.

■ ■ ■

In contrast to the success of the Bandidos investigation, the CISPES investigation blackened the FBI's reputation and raised troubling questions about whether the new bureau was really that different from the old, when Hoover assigned agents to investigate people because of their political beliefs.

The CISPES investigation began in June 1981, when Frank Varelli, a native of El Salvador, met with Daniel Flanagan, an agent in the Dallas Field Office, and gave him a wild story about right-wing Salvadoran death squads targeting people in the United States.

The Dallas office knew nothing about El Salvador or its politics. But Gary L. Penrith, then an assistant special agent in charge in Dallas, thought Varelli's story was worth checking out. When the FBI asked the CIA, the agency said it thought Varelli knew what he was talking about. Then Varelli came up with a new story about the Committee in Solidarity with the People of El Salvador (CISPES), an amorphous left-wing group that raised money in America for humanitarian aid to El Salvador. Varelli claimed that it, too, was targeting Americans for death. After six months of investigation, Penrith decided to close the case. There was nothing to Varelli's claims.

Because of poor supervision by headquarters, the Dallas office reopened the CISPES case two years later. This time, in trying to establish criminal activity, FBI agents attended political rallies, conducted surveillance of nuns, took notes on what people said in political gabfests, and opened files on 2,375 individuals.

Unlike the bureau's activities under Hoover, the investigation had no political motive. But a later review by the FBI's inspectors determined that there were two major problems with the CISPES investigation: Varelli's information was false, and even if it had been correct, the techniques used were too broad, unfocused, and chilling—a fact that some agents in the field noted at the time.

Since the days of COINTELPRO and the abuses of the Hoover era, the bureau had established elaborate procedures and guidelines that had to be followed before a case was opened. But these reviews came into play only if intrusive techniques like wiretapping were to be used. In the CISPES investigation, no one was wiretapped, no homes were broken into. For that reason, the case did not get the kind of scrutiny it would otherwise have received. Webster never knew about it.

The bureau started its own review of the CISPES investigation only after members of Congress and the media began asking questions. While the bureau had not done anything illegal, it had improperly conducted investigations into political beliefs and constitutionally protected free speech.

"We found an unreliable informant and a case agent who was inept and a supervisor who didn't do his job," said Buck Revell.

Eventually Daniel Flanagan, Varelli's case agent, resigned from the bureau after admitting he had withheld FBI payments meant for Varelli. He also made $1,000 in restitution to the FBI.[139]

■　■　■

Nothing symbolized the change to the new FBI so much as ABSCAM, which began as a sting to recover stolen securities and paintings. The FBI used a convicted swindler named Mel Weinberg to act as an intermediary to convince thieves to bring stolen property to fencing fronts on Long Island. There, undercover FBI agents posed as representatives of a phony Arab sheik.

In the fall of 1978, the focus of ABSCAM shifted to political corruption in New Jersey and then to Washington. In a two-story house rented on W Street in Washington, undercover agents expressed an interest in obtaining political favors for the sheik from congressmen. Agents videotaped congressmen receiving cash in exchange for favors. Seven members of Congress, including Senator Harrison A. Williams Jr. of New Jersey, were convicted. Webster made sure that no member of Congress was pressured into taking a bribe.

"We had put all these protective mechanisms into place in AB-SCAM," Webster said. " 'Don't bring anybody to the sheik who wasn't ready to deal. We're not going to sell him. Bring him if he wants to deal. Don't try to persuade him. If he wants to leave, let him leave.' "

With some misgivings, Webster approved the first bug placed by the FBI in a judge's chambers in operation GREYLORD, which attacked a corrupt judicial system in Cook County, Illinois. The FBI brought in agents from all over the country to pose as defendants who paid off judges.

To carry off the ruse, the FBI arranged for the first time to permit agents to testify falsely under oath. The Justice Department decided that under the constitutional provision giving the federal government supremacy, the bureau could supersede state perjury laws. To be on the safe side, the bureau informed several key Illinois officials who were deemed honest, including Governor James Thompson. The sting resulted in some ninety-one convictions of judges, lawyers, sheriffs, and police officers.

"I was always concerned about getting into privileged territory," Webster told me. "Unless the judge invited an undercover agent back to his chambers, I had concern about it. I felt we could not be indifferent to privacy interests. I usually looked to be sure that there were exclusions from putting audio capability in bedrooms, particularly in view of the history of the Martin Luther King episode. I didn't believe we should be in the bedroom unless there were some overriding reason that could be documented and then controlled. They should turn it off when they were not getting things they were supposed to be hearing."

With anything involving the FBI, Webster said, "You have to have thought through the reality and perception of your actions. It must not only be legal but also not be seen to be so offensive that we might lose the technique because of outrage."

■　■　■

Under Webster, the focus of the bureau's Intelligence Division shifted from going after assorted antiwar protesters and aging Communists in wheelchairs to real spies from other nations and the American traitors who helped them. But because it was embarrassing to acknowledge traitors in their midst, the CIA, Defense Department, and other national security agencies had succeeded over the years in convincing the Justice Department not to prosecute spies. Instead, spies would be allowed to quietly resign from jobs that gave them access to sensitive information.

"Every time we would present [a spy case for prosecution], the attorney general would take it up with the secretary of state and even the president," said W. Raymond Wannall Jr., who headed the Intelligence Division. "You'd always go through the procedure [of trying to get a prosecution]. Some years there were none, some years two [such cases]."[140]

In 1977, Attorney General Bell changed the policy and began prosecution of spies to deter espionage. "I didn't see why spies should not be prosecuted," Bell told me. "The problem was many people in the bureaucracies didn't want to be embarrassed because spies had stolen their secrets."[141]

The architect of the Justice Department's aggressive policy in prosecuting spies was John L. Martin, who, after heading a key unit in 1973, became chief of the Justice Department's Internal Security Section in 1980. Born in Utica, New York, Martin attended Syracuse University College of Law. One summer, he sold ice cream off a truck at Camp Drum, a military facility outside of Watertown, New York. When he had downtime, he read transcripts published in the *New York Times* of the trial of Francis Gary Powers, the American shot out of the sky in May 1960 while taking clandestine photos in the U-2 reconnaissance plane sixty thousand feet over the Soviet Union. It fascinated Martin that the U.S. government denied that Powers had been spying and that the Soviets had retaliated by producing the live pilot, placing him on trial, and later trading him for Soviet spy Rudolf Abel.

Martin joined the FBI in 1962 and left in 1968 to practice law. He joined Justice in 1971. Having become involved in prosecuting Daniel Ellsburg, Martin, handsome enough to be the lead in a Hollywood movie, had become suspicious of the way the government handled national security cases.

"It was ironic that, as the administration preoccupied itself with these documents, most of which were eventually declassified, John A. Walker had already been working for the Soviets for three years," Martin told me. Undetected by FBI surveillance, he had begun his spying by walking into the Soviet embassy in Washington. The Navy would later say that because Walker gave the Soviets Navy codes, the United States could well have lost a war to them.

"Yet," said Martin, "here we were spending our time hunting for the source of a leak of information that portrayed the truth about our involvement in a war that ultimately cost more than fifty thousand American lives. I began to equate the government's obtuse attitude in the Ellsberg case with its approach to the Vietnam War itself. In addition to losing the war, the defense and intelligence communities were prepared to lose the domestic wars in federal courtrooms."

Before Martin took over the job, no spies had been prosecuted in federal courts for nearly a decade. By the time he retired in August 1997, Martin had supervised the prosecution of seventy-six spies. Only one of the prosecutions resulted in an acquittal.

Martin's office was on the ninth floor of the Bond Building at 1400 New York Avenue NW. In addition to having a top-secret clearance, Martin was cleared for special compartmented intelligence. Designated by code words, this included TK, for Talent Keyhole, which gave him access to information about spy satellites; M, which is the first initial of a code word for sensitive covert operations; SI, for signal intelligence, which gave him access to intercepted and decoded communications from NSA; Byeman, which related to satellite reconnaissance and material from the National Reconnaissance Office; and Q, which is issued by the Energy Department and allows access to information about nuclear weapons. Martin had clearance to still other compartments, referred to by initials only because the very existence of those clearances is secret.

Martin preached that the government could achieve two goals at once: prosecute spies to deter future espionage and retain any secrets that legitimately needed to be protected. Moreover, he maintained, the government could learn what the spy had given away and protect his rights, all at the same time.

"I'm a firm believer in giving them their full constitutional rights and then sending them to jail for a lifetime," Martin would say.

As chief prosecutor of spies for more than twenty-five years, Martin had one of the toughest jobs in the government. Once the program of prosecuting espionage became successful, Martin had to withstand pressure from the FBI to prosecute on evidence that he did not, in some cases, think was strong enough. As a result, FBI agents would grouse that Martin was too cautious. When national security is involved, it is easy for people to become hysterical and forget about constitutional rights, Martin would say.

Martin also had to withstand pressure from the intelligence community in the opposite direction. The CIA and NSA, in particular, would claim that prosecuting spies would disclose too many secrets. In fact, Martin would say, these agencies wanted to bury their mistakes. Powerful as they were, Martin had the intellect and courage to take on all the agencies.

"The intelligence community often believes that nothing is known unless it originates with them, and that revealing anything previously kept secret helps the other side," Martin told me. "That ignores the reality that our adversaries know much more than we publicly admit, and that the national interest will inevitably be better served by a public trial revealing and re-creating precisely what took place. Not only does it expose and punish the defendant, it is a way of impressing upon the bureaucracy the ultimate consequences of its oversights, if any. The purpose should be to deter the American who is tempted to spy and to correct within the government the reasons why things went wrong."

In 1980, Congress passed the Classified Information Procedures Act, which Martin helped draft. The law became known as the greymail statute because it was intended to prevent defendants from trying to use the threat of exposure to win dismissal of the charges against them. The law permitted judges and defense lawyers to examine outside of public view classified information relating to their cases. But that did not stop objections from the intelligence community to prosecuting spies.

While the FBI was back in the business of catching spies so they could be prosecuted, it needed tutoring. During their in-service training at the FBI Academy at Quantico, Martin taught agents that the kind of blunderbuss approach to intelligence gathering fostered by

Hoover was improper and ineffective. Nor was the approach of James Angleton, the CIA's legendary chief of counterintelligence, useful.

"Angleton fostered the misconception that counterintelligence officers need to be a different breed—suspicious to the point of paranoia," Martin said. "Often, this outlook is referred to as a 'counterintelligence mentality.' This is pure malarkey. People who catch spies need to be no more and no less suspicious than people who catch murderers, bank robbers, or white-collar criminals. To be effective, any professional investigator must bring a balanced approach."

Angleton called counterintelligence a "wilderness of mirrors" and saw catching spies as a game. Martin saw it as deadly serious business.

"Homicide, kidnapping, bank robbery have individual victims, but the victims of espionage by definition are the people of a country," Martin said. "If espionage is continually successful, we lose the ability to win a war. Ultimately, we can lose our freedom."

So that their cases would hold up in court, Martin wanted FBI agents to give him a heads-up on investigations so he could advise them on how best to proceed. While the FBI did the investigating and arresting, Martin was the one who supervised the bureau's work. Agents worked closely with Martin on the cases of Christopher J. Boyce and Andrew Daulton Lee, who sold classified information to the Soviets from a TRW Inc. communications center; William Kampiles, a CIA employee who sold the Soviets a top-secret technical manual on a spy satellite; David H. Barnett, a CIA officer who sold the Soviets information on a sensitive CIA operation; Jonathan J. Pollard, a Naval Investigative Service analyst who gave the Israelis a roomful of secret documents in return for $50,000 in cash; Ronald Pelton, an NSA employee who told the Soviets the agency had tapped into an underwater cable carrying secret military communications; and Aldrich H. Ames, the CIA counterintelligence officer who gave up dozens of operations and agents to the Soviets. The cases went smoothly, and all were convicted or pleaded guilty.

In the Pelton case, for example, Martin met with David E. Faulkner, the case agent, and his partner, Dudley F. B. Hodgson, to review strategy before the agents confronted Pelton and interviewed him. When they saw him, the agents played a tape of Pelton calling the Soviet embassy in Washington.

"You have no case," Pelton said. "That was not me. Whoever it was would be crazy to say anything that would hang him."

Hodgson told him it was ridiculous for him to claim that it was not his voice on the tape, because it clearly was him.

"People have identified you as the voice, and people in the FBI lab have made comparisons indicating that your voice was on the calls," the agent said.

The statement was only partly true. Everyone who heard the tape of the call to the embassy and a tape of Pelton's voice from his wiretapped telephone calls thought the voices were the same. But using voiceprints, the FBI lab had been unable to match the voices. Apparently, the lab needed a longer sample, or samples using similar words, to establish a link scientifically. Even if the voiceprints had matched, a lawyer would have advised Pelton that voiceprints are not admissible as evidence in court. Moreover, his call was not evidence of a crime. But to Pelton, the recording seemed damning. He told the agents he would not say anything that would help "hang me."

As Martin had instructed, Faulkner told Pelton, "You have the right to have an attorney if you so desire." Then he placed an obstacle in the way. He said any attorney would need to have a top-secret security clearance to delve into the matters Pelton knew about at NSA. To Pelton, it seemed unlikely he could find such a lawyer. In fact, the law provides a procedure for clearing any lawyer chosen by a defendant. Then Faulkner gave Pelton another reason for not getting a lawyer.

"If anybody else is involved in these discussions," he said, "the agents here will lose control of the situation, and the options we have would be reduced." In fact, the agents had only one option: to obtain Pelton's confession. But Pelton was hoping against hope that the agents would somehow give him a way out, perhaps by enlisting him to penetrate the Soviets or helping to assess the damage he had done.

Eventually, Pelton admitted enough to incriminate himself. Asked how much money he received from the Soviets, Pelton said, "Thirty to thirty-five thousand, plus expenses." However, Pelton still had not told the agents exactly what classified information he had given the Soviets. Without that, a good defense lawyer might convince a jury that Pelton had only been leading on the Soviets. Faulkner suggested that Pelton tell the agents what information he had given the Soviets, since they already knew about it. In that way, he suggested, Pelton could still avoid giving out new details until he got the "guarantees" he wanted.

It was tortuous reasoning, but Pelton fell for it. If criminals were smart, they would not be criminals. The agents asked him about project Ivy Bells, which allowed NSA to tap into an undersea cable carrying Soviet military communications, and the location of another intercept inside the Soviet embassy in Washington. Asked why he had chosen to disclose these projects to the Soviets, Pelton said he thought they might already have known about them.

The agents placed handcuffs on Pelton, read him his rights, and took him first to the Baltimore Field Office and then to the Anne Arundel County Detention Center in Maryland. Despite his confession, Pelton claimed he was not guilty and had not been adequately apprised of his rights when he spoke with the FBI. But on June 5, 1986, a federal jury in Baltimore convicted Pelton of espionage. In the hope of getting a lighter sentence, Pelton briefed NSA officials on what he had told the Soviets. Saying he had done "inestimable damage" to U.S. security, U.S. District Court Judge Herbert F. Murray upheld the legality of Pelton's confession and sentenced him to life in prison.

In contrast to this case, the FBI did not inform Martin that agents had begun pursuing a highly unusual case in early 1982. The results would be disastrous.

16

SWINGING SPIES

From a defector, the FBI learned that Karl Koecher, a high-level translator at the CIA, was actually working for the Czech Intelligence Service, an arm of the KGB. Claiming themselves to be defectors, Karl and his wife, Hana, had come to the United States from Czechoslovakia in 1965. In fact, Karl secretly was an officer of the Czech Intelligence Service, assigned to become a mole in the U.S. government, preferably in the CIA. Hana acted as his courier, providing him with cash she obtained from the Czechs when she traveled as a diamond merchant. Like Rudolf Abel, Koecher was an illegal who operated without benefit of diplomatic cover. If arrested, he and his wife could be prosecuted.

The Czechs began training Karel Frantisek Köcher—his original name—to become a mole in 1962. While not formally part of intelligence terminology, "mole" is commonly used to describe an agent or spy who obtains a job with an opposing intelligence service to provide classified information on a continuing basis to his own intelligence service.

At a party in 1963, Koecher met Hana Pardamcova, a nineteen-year-old translator who was also a member of the Communist Party. Five feet two inches tall, Hana was gorgeous, warm, and outgoing. Three months later, they married.

After he entered the United States, Koecher attended Columbia University. In 1970, he obtained a Ph.D. in philosophy and a certificate from Columbia's Research Institute for Communist Affairs. One of his teachers was Zbigniew Brzezinski, later President Carter's national security adviser.

A brilliant Renaissance man, Koecher developed an elaborate legend or cover story. Pretending to be a rabid anticommunist, he claimed that Czechoslovakia Radio in Prague fired him because of his biting commentary about life under the Communists. He obtained excellent recommendations from professors and used them for his application to the CIA.

Before being hired, Koecher took a CIA polygraph test and failed. But when confronted with the evidence of deception, he invented a tale about a previous encounter with the FBI to explain why he had been nervous and showed signs of deception. The polygraph operator bought his story, marking him as having passed.

On February 5, 1973, Koecher became a CIA translator with a top-secret clearance. The first known mole in the CIA, Koecher translated written or tape-recorded reports from CIA assets. Because of Koecher's knowledge of science and engineering terms, the CIA gave him some of its most sensitive material to translate from Russian and Czech. Because his information was so important, Koecher reported directly to the KGB. For his efforts, Koecher won multiple decorations from the KGB and the Czech Intelligence Service.

Through his translation duties, Koecher was able to piece together the identity of Aleksandr D. Ogorodnik, a critically important CIA asset. Ogorodnik—code-named TRIGON—worked for the Soviet Ministry of Foreign Affairs in Moscow. He provided the CIA with microfilms of hundreds of classified Soviet documents, including reports from Soviet ambassadors. The information was so valuable that it was circulated to the White House.

In conducting surveillance of Ogorodnik in 1977, the KGB caught him photographing documents. He agreed to confess and asked his interrogators for pen and paper. "By the way, for some years, I have written with the same pen, a Mont Blanc pen," he said. "I think it's on top of my desk. If one of your people happens to go near my apartment in the next few days, I'd like to have it."

The KGB delivered the pen, which contained a poison pill carefully concealed by the CIA. Ogorodnik opened the pen and swallowed the pill. Within ten seconds, he was dead.

Aside from his translation duties, Koecher had an unusual way of obtaining classified information—attending sex parties. A red-headed man of slight build with a graying mustache, Koecher introduced his wife to mate-swapping. Hana liked it so well that she became a far more avid swinger than he was. Karl and Hana regularly attended sex parties and orgies in Washington and New York. They frequented Plato's Retreat and the Hellfire, two sex emporiums in New York. They also enjoyed Capitol Couples in the Exchange, a bar in Washington, and the Swinging Gate in Jessup, Maryland. Known as the Gate, it was a country home outfitted with wall-to-wall mattresses and equipment for engaging in acrobatic threesomes.

Karl and Hana had a wide circle of married friends with whom they swapped spouses. On the side, they both had affairs going.

Because of her extreme sexual proclivities, Hana quickly became a favorite on the orgy circuit. A sexy blonde with enormous blue eyes, Hana liked to accompany Karl to Virginia's In Place, an elite private club organized in 1972 by a suburban Virginia real estate man who was bored with his wife. For the club, the man rented a spacious home in Fairfax, Virginia, just minutes from Koecher's CIA office in Rosslyn, Virginia, across the Potomac River from Washington. The home had a large circular driveway and was framed by four tall white pillars. In those pre-AIDS days, the home was a rendezvous for weekend sex parties.

Beyond a prohibition on drugs, the only rule was that each participant bring a spouse or a date. More than three-fourths of the couples were married. When the couples arrived, they paid $20, which covered drinks and contributed to the maintenance of the house. Couples paired off at the bar in the living room. They engaged in sex on mattresses laid out on the floors in bedrooms upstairs or downstairs in the recreation room. An exception to the couples rule was made when two nubile, blonde high school girls who lived in the neighborhood showed up and were allowed to participate.

"They were wild," the organizer of the parties told me.

A favorite form of entertainment was the bunny hop. Men and

women would dance naked in a line and then fall on the floor, where they had group sex with anyone who landed nearby. A double bed in the recreation room was also used for group sex. Anyone who wanted to joined in.

Some of the partygoers preferred to take on many different partners throughout the evening. One woman decided to have sex with each of the twenty-one men at a party. She succeeded in making it with only nineteen. Another young woman kept a tally of how many men she had had sexual intercourse with at the parties: 426.

Hana was one of the most active partygoers. Described by one of her partners as "strikingly beautiful" and "incredibly orgasmic," Hana loved having sex with three or four men on the double bed. Although Karl participated, he often retreated to the living room and chatted.

"I remember him because he used a few Czech words, and I would tell his accent; my mother-in-law was part Czech," the organizer said. "We got talking, and he said he was Czech. He was sitting on the sofa while his wife was partying. She was a very attractive girl and a very active young lady. She was doing group things."

If both spies enjoyed swinging, they also found the orgies a good way to meet others who worked for the CIA or other sensitive Washington agencies. Because security rules at agencies like the CIA banned such activities, participants placed themselves in a compromising position in more ways than one. The Koechers took full advantage and picked up valuable information from other partygoers who were officials of the Defense Department and White House, as well as the CIA.

By early 1982, when the FBI finally learned from a defector about the Koechers and began conducting surveillance of them, they had moved to New York, where Koecher became a CIA contract employee. Once the FBI was on to him, the CIA moved him into less sensitive activities.

With little new to show for his spying efforts, the Koechers in June 1984 decided to return to Czechoslovakia. Their cover story was they were moving to Austria. The FBI, in conjunction with the CIA, decided to close in and arrest them. Since the FBI did not have enough evidence to support a prosecution, the bureau needed to elicit confessions. On November 15, 1984, Kenneth M. Geide, the FBI case agent, and nine other agents watched as Karl and Hana walked out of a bank building at 9 West Fifty-seventh Street. As other agents followed the Koechers in cars, Geide and two other agents followed the Koechers on foot a block or two away. On Forty-seventh Street, they saw them enter the Diamond Club Building, where Hana's office was. When Karl came out of the building alone, Geide and another FBI agent who worked out with Karl at the Ninety-second Street Young Men's Hebrew Association approached him.

"Hello, Karl. I'd like to introduce someone to you," the agent said, according to a transcript of the exchange later filed in court.

"Hello, Karl. I am Ken Geide, a special agent of the FBI," Geide said.

Geide referred to Karl's CIA employment and suggested they talk. Koecher was calm, as if being approached by the FBI happened every day.

"I think we should, all right," Koecher said.

They drove to the Barbizon Plaza Hotel at Fifty-eighth Street and Sixth Avenue and took the elevator to the twenty-sixth floor. They walked into Room 2640, one of a series of rooms the FBI had rented under a phony name.

The CIA's Jerry Brown was sitting on one of two overstuffed love seats. Having a CIA officer participate with the FBI in an interview of a suspect was ill-advised—an indication that the FBI and CIA had no idea what they were doing.

As Koecher sat on the other love seat and a video camera secretly recorded the interview, Geide began in a friendly, confiding tone. But what he had to say was clearly threatening.

"I think we should establish one thing," he said. "We know who you are and what you've done since you arrived in this country. Um, in other words, your association with the, as we would term it, the opposition, hostile intelligence services, and we don't really want to sit and discuss that. We, we just want to establish right away that we do know who you and who your wife are, and your activities on behalf of those folks over the years.

"With that established," Geide said, "what we want to do is talk about a proposition for you, and talk about your future—your future and your wife's future—and that future I think is going to depend on . what we accomplish today in our conversation with you."

"Yes, yes," Koecher said.

"We appreciate who you are, and your abilities, and we would like to look at this as where we will mutually help one another and, uh, hopefully, as they say, as we go on, we will be able to make certain proposals to you that I think you'll find very, very attractive," the agent said.

What he had in mind would cause no disruption to the Koechers' lives, Geide promised. "But, uh, on the contrary, and in your, you know how things can happen? Certainly we don't want anything like that to happen to you and Hana," Geide said.

Geide did not specify what could happen to them. But he said that it would not happen if Koecher helped them fill in some "blanks."

"Okay," Koecher said.

"And, I think you can look forward to a harmonious relationship, and we are not going to try to do anything which will harm you or Hana in any way or any of your relatives."

"I'll certainly go along," Koecher said, "certainly if you will."

"Well, we chose to do it this way. Certainly, there were a lot of other choices," Geide said.

"Because you know," Brown said, "if you leave, it could be a major thing and my God, the flaw. And you know something could happen, terrible could happen."

"Yes," Koecher said.

By now in this elliptical conversation, the agents had established that, in return for not harming Karl or his wife, the FBI would "turn" Koecher, making him a double agent. "I give you my absolute, guaranteed assurance right now," Brown said. "We can't run this that long—very short time, we will be through with it."

Brown promised Koecher that he could eventually go to Austria.

"It's a new beginning for you," Geide said.

"It's the way I also feel," Koecher said.

On that joyous note, Koecher began giving the agents a detailed confession. He said the Czechoslovak Intelligence Service recruited him in 1962 to become a mole in a sensitive U.S. government agency. During her trips overseas to buy diamonds, Hana often picked up money for Koecher from the Czech Intelligence Service. Over the years, Karl estimated, he had received $50,000 to $70,000 from the Czechs, in addition to a $20,000 bonus so he could buy his co-op.

The FBI had picked up Hana and was interviewing her in another room. Not as gullible as Karl, she demanded to see a lawyer. On the phone, and then later that evening over dinner, Karl and Hana talked with each other with the agents present. Calmly, Karl urged her to help the agents. But she was distraught and tried to tell him to shut up.

"I understand your shock," Koecher told her. "You're worried, and you don't want to get into trouble."

"Well, I think you are in trouble," she said. "I don't think you see it even."

"What you have to understand is that we're gonna work together for the future," Geide said.

Hana said that if she didn't end up in prison now, she would surely have to carry something for Karl again. "I delivered things," she said in tears. "That's all I can offer because I don't want to, to really be, I'm not a spy; I'm not by nature a spy. I don't ever want to be in my whole life."

Brown insisted that Hana would still be free to go to Austria in two weeks. Hana doubted that. "I'd rather be in prison. If I have to go, I will go," she said.

Based on Koecher's admissions, Geide drew up an eight-page confession, which Koecher corrected and signed. In the first four minutes of the interview, Koecher admitted enough to warrant his arrest. Yet it was not until six days later that he was finally given his rights by Special Agent James K. Murphy, a supervisor of polygraph examiners. At the time, Koecher signed a form stating that the agents had not promised him anything and that he had not been threatened—all patently untrue.

Still pretending the FBI would allow Koecher to become a double agent, the bureau allowed Karl and Hana to return to their apartment, number 12-B at 50 East Eighty-ninth Street, that night. The FBI still had them under surveillance and heard the Koechers have what would be their last swing in America with one of their favorite couples. The husband looked like Cary Grant, with elegant white hair and a tan. The

J. Edgar Hoover created the FBI. *FBI*

Stanley W. Finch was appointed chief examiner to head a Justice Department force of special agents in 1908. *FBI*

Director William J. Burns enmeshed the bureau in the Teapot Dome scandal. *FBI*

Clyde Tolson, associate FBI director, was Hoover's constant companion. *FBI*

The FBI distributed this photo to show that Hoover had a lighter side. *FBI*

Agents killed desperado John Dillinger as he left the Biograph Theater in Chicago on July 22, 1934. *AP/Wide World Photo*

Hoover made up the story that Louis "Lepke" Buchalter turned himself in to him. *AP/Wide World Photo*

Bureau agents and police tracked Clyde Barrow and Bonnie Parker—the infamous outlaws known as Bonnie and Clyde—to Louisiana, where police arrested them. *FBI*

When agents searched the apartment of KGB officer Rudolf Abel, *left,* they found cipher pads used for sending messages in code, a hollow shaving brush, and hollow pencils for concealing microfilm. *FBI*

Cartha D. "Deke" DeLoach, one of Hoover's closest aides, told Roy L. Elson, administrative assistant to Senator Carl T. Hayden, he had compromising photos of Elson, according to Elson. *AP/Wide World Photo*

During World War II, George John Dasch told the FBI he had been sent by the Nazis to commit sabotage. *AP/Wide World Photo*

Susan L. Rostenstiel, who married Schenley chief Lewis S. Rostenstiel in 1951, claimed she saw Hoover wearing a dress at the Plaza Hotel in New York.
AP/Wide World Photo

Bob Woodward paid a mysterious visit to former FBI official W. Mark Felt in Santa Rosa, California, in the early summer of 2000, lending support to the notion that Felt was Deep Throat.
Ronald Kessler

Clarence M. Kelley moved the bureau toward pursuing quality cases. *FBI*

Acting Director L. Patrick Gray disgraced the FBI by destroying Watergate evidence. *FBI*

wife had blond hair cropped short and skin from an Ivory Soap commercial.

The couple lived in New Paltz, New York. They told me they met the Koechers at a swinging party in New Jersey in 1981. Hana was sitting on a sofa, and the husband sat down beside her. After introducing himself, they went up to a bedroom and engaged in sex. After that, they swung at least every other month, alternating homes. In New Paltz, the couple and their eighteen-year-old daughter ran around nude.

On the night of their last swing, as was their practice, Karl had sex in his den with the other man's wife, while Hana had sex in the master bedroom with the other woman's husband. They rejoined their own spouses for the night.

The FBI wanted to arrest the Koechers the next day on their way to the airport. Because it was an espionage case, the FBI first had to obtain John Martin's authorization.

When he learned about the case, Martin was livid. First, the FBI had not told him about the matter until agents moved in. Second, the FBI and CIA had no clear idea of what they were trying to do with the Koechers.

"They didn't seem to know whether they wanted to turn him or obtain a confession so they could prosecute him." Martin said. "Still, I authorized the FBI to arrest the Koechers. I had no idea then how disastrously the FBI and CIA had bungled the case."

In a press release, the bureau said Koecher had worked for the CIA from 1973 to 1975. The FBI said nothing about the fact that Koecher had continued as a CIA contract employee until his arrest. Frequently, the bureau summarizes the case against suspects, proud to show how dangerous they are. In this instance, the FBI said Koecher had been recruited by the Czechoslovak Intelligence Service but gave no details about his activities.

The CIA wanted it that way. Disclosing that the agency had been fooled by a mole who was still a contract employee was simply too embarrassing. The story ran only 448 words on page 4 of the *Washington Post* and only 969 words on page 1 of the *New York Times*. In the next two months, the *Times* ran two longer front-page stories on Koecher.

The day of the arrest, the FBI played the videotape of the interrogation for Martin.

"My stomach turned. The tapes were devastating," Martin said. "Not only had Koecher been given promises that the FBI and CIA were not authorized to give, his rights and those of his wife had been violated. The FBI and CIA had pulled them into a hotel and started grilling them without giving them Miranda warnings. Moreover, in offering Koecher immunity, the FBI clearly had made a promise it knew it could not keep. Only I or people above me could authorize a grant of immunity."[142]

Beyond that, the agents ignored Hana's request to see a lawyer. "The law requires that as soon as the suspect asks for a lawyer, an interrogation is to cease until a lawyer is obtained. The FBI and CIA ignored Hana's request and continued the interrogation anyway," Martin said.

Still, Martin thought the case could be salvaged. Koecher had repeated many of his admissions even after Jim Murphy, the polygrapher, gave him his Miranda warnings. "We could use that portion of the confession to prosecute Koecher for espionage. While Hana did not make admissions after being given her rights, we could still charge her as a material witness," Martin said.

To avoid further litigation, Martin was able to arrange to include the Koechers in a prisoner exchange that included Soviet dissident Natan Sharansky. Martin had a firm policy against trading American traitors. Moreover, the Soviets did not particularly want such people. Once they lost their access to classified information, they were expendable. But Martin was perfectly willing to trade foreign intelligence officers if it meant the United States could free spies or dissidents who were considered important.

After Koecher pleaded guilty in a secret court proceeding in New York, the Koechers, with Martin there observing, were swapped on a snowy day in February 1986 over the Glienecker Bridge, which joined East Germany with West Berlin. It was the same bridge where the United States exchanged U-2 pilot Francis Gary Powers for Rudolf Abel more than twenty years earlier. Under the terms of an agreement, the Koechers were barred from ever entering the United States again. They had to surrender their fraudulently obtained U.S. citizenship.

During five days of interviews that began on April 29, 1987, in Prague, Karl Koecher told me that attending the orgies was useful. "Even knowing that somebody attends parties like that—maybe a GS-17 in the CIA—is interesting stuff," Koecher said. "Or you just pass it on to someone else [another intelligence officer], who takes over. That's the way it's done."

The group sex was "just the thing to do at that time," Hana Koecher told me. "All our friends somehow went to a little club or something. So we went there too, to see how things are."

Asked how he felt about Ogorodnik's death, Koecher said, "I'm deeply sorry about that. But the people who did him in were the CIA and he himself. They recruited him in such a clumsy manner."

17

MEGAHUT

Over the years, the FBI investigated its own agents when they were suspected of dealing with the Soviets, placing them under surveillance and following them to parks where they might have planned dead drops. Aleksei Kulak, a Soviet code-named Fedora, told the FBI that he had heard that an FBI agent in New York was working for the Soviets. But the FBI was never able to bring a case involving one of its own to completion.

That changed when the FBI began investigating Svetlana Ogorodnikov, a Russian émigré. Ogorodnikov made the mistake of visiting the Soviet consulate in San Francisco on a Saturday, calling attention to herself. Surveillance established that she had recruited Richard W. Miller, an FBI agent assigned to foreign counterintelligence work in San Francisco, to work for the KGB in August 1984. She would give him oral sex in the front seat of his Volkswagen. Further investigation established that Miller, like most spies, was greedy. Miller had given Ogorodnikov and her husband, Nikolai, both of whom worked for the KGB, a classified document outlining the types of intelligence information the United States was seeking. In return, Miller demanded $50,000 in gold and $15,000 in cash.

Miller barely made it through training at Quantico. His reports were badly written and often late. He repeatedly called other agents to ask the most basic questions. Weighing 250 pounds, Miller snacked on doughnuts and Twinkies. He car-pooled with an agent known for his neatness. The agent regularly got mad at Miller over his untidy habits. Once, the agent emerged from Miller's car with a half-eaten peanut butter sandwich stuck to his back.

The bureau still did not have enough for an arrest when it confronted Miller and asked him to take a polygraph test. While polygraphs get a bad rap because of inexperienced polygraphers, the FBI has some extremely capable polygraph operators. When polygraphers obtain confessions, they can make or break a case. Miller failed a polygraph test on whether he had given away classified documents. During a second test, Miller admitted giving a classified FBI foreign counterintelligence manual to Svetlana Ogorodnikov.

John Martin authorized Miller's arrest for espionage on October 3, 1984. In a public relations touch, the FBI insisted on firing Miller just before his arrest. That way, the news stories would report the arrest of a *former* FBI agent. Still, when the news broke, agents were devastated by the betrayal by one of their own. After three trials, Miller was convicted of espionage in 1991 and sentenced to twenty years in prison.

"How many other Richard Millers were operating without having been caught?" Martin asked. "We didn't know. Espionage is an unusual crime because there is no way to know its full extent. If you have a bank robbery, you know it. But if you uncover six espionage cases, you don't know if you have detected 2 percent of the spying activities, 20 percent, or 98. If you have an increase in espionage cases, you don't know if you are getting better at detecting espionage or the extent of spying is increasing. But hindsight made it clear that if you were sitting at the American desk at KGB headquarters in Moscow, you would be very happy."

■ ■ ■

Under Webster, the FBI began developing sophisticated techniques for combating spying. Instead of merely conducting surveillance of KGB officers assigned to the United States as diplomats, the FBI took what it likes to call a proactive approach, by operating double agents to eat up their time, learn what they were after, and eventually help expel them. In what became known as the foreign counterintelligence program, the FBI's Intelligence Division engaged in a secret and highly effective dance with the KGB and the GRU—Soviet military intelligence—watching, learning, and moving in when necessary to thwart a spy operation.

Because the largest contingents of KGB operatives were in Washington and New York, those were the main cities where spy operations took place. Under the nose of the press, the FBI kept secret the fact that many utility boxes contained video cameras for watching KGB operations. Some stereo equipment stores were operated by the FBI so undercover agents could befriend KGB officers. The guests at some parties given by neighbors of KGB officers were all undercover FBI agents. A nondescript office in Springfield, Virginia, was in fact headquarters for a highly effective joint FBI-CIA operation known as COURTSHIP that resulted in the recruitment of at least one KGB officer within the Soviet embassy in Washington. The FBI on its own recruited a second officer within the embassy, giving the bureau a grand view of the KGB's plans and operations.

Many of the cars driven by KGB officers in Washington were equipped with FBI bugs. Through sensors implanted in the cars, agents could track the location of KGB officers. An artificial intelligence program signaled when an officer had departed from his normal daily routine.

Through the bureau's Technical Division, agents broke into embassies to plant bugs and obtain documents. Although the Soviet embassy was never penetrated, agents entered the embassies of some Soviet bloc countries. To make sure they would not be surprised by embassy employees unexpectedly returning to their office, agents followed the employees to their homes, where they watched to make sure they did not return. Agents could remotely freeze the view on closed-circuit television so embassy guards watching for intruders would not see agents enter. Agents fed watchdogs tasty meatballs laced with tranquilizers.

In carrying out these schemes, the FBI had the help of a new law permitting electronic surveillance in foreign counterintelligence or counterterrorism cases. The Foreign Intelligence Surveillance Act of 1978 (FISA) established a court that hears requests for electronic intercepts in those cases.

A secret FBI facility coordinates the work of the FBI and NSA in installing bugs and intercepting conversations in the United States. Code-named MEGAHUT, it operates from a four-story brownstone in midtown Manhattan. In addition, MEGAHUT has several offices throughout the country, known in FBI parlance as offsites. Altogether, some hundred FBI agents are assigned to MEGAHUT. In a typical scenario, FBI agents might break into a foreign embassy in the United States so NSA can install listening devices.

James Murphy, who was assigned to MEGAHUT for twenty years, said he occasionally found wiretaps placed by the Israelis on the telephone lines of the diplomatic establishments of other Middle Eastern countries. Murphy would notify FBI headquarters, which told the State Department, which told the Israelis. The wiretaps would then be removed.

"The Israelis know no boundaries," he said. "If we were doing it, they were doing it."[143]

Occasionally, FBI wiretaps and bugs picked up crimes taking place. In a chilling episode, an FBI bug approved by the FISA court picked up the sounds of Zein Isa, a Palestinian American, murdering his sixteen-year-old daughter. For two years, the FBI had been listening to conversations in the tiny St. Louis apartment Zein shared with his wife, Maria. The bureau believed that Zein Isa was involved in terrorist activities.

Isa disapproved of the fact that his daughter Palestina had gotten a job at Wendy's and, without his permission, was seeing a young man. When Tina, as she was called, arrived home from work on the evening of November 6, 1989, her mother asked in Arabic, "Where were you, bitch?"

"Working!" Tina shot back, according to the FBI tape.

"We do not accept that you go to work," Isa interrupted.

"Why are you doing this to us?" her mother asked angrily.

"I am not doing anything to you," Tina said.

"You are a she-devil," her father hissed.

Isa then asked about Tina's boyfriend and accused her of engaging in "fornication." Her parents threatened to throw her out of the apartment. Tina challenged them to do it.

"Listen, my dear daughter," Isa said. "Do you know that this is the last day? Today you're going to die?"

"Huh?" Tina asked, bewildered.

"Do you know that you are going to die tonight?"

Realizing he was serious, Tina let out a long scream. There was a crash, and Tina's screams became muffled.

"Keep still, Tina!" her father yelled.

"Mother, please help me!" she cried.

Instead of helping her, her mother held her down as Isa began stabbing Tina in the chest with a seven-inch boning knife.

"No, please!" Tina cried.

"Shut up!" her mother said.

"No! No!" Tina shrieked.

"Die! Die quickly! Die quickly!" her father shouted, panting from his exertion.

Tina screamed one more time. By then, Isa had punctured her lungs. Only the sound of air being expelled could be heard.

"Quiet, little one!" her father said, stabbing her the sixth and last time.

"Die, my daughter! Die!"

Then there was silence.[144]

"We translated it the next day from Arabic," said Neil J. Gallagher, then chief of the FBI's Counterterrorism Section. "It [the investigation] wasn't so active that you had to have people listening live. We were always one day behind because of the limited number of agents who speak Arabic."

The agent who came to work the next day to translate the tape heard the tragedy played out. The tape even picked up Isa calling the police the night of the murder and claiming he had killed his daughter in self-defense.

There was never any question that the Justice Department would inform the police and local prosecutors about the recording. St. Louis police arrested the couple. Based on the tape, Isa and his wife were convicted of first-degree murder and sentenced to death by lethal injection. While he was on death row, Zein Isa and three others were indicted for allegedly plotting to kill thousands of Jews, blow up the Israeli embassy in Washington, and smuggle money to members of the Abu Nidal terrorist organization.

Contrary to the impression given by the transcript of Isa killing his daughter, Isa killed her because she was rebellious and knew too much about the group's activities. One of the other terrorists suggested he kill her to keep her from talking. Her father agreed, telling a relative, "This one should live under the ground."[145]

18

FREEZE!

Based on a tip from a defector, the FBI assigned agents to ask New York scientific and technical libraries to let them know about patrons who perused certain technical publications. The bureau was looking for real spies—KGB and GRU officers who may have been engaged in espionage and who consulted technical books as part of their work. But the FBI's effort, called the Library Awareness Program, was a hamhanded effort that betrayed insensitivity to the fact that libraries are symbols of Americans' First Amendment rights. The idea of government agents scrutinizing the reading material of library patrons was chilling.

In the end, the program produced very little useful information. Headquarters rejected the idea of extending the program to other cities, saying it had not produced enough to justify the effort. Aside from that lapse, Webster turned the FBI's counterintelligence program into a tool that was both effective and lawful. Spurned by many agents because of its tarnished reputation, the counterintelligence program became a big draw.

"People who are inclined to go into law enforcement are results-oriented," James H. Geer, who headed the division from 1985 to 1989, said. "Seeing these espionage cases going to trial, we moved into a situation where we had a waiting list of people who wanted to go into foreign counterintelligence."

The climax to the bureau's effort to perfect its counterintelligence program came in 1985, known as the Year of the Spy, when the FBI arrested eleven spies. They included John A. Walker Jr., a Navy warrant officer; Jonathan J. Pollard, the Israeli spy; Ronald Pelton, a former NSA employee; and Lawrence Wu-Tai Chin, a spy for the Chinese. All pleaded guilty or were convicted.[146]

Not included on that list was Edward Lee Howard, a former CIA officer who escaped FBI surveillance in 1985 and fled to the Soviet Union. An inexperienced FBI agent conducting the surveillance of Howard's home in Santa Fe, New Mexico, simply did not notice Howard leaving. The agent was suspended for forty-five days and then left the bureau. After the Cold War ended, Howard became an insurance agent in Moscow.

Because of the FBI's initial handling of the case, Walker—one of the most damaging spies in American history—almost did not make the list either. On November 17, 1984, six weeks after John Martin authorized the arrest of Richard Miller, Walker's former wife Barbara called the Boston Field Office of the FBI. Since 1968, when she inadvertently discovered his activities, Barbara Walker had known about her husband's spying. She had even accompanied him on two trips to northern Virginia to leave documents at dead drops. Scorned by her husband, she had often thought about turning him in. Finally, she took the step.

The FBI clerk who took her call referred it to an agent in the FBI's Hyannis office. He interviewed her and was unimpressed. She rambled on, downing one glass of vodka after another and slurring her words. Her story seemed dated. She had not lived with Walker for ten years. And she made no secret of her hatred of her former husband, who was living with a pretty blonde young enough to be his daughter. The FBI's greatest slipup was sending an agent with no experience in foreign counterintelligence. He failed to recognize that the details she cited were genuine signs of a Soviet spy operation.

The agent could have obtained more corroboration by interviewing Barbara's daughter, Laura Walker, who was aware of her father's activities and had urged her mother to turn him in. Instead, the agent wrote up the report and recommended that it not be pursued. As a result, the FBI almost missed catching Walker, just as the bureau had failed to detect him walking into the Soviet embassy at Sixteenth and

L streets NW in Washington when he began his spying activities in
1968.

Back then, to show the Soviets he was genuine, Walker had brought
with him a top-secret list of cryptographic key settings that would en-
able the Soviets to decode messages sent by the Navy's KL-47 cipher
machine over a period of thirty days. That let them read naval commands that would be given in time of war. Impressed, the Soviets gave
him $2,000. In return for more information, Walker asked for $1,000
a week. The Soviets agreed. After meeting for an hour, the Soviets bundled him between two Russians in the backseat of a car. They sped
away from the rear of the embassy. Walker would make his first drop
the following month, leaving top-secret documents in a locker at National Airport.

Three months after the Hyannis agent interviewed Walker's ex-wife,
an agent in Boston reviewed his report. Thinking it worth pursuing, the
agent sent a copy to FBI headquarters and to the FBI's Norfolk Field
Office, where Walker lived. Officials in both offices immediately recognized details of spy operations that Barbara Walker could not have
picked up from reading spy novels. The Norfolk agents ordered new
interviews with her and one with Laura Walker, who corroborated
many of her mother's allegations. After both women passed lie detector
tests, FBI counterintelligence officials were convinced the case was real.

Walker had retired from the Navy in 1976 and now, at age forty-
eight, ran his own private detective agency, Confidential Reports Inc.
in Virginia Beach. Because of his new occupation as detective, Walker
was likely to be on the lookout for surveillance. Above all, the agents
assigned to the Walker case—code-named WINDFLYER—did not
want to tip their hand.

The FBI obtained approval from the Foreign Intelligence Surveillance
Court to wiretap Walker's home phones at 8524 Old Ocean View Road
in Norfolk and his business phones at 405 South Parliament Drive in
Virginia Beach. After six weeks, the intercepts produced no hint of his
spying activities. But during the week of May 13, 1985, the agents heard
Walker chatting about a business trip planned for Sunday, May 19. To
some of his friends, he said he was going to Charlotte. To others, he
said he was going elsewhere. When his favorite aunt died that week in

Pennsylvania, Walker insisted he could not attend the funeral. His business trip could not be postponed, nor could his partner in the detective agency handle the assignment.

To the agents assigned to the case, it meant Walker might be planning a drop. On Saturday, they placed him under constant surveillance. The next day, they watched as Walker, wearing blue jeans, a dark blue pullover, and a black nylon windbreaker, got in his blue-and-silver 1985 Chevrolet Astro Van and began driving into driveways and dead ends. Clearly, he was dry-cleaning himself—spy jargon for shaking surveillance—and was about to go operational. Overhead, a single-engine FBI plane radioed scrambled reports to the command car. At 2 P.M., the plane radioed that Walker was driving north, not south toward Charlotte, along Interstate 95 toward Washington.

Twenty FBI cars followed him. Never looking directly at him, the agents would pass him, turn off the road, then come back and pass him again. In case they were observed during that time, agents changed disguises en route.

Because the FBI had decided that Walker probably would continue dealing with the Soviets in Washington, it had devised a special surveillance plan. Joseph Wolfinger, head of operations in Norfolk, called the Washington Field Office to activate the command center—a cluster of secure phones, television screens, radio transmitters, and blackboards on the tenth floor of the Washington Field Office, then overlooking the Anacostia River. The command center, in turn, notified another forty agents assigned to the two FBI squads targeting operations of the GRU, the Soviet military intelligence, which usually targets military personnel like Walker. Members of the FBI's Special Support Group also went into action. Known as Gs, they are lower-paid surveillance people used in counterintelligence cases. They might pose as joggers, derelicts, skaters, priests, or secretaries. Instead of using FBI cars, they employ anything from skateboards or bicycles-built-for-two to moving vans, bulldozers, and helicopters.

At 4 P.M., Walker crossed the Potomac River on Route 495 into the Maryland suburbs outside of Washington. To blend in, many of the agents changed their license plates from Virginia to Maryland tags. They changed into camouflage garb.

Walker began traversing the countryside in Potomac, Maryland, just off River Road, slowing down at certain intersections and peering at utility poles. Having received instructions from the Soviets on where to leave documents and pick up his cash, he was casing the locations first so he could find them easily later that night. Just in case he returned, the agents noted the locations.

The lush area has long steep hills and multimillion-dollar homes equipped with lighted tennis courts and swimming pools. Ponds dot the front yards, and golden retrievers romp near the swing sets. It is hunt country, and the residents groom their horses on the lawn.

The site was not only beautiful, it was perfect for the Soviets' purposes. Because it was so deserted, Walker could easily detect anyone following him. At 4:45 P.M., the agents lost him. To avoid being spotted, they had to stay two to three blocks behind him. The agents later learned that Walker had checked in at a Ramada Inn in nearby Rockville, registering as "Joe Johnson."

Behind the Safeway at a shopping center at River and Falls roads, the agents regrouped. There, more than fifty agents and Gs were wringing their hands until William P. O'Keefe and A. Jackson Lowe, the supervisors in charge of the two FBI squads in Washington that tracked Soviet GRU officers, came up with a plan. Figuring that Walker would return, the two ordered the agents to conduct picket surveillance—a fence of stationary surveillance at intersections leading to the area. At 7:48, their hunch proved right. Over the radio, the agents heard the voice of a female G exclaiming that she had spotted the target.

Walker was driving up River Road near the shopping center. By now, another FBI reconnaissance plane was flying overhead. Since Walker had turned on his headlights, the agent in the plane could easily locate him.

Walker began following a set of instructions his Soviet handlers had written. The instructions described an intricate dance that Walker would follow for the next four hours. While spies may communicate using the most modern equipment available, the preferred way is still through dead drops.

"Normally, you have physical evidence," said J. Stephen Ramey, a counterintelligence agent who worked the Walker case that night. "In a bank robbery, for example, the individual hands over a demand note. He has written it in longhand, and there are fingerprints on it. Sometimes they touch the countertops. You have a dye pack that explodes as they run down the street. You have surveillance cameras taking their photographs. Even though they may wear a mask, you can pick out an unusual feature or type of clothing." In an espionage case involving the Russians, the only physical evidence is usually documents that are already in Moscow, he said.

The instructions to Walker included a way of communicating by placing 7-Up cans in particular locations. If for any reason Walker could not leave his documents where he was supposed to leave them, or the Soviet could not leave his cash, the instructions included alternate sites. While the drop points were within a twenty-square-mile area, it would take two hours of driving to hit them all.

At 8:20, the agents noticed a 1983 blue Malibu with diplomatic plates. It was driven by a man accompanied by a woman and a child. Running the tag number through an FBI computer, the agents learned that the car belonged to Aleksey Gavrilovich Tkachenko, third secretary of the Soviet embassy and a KGB officer. Because Walker was so important, the KGB, rather than the less powerful GRU, had taken over running him. A few minutes later, the agents again spotted Tkachenko. Then, a mile and a half away at 8:30, Walker dropped the 7-Up can at the bottom of a utility pole on Quince Orchard Road at Dufief Mill Road, signaling that he was ready for the exchange of documents.

Over the scrambled radio, Lowe told the agents to make sure to preserve the can as evidence. They misinterpreted what he said and scooped up the 7-Up can immediately after Walker drove away. This was a mistake, since the can signaled that the coast was clear and Tkachenko could pick up the documents. If he had gone to the place where Walker had hidden the documents, and the FBI had left the documents in place, the agents could have taken the KGB officer into custody. Instead, the Soviet took off without retrieving any documents or leaving any cash for Walker.

Walker sped off toward Partnership Road and got out of his van. After he left, a member of one of the squads found a brown paper bag near a large tree. The bag was filled with what looked like trash—empty

Coke bottles and cereal boxes. But the bottles had been carefully rinsed out, and there was no food inside the discarded boxes. The garbage concealed another bag. Inside that bag, the agents found 129 classified documents and a note to Walker's handlers.

Agents rushed the documents to the command center at FBI headquarters. The documents were from the aircraft carrier USS *Nimitz* and were marked top secret. By letter code, a note to Walker's KGB handlers referred to others who were supplying him with documents now that he had left the military. Using a technique that employs lasers to detect fingerprints on paper, the lab found a print of Walker's son, Michael L. Walker, a sailor aboard the *Nimitz*.

Still not realizing anything was amiss, Walker drove to a forked tree where he was to get his cash at 10:30. Walker searched for his money but couldn't find it. He directed a flashlight at the nearby trees. Ramey, a powerfully built agent, was standing behind a small tree. He was sure Walker saw him. Ramey pointed his .357 Magnum at Walker as the spy shined the light directly on him. Somehow, Walker didn't see him and continued to search for the money.

Finally, at midnight, Walker gave up looking and headed back toward the Ramada Inn. He entered the hotel at 12:17 A.M. and went directly to his room on the seventh floor. By 3:30, Walker was presumably asleep. Special Agent William Wang posed as the hotel clerk and called him in his room. Wang apologized for waking him but said another guest had smashed into his van. Would he mind coming down to look at the damage and exchange insurance information?

Warily, Walker opened the door. He saw no one. He closed the door, walked to his window, and looked out. He couldn't see his van. Shoving a .38-caliber Smith & Wesson revolver in his belt, he opened the door and walked into the hallway. As he approached the elevators, Robert W. Hunter, the case agent from Norfolk, and James L. Kolouch, the case agent in Washington, accosted him, their guns drawn.

"FBI, freeze!" Kolouch said.

Walker drew his gun and pointed it at the agents, who were both wearing bulletproof vests. There was no way he could have gotten away. Agents had surrounded the hotel and blocked off the stairways and elevators. Others waited in a room near Walker's.

Walker hesitated a moment, then dropped the gun, along with a manila envelope. The envelope turned out to contain instructions from his Soviet handlers. Throwing Walker against a wall, the agents ripped off his toupee and searched him. Placing handcuffs on him, Hunter told him, "You are under arrest for violation of the espionage laws of the United States."

For eighteen years, Walker had been giving the Soviets information on future naval plans, ship and submarine locations, weapons data, naval tactics, covert military and counterintelligence operations, and emergency plans in the event of a nuclear war. In all, Walker received more than $1 million from the Soviets.

As he did in other cases where a family member was involved in spying, John Martin offered a reduced sentence for the relative if the principal pleaded guilty. As a result, Walker's son Michael got twenty-five years. John Walker and his brother Arthur, who was involved in giving John classified information, got life in prison.

The fact that the Navy later said the U.S. could have lost a war with the Soviets because of Walker's spying underscored the importance of uncovering and deterring espionage.

19

MORE ROAST BEEF

According to bureau legend, a New York FBI agent went to lunch at a deli around the corner from where the field office previously was located on Sixty-ninth Street at Third Avenue. The agent thought that the deli was an establishment that offered a discount or more food to FBI agents and police officers. He ordered a roast beef sandwich and watched as the counterman piled on the slices. The deli man slid the plate toward the agent. To the agent's chagrin, the sandwich looked no bigger than any other roast beef sandwich. Showing the deli man his credentials, the agent said, "FBI! More roast beef."

Not knowing anything about any special deals, the counterman looked at the agent, dumbfounded. The story soon spread to the FBI's fifty-six field offices, four hundred resident agencies, and twenty legal attaché offices overseas. Probably no story is more widely known within the bureau, and no story is so sure to send agents into peals of laughter. When they are dissatisfied with anything, agents say, "More roast beef!" When they tell their bosses they showed their credentials, they say, "I roast beefed him."

Kevin D. Flynn, the New York agent who is the subject of the story, says it was not a roast beef sandwich; it was a corned beef sandwich. It was not that he wanted more meat; it was that he wanted leaner meat. As for pulling his credentials, according to Flynn, an engaging man with a light brown mustache and a round head that is almost totally bald, "I . . . mentioned that the sandwich was very, very fatty. I said I would appreciate it if he would take the sandwich back and show the chef. I was very civil about it. I did not identify myself. As a matter of fact, being in New York, and just being myself, I am very sensitive to not identifying myself unless on official business."

True or not, the story is appealing because it goes to the heart of what it means to be an agent. FBI agents have awesome power. They are authorized to carry weapons and can shoot to kill. They can deprive a suspect of his freedom and send him to jail for life. They can eavesdrop on private phone conversations, videotape what goes on in bedrooms, subpoena witnesses to testify before a grand jury, open mailboxes and read mail, and obtain telephone toll records and other confidential documents, including income tax returns. By consulting their files, they can find out the most damaging personal information. By showing their credentials, they can bypass airport security, take their weapons on airplanes, get into movie theaters free, and park illegally without getting a ticket. But unless an agent is on bureau business, has proper authorization, and, in many cases, has a court order, he or she has no more power than any other citizen. Showing "creds," as they are called, to obtain more food at the local deli violates the most basic credo of the FBI.

"When you mow the lawn, you're still the FBI," James T. Reese would instruct new agents at Quantico. Agents may be asked by neighbors to intervene in situations they should avoid. "You should tell them to call the police," Reese told them. "What you do is give them a logical explanation for why we are not Batman."

While most agents understand that, since the Hoover days, FBI discipline had broken down. Webster tended to look for extenuating circumstances when deciding whether an agent should be fired. Considering how much trust the public places in agents, it was alarming that falsifying reports of interviews, obtaining information from bureau files for friends, and lying during administrative inquiries were not by themselves firing offenses. An incompetent like Richard Miller should have been fired long before he began spying.

"Webster tried to differentiate on each case and look at mitigating factors," said Buck Revell, the former associate deputy director under

Webster. "There are certain standards you shouldn't do that with, and that includes integrity. There should be a bright line that you simply don't cross. You don't make false statements. You do not lie. You do not give false testimony. If you do, you will not be employed."

Over time, the more lenient approach began to have an effect.

■　■　■

At 5:30 P.M. on April 16, 1980, janitor Earl Thornton opened the door to the Federal Credit Union on the eighth floor of the new FBI headquarters. Thornton turned on the lights. He was about to start vacuuming when he saw behind the counter a stocky man with brown hair in front of an open safe. After a pause, the man behind the counter jumped up.

"FBI! Freeze!" he said.

The janitor quickly recognized the intruder as H. Edward Tickel Jr., the FBI's top break-in artist. Tickel could pick almost any lock, crack any safe, and enter any home or embassy without leaving a trace. Because of his specialty, some of the bureau's most precious secrets were entrusted to him, including the fact that the FBI had bugged certain Soviet bloc embassies as well as the homes of leading Mafia figures. After Webster became FBI director, as a security precaution, Tickel changed the locks at his home in Bethesda, Maryland.

The son of a former FBI agent, Tickel was widely admired within the bureau and had many bureau friends, including James W. Greenleaf, who was then assistant director over the laboratory and later became associate deputy director of the FBI. Tickel gave lavish parties and had a collection of Porsches and horses at his house on a five-acre lot in Virginia. He owned a $10,000 boat as well.

"He was so highly regarded and so highly respected," Greenleaf said. "He was living a little above his means, but we thought it was from royalties from inventing a lock."

Tickel told Thornton he had been called to the credit union, which had $260,000 in cash in the safe, because of a report the door was unlocked. He placed Thornton under arrest. But Tickel's story unraveled when he could not identify who had called him to the credit union, and Thornton said the door was locked.

"I polygraphed him [Tickel], and he failed," Paul Minor, the agent who conducted the test, said. "There were no admissions. Except when he left [the polygraph room], he said, 'From the beginning, I knew this might come down to a contest between experts. I respect you very much.'"

An investigation determined that, aside from his activities in the credit union, Tickel had been selling stolen rings and loose diamonds. He also was involved in selling stolen cars and stealing two-way FBI radios for friends.

Tickel was acquitted in federal court in Washington of breaking into the credit union. However, he pleaded guilty to having taken the radios. After a nine-day trial, Tickel also was convicted in Alexandria, Virginia, of charges connected with jewelry theft—interstate transportation of stolen goods, making false statements, obstruction of justice, and tax evasion. For these charges, he received a prison term of eight years. In addition, in Loudoun County in Virginia, he was convicted of receiving $120,000 in stolen cars and other items.[147]

At the end of the proceedings, Tickel was charged in Prince George's County with having sex with a daughter of one of his many lawyers. The daughter, who was twenty at the time, had a learning disability and epilepsy. Tickel pleaded guilty to a second-degree sex offense—having sex with force or the threat of force. His twenty-year sentence for that crime ran concurrently with federal sentences he was already serving.

■ ■ ■

If the Tickel case was bizarre, it was nothing compared with the case of Frank and Suzanne Monserrate, married FBI agents who were held up at gunpoint after leaving the Playhouse in Perrine, a suburb south of Miami.[148] Paul Miller, the media representative in the Miami Field Office, learned that there was a problem when the office called him just after two o'clock on Sunday morning, January 4, 1987.

"They said there had been a shooting of one of our agents, Sue Monserrate, whom I knew," Miller said.

To Miller, the Playhouse sounded like a dinner theater. He had no idea it was a sex club. Miller turned on his siren and flashing blue light and raced to the scene at 9551 SW 168th Street. National network reporters, not just local television stations, had already arrived. Miller wondered why the networks would send reporters to cover a shooting of an off-duty FBI agent in Miami.

From police on the scene, he picked up the basic facts: The Monserrates had just left the club at 2:05 A.M. when Chester Williams confronted them and demanded their money. Williams, who had an extensive criminal record, began ripping the gold chains off Sue Monserrate's neck. Frank Monserrate did not have his gun on him, but he knew his wife had hers in her purse. When Williams demanded money, Suzanne Monserrate reached into her purse to get her wallet. At that point, Frank Monserrate grabbed his wife's .38-caliber revolver and shot Williams several times, killing him. Meanwhile, Williams had shot and wounded Sue Monserrate in the back.

"I saw Bill Johnson, the media person for the police department," Miller said. "I asked, 'How is she doing?' He said, 'I can tell you don't know what this is about. Do you know what this Playhouse is? It's a swingers' club.' "

Like other agents who knew Suzanne Monserrate, Miller was shocked. Pretty and blonde, Monserrate was a respected agent who had a fresh Midwestern look to her. She was the principal relief supervisor on a squad that handled background investigations and coordinated the work of three of Miami's resident agencies or satellite offices. Frank Monserrate worked on a terrorism squad. Both agents had received performance appraisals of "superior." The only rating higher is "exceptional."

"She acted very professionally," Miller said. "I always thought she was very prim and proper. The last thing in my mind was that she might be involved in swinging."

Standard in any shooting, the bureau's inspectors began an investigation. At first, the couple lied about their activities, but their stories fell apart. Eventually, Frank "disclosed that he and his wife did, in fact, fully participate in sexual activities at [the club], to include swapping spouses," according to the report by the FBI's Office of Professional Responsibility. The swapping was both with the other couple who had been interviewed the night before and with "several other couples whose identities he does not know and whose names he could not now recall."

After several interviews, Suzanne Monserrate admitted for the first time that she and Frank "engaged in sexual intercourse with other people" at the club during their two years of membership. Retracting information she had given previously, she said that she "also participated in oral sex and engaged in sexual activity with other females at the club."

In July 1987, the FBI fired both Monserrates. What it came down to was that FBI agents simply don't go to sex clubs. The Monserrates might have received only suspensions, had they not lied about their activities. Moreover, Suzanne Monserrate had committed a sin almost as bad as going to a sex club—checking her handgun and FBI credentials with a club employee. Clearly, it would be difficult to have sex while wearing a gun and a badge, but FBI agents are never supposed to relinquish them.

Within the bureau, it is an article of faith that Hoover—who never wanted female FBI agents in the first place—would return from the dead to settle scores over the direction the bureau had taken. If there were ever a reason for his return, this case was it.

20

PROFILING

When Howard D. Teten began teaching police officers who attended the FBI National Academy the rudiments of what became known as criminal profiling, Teten and his supervisors were afraid that Hoover would veto the innovative idea, so they never told him what they were doing.

Teten began developing his ideas on profiling as an evidence officer in the San Leandro, California, police department near Oakland. At the same time Teten was examining murder scenes, he was finishing a bachelor's degree in criminology at the University of California at Berkeley. There he was heavily influenced by such world-famous criminalists as Douglas Kelly, Paul Kirk, and O. W. Wilson.

Teten began to see a correlation between the crime scene and the person who committed the crime. Whatever they do, criminals and noncriminals act in particular ways. Some writers use computers, others pen and paper. Some write in the morning, some at night. Each writer has a distinct style, with variations in grammar, sentence structure, and voice.

In the same way, criminals carry out their crimes in their own characteristic ways. What they do, rather than what they say, betrays who they are. By reading those signs, profilers can often determine from the crime scene the kind of person who committed the crime and the fantasies that propelled him—in effect, the criminal's signature.

In some respects, profiling is simply good detective work. Profilers look at every aspect of the crime, including interviews, photographs, investigative reports, autopsy reports, and laboratory reports. What sets profiling apart from good police work is that the conclusions are based on the patterns that emerge by comparing crime scenes in thousands of similar cases with the characteristics of the actual perpetrators apprehended in those cases.

To the uninitiated, a profile can seem so uncannily accurate as to be clairvoyant. When police found the mutilated torsos of two teenagers floating in a river, they identified them as a boy and girl who were missing. The profile the FBI drew up said the killer was a male in his forties who knew the children. He probably led a macho lifestyle, wore western boots, often hunted and fished, and drove a four-wheel vehicle. He was self-employed, divorced several times, and had a minor criminal record.

With the profile, the police focused on the children's stepfather, who fit the description perfectly but had not previously been a suspect. They were able to develop enough additional information from witnesses to convict him of murder the following year.

The FBI had found that a person who is careful enough to dispose of a body in a river is usually more sophisticated and often older. If the body is dumped in a remote area, the killer is probably an outdoors person with a knowledge of the area. When the slashes on the victim's body are vicious and directed at the sex organs, the assailant usually knows the person. If there is no sign of forced entry and the assailant stayed around at the crime scene to have a snack after killing the victim, he probably lived in the neighborhood and knew the victim. In contrast, killers who don't feel comfortable in an apartment leave immediately.

Thus, based on a few elementary facts from the crime scene, the FBI can draw a profile of the killer as an older man who likes the outdoors, is familiar with the area where the body was left, knows the victim, and lived in the neighborhood. In many cases, armed with the profile, police can focus on one or two suspects and solve the crime.

Ironically, it was Sir Arthur Conan Doyle, British author of the Sherlock Holmes detective mysteries, who came up with some of the techniques profilers use long before Teten and his FBI colleagues perfected them.

Now known as the father of profiling, Teten is a beefy six-footer. A former Marine, he has a Marine Corps tattoo on his right arm—a skull and crossbones over the words "U.S. embassy." Even though Teten began what has turned out to be the sexiest technique in the FBI's arsenal of crime-solving tricks, he has always avoided publicity. With the exception of interviews with me, the soft-spoken former agent has never talked with the press about profiling.

Teten joined the FBI in 1962 and began teaching police management at the National Academy. In 1969, he suggested a course in what he called applied criminology. It focused more on crime scenes than did the traditional criminology course.

Teten taught the new course by asking police to bring him their unsolved homicides. "Law enforcement officers have psychological baggage," said Roger Depue, who began working with Teten in 1973 and later headed the profiling unit at the FBI Academy. A brilliant agent with a doctoral degree in counseling and development, Depue is boyish looking, with almost a mischievous smile. Depue with a baseball cap would look like he belonged in the Little League. "If you've ever worked a case, a kidnapping for instance, and you've done everything you could possibly do, and you sleep at your desk, and you try as hard as you can with everything you possibly know, and the child is found killed anyway, you carry that around. It bothers you. I've known law enforcement officers who are still working a case ten years after retiring," he said.

As officers described the cases in class, other officers recalled similar cases they had worked on. They brainstormed, analyzing the crimes' similarities and the strategies that had worked best in solving them. Before long, officers were toting to class briefcases crammed with records of their unsolved cases.

By now, Teten had associated some crime scene patterns with particular mental disorders. One such disorder was referred to at the time as simple schizophrenia. Now called undifferentiated schizophrenia, it usually manifests itself at puberty. "It results in an individual becoming more and more of a loner, distancing himself from the family," Teten said. "The simple schizophrenic never went out of his way to do something. But if things were put in his way, particularly sexually oriented potentials, like a woman who was pretty and might flirt with him, he seemed to retreat from reality because of a fear of this type of contact. He would act defensively. His method of defensive action was to kill."

Most schizophrenics are harmless. But when they do kill, they do it in a particular way.

"The simple schizophrenic will always kill first, and then, because he is so curious, he's going to look it over," Teten said. "It's almost as if the sexual organs are magic. The way he does it depends on his age. If he is younger, he will touch, but as he gets older, he will somehow try to remove them or change them to make a woman a man. He will place a stick in the vagina. He might cut off the breasts, something like that. In spite of his actions, he is not an ogre looking for people to kill. He doesn't do that. He is defending himself against what he believes to be a threat."

Teten found that because killers' behavior changed with age, he could estimate their ages based on the way they had killed. A younger person will "take part of the clothes off, expose the breasts and maybe feel them, examine the vagina. Often you can see that they have blood on their hands, and you can see the marks of the blood. They don't damage anything. They remove the danger, so to speak, but they are fascinated by it." On the other hand, to an older person, the danger appears greater. "They try to remove the evidence and change the sex," Teten said.

In contrast to the simple schizophrenic, a psychopath is outgoing and articulate. "A psychopath will actually kill someone and then sit where the police drink coffee and listen," Teten said. "He gets a great thrill from hearing the police discussing how this crime happened. This gives him a sense of superiority, that he knows something they don't know, and they'll never figure it out. If they stop investigating, he may commit another crime to get the police going. He may even write them a taunting letter."

Psychopaths often go back to the crime scene or to the cemetery, Teten said. "So will some schizophrenics for different reasons. . . . A simple schizophrenic may kill a woman, but under no circumstances will he ever rape her until after she is dead. A psychopath would probably never rape one after she is dead. A schizophrenic would never torture a woman. He would just never do that. A psychopath, on the other hand, might enjoy torturing his victim. He would take pliers and squeeze the nipples of a woman before she is dead. This power over her is his sexual stimulant."

By 1972, Teten had learned that Dr. James A. Brussel, a New York psychiatrist, was following the same train of thought. Brussel, who had written *Case Book of a Crime Psychiatrist*, had served as a consultant to local police on several serial killings, including the 1956 case of the Mad Bomber in New York. In that case, Brussel said the bomber was an Eastern immigrant in his forties who lived with his mother. He even said he usually wore a neatly buttoned double-breasted suit. When arrested, the bomber, George Metesky, was wearing a double-breasted suit and fit the profile in most other respects.

Teten asked Dr. Brussel to tutor him and inquired about his fees.

"You can't afford it," Brussel said. "But I'm a patriot, and I cannot reduce my rates. So I'll have to do it for free."

Patrick J. Mullaney, a New York agent with a degree in psychology, had become interested in Teten's work. Teten helped to get him transferred to the FBI Academy so they could both teach and conduct research. If some of the profiles were wrong, as they inevitably were, Teten and Mullaney were afraid Hoover or the loyalists in control after his death would find out and stop the profiling program.

"When we first started, we were in the period when the bureau didn't like to be 'embarrassed' was the word," Mullaney said. "It was a whole different era. My personal belief is if you make a mistake or don't have the answers, you show more strength by admitting it than if you don't have the answers and are unwilling to admit it," Mullaney said.

As word spread that the profiles had actually solved some of law enforcement's most intractable cases, police graduates of the FBI National Academy would call in with cases similar to ones they had studied. "So we got heavily into the consultation business. It was on a time-available basis. The FBI was not involved very much at this time. By and large the FBI was the last to recognize we had a contribution to make," Depue said.

By 1976 or 1977, they still had more questions than answers: How does the criminal gain control of his victim? How does he manipulate the victim? How does he maintain control? How does he select his victim in the first place?

The agents found nothing in the academic literature. By and large, academics studied crime from afar. They generally focused on theories and likely would not think of asking criminals how they did their crimes. So the FBI's Behavioral Science Unit, under the direction of Depue, began research projects on certain types of crimes. They began with assassination. In conducting the research, John E. Douglas and Robert K. Ressler interviewed assassins in prison, including Sirhan Sirhan, Sarah Jane Moore, and Lynette "Squeaky" Fromme. Robert R. "Roy" Hazelwood, another agent in the unit, developed a protocol with questions covering fifty-seven pages. The agents found assassins to be generally unstable individuals seeking attention. They often kept diaries to underscore their importance. The agents also learned how assassins go about planning their crimes.

The agents went on to conduct research into serial killers and serial rapists. These assailants enjoyed sitting down with professionals who had researched their crimes. It made them feel important and gave them a chance to relive what they had done.

At one point, Bob Ressler was interviewing Edmund E. Kemper III, who had killed his mother, grandparents, and six other people and was serving multiple life sentences in California. Hannibal Lecter, the serial killer played by Anthony Hopkins in *The Silence of the Lambs*, was a composite of serial killers like Kemper, who removed people's heads and saved them as trophies; Edward Gein, who decorated his home with human skin; and Richard Trent Chase, who ate the organs of his victims.

When he was finished talking with Kemper in his cell just off death row, Ressler rang a buzzer to summon a guard to let him out. When the guard didn't come, the 295-pound prisoner told Ressler to "relax," because the guards were changing shifts and delivering meals.

"If I went ape-shit in here, you'd be in a lot of trouble, wouldn't you?" Kemper asked menacingly. "I could screw your head off and place it on the table to greet the guard."

Ressler was able to cool Kemper off by suggesting that he might have a concealed weapon. After that, agents interviewed inmates only in pairs. And contrary to the impression created by Jodie Foster's role in *The Silence of the Lambs*, the FBI would never send a trainee to interview anyone.

A clear pattern emerged from the interviews. Most of the perpetrators lived a fantasy life that included enacting the types of crimes they had committed. The crime allowed them to realize their fantasies. Now that the agents knew what was inside the killers' heads, they could better match what they saw at the crime scene with the way the crimes were carried out. They learned when the perpetrators cased the area before choosing a victim. What did they look for in a rape victim? Could a victim have said anything that would have prevented the rape? Did they keep trophies to remind them of their victims? If so, what were they? Did they tell anyone about their crimes or contact the victim after the crime?

Depue made profiling part of the FBI's operations, assigning agents to do nothing but profiles to help both the police and the FBI solve crimes. The agents worked in cramped basement offices at the FBI Academy at Quantico.

When I wrote the first national story on the subject in the February 20, 1984, *Washington Post*, the term "profiling" had no law enforcement connotation. It has since taken on a sinister meaning, referring to singling out suspects solely because of their race. That is neither good profiling nor good law enforcement.

Many times, the agents' profiles conflicted with the leads police had received or what appeared to be common sense. For example, the profilers said a man who had killed a series of black children in Atlanta was himself black. Everyone had assumed that since the victims were all black, the killer must be a white man who hated blacks. In fact, John Douglas concluded, "There was no way a white person could go in these areas and not be spotted." In addition, as a rule, serial killers turn on people of their own race. The killer turned out to be Wayne B. Williams, who is black and is now serving two consecutive life terms.

From interviews with serial killers, the agents learned that some killers carefully read the newspapers for references to their crimes. The profilers would suggest planting stories in local papers pointing out that the anniversary of an unsolved crime was coming up. The stories might also mention where the victim was buried. The story would trigger the killer's fantasy, and he might decide to visit his victim's grave around the anniversary of the crime. In videotaping the site of the grave, police have actually heard assailants confessing. Sometimes, killers have enumerated details of the crime that no one else knew. They will even say things like, "You bitch! The reason you're here is . . . ."

Police who have ignored the profilers' advice sometimes have done so to their sorrow. Police from an Illinois town staked out a cemetery all day, hoping an assailant would show up. Because the weather was nasty, they finally gave up. They left their video cameras in place, rigged to start when they sensed motion. Sure enough, the killer showed up. But the police were not there to identify him. They have a videotape of a man, but they have no idea who he is.

■ ■ ■

The profilers divided killers into two broad categories: organized and disorganized. Each type has a different kind of fantasy. Each leaves his distinctive characteristics at the crime scene. And each has a set of personal characteristics that can help identify him. Although profiling can be used to help solve any crime, it is usually used for the most vicious and emotionally charged crimes—murder and rape. The broad classifications of organized and disorganized perpetrators can apply to both murderers and rapists, but they are especially useful when trying to identify serial killers.

"The disorganized killer is the least sophisticated," Depue said. "At the crime scene, agents see signs of rage and poor planning because he commits the crime spontaneously. He says nothing or very little to the victim. Suddenly, he engages in violence. The weapon is a weapon of opportunity. For example, the killer may use a rock to beat a victim. He will leave the weapon at the crime scene. The scene has a lot of evidence, including blood, fibers, and hair. The body is found where the murder took place. No effort is made to conceal where it is."

The disorganized killer generally has below-average intelligence and is socially inadequate. "He prefers unskilled work and is sexually incompetent," Depue said. "He tends to be a younger sibling in his family. His father's work was unstable, and he often received harsh discipline as a child. He lives alone. Before the crime, he appears anxious. He usually does not use alcohol before committing the crime. He has minimal interest in news of the crime. After the crime, his behavior changes significantly. He may go on a drinking or drug binge or become highly religious."

The vast majority of organized killers are legally sane. They know that what they're doing is wrong and illegal, and they are capable of controlling their behavior—the two tests of legal sanity. On the other hand, disorganized killers often are legally insane. The more mentally disturbed the person is, the more disorganized and bizarre the crime scene is. Such a killer might kill the victim and then have sex with her.

In California, Richard Trent Chase knocked on the door of his victims, shot and killed them, then slit open their body cavities, exposing their organs. Sometimes, he partially removed the victims' intestines. In almost every case, police found a ring of blood on the floor near the bodies, as if a cup dripping with blood had been placed there.

"We determined that this was a vampire killing, carried out by a person who opened his victim's body so he could scoop out a cup of blood, then drink the blood," Depue said. "The killer was so disorganized that he did not care how much evidence he left. Instead of fleeing immediately to avoid being caught, he stayed around to sip his victim's blood."

In contrast, the organized killer's fantasy is more thought out. Planning the crime becomes part of the fantasy. He may even pack a murder kit, including ligatures, tape, binoculars, gloves, a different set of clothing, and weapons. Often, he abducts the victim in one place, kills him or her in another, and disposes of the body in a third. He hides the body. He engages in controlled conversation with the victim and makes demands of the victim.

Edmund E. Kemper III, John Wayne Gacy Jr., David "Son of Sam" Berkowitz, Ted Bundy, and Henry Lee Lucas were all organized serial killers. The organized killer is the typical serial killer. He has average to above-average intelligence. He prefers skilled work and is sexually competent. His father had stable work, but he experienced inconsistent childhood discipline. He is usually an older sibling.

"The organized killer enjoys the predatory aspect of killing—hunting, manipulating, and gaining control of the victim," Depue told me. "He may select a certain kind of weapon, and he learns from experience. He often drinks before committing the crime and possesses social skills. He usually lives with someone. His car is in good condition. He follows the crime in the news media. After the crime, he may change jobs or leave town. He interacts with victims. Because he is so skilled, it is difficult to catch him. And when he is caught, everyone says, 'I can't believe he did it.' "

Gacy, for example, volunteered to help children in hospitals. He would troll the streets of Chicago, looking for young male hustlers and runaways. He would invite his victim home for a drink and wind up strangling him, burying him in a crawl space under his house.

An organized killer has a fantasy that drives him. "For example, Edmund Kemper told us he needed to have particular experiences with people. In order to do that, he had to 'evict them from their bodies.' In other words, he had to kill them," Depue said.

Many killers revisit the scene just to rekindle their fantasy. When he decided that killing a particular woman was too risky, David Berkowitz would return to the scene of a previous crime and reenact the murder, aiming his gun just as he had aimed it when he killed his victim. Jeffrey L. Dahmer kept photographs of his dismembered victims.

What unites organized and disorganized serial killers is the sexual aspect of their acts. That does not necessarily mean that serial killers engage in sex with their victims. Instead, whether because of genetic defects or deviant experiences in their childhoods, serial killers derive sexual satisfaction from killing or from the events leading up to death. The sight of his victims' spilled blood turned on Jack the Ripper, who stalked prostitutes in the East End slums of London beginning in 1888. He usually cut out the uteruses of his victims, increasing his pleasure.

Vincenz Verzeni, who murdered and sucked out the blood of several young women in the late 1860s, told an interviewer that choking his victims caused him to have orgasms. Whether his victim was young or old, beautiful or plain, made no difference. Verzeni also enjoyed cutting out the intestines of his victims and keeping them in his room.

Most perpetrators engage in ritualistic behavior that never changes. For example, after entering a home, a rapist might confront the victim in a particular way, while she is sleeping. He may stand over her and watch her as she sleeps, enjoying the sense of control he feels. He derives pleasure from the victim's feeling of helplessness when she wakes up and sees him standing there, perhaps nude. As he improves his methods and becomes more organized, his ritual remains the same because he commits the crime in order to enjoy the ritual.

Some offenders like Dahmer have a mixture of traits. Dahmer confessed to murdering seventeen young men and cutting them up. In some cases, he cannibalized them after having sex with their dead bodies. While most of his methods were disorganized, Dahmer cleverly used acid to dispose of some of the bodies. He tortured victims by drilling holes in their skulls and pouring acid into their brains. Just before he was caught, Dahmer became more sloppy and disorganized.

Just as they had with serial murderers, the profilers went about interviewing rapists and matching what they revealed about their crimes with evidence found at the crime scene. Unfortunately, they found that different types of rapists respond in opposite ways to a woman's efforts to dissuade them from going ahead with their plans.

The profilers called the most common rapist the power reassurance or inadequate rapist. He tries to assure himself of his own masculinity and to prove himself to the opposite sex. His fantasy is that his victim is actually attracted to him and even romantically involved with him. Since he is an inadequate personality, it is possible to elicit sympathy from him. If a woman says she was an abused child or her mother is dying of cancer, he may leave her alone.

"A woman could refuse to perform a sex act with the inadequate rapist, and it would probably work," Depue said. "For example, when asked to perform oral sex, she might say, 'I can't do that.' We've had cases where the rapist then withdrew his demand, although he might have requested some other kind of sex. On the other hand, the woman-hater rapist reacts in the opposite way." This rapist hates women and wants to hurt, dominate, and control them. His fantasy is that he is getting even with women for perceived wrongs.

"Faced with refusal to perform oral sex, the woman-hater rapist will crave it even more because it degrades the victim more," Depue said. "Performing sex with an unwilling victim is exactly what he wants—to hurt the opposite sex."

If the victim tries to ingratiate herself with this kind of rapist or to manipulate him, he becomes even more angry. To him, this kind of behavior means the woman is exactly what he suspected all along, a sniveling female whom he has every right to exploit.

"When a woman is being victimized, it's not the time for trial and error," Depue said. "Once a rapist gains control, a woman can only use her intuition to determine what approach might work best. The best thing is to get away immediately, before the rapist gains full control."

■　■　■

Besides profiling, the agents began working on a number of other techniques for helping FBI agents solve crimes, such as how to confront suspects during interviews and how to evaluate their language. Based on an evaluation of the suspect, the profilers tell agents whether they should interview a suspect in the morning or at night, and whether to use a hard or a soft approach.

"If someone says, 'My wife and I and our children went out shopping, and the kids got a little bit unruly'—in other words, we went from 'our kids' to 'the kids'—a suspect is unconsciously distancing himself from the kids," Teten said. "You would listen for that where there was no logical reason for distancing, perhaps suggesting that the father killed his own children."

The same kinds of observations led profilers to conclude that when a right-handed person looks to his left when asked a question, it may mean he is genuinely trying to remember the answer and attempting to tell the truth. If such a person looks to his right, he may be trying to create information—in other words, to lie. Conversely, left-handed people usually look to the left when they are lying.

"If we are talking about memory, you shouldn't be creating," Teten said.

21

QUANTICO

Under Webster, competition to join the FBI became keen. To become FBI agents, candidates had to be U.S. citizens between the ages of twenty-three and thirty-seven. They had to hold a degree from a four-year college and pass a background check for a top-secret security clearance. In later years, a polygraph test was added to the requirements.

Instead of focusing primarily on recruiting lawyers and accountants, under Webster the bureau began seeking applicants who had work experience ranging from banking and commercial flying to art gallery sales. The average age of new agents was roughly twenty-nine. Close to 15 percent had law degrees and 15 percent had accounting degrees, proportions that roughly apply to existing agents as well. Only three hundred to five hundred agents were accepted out of the five thousand to eleven thousand who took the applicant test each year.

Before the new FBI Academy opened in Quantico, Virginia, on May 8, 1972, the FBI trained new agents in a handful of classrooms on the sixth floor of the Old Post Office Building in Washington and in a classroom and gym at the Justice Department. Trainees spent three weeks on the U.S. Marine Corps Base learning to fire weapons and make arrests.

The FBI Academy is off Interstate Route 95 some forty miles south of Washington. It is reached by a long, wooded, two-lane road through Quantico Marine Base, from which its 385 acres are carved. Signs like

"Danger—Government field reservation—Firing in progress" pepper the roadside.

The complex of twenty-one tan brick buildings that comprise the academy looks like a comfortable, well-kept community college. At the entrance to the administration building, an inscription on a pillar on the overhang over the driveway reminds visitors that construction was started in 1970 during Hoover's reign. Inside, high up on the walls of the sunny atrium, the expected exhortations are carved, relating to the letters FBI and its slogan. For fidelity: "Prosperity asks for fidelity; adversity exacts it"—Seneca. For bravery: "Courage is resistance to fear, mastery of fear—not absence of fear."—Mark Twain. For integrity: "Integrity without knowledge is weak and useless, and knowledge without integrity is dangerous and dreadful."—Samuel Johnson.

Once an FBI trainee steps through the entrance to the academy, he or she need never leave during sixteen weeks of training. There's a student cafeteria where the food is free, laundry service, a swimming pool, a student store that sells everything from greeting cards to FBI mugs, a pub that doubles as a cafeteria during the day, a nurse's office, and a trainer for athletic injuries.

Glass-walled corridors interconnect all the buildings. The configuration of the buildings produces a quad in the middle. Like high school, there is mayhem in the halls when classes change. Everyone wears a T-shirt with appropriate insignia and khaki pants. Each FBI class chooses its own special T-shirt color and class slogan.

Quantico represents the best in the FBI, all of the agency's values on display. Agents are taught that brains are more important than brawn, that the FBI is all about getting information, and the way to get information is to treat everyone—even suspects who have committed terrible crimes—like your mother.

There is an honesty to the place. In firearms training, agents are told they will be scared during a shootout. Because of that, and the speed at which events unfold, only 20 percent of their rounds will find their target.

Agents must make split-second decisions about using deadly force. No warning shots may be fired. Agents may shoot a fleeing subject only if the suspect has committed a felony involving death or serious physical injury and his escape would pose an imminent threat of death or serious injury to the agent or others.

"We do not shoot to wound," Michael Brooks told a class. "We don't shoot to kill but to eliminate the threat."[149]

Nothing illustrates how difficult an agent's job is so much as the Firearms Training System, a simulator that tests agents on their judgment and marksmanship. On a large screen in front of them, agents watch different arrest scenarios. Where appropriate, they shoot a wired gun that can no longer take ammunition. A slim, blond woman in a carpet warehouse refuses to drop to the floor when told she is under arrest. She uses a karate kick on the agent, pulls out a gun, and begins firing at him. Trainees are to kill her before she shoots the agent. Most do not.

In another video, a suspect wounds a female agent in the eyes as she and her partner park in the driveway of his house. The suspect falls, drops his gun, then runs. Can the agent's partner shoot him in the back as he runs away? Trainees must make the call instantly, in fear for their lives. Because he has already wounded an agent and poses a potential threat, the answer is yes. What about a suspect who darts behind a tree, firing at agents? Just beyond the tree is a home, where the occupants may be looking out the windows. Returning fire could kill innocent bystanders. When deciding whether to return fire, trainees must consider that, and the interactive program scores them accordingly.

During training on indoor and outdoor firing ranges, students fire a total of three thousand five hundred rounds from a Glock semiautomatic .40-caliber pistol, three hundred rounds from a Remington Model 870 shotgun, and three hundred rounds from an H&K submachine gun. Besides firearms instruction, they receive training in the law, defensive tactics, making arrests, emergency driving, computers, white-collar crime, foreign counterintelligence, profiling, civil rights cases, polygraph, undercover work, forensic science, organized crime and drug cases, the history of the FBI, and ethics. Agents who can relate their personal experiences teach the classes.

In an ethics class, Walt H. Sirene reviewed the case of Dan Mitrione Jr., a Miami agent who began taking a cut of cocaine from the traffickers he was supposed to be arresting.

"There will be temptations," Sirene told the class. "As the small gifts build up, we don't know for sure that the slippery slope works. But it probably does. Pretty soon you make bigger and bigger rationalizations."

"To whom are we obligated?" Sirene asked.

"The public," a trainee answered.

"To the accused and the public as a whole to assure that equal justice is provided for everyone," Sirene said. "We have an obligation to the accused to search out every bit of evidence. Isn't that what our obligation is? Our obligation is justice."

Then Sirene made a point made by many FBI agents: "The greatest satisfaction you will someday get is when you will see all the evidence pointing to one individual or group of people and, by getting to the bottom of the facts, you will prove their innocence. That is our obligation to the justice system as a whole, to find out the facts, find the truth, wherever it lies."

About 5 percent of the trainees flunk out or withdraw. Some come to realize they could not take another person's life. When he was assistant director over training, James D. McKenzie was walking through the academy when he saw a trainee buy a candy bar from a vending machine, rip it open, throw away the candy, and eat the wrapping. McKenzie called him into his office.

"I was walking down this hall, and I saw you buy a candy bar, throw the candy bar away, and eat the paper," he said to the trainee.

"Yes," the man said.

"What did you do that for?"

The trainee said that when he was a small child, his parents would not let him have candy in his room, so he would sneak it. "I would eat the candy, and then I would eat the paper so there wouldn't be any evidence. After a while, I started to like the paper," he told McKenzie.

"He's sitting there telling me that," McKenzie recalled. "Now, can you imagine this guy being an FBI agent? Now this guy is out on a surveillance and gets hungry and eats the surveillance log. The guy is a couple of bubbles off center. Naturally, people like that don't become FBI agents. He resigned based on that."

■　■　■

In testimony before the House Appropriations Committee in 1966, Hoover spoke about the qualities he looked for in agents. "I will not appoint any man merely because of the color of his skin," Hoover said.

"I will not lower the qualifications. I must insist that appointees be above average in intelligence and reputation, of good character, and be above average in personal appearance." In that regard, Hoover cited Efrem Zimbalist Jr., who played the FBI inspector in the television series *The FBI*.

"In other words," Hoover said, "there is an image that people have of the FBI. I want our agents to live up to that image."

To Webster, Efrem Zimbalist Jr. was no more an example of what an agent should be than was Bill Cosby. There was a need for FBI agents to reflect society in general. It was not only the right thing to do, it was the practical thing to do. Black agents might have a better chance of gaining the confidence of black informants or witnesses than white agents. Undercover operations demanded agents of all races and both sexes. Whatever their race, agents were more likely to obtain information from minorities if the FBI as a whole was perceived as an integrated agency. Subsequent litigation by black agents further underscored the need to integrate.

Webster tried to devise a way to accept more minorities and women without running afoul of laws banning preferential treatment. He divided applicants into seven pools—minorities, women, lawyers, accountants, and applicants who spoke needed languages or had a scientific or an engineering background. An eighth category, called diversified, was for white males. Saying the bureau might need more of one category than another at any given time, Webster then weighted applicant test results. A white male had to score at least 34, while a minority applicant had to score 31, an attorney or accountant 31.5, a female 32, and an applicant who spoke a critical language 29.5. While women, minorities, and applicants with special skills had an edge getting into the training program, in the end everyone had had to pass the same tests before graduating from the academy. The only exception to that was women, who had to pass less rigorous physical tests.

On a card he kept in his wallet, Webster recorded the number of minority and women agents. During his nearly ten years as director, the number of black agents increased from 185 to 393. Hispanic agents increased from 173 to 400. The number of women agents rose from 147 to 787. By the time Webster left the FBI, 10 percent of the FBI's agents were minorities—including native Americans and Asians—and 8 percent were women.

Under Webster, training of new agents at Quantico became far more sophisticated. Courses made heavy use of role playing. Secretaries, agents, and cooks were enlisted to play the bad guy or gal. A typical classroom was amphitheater-style, with mustard-colored chairs behind five semicircular tables that rose on tiers. The students kept the same seat through their training; teachers who were FBI agents came to them.

At Hogan's Alley, a mock town within the academy, students learned how to make arrests. Hogan's Alley has all the comforts of small-town America—the Co-Op Laundromat, the All-Med Drug Store, the post office (zip code 22135), while at the same time being a little seedy and down-at-the-heels with its billiard parlor and pawnshop. If the town were more like a pristine New England town with clapboard houses and church steeples, it would be hard to believe the crime wave that comes over it five days a week. Or that the Pastime Lounge conceals a casino where FBI agents who will work undercover learn the ins and outs of playing blackjack, roulette, and craps.

Down the street, the Biograph is screening *Manhattan Melodrama*, with Clark Gable and Myrna Loy. This movie was showing when FBI agents gunned down John H. Dillinger as he left the Biograph Theater in Chicago on July 22, 1934. In the center of town is a no-tell motel with about thirty rooms behind orange doors. The Dogwood Inn takes Visa and MasterCard, and guests don't have to check their guns.

The bad guys are paid actors like Bryan L. Barnhart, a twenty-four-year-old with a light brown ponytail. "I've done everything from bank robberies to kidnappings," he boasted, then launched into an animated description of how he poisoned a federal judge.

An FBI car, siren screaming and tires burning, screeched to a halt outside the drugstore where Barnhart was standing. Another FBI car pulled up in front of the Bank of Hogan next door. Shouted commands blasted from loudspeakers mounted on FBI cars, as agent trainees leaped from their vehicles.

"Halt! FBI!" one called out from behind a shotgun.

Soon, Barnhart was under arrest for robbing the Bank of Hogan. If the bank is not robbed twice a week, it could go out of business.

Just then, a new crime wave started. Three cars appeared from nowhere, two with sirens wailing. A weather-beaten gray Oldsmobile was in the lead. The car behind it passed it and nearly jumped the sidewalk, in order to block the Olds, now in the middle. Trainees in the car behind the Olds jumped out, holding their guns and yelling at the driver with an anger all out of proportion to the actual situation.

"Do exactly as I say! Reach your left arm out the window and open your door from the outside." The trainee had not made allowances for the possibility that the door could be locked, but apparently it wasn't, because it opened.

When the suspect left the car, a trainee barked, "Drop to your knees right now!"

"Driver, face forward," someone else yelled.

"There's someone in the car," a surprised trainee called out.

"Open the right rear door. Open it all the way," a trainee said. When there was no response, he said, "If there's someone in the car, get out with your hands up."

Until Hogan's Alley was built, trainees chased FBI agents who posed as criminals at the academy. One day, Vincent P. Doherty, then the academy's feisty comptroller, was showing the facilities to official guests. Doherty happened to match a description given to a training class of the perpetrator of a bank fraud. A trainee spotted Doherty and gave the usual warning: "Freeze, FBI!"

Saying he was giving a tour, Doherty said, "Get lost."

Whereupon she flipped Doherty, who found himself lying on the carpet.

22

THE CODIRECTOR

Given how successful William Webster had been as FBI director, after Ronald Reagan chose him to be director of Central Intelligence in May 1987, the president cast about for another judge to head the FBI. On the recommendation of Edwin Meese III, his attorney general, Reagan chose William S. Sessions in July 1987.

By all accounts, Sessions was an excellent judge. With white hair that framed his face, Sessions had a wide smile and riveting eyes through glasses with large round lenses. He looked like a country boy, farm-raised, with enough of a Texas twang to make the stories he liked to tell sound authentic. It was the Texas congressional delegation that had suggested him to Meese.

The son of a minister in the Disciples of Christ Church, William Steele Sessions was born on May 27, 1930, in Fort Smith, Arkansas. He graduated from Northeast High School in Kansas City, which Clarence Kelley had attended. When he was a sophomore, he met his wife, Alice, who was going to the same school. She was also the daughter of a minister, but from a different church—the Reorganized Church of Jesus Christ of Latter Day Saints. She later became a Methodist.

Sessions attended the University of Kansas and Florida State University before graduating in 1956 from Baylor University and, two years later, from its law school. He served as a first lieutenant in the Air Force and, after ten years of practicing law in Waco, Texas, joined the Justice

Department in 1969. There he headed a section that prosecuted draft evasion, pornography, election fraud, and violations of the Foreign Corrupt Practices Act. Having served in 1966 as a county chairman for Senator John Tower, the Texas Republican, Sessions was connected politically. In 1971, he was named U.S. attorney in San Antonio. Three years later, he became a judge at the U.S. District Court in San Antonio and, in 1980, chief judge.

As a judge, Sessions was known for his fairness, toughness, and attention to decorum. He had a self-deprecating sense of humor and put people at ease. Despite a bout with polio when he was sixteen, Sessions was a mountain climber who made two treks up to the eighteen-thousand-foot level of Mount Everest.

Sessions gained national attention when he presided over the trials of defendants charged with assassinating U.S. District Court Judge John H. Wood. Known as a tough judge, Wood was killed just before sentencing Jamiel "Jimmy" Chagra. The bureau solved the case by planting rumors in the prison where Chagra was incarcerated. The rumors prompted Chagra, in conversation with others, to make admissions that the bureau picked up through electronic bugs and wiretaps. Apparently, he hoped to get a lighter sentence by having another judge sentence him.

Accusing Sessions of "unspeakable evil" and the government of "Gestapo tactics," Charles V. Harrelson, who killed Wood at Chagra's direction, ranted in Sessions's courtroom in San Antonio: "I think the court should consider a charge against itself for rape and murder." Sessions never flinched. He quietly sentenced him to two consecutive life terms for murder and conspiracy to murder, to be served after he finished a forty-year state sentence for drug trafficking. Chagra also was convicted.

Before recommending Sessions to succeed Webster, Meese consulted Jack Lawn, who was the FBI's SAC in San Antonio and had directed the investigation into Wood's killing. Lawn spoke highly of him.

"I thought he would be the ideal candidate for the FBI," Lawn said. "He is a people person. I thought that was important. As chief judge, he listened. I thought that would be a wonderful attribute for him to bring to FBI headquarters."[150]

But even before Sessions was sworn in, John E. Otto, the acting FBI director, had odd encounters with him. Because Sessions had a stomach ailment, his swearing in had to be postponed twice after he was confirmed by the Senate on September 25, 1987. In the interim, Otto would call Sessions at home to discuss the arrangements. Each time, Alice Sessions would take the phone from Sessions and berate Otto.

"Alice would interject and criticize the swearing-in procedures," Otto said. "I finally said we cannot accept having a Martha Mitchell dictating to the bureau. He said he agreed."[151]

Sessions was finally sworn in on November 2, 1987. Contrary to expectations, Sessions turned out to be quite different from Webster and a man of many contradictions. Whenever agents thought they had a handle on him, he proved them wrong.

Despite advice from bureau officials that he stay at headquarters and learn how the FBI works, Sessions spent his first several years visiting all but four of the FBI's fifty-six field offices. In 1988, he gave 88 speeches and in 1989, he gave 101 to the likes of the Rotary Club of Cincinnati and the El Paso Chamber of Commerce. When visiting field offices, he made a point of shaking every agent's hand.

Like Webster, Sessions talked about the need to adhere to the rule of law and the Constitution. To those who remembered the Hoover days, it was reassuring stuff. But the speeches burst with platitudes, and in person, Sessions spoke the same way. He developed a reputation among agents as a cheerleader who engages in "Sessions-speak."

"He just babbled," said Larry Lawler, an SAC under Sessions. "At the SAC conferences, there was the gibberish meter. Sessions would get up, and the meter would start beeping. He thought he was a very good orator. He talked, and everyone looked at each other and said, 'What the hell is he saying?' "

Sessions loved the perquisites of his job. He wore his brass FBI badge pinned to his shirt at all times. Even when talking to retired agents, Sessions referred to himself in the third person as "your director." These idiosyncrasies annoyed some agents, who pointed out that unless agents are going on an arrest, they pin the badge to the inside of their credentials case.

Asked why he wore the badge on his shirt, Sessions gave an example of "Sessions-speak": "The badge was given to me at the ceremony when I was sworn in. When I got it, I said to myself I would wear it. I knew that agents all have their credentials, and I knew I had my credentials. I knew I wasn't an agent. I knew I wasn't an investigator. But it's my identification really more with the bureau than anything else. I know that right now I'm on bureau business. If I go to an embassy party tonight, I'll be on bureau business."

Many agents reported trying to brief him on important subjects in his office, only to find him looking past them to his television set, which he kept tuned to CNN with the volume off. His most memorable contribution was offering them cookies. When traveling, he would interrupt a serious briefing to ask about the sights.

Sessions kept a neat office and was proud of the fact that he emptied his in box each day. But the way he ran the bureau was frenetic. A fan of technology, he peppered assistant directors with questions by E-mail, requiring them to conduct research that was often pointless because Sessions did not remember asking the questions.

Once Sessions asked a question of Joe Stehr, the head of Sessions's security detail, and when Stehr came with the answer, instead of listening, Sessions began whistling "The Yellow Rose of Texas" as he walked away.

In December 1990, Sessions traveled to Atlantic City to publicly announce, with then Attorney General Dick Thornburgh, that based on an FBI investigation, the Justice Department was filing a civil suit against the largest casino workers' union in the city. On the way, Sessions asked agents from the Newark Field Office to brief him on the case. In the middle of the briefing, he began singing a commercial: "Brylcreem, a little dab will do you. Brylcreem, you'll look so debonair."

Shocked, baffled, and hurt, the agents stopped briefing him, aware that he had not been listening to them. Another official who went to Sessions's office to brief him about an espionage case was startled when Sessions looked beyond him at a television set. On the screen was the image of some large pots. "Those moujahedeen do everything in those pots," Sessions intoned, according to a *Los Angeles Times* story by Ronald J. Ostrow. "They cook in them. They shave in them."

A few days after the start of the air war against Iraq in January 1991, Sessions met with Thornburgh and other top officials in a Justice Department room shielded to prevent electronic eavesdropping. Off-handedly, Thornburgh said he had learned about the start of the air war initially from the president. He asked how the others had learned about it. When it was his turn to speak, Sessions, sitting bolt upright, said the information was classified. When Thornburgh pointed out that everyone in the room was cleared to receive top-secret information, Sessions stiffly said he had been asked not to talk about the air strike.

"I liken him to a shorebird who runs along the shore, looks up a little startled, dashes off in another direction, and does the same thing," said William M. Baker, who headed the Criminal Investigative Division under Sessions.

Sessions made it clear he saw no reason to learn the details of investigations, and he displayed little interest in them.

"Sessions is an individual who, by his own admission, said, 'I am not an investigator. You people are the career investigators. You have a wealth of experience. That's your business,' " Floyd Clarke, the deputy FBI director under Sessions, said. "So he didn't try to get into the details of the investigative process to the extent some of the directors have, especially Webster."

Instead, Sessions focused on the personnel, technical, and systems aspects of the bureau, trying to improve advancement opportunities for women and minorities, pushing such techniques as DNA typing, closing field offices that were no longer needed, trying to change practices like keeping paper needlessly—practices that in many cases dated to Hoover's time and were archaic. Sessions worked on such unglamorous but vital issues as how the FBI coordinates with the states what data goes into the National Crime Information Center, the national computer network that stores data for police on stolen cars and other property.

When Sessions became director, he was appalled at how much material he was given to read and how many decisions he had to make. Pointing to his in box, he told me, "I would come in routinely, and the in basket you see there would have sixteen to eighteen inches of material that would flow across my desk each day. It was flowing from three executive assistant directors, all of whom were highly energetic. I would get here at 7:30 or 7:45 A.M. They would already be here. I would leave at 7 to 7:30 at night, and they would still be here. I would talk to them on the weekends. I was here, and they were here or at home working."[152]

Sessions decided to give lower-level managers more responsibility. He reorganized the hierarchy at the top so that instead of three executive assistant directors, he had a deputy director and two associate deputy directors.

At an executive conference breakfast I attended, Sessions appeared to be firmly in command. Over sausage and pancakes, he went around the room asking the bureau's top officials what was going on in their divisions or offices. They talked about the latest kidnapping case, technological changes, the backlog in matching fingerprints, and locations of field offices.

John W. Hicks, the assistant director over the laboratory, described plans to make over the front of the J. Edgar Hoover FBI Building to give it a more hospitable look. One idea was to erect green granite slabs along the front and decorate them with ivy planters and bronze bands. D. Caroll Toohey, the assistant director over inspections, said he thought the marble would make the building look like a mausoleum. Sessions wanted to know what the costs were and if the granite could be easily defaced.

"Congress is taking steps to limit their own appropriations [for their own operations], which is unusual and a bad sign," said John E. Collingwood, who headed the Office of Public and Congressional Affairs.

"It may not be a bad sign. It may be a good sign," Sessions said.

"It depends on whether you are a taxpayer or trying to get more money to the FBI," Collingwood said.

"What if you are both?" Sessions said.

Like Webster, Sessions picked highly capable agents to run the bureau—Floyd Clarke, James Greenleaf, and William Baker, an assistant FBI director who headed Congressional and Public affairs under Webster and headed the Criminal Investigative Division under Sessions.

Baker was one of the sharpest, most liked, most experienced, and most respected bureau executives. The son of an American Airlines pilot, Baker graduated from the University of Virginia in 1961 with a

B.A. in history. After serving in the Air Force Office of Special Investigations, he became an FBI agent in 1965. While he held extremely powerful positions at the FBI, then at the CIA under Webster, then back at the FBI, Baker never lost the street agent's touch. He was charming, slightly roguish, and able to cut through bureaucracy like a razor blade. He moved confidently between the cloistered world of FBI agents on the one hand, and the politicians and media stars who dominate Washington on the other.

When agents talked about Baker, they often compared him with Thomas E. DuHadway, a loved and admired agent who had headed the Intelligence Division until his sudden death from a heart attack in 1991. Two thousand FBI employees attended his funeral, placing a piece of black tape across their badges, a demonstration of mourning.

When Buck Revell chose to become SAC in Dallas, Sessions replaced him as associate deputy director with W. Douglas Gow instead of Baker. Gow was rated lower than Baker by the FBI's career board. Baker left the FBI to become a senior vice president of the Motion Picture Association of America in Los Angeles, then became president of its Motion Picture Association, which represents Hollywood overseas.

There was considerable evidence that Sessions had followed his wife Alice's advice. For reasons unknown, Alice Sessions detested Baker but liked Gow. When it came to such key decisions, Sessions allowed Alice and his longtime assistant, Sarah Munford, to interfere.

Alice Sessions is a down-home, just-plain-folks woman who speaks with a nasal twang and has pretty blue eyes. Having earned a master's degree in historical costuming, she designed and made costumes for the San Antonio ballet and other dance companies. In Waco, Texas, she worked on local antidrug and antipornography efforts.

Alice Sessions saw herself as a codirector of the FBI. When referring to her husband becoming FBI director, Alice Sessions said, "When we were sworn in." She called herself her husband's "eyes and ears." Referring to gossip she picks up, she said, "I learn things in the elevator."

After describing how his wife helped him in representing the FBI, Sessions said, "So I think it's kind of a two-for-one proposition. You have a director, and you also have a director's wife—very important to the bureau."

But her judgment and perceptions were open to question. In giving her opinion of Bill Baker, Alice Sessions said, "Baker was known among agents as not being bright." In fact, Baker was considered one of the smartest agents ever to hit the FBI, one who was selected by both Sessions and Webster for high-level posts both at the FBI and the CIA.

"We are probably being recorded," Alice Sessions told me ominously during a phone interview patched through the FBI headquarters switchboard. Asked in another interview if she believed the FBI was wiretapping all her calls or only those calls routed to her home through headquarters, she said, "My other line often gives me indications of compromise," referring to a second line to her home. "I have no idea if they are doing it on other calls." Referring to the FBI's wiretapping capabilities, Alice Sessions said, "I have consulted some other people professionally about this. In fact, I had the telephone company in a year ago."[153]

When something she had told the director in their bedroom was later repeated to her, she suggested to Ronald H. McCall, then the head of the director's FBI security detail, that the bureau had placed an electronic bugging device in their bedroom. Alice Sessions said she thought the bug was in a transmitter supplied to Sessions by the bureau for coded communications.

"I began thinking that the radio was kind of funny, you know," she said.

The allegation was reported through the chain of command of the Administrative Services Division up to the level of assistant director, startling the entire bureau.

Alice Sessions freely advised her husband on matters ranging from the qualifications of bureau officials to the handling of maternity leave. Her opinions, which she shared freely with wives of bureau officials, were overwhelmingly negative. In her view, the bureau was full of self-serving, inept officials with their own agendas.

A teetotaler like her husband, Alice Sessions criticized agents she saw with drinks in their hands at parties. Referring to a successful Washington lawyer who was the wife of one bureau official, Alice Sessions confided that when she talked with her at an FBI party, she thought she "probably had been drinking. At least I felt she had. . . . They had probably been at a party before." Bureau officials, she said, are "not well educated or intellectually bright, but they are cunning. . . . They leave no fingerprints. They have to drink to facilitate things."

Her husband did not escape criticism. The FBI director had a "fatal" flaw, she said. He was a "Pollyanna" who was "not curious." His problem, she said, is that he "thinks everyone is as up front as he is."

When Bill Baker retired, Alice Sessions did not go to the dinner, which was attended by five hundred people, including both Sessions and Webster. She explained that she knew the jokes would include remarks she considers offensive. She later found out from her husband that she had been right. As master of ceremonies, William Gavin, the Miami SAC, had referred to the airline stewardesses Baker, who is dashingly handsome, had dated before marrying Robin Baker, who is herself an attractive, savvy Delta flight attendant. Baker was forty-six when he married her.

"I think it would have been embarrassing for me to sit in front of Robin and hear this," Alice Sessions said. "I didn't want to dignify it."

But Robin Baker said, "I laughed harder at that than anything else. I called Gavin before the party and said, 'Don't hold back on account of me.' "

What offended Alice Sessions the most was that she learned that then Attorney General William Barr had invited Floyd Clarke, the deputy director, and Bill Baker, the assistant director, to his home and had not invited her and her husband.

Before being named attorney general, Barr had attended a speech that Sessions gave at the FBI. Barr, then an assistant attorney general, was appalled. The talk was nothing but pithy maxims. Once he became attorney general, Barr developed disdain for the FBI director. Six months into his new job, Barr learned that Sessions had been using FBI planes to visit his family and friends. Invariably, Alice Sessions went along on these trips. Barr talked to Sessions about it, rebuking him for taking his wife. Barr pointed out that as attorney general, he could make up excuses to take his wife anywhere in the world, yet he had never taken her on a trip. Sessions launched into a defense that Barr found laughable: that Alice Sessions was somehow important to maintaining the morale of the FBI.

Barr made it clear he did not accept Sessions's explanation, but he never followed up to make sure Sessions was not abusing his position. Instead, Barr became convinced that Sessions had to go simply because he was not a good FBI director. His responses in discussions seemed bizarre, and Barr tried to avoid him. For example, when deciding how to respond to riots in Los Angeles, Sessions started talking about the FBI's Hostage Rescue Team, as if such a small force would solve the problem.

Barr learned that his predecessor, Dick Thornburgh, had had so little respect for Sessions that he generally refused his calls. It appeared to Barr that Sessions's chief concern was getting invited to the right parties, taking trips to Europe, and appearing at important ceremonial functions. In one nineteen-day period, Sessions and his wife attended nineteen parties. Barr would mock the way Sessions strutted and talked, imitating his baritone voice, mouthing bromides. Barr decided that aside from the abuses, he would like to fire Sessions for incompetence. He found that President George H. W. Bush was also appalled by Sessions's shallowness. When Bush wondered aloud how Barr could put up with him, Barr expressed his determination to get rid of him after the 1992 election. The president agreed.

When Barr was an assistant attorney general, he had come to know Floyd Clarke and was impressed by his professionalism, brightness, and knowledge. He much preferred the company of Clarke and Bill Baker to Sessions's. His failure to invite Sessions to his home was intentional. As much as possible, Barr tried to deal with Clarke rather than Sessions. But Sessions constantly tried to interpose himself so he would not be cut out of the loop.

Barr was also put off by the surly way Sessions and his wife treated FBI agents. After her husband had given out awards to agents in New York one day, Alice Sessions asked an agent from the security detail what had happened to the platter of sliced fruit that had been on the FBI plane on the way up from Washington.

"It's gone," he said.

"Gone?" she snapped.

"It was just fruit," he said.

"Just fruit?" she groused.

Alice Sessions would startle members of the security detail by asking for doggie bags at receptions given by foreign embassies. While attending a meeting of Interpol in Lyons, France, Alice and William Sessions and Interpol officials dined at Le Tour Rouge, one of France's best restaurants. Alice Sessions complained to astonished FBI agents that the food was terrible.

When her husband was a judge, Alice Sessions displayed little interest in the court. Now that Sessions was FBI director, she saw an opportunity to enhance her own status and lifestyle. When shopping in downtown Washington, Alice Sessions routinely asked FBI security guards to park her car for her in the garage under the Hoover building. On one occasion, she asked a startled FBI guard to park her car and look after the director's elderly father, Will, who was sitting in the car.

When she accompanied her husband to a speech in Baltimore, she had Sessions divert the procession of FBI cars to an appliance plant so that she could return a toaster. Seeing the motorcade, a guard at the plant asked, "This is necessary to return a toaster?"

When the FBI decided the director's home off Sixteenth Street in Washington needed better security, Alice Sessions suggested that the security detail use Donald Munford. Then the husband of Sarah Munford, Sessions's longtime assistant, Don Munford was in the home security alarm business—not in Washington but in San Antonio. Alice Sessions recommended him because she knew him. Because she was the director's wife, and she was determined, the security detail acceded to her request.

"When she gets her mind set on something, she won't let it go," said an agent involved in the matter. "A month may pass, but it is in the inventory."

Don Munford proposed a system that would have cost $97,046—roughly a quarter of the $435,000 the Sessionses paid for the three-bedroom home in 1989. Bureau officials vetoed the proposal. If allowed to proceed, it would have violated government procurement rules because of the lack of competitive bidding. In addition, bureau officials decided it would have been improper to award the contract to Don Munford because of his relationship to the director's special assistant. Although he asked for considerably more, the bureau paid him $5,822 for time he spent doing the survey.

In the end, the FBI hired another private firm to improve security, including installing a fence. So intruders could be seen, the FBI wanted to install what is known as a security fence with vertical iron pickets, the same kind used around the White House and foreign embassies in Washington. But Alice Sessions insisted on a six-foot wooden fence with slats almost touching each other. It would give her more privacy, she said. FBI security officials objected. They said the FBI should not pay for the fence she wanted because it would allow snipers to hide behind it and would not enhance security. They believed that Alice Sessions wanted the fence to enclose the Sessionses' dog, Petey.

William Sessions washed his hands of the issue. He walked out of an FBI meeting called to discuss it, leaving Alice Sessions in charge. Similarly, when Alice Sessions demanded a pass so she could enter FBI headquarters without being escorted in, the director ordered it done. Only employees with a top-secret security clearance are allowed to have the pass, yet the FBI issued her building pass No. 14592, which entitled her to the special privileges accorded an assistant director or above. With the special gold pass, Alice Sessions could bring in visitors without signing them in.

When headquarters employees forget their passes, their supervisors are notified in writing. But because she often forgot to bring the pass, Alice Sessions and her friends were admitted without any pass. Realizing that the director exempted his wife from such regulations, FBI security officials were afraid to challenge her.

"The building guard [at the parking garage entrance] called me and said, 'Mrs. Sessions just went by the post with a car full of ladies. What do I do?' I said, 'Get out of the way,' " said a former member of the security detail.

Even this level of access was not enough for Alice Sessions, who asked for and received a four-digit code that allowed her access to the director's suite without going through receptionists. Entry is controlled in this way because of the extraordinarily sensitive information the suite contains. On an official's desk could be the name of a Mafia informant or a spy the FBI is watching, or documents from other supersecret agencies like the CIA or NSA. In general, only those FBI officials who work in this high-security area—known as mahogany row because of its wood paneling—have a code to enter the suite.

When I asked about her special access, Alice Sessions said she did not know that a top-secret clearance was required. "Why shouldn't I be able to go in and out of Bill's office?" she asked. "They better get on to investigating me for a top-secret clearance because, believe me, I hear a lot more things than the girls in the telephone room do. I'm privy to a lot more things than that."

■ ■ ■

An attractive woman with a Texas drawl, Sarah Munford began working for Sessions in 1980, when Sessions became chief judge in San Antonio and she was deputy clerk of the court. When he became FBI director, Sessions brought her to the bureau as his special assistant in charge of scheduling.

As scheduler, Munford's job was relatively limited. But according to bureau officials and other assistants who worked with her, she saw her role as helping to formulate policy. Referring to Munford, John Hicks, the assistant director over the laboratory, said, "You have an individual who doesn't have a full appreciation or understanding of how this organization functions exactly. But she has found where the special projects section is, where we do plaques and photographs. Invariably she wants things done on short notice. Many requests require reviews and approvals. She is not familiar with that."

Bill Baker found that Munford would try to refer to him people who wanted to talk about pending criminal cases, not realizing such contacts would be improper. He ignored her.

According to former assistants who worked closely with her, Munford often claimed that the director had asked her to take action or obtain information that he had not requested. Moreover, these former assistants said, Munford was in the habit of making things up.

"I would never think of calling someone and telling them the director asked me to say a certain thing, when in fact he had not done that," said John L. McKay Jr., a lawyer who was a special assistant to Sessions. "I have seen that many times [with Munford], and I think others have. It made him [Sessions] look bad, and that is very unfortunate." He added, "I would just say that by the time I left the FBI, I did not rely on anything she [Munford] told me." A White House fellow who had been assigned to the FBI, McKay said Sessions had no idea that Munford lied. "He would be absolutely appalled," he said.[154]

James J. Hogan, a veteran agent who also served as one of Sessions's special assistants, said that one Monday, Munford mentioned that she had been in working all weekend. As it happened, Hogan had been in working all day Sunday and had not seen her. Nor had his eight-year-old daughter, who had watched television in Munford's office during the day. When Hogan said he had not seen her, Munford questioned whether *he* had been in.

"She then proceeded to tell me *I* wasn't in," Hogan said.

In the FBI, honesty is a prerequisite. Not only is the FBI accountable to the courts for its veracity, agents have to trust each other when they face danger together. Moreover, the people who worked in the director's suite were entrusted with some of the most sensitive secrets in the government. Everyone who worked there had to be above reproach. While it did not involve a matter of consequence, Munford's claim that she had been in all weekend shook up Hogan. He mentioned it to Ron McCall, the head of Sessions's security detail, saying that Munford "would just make things up, and that he should be careful when dealing with her." McCall proceeded to warn the detail to be careful around Munford because she was a "pathological liar."

Eventually, Sessions removed McCall from his position. An agent who is a lawyer, FBI pilot, and accountant, McCall subsequently found himself passed over for a promotion as well. His removal followed his warning to the security detail that Munford dissembled. When Munford heard about it, she confronted him and threatened to have him fired if he ever called her a liar again.

About the same time, McCall gave copies of the key to the Sessionses' home to each member of the director's security detail. He felt that to protect the director, the security detail needed to be able to enter his home easily if he were in trouble. In addition, Alice Sessions periodically asked the detail to let her into her house because she had forgotten her key. But McCall's action was contrary to Alice Sessions's request that the detail have no copies or only one. Thus, McCall was in both Alice Sessions's and Munford's crosshairs, and his removal became a foregone conclusion.

Sarah Munford and Alice Sessions would talk on the phone for hours each day, often manipulating each other and blaming the security detail for not delivering to Alice Sessions personal invitations or copies of the director's daily and future schedules.

Alice Sessions told me that before he was removed, she had found McCall in her bedroom without permission. But she had her facts confused. An FBI OPR investigation found that a previous member of the FBI security detail had entered the Sessionses' bedroom with William Sessions's permission to change the codes on the FBI director's two-way radio.

Some tried to attribute Munford's problems to the fact that she was an outsider and a woman. But Nancy McGregor, Webster's assistant, was widely admired by bureau officials and experienced no problems at the FBI.

What concerned headquarters officials the most was that, after having lived in Virginia for five years, Sarah Munford continued to register her Cadillac in Texas. Virginia law required Virginia registration after living in the state thirty days. To agents, who stand to be disciplined if they disobey local laws, Sessions's refusal to require his assistant to comply with the law was seen as another example of the double standard he applied when it came to his wife and his assistant.

Munford said that the Virginia Department of Motor Vehicles had granted her permission to continue to register her car in Texas. She said the exemption was granted because she was in Washington for a fixed term and had property in Texas. However, Charles E. Murphy, the department's director of investigations in Richmond, said, "There is no such thing as a waiver. The Virginia statute doesn't give anyone the authority to waive anything. Even Jesus Christ doesn't have the authority to waive the laws of the Commonwealth of Virginia."

Munford again demonstrated her belief that she was above the law on December 24, 1991, when two Texas state troopers stopped her and her son Glenn one mile west of San Saba, Texas, for having tinted side windows. Too much tinting is considered a safety hazard. Munford was on the passenger side of the 1989 Chevrolet Blazer, which was owned by her son. According to trooper Stephen L. Boyd, as he approached the driver's side of the car, Munford rolled down the passenger window

and displayed her FBI credentials. Although she was a support employee, Munford had so-called soft credentials that look like an agent's
and are kept in a credentials case. Apparently, she thought that waving
the credentials out the window would take care of the ticket. Saying
she was the assistant to the director of the FBI and that her family was
in law enforcement, Munford told the trooper, "You go home at night,
and your kids think you are a decent person, and then you go and do
something like this."[155]

Boyd ignored her and wrote her son a ticket, explaining that the
judge would probably dismiss the case if the son mailed in a photo
showing that the tinting had been removed.

"If I'm not mistaken, there was a row about selective law enforcement with Idaho state troopers. They were letting other troopers go
when they stopped them. The FBI did an investigation of them," Boyd
told me. "She was saying her family was in law enforcement, and she
was an FBI employee, and I should have let them go," Boyd said. "I
take my kids to church and make sure they do what is right," he said.
"Who is this lady telling me what my kids think of me?"

Munford had attached her FBI business card to Boyd's copy of the
ticket, and the following week, he decided to call the number on the
card and complain. He was quickly transferred to the FBI's Office of
Professional Responsibility, which opened an investigation into Munford's actions.

"Dad-gum, I thought they ought to know about it," he said. "I felt
she was abusing her position by flashing her credentials. She was wanting off just because she was an FBI employee. I thought that's not
right."

At the direction of OPR, the FBI sent two agents from its San Antonio office to interview Boyd and his partner. As a result of the investigation, the administrative summary unit recommended that Munford
be suspended without pay for seven days.

The fact that Munford continued to register her car in Texas five
years after she had moved to Virginia grated on many headquarters
agents, who had to follow the law when they were transferred to the
Washington area from other parts of the country that have lower car
insurance rates.

Sessions was aware that Munford registered her car in Texas and that his wife had a building pass in violation of regulations. Any local police department would have quickly taken action against an employee who violated the law by failing to register her car in the state where she lived or who violated security regulations. Yet Sessions turned a deaf ear.

In his own dealings, Sessions seemed to go out of his way to demonstrate his propriety. For example, he returned FBI paper clips attached to documents that had been sent to his home. In his courtroom, he had been a stickler for rules and procedures. In his speeches, he talked about the importance of following regulations and laws. But in other settings, Sessions betrayed a lack of sensitivity about the way he conducted himself. As director, he repeatedly steered his speaking engagements toward his home state of Texas. In his first four years as director, one of every five of his official trips was to his home state— an average of one trip every two months. While Sessions could justify each trip as being related to business, the pattern made it clear he was taking advantage of his position to see his family, friends, and his old doctor and dentist back in Texas.

Just before he was to leave on a trip, Sessions would run the trip by Joseph R. Davis, the FBI's assistant director in charge of the Legal Division. When Davis would tell him the trip violated FBI regulations, Sessions would ask him to explain it to his wife. Alice Sessions would argue about it. When Davis would go back to Sessions, he would say, "Deal with Alice on this."

At various times, most of the FBI's top officials like Floyd Clarke, Jim Greenleaf, John Otto, and Buck Revell warned Sessions about his abuses and the problems caused by Munford and Alice Sessions. Revell issued standing orders that any agent in his Dallas Field Office who received a call from Alice Sessions or Sarah Munford was to take no action on the request and to refer it to him. Prophetically, Revell and the other top FBI officials speculated that Sessions could lose his directorship if the abuses got out. While the FBI director can serve no longer than ten years, the president can remove him at any time.

23

SABRELINER

Since its inception, the FBI has had a penchant for controlling the media. For an ABC television show called *FBI: The Untold Stories*, for example, the FBI had complete veto power over content. When the program wanted to air the story of Mark S. Putnam, an FBI agent who killed an informant he had impregnated, the press office under Sessions told the production company to forget it, and it did.

Thus, when I began writing a book on the bureau that focused on the Webster and Sessions era, the FBI's press office insisted that I clear any contact with them. Even if I wanted to call longtime sources and friends who were agents, I had to go through the press office first, I was told. In effect the press office was asking me to break my word to these sources that their identities would remain confidential. When I pointed that out, a press officer said, "Just blame us." It was an invitation to commit professional suicide. I later learned that the press office planned to cut off cooperation if it believed my questioning became too negative.

The issue came to a head when the press office called me to complain that I had been seen interviewing Bill Baker in his office, and that Baker had not cleared the interview with them. Apparently, they expected me to tell an assistant director who headed the Criminal Investigative Division to follow FBI directives. In fact, by writing a memo about me to Thomas F. Jones, who headed the press office, Baker had already given the press officers notice that I was interviewing him. But a press officer told me if I talked with Baker again without calling them first, the FBI's cooperation would end.

I called Baker at home on a Sunday and poured out my frustration. As a sophisticated former public affairs officer himself, Baker realized that only an objective account of the FBI, with all the warts, would be credible. As he later told FBI executives, I needed to be able to "test" what FBI officials told me. To do that, I needed to have free access to the bureau. Baker said he would take care of it.

At the end of the next day, Baker called from his car phone. He said he had talked the matter over with Jim Greenleaf, the FBI's associate deputy director for administration. Both men recommended to Floyd Clarke, the FBI's deputy director, that the bureau cooperate fully. After Clarke raised the issue with Sessions, the director issued a teletype to all FBI employees requesting their cooperation on the project and waiving most of the usual rules governing contacts with the press. For *The FBI: Inside the World's Most Powerful Law Enforcement Agency*, I interviewed 314 current or retired agents.

In the course of the research, I learned from a longtime FBI source that Alice Sessions had been trying to get the bureau to hire Donald Munford, Sarah Munford's then husband, to install a security system in the Sessionses' Washington home. Quietly, so I would not impair the access I had, I followed up and learned of other abuses by the director, including the installation of a fence that was of no security value, misuse of the FBI plane, and issuance of a building pass to Alice Sessions.

When I asked for another interview with Sessions to go over the items, the FBI's press office refused. Tom Jones, the head of the press office, had just been named SAC in Cleveland, and the last thing he wanted to do was confront the director over his own wrongdoing. However, higher-level officials like Greenleaf intervened. They told Jones to ask me to put in writing the issues to be discussed. Sessions could then determine if he wanted to grant another interview.

In a June 24, 1992, letter, I outlined many of the abuses. Sessions took a month and a half to decide whether to accede to my request. An FBI official said Sessions was "pondering" how to respond. When he finally met with me in his conference room, Sessions declared he would not answer any of the questions raised in the letter. Instead, the FBI director launched into a half-hour tongue-lashing. He noted that he had given me unprecedented access to the FBI, making sure that everyone cooperated. He said he thought the book would focus exclusively on the great work the FBI does. He said he was "offended" and "disappointed" that I had delved into any FBI personnel matters, particularly the issues relating to his wife.[156]

Sessions said his wife occupied a special and important place in the bureau. He said wives of other directors had been sick or had stayed in Kansas City, an apparent reference to the fact that Clarence Kelley's wife had been sick and never moved to Washington. Webster's first wife, Drusilla, who was widely admired and loved by agents, died six years after Webster became FBI director. In stressing his own wife's importance to the FBI, Sessions did not address the fact that Alice Sessions had accused the bureau of wiretapping her calls and bugging their bedroom.

Without my knowledge, on the grounds that the FBI is obligated to make its Office of Professional Responsibility aware of any specific allegations of wrongdoing by bureau officials, high-level FBI officials turned over my ten-page, single-spaced letter summarizing Sessions's abuses to the FBI's OPR. That office then officially gave the letter to the Justice Department's OPR.

Meanwhile, Attorney General William Barr received a second, anonymous letter purportedly written by a retired FBI agent. Dated June 25, 1992, it focused on Sessions's practice of disguising personal trips as official business. The fact that the second letter was dated a day after the FBI received my letter suggested that the anonymous writer was aware of my letter.

Based on the two letters, Justice's OPR opened an investigation into Sessions's actions and broadened the previous FBI OPR investigation into Sarah Munford's activities. Michael E. Shaheen Jr., who headed Justice's OPR, later wrote that the investigation of Sessions "was predicated upon two letters, one dated June 24, 1992, and the other June 25, 1992. The allegations contained in those letters were very specific and detailed."

FBI agents pursued the investigation for Justice's OPR in unusual secrecy. But on October 11, at the height of the presidential campaign, Sam Donaldson broke the story of the investigation on ABC-TV.

As a result of the investigation, the Justice Department put Sarah

Munford on administrative leave, pending her dismissal from the FBI, for misusing her position. Among other abuses, Justice OPR found that Munford had used FBI telephone lines to make personal long-distance calls and had lied to FBI officials about her car registration. Her dismissal was also over the fact that she had flashed her FBI credentials to try to avoid a ticket for her son. In keeping with normal practice when FBI employees are fired, FBI security police escorted Munford out of the building. In taking the action, Justice had to bypass Sessions, who would not fire her himself.

Predictably, Alice Sessions weighed in with her own analysis. In an interview with the *San Antonio Light*, she suggested that evidence had been manufactured and that her husband was "waking up out of a stupor, realizing he's been had." Someone tacked a copy of the article to a bulletin board in FBI headquarters with the inscription, "Alice in Wonderland."

While Sessions had little popular support within the bureau, some high-ranking bureau officials saw the negative publicity as an attack on the FBI. While they had little respect for Sessions personally, they resented the fact that the position of the director had been cast in a bad light. Their reaction was a holdover from the Hoover years, when the director was equated with the bureau, and upholding the image of the FBI was more important than correcting problems.

Other high-level FBI officials took a more objective view. As FBI agents, they had sworn faithfully to uphold the laws of the United States. The laws contained no exceptions for the FBI director. Agents were routinely fired or suspended without pay for up to a month for failing to register their cars properly or for having abused their positions. Why should Sessions, his wife, and his aide be treated any differently?

There were those who questioned why the investigation had been leaked to ABC at the peak of a political campaign. The real question was, how had the FBI been able to keep the abuses secret for so long? That went back to the issues of loyalty and image. The fact that high-ranking FBI officials did not themselves report the abuses to Justice raised questions about whether the FBI could police itself.

"They [FBI officials under Sessions] had an affirmative obligation to report his abuses to OPR," John L. Werner, the agent who conducted the investigation of Sessions for the Justice Department's OPR, told me. "They left us to take care of their mess. I didn't have many friends in the bureau left after that."[157]

Self-destructive or self-deluding, at the height of the investigation into his improper use of FBI planes, Sessions flew with his wife on the FBI's Sabreliner jet aircraft to attend a performance of the Bolshoi Ballet at the Sands Hotel & Casino in Atlantic City on November 27, 1992. The Sands picked up the $100 tab for the tickets. After the story hit the press, there were the usual tortured justifications: The Russian ambassador, Vladimir Lukin, had invited him. They had planned to discuss the possibility of giving FBI training to Russian law enforcement personnel. Sessions thought the Russian government, not the Sands, would be paying for the ballet tickets. And the ambassador was "reaching out to him [Sessions] to make official contact," according to an FBI spokesman.

After all the leaks to the press, it would have been hard to imagine the Justice Department's OPR report doing much more than confirming what was already known. But when the report finally came out in January 1993, it contained so many additional examples of Sessions's abuses and lack of judgment that it hit like a bombshell. The 161-page report, prepared by Shaheen, disclosed what the *New York Times* called "a seemingly endless record of chiseling and expense account padding."

The report said Sessions had kept an unloaded gun in a locked briefcase in the trunk of his FBI limousine as part of a "sham arrangement" to avoid paying income taxes on the value of FBI transportation to and from work; he had the FBI pay for the fence around his house even though it detracted from the security of his home; he took nonofficial passengers in his limousine in violation of regulations; he abused government travel for personal gain; he systematically used his security detail for personal purposes; and he allowed his wife to have an FBI building pass without the required clearance.

The report said that four times while he was director, Sessions and his wife took the FBI plane to San Francisco, where their daughter lived, for Christmas. There, in an effort to justify the trip as official business, they had the FBI generate excuses for making the trip. Indeed, after Alice Sessions attended a breakfast meeting to which she had not been invited, she confided to an agent that she had come to the meeting because she had to justify her trip. Even as the report was being written, Sessions made a similar trip to San Francisco for Christmas 1992. On trips to Australia and France, Sessions collected per diem reimbursement for days when he transacted no official business. Because they had so much baggage, he ordered a larger FBI plane sent to San Antonio to pick up his wife and their daughter. On another trip, Sessions had FBI agents load firewood into the FBI car and drive it from Salisbury, Connecticut, to Poughkeepsie, New York, then fly the firewood to Washington.

As a result of an anonymous tip, OPR also looked into the Sessions's purchase of their home. OPR concluded that on his salary, Sessions could not have afforded to buy the $435,000 house unless he had received a break from Riggs National Bank in Washington, either on the interest rate on the mortgage or the income standards needed to qualify for such a loan. Such a "sweetheart" arrangement would have been only because of the bank's interest in accommodating the FBI director, the report said. When asked for the mortgage document, Sessions refused, saying the request related to an issue that was "entirely new" and came as the press was reporting leaks from the investigation.

The irony of an FBI director making such a disingenuous argument was exquisite. Every day, FBI agents probed into the personal and financial affairs of thousands of Americans, each of whom would dearly love to brush aside the requests by saying there seems no end to the inquiries.

Most revealing was the report's characterization of Sessions's attempts to obtain prior approval of his actions. When it suited his purposes, the report said, Sessions cited officials who allegedly approved his trips and other benefits in advance. When it did not, Sessions blamed authorities for not having told him that his actions would have been improper. "Yet," the report said, "when the independent review does not produce the desired opinion, he seeks another forum until he finds an acceptable answer." For example, in seeking approval for his trip to attend the Bolshoi Ballet in Atlantic City, Sessions first sought the advice of Wayne Gilbert, who headed counterintelligence, and Doug Gow, the associate deputy director. When they recommended that Sessions not take the trip, Sessions asked Lawrence S. Eagleburger, the secretary of state. When the secretary of state did not object, Sessions took the trip.

The OPR report concluded that the issues raised by the internal investigation were so serious that the president should decide whether Sessions should remain in office. Barr sent the report to President Bush. He also ordered Sessions to reimburse the government $9,890 for the fence around his property, pay taxes on the value of his FBI transportation to and from work, release his mortgage documents to OPR, and pay back the government for travel and per diem payments for personal trips.

"Given that you are a former U.S. attorney and federal judge, and that you are currently director of the premier federal law enforcement agency, I must conclude that there is no excuse for your conduct," Barr wrote to him.[158]

In comments to the press, Sessions blamed everyone but himself. He claimed that Joe Davis, the FBI's legal counsel, had approved each of the 126 trips he and his wife took. In fact, Davis approved only a handful of them, according to a Justice OPR analysis.

Sessions also claimed the OPR report had accepted uncritically the statements of Ron McCall, whom Sessions had removed as head of the security detail because of what Sessions referred to ominously as his "conduct." In fact, the OPR report was based on statements under oath by dozens of FBI agents and hundreds of internal memos written contemporaneously by those agents. McCall's "conduct" had consisted of standing up to Sessions and his wife at the risk of his job when their requests were improper.

The OPR report came out the day before Bill Clinton became president. Asked about the report, Clinton spokesman George Stephanopoulos called it "disturbing." In an editorial titled "Time's Up for William Sessions," the *New York Times* called for his removal. That Sessions was choosing to attack the bureau itself for his own wrongdoing infuriated agents and made them more willing to leak evidence of his abuses.

After considering going public to show their lack of support of the director, FBI officials decided such an action would not be appropriate or even helpful. However, Weldon L. Kennedy, who replaced Greenleaf as associate deputy director for administration, ordered a halt to discipline of agents for infractions similar to Sessions's. That included unauthorized use of bureau cars, an abuse that requires a suspension of thirty days without pay. Kennedy reasoned that he could not in good conscience discipline agents for what the director was doing with impunity. Moreover, agents disciplined for what the director was getting away with could conceivably mount a successful legal challenge to the punishment. Only if and when Sessions was replaced, Kennedy said, would normal disciplining of agents resume. Kennedy did not tell Sessions about his action, but when he learned of it, Sessions ordered disciplining to proceed.

■ ■ ■

Notoriously indecisive, Clinton wanted to name an attorney general before taking action on removing the FBI director. However, if there was any question about how Clinton felt about Sessions, it was dispelled when the White House refused to invite Sessions to the new president's State of the Union address to Congress. Sessions had been at all four previous addresses while he was director. Miffed, he asked John Collingwood, who headed congressional affairs, to try every avenue possible to get an invitation, to no avail. Earlier, Alice Sessions, distraught at not receiving enough invitations to Clinton inauguration festivities, had accused a Sessions assistant of throwing away her mail.

For all their idiosyncrasies, both William and Alice Sessions mounted an impressive lobbying campaign, apparently convincing the usually savvy *Washingtonian* magazine that Sessions was the victim of a conspiracy that included me, Hooverites, bigoted FBI agents, Shaheen, and Barr, among others.

"If they get Sessions," the magazine's March 1993 issue quoted a former law enforcement official as saying, "it means you're going to have a tough time convincing the American people that the bureau can do its job independently. It's important to know the bureau can't be bought off or ordered off."[159]

In fact, it was Sessions's abuse of his position that had undermined faith in the FBI. Many agents were afraid that because of the controversy, their own credibility and effectiveness in conducting investigations had been impaired.

Thus Sessions emerged as an enigma, not at all a clone of Webster, who would have found it unthinkable to break the rules for anyone, who would have fired any assistant who abused his or her position, and who leaned over backward not to create even the appearance of impropriety. While Sessions acted as a cheerleader for the bureau, the reality was that he—like his wife—mistrusted the FBI and had disdain for its agents.

Instead of the pleasant man Sessions appeared to be, Barr and other Justice and FBI officials concluded he was, in fact, arrogant. How else to explain Sessions's position that he was not subject to the rules that governed everyone else? Sessions's comment that wives of other FBI directors had been sick revealed a nastiness that conflicted with his affable image.

After Clinton became president, Stuart M. Gerson briefly became acting attorney general. His opinion of Sessions was similar to Barr's. Gerson expressed his view both to the Clinton White House and to Barr's successor, Janet Reno, who was sworn in as attorney general on March 12, 1993.

As the former prosecutor in Dade County, Florida, Reno had been so careful about avoiding even the appearance of impropriety that she had refused to use restaurant discount coupons. When parking her official car at parking meters, she had fed the meters quarters.

"The issue is respect," Gerson told Reno and the White House. "Sessions doesn't have it."

24

KORESH

In the middle of the standoff over Sessions, the FBI became involved in a far more serious imbroglio. On February 28, 1993, the Treasury Department's Bureau of Alcohol, Tobacco and Firearms (ATF) staged a disastrous raid on a ramshackle compound in Mount Carmel, Texas, ten miles east of Waco. There, thirty-three-year-old David Koresh and his group of religious fanatics had been arming themselves with illegal machine guns and explosive devices, preparing for what Koresh said would be a bloody confrontation with nonbelievers.

Koresh was an unlikely prophet. Born Vernon W. Howell in Houston, Koresh was a high school dropout with a history of learning disabilities. As a young man, Koresh attended services of the Seventh-Day Adventists. He had a knack for interpreting the Bible's Book of Revelation and its doomsday prophecies to make any point he wished. His seventeen-hour dissertations attracted members of the Waco-based Branch Davidian sect, which had splintered from Seventh-Day Adventists in 1934. Koresh briefly lived in the sect's compound but moved in the mid-1970s to Southern California, where he began recruiting for the sect.

In 1987, Koresh returned to the compound and, in a fierce gun battle, took it away from George Roden, who had led the sect. The two had feuded since Koresh had started having sex with Roden's mother, then in her late sixties. Roden was injured in the gun battle, and Koresh was charged with attempted murder but acquitted.

In 1990, the charismatic leader changed his name to David Koresh—David to reflect his conviction that he was the head of the biblical House of David, and Koresh because it is the Hebrew transliteration of Cyrus, the Persian emperor who allowed the Jews being held captive in Babylon to return to Israel. With wavy hair and soft eyes, the guitar-strumming Koresh was particularly attractive to women, who flocked to his cult. By the time he had taken over the compound, Koresh was proclaiming himself the Messiah. Part con artist, part paranoid personality, part frustrated rock star, Koresh had some 120 followers whose only wish was to serve his will.

The ATF first learned of the group on June 4, 1992, when a member of the local sheriff's department told an ATF agent about vast quantities of arms and explosives being shipped to Koresh's seventy-acre compound on Route 7.

The ATF interviewed a number of former Branch Davidians and traced some of the shipments back to arms dealers. From these inquiries, the ATF learned that Koresh preached that by having sex with him, female members of the group would become his disciples. Koresh had already fathered at least fifteen children by different women whom he called his wives. Many of the "wives" were as young as twelve. For those who were married when they entered his cult, Koresh had a simple solution. He purported to annul their marriages and reserved the right to have sex with any of the wives himself. Their husbands were to remain celibate.

Koresh used all the mind manipulation of traditional cults. He created a spartan environment, required members to surrender all their worldly possessions, and insisted on slavish loyalty. At times, the cultists subsisted for days on popcorn or fruit. He would ban sugar and ice cream. Then, for no apparent reason, Koresh would declare that sugar and ice cream were desirable. At one point, he decided hot dogs made with chicken were acceptable. When cultists brought him bologna made with chicken, he flew into a rage.

Koresh administered discipline by paddling children as young as eight months for as long as forty-five minutes until they bled. Adults were forced into a pit of raw sewage. Afterward, they were not allowed to bathe. Children were to call their parents "dogs." Only Koresh was to be referred to as their father. When a girl reached the age of ten or eleven, Koresh gave her a plastic Star of David to wear, signifying that she possessed "the light," meaning she was ready to have sex with him.

Of more interest to the ATF, the firearms accumulated by the group could have held off a battalion during the Persian Gulf War. In a year and a half, the group had spent an estimated $200,000 on such purchases as three hundred assault rifles, hundreds of thousands of rounds of ammunition, two hundred grenades, thirty pounds of potassium nitrate for making explosives, and hundreds of parts for making machine guns. As the Davidians had no license to make machine guns, this was a violation of federal law.

Based on the information gathered, the ATF obtained a warrant to arrest Koresh and seize material within his compound, Ranch Apocalypse. Given the degree of danger and the fact that the compound held innocent women and children who could be used as hostages, it would have been foolhardy to try to arrest Koresh while he was still in the compound. Koresh periodically jogged around the compound on Double EE Ranch Road, or he ran errands in town; that would have been the time to arrest him. Yet the ATF made the fatal mistake of trying to arrest Koresh in the compound. Moreover, in any raid, surprise is critical. As a rule, raids are conducted in the early morning hours when people are still asleep.

ATF supervisors knew, before their agents went in, that the Davidians were expecting them. In an effort to burnish its image, ATF had alerted eleven media outlets of the raid. Television cameramen and reporters were waiting for the ATF agents when they arrived to storm the fortress. Forty minutes before the raid, Robert Rodriguez, an ATF undercover agent who had managed to infiltrate the Davidians, scurried out to warn supervisors that Koresh knew the ATF was coming. A cult member had encountered a local TV cameraman on the road, who said the ATF had tipped the television station about the impending raid.

"Neither the ATF nor the National Guard will ever get me," Koresh told Rodriguez. "They got me once, and they'll never get me again."

Rodriguez rushed to tell his supervisors, who brushed him off. In a splendid non sequitur, ATF intelligence chief David Troy explained, "The element of surprise does not mean they don't know you're coming. Only that they can't take control."

The ATF also knew that the Davidians had .50 caliber rifles capable of shooting a round a mile and a half, not to mention assault rifles, machine guns, and shotguns. Yet many of the ATF agents were armed with only semiautomatic weapons.

Despite protests by some ATF agents, the agency ordered the raid to proceed. Brandishing a search warrant and a warrant for Koresh's arrest, ninety-one ATF agents stormed the compound at 10 A.M. on Sunday, February 28.

Given the criminally negligent planning, it was a wonder more lives were not lost. As it was, in the ensuing forty-five-minute gun battle, the Davidians killed four ATF agents and wounded or injured another fifteen. The ATF had to withdraw.

Later that same day, President Clinton ordered the FBI to take over. Thus from the start the bureau was at a disadvantage. From their first days at Quantico, FBI agents are taught to plan such raids thoroughly. Unlike police, FBI agents usually have the luxury of choosing the best time and place to confront suspects. Traditionally, the FBI overpowers targets with superior manpower and weapons. The ATF's fumbling had deprived the FBI of these natural advantages.

Under the direction of Jeffrey Jamar, the beefy FBI special agent in charge in San Antonio, members of the FBI's Hostage Rescue Team (HRT) began surrounding the compound that afternoon, hoping to negotiate an end to the standoff.

■　■　■

As originally proposed, the HRT would operate as a critical response team that would take command of a siege and combine the expertise of a special weapons and tactics (SWAT) team, hostage negotiators, profilers, and other technical experts. Donald A. Bassett, a firearms instructor at Quantico, began to see the need for such a team in 1977, when twelve Hanafi Muslims took 149 hostages at three Washington buildings, including the headquarters of B'nai B'rith's Anti-Defamation League. Even though the Metropolitan police were in charge, the FBI gave tactical advice and offered FBI pilots so the police could land helicopters on the top floor of the B'nai B'rith building. By then, each field office had a SWAT team, created in response to a terrorist massacre at the 1972 Olympics in Munich. But the SWAT teams, which were started in 1973, consisted of agents who were marksmen only part-time.

In the 1977 case, if the Hanafi Muslims had not agreed to leave the buildings peacefully, "It would have been a bloodbath. These [police] officers had never been trained to do airborne assaults," said Bassett, who was one of the tactical advisers.

That same year, GSG9, a German hostage rescue team, succeeded in liberating hostages taken during the hijacking of a Lufthansa airliner bound for Mogadishu, the capital of Somalia. As a result of the two events, Bassett, Roger Nisley, and others in the FBI's firearms training unit at Quantico proposed an FBI hostage rescue unit that would train full-time and respond to hostage takings and other extremely dangerous threats all over the country. Meanwhile, Buck Revell had attended a demonstration by Delta, a military special unit. He saw the need for an FBI force, but one that would take a more surgical approach. Jim McKenzie, who was over the Training Division, supported the idea, and Webster approved it. By 1983, the team was operational.

In naming the new force, the bureau did not want to create the impression it was an elite group. "Super SWAT" was proposed and shot down for that reason. Hostage Rescue Team (HRT) sounded less elitist and more benign.

Instead of adopting the more comprehensive approach proposed by Bassett and Nisley, the bureau established the HRT as only a tactical unit that would take control of armed suspects in buildings, airplanes, or vehicles. The lack of a coordinated approach would lead to problems at Waco.

■　■　■

By early April, after more than a month had elapsed since the ATF raid, the FBI realized that its strategy for dealing with Koresh was not working. Koresh would promise to come out but then say God had told him to wait. Meanwhile, conditions within the compound were deteriorating. From several people who had chosen to leave, FBI agents learned that the Davidians were surrounded by human waste and dead bodies from the ATF raid. Koresh continued to live with his twelve-year-old wives, an abuse of children and a violation of statutory rape laws.

The FBI's strategy was to negotiate while shrinking the perimeter, removing a fence and sending in armored vehicles to surround the compound. The bureau also sought to make life inside the compound increasingly hellish, shining searchlights into the windows at night. Headquarters came up with the idea of playing tapes of ear-splitting noises—chants of Tibetan monks and the sounds of rabbits being slaughtered. Jamar, the San Antonio SAC, and Bob A. Ricks, another SAC on the scene, opposed the idea.

"What we got from headquarters is we're going to put pressure on them, and they're going to give up," Ricks said. "I would try to explain this is not the case. They had lived before in wooden crates in hundred-degree weather with no plumbing facilities. To think we're going to play a few tapes, and they're going to run out was somewhat silly."

The last straw was when Koresh said he would come out after finishing his manuscript on the Seven Seals of the Book of Revelation. Steve Schneider, Koresh's deputy, resented Koresh because he had taken away his wife. He told the FBI that Koresh was not even working on the manuscript.

In an April 9 letter to the FBI, Koresh predicted calamities at the compound. He said there would be an earthquake, and a dam would burst. "I AM your God," he wrote to the FBI, "and you will bow under my feet. . . . Do you think you have the power to stop My will?" From his actions and statements, and from conversations sporadically picked up through electronic surveillance, the FBI determined that Koresh had no intention of coming out peacefully.

The Davidians had their own water supply and enough food for at least a year. The prospect of armed criminals who had killed four federal agents biding their time grated on the agents. At the end of the year, the Davidians could still use the children as hostages or kill them in an effort to save themselves. What's more, according to an internal FBI position paper, there was "increasing risk, as the standoff continues, of injury to federal agents, whether by accident or . . . shooting from inside the compound."

By waiting, the FBI had achieved the end of allowing thirty-four people, including twenty-one children, to leave the compound voluntarily. But by now, the defections had stopped.

After meeting with FBI negotiators and tactical commanders sepa-

rately, Jamar proposed to step up the pressure by inserting CS gas—
more effective than tear gas—into the compound. Jamar was aware of
the possibility that the Davidians might commit mass suicide, as had
the religious fanatics led by Jim Jones, who committed suicide with
more than nine hundred of his followers at the People's Temple in Guy-
ana in 1978. Former Branch Davidians had told the FBI that there had
been rehearsals of mass suicide. One member said Koresh was toying
with the idea of leaving the compound with grenades strapped to himself so he could blow up agents as they arrested him.

As Jamar's plan moved up the FBI hierarchy, the bureau's top officials decided this was the best way to end the standoff. No one could
say with certainty what the Davidians would do if confronted. But the
majority view was that the status quo was unacceptable. Sooner or later,
criminals must be held accountable for their crimes.

During the deliberations at headquarters, Sessions took his usual
posture of letting the experts work out strategy. Unlike William Webster, who would have cross-examined FBI officials for days if such a
plan had been proposed, Sessions for the most part was passive—unless
he saw a chance to take another trip back home at government expense.
In the middle of the standoff, Sessions decided he wanted to go to Waco,
where he had once practiced law. It was not clear whether Sessions
thought he would rally FBI agents in Waco or stand Koresh down
Texas-style. In any case, Stuart Gerson was appalled. He thought Sessions's idea was "stupid," showed poor judgment, and was probably a
ploy to help him retain his job. As acting attorney general, he ordered
him not to go.

As soon as Janet Reno took over, she was faced with approving the
FBI's proposal. On April 12, Sessions, Deputy Director Floyd Clarke,
and Larry A. Potts, the chief of the Criminal Investigative Division,
presented the plan to Reno. The bureau officials told Reno that since
the Davidians might choose to attack at any time, the Hostage Rescue
Team had to be in a constant state of readiness, with rifle scopes trained
on the compound. Local FBI SWAT teams came in to relieve HRT
members, but they were not as highly trained. If another crisis occurred
elsewhere, the HRT would have been unprepared to deal with it. Already, the FBI's presence at the compound had cost taxpayers $6 mil-

lion, not including regular salary payments or the cost of repairing an FBI helicopter that crashed when it hit a power line.

Instead of accepting on the spot the bureau's plan, Reno asked the FBI to find out the answers to dozens of questions: Would the gas harm the children? Can anything else be done? For hours, Reno personally quizzed two army experts on the subject of CS gas. They assured her that the gas was nonlethal, would not permanently harm adults or children, and would not start a fire on delivery. On the other hand, if the FBI used an anesthetic gas, it might kill the weaker adults and children. Reno lived in fear that if the siege were to continue, she would find many children dead from disease, starvation, or beatings.

Reno would wake up at 4 A.M., trying to come up with a better solution. There appeared to be none. As she would later say, "In some cases, there is no right answer. What you've got to try to do is do the best you can, based on all the information you can assimilate, and then be as candid as you can."

On April 15, the FBI officials met again in Reno's private office. Carl Stern, Reno's public information officer, argued against using gas. "Saddam Hussein uses gas against civilians," he said. "We don't do that. We can be patient."[160]

In a late afternoon meeting in Reno's conference room on Saturday, April 17, Sessions was emotional, flailing his arms in the air.

"They're making monkeys of the FBI," he said.

Potts and Clarke said the HRT would have to withdraw for training—an overblown issue. They said the experts had said Koresh would not likely kill himself and take his followers along. That was not entirely true. FBI profilers assessed Koresh as having "significant characteristics associated with psychopaths; that is, he will generally act only in his self-interest, rarely accepts blame for his actions, is manipulative, cunning, and has the ability of controlling the actions of others. He will display rapid flashes of anger if provoked and will act impulsively."

Koresh's followers, the profilers said, possess "low self-esteem, are unable to act or think for themselves, and are easily manipulated by dominant individuals like Koresh. When faced with a crisis, they would be expected to follow the dictates of Koresh, not think for themselves, nor question his authority."

With that said, the profilers and psychologists differed on how to handle him. But a March 5 memo by profilers Peter A. Smerick and Mark C. Young was remarkably clairvoyant. In traditional hostage situations, they wrote, "a strategy which has been successful has been negotiations coupled with ever-increasing tactical pressure. In this situation, however, it is believed this strategy, if carried out to excess, could eventually be counterproductive and could result in loss of life."[161]

A March 8 memo noted that Koresh had told his followers that the end was closer than they thought. If Koresh were to die first, the women were to kill themselves and the children. If the women were unable to do so, the men were to help them.

Smerick and Young noted that every movement of tactical personnel "validates" Koresh's prophetic warnings that an "attack is forthcoming, and they are going to have to defend themselves." They recommended a "temporary de-escalation of the forward movement of tactical personnel. Instead, an effort must be made to reduce the influence Koresh has on the minds of his followers to convince them that a battle is not inevitable, and that Koresh's predictions are wrong."

However, other experts pointed to the fact that Koresh had been planning to write a book and seemed concerned about selling the rights. Potts and Clarke pointed out that when FBI agents towed his black 1968 Camaro in preparation for the raid, Koresh became furious. Based on talks with his client inside the compound, Koresh's attorney Dick DeGuerin said he was sure Koresh would not commit suicide. Four times, the FBI negotiators had asked Koresh if he planned to kill himself, and four times he said he would not.

Reno decided to go ahead. The next evening, she called Clinton and discussed the plan for fifteen minutes. Clinton said to go ahead. Having received approval, Jamar chose the morning of April 19 for the raid. At 5:55 A.M., when the wind had died down, the FBI warned Koresh and his followers over loudspeakers, "This is not an assault! Do not fire! Come out now and you will not be harmed!" For some, this only confirmed Koresh's predictions that the world was coming to an end. Schneider, Koresh's lieutenant, broke off communication by defiantly throwing the telephone out a front window. At 6:04, a modified M-60 tank began battering holes near the entrance to the compound and spraying a mist of CS gas through a boom on the tank. The Davidians began firing at the tanks, but agents held their fire. At 9 A.M., a tank bashed in the front door of the compound to make it easier for the occupants to leave. It also bashed a hole in the wall near the northwest corner of the compound. At noon the FBI demolished whole sections of the exterior. The fifty-one-day standoff was over.

No one in the FBI thought the Davidians would come out immediately. Rather, the strategy was gradually to build up the pressure until Koresh and his followers became so uncomfortable that they would give up. Over the next two days, the FBI planned to peel back the walls of the compound if necessary and dismantle it.

At 12:05 P.M., a wisp of smoke followed by a small tongue of flame appeared at the southwest corner of the compound. By 12:20, fire was whipping along the west side of the compound, fanned by thirty-mile-per-hour prairie winds. Two minutes later, FBI agents climbed out of their tanks and surrounded the compound. One cult member fell from the roof, engulfed in flames. As he tried to wave them off, agents tore off his burning clothing and placed him inside an armored vehicle. A distraught woman emerged from the flames, her clothes smoking. An agent snatched her as she tried to run back into the burning compound. The agents entered the building and tried to find children, wading thigh-deep into a concrete pit filled with water, human excrement, floating body parts, and rats.

From the FBI officials on the ground to those back at headquarters watching the events unfold in the Strategic Information and Operations Center (SIOC), everyone was stunned.

"Oh, my God, they're killing themselves!" exclaimed Bob Ricks, whose deadpan descriptions of Koresh's religious ranting had appeared on television networks throughout the siege. In SIOC, there was silence. Danny O. Coulson, who had founded the HRT and now headed the Violent Crimes Section in the Criminal Investigative Division, assumed Koresh was merely trying to burn firearms to destroy evidence. He was sure the mothers in the compound would get their own children out alive. But they did not come out.

The FBI had considered the possibility that fire would break out as a result of the raid; gunfights always carry that risk. But the bureau decided it would not ask fire trucks to remain at the scene because the Davidians would try to shoot the firefighters. But now, even if fire trucks had been on the scene, they would have been useless. The winds quickly turned the wooden structure into an incinerator, and there was something else fanning the flames.

A few of the nine cultists who escaped would later claim that the fire started when the FBI's battering rams knocked over kerosene lanterns. Over time, the conspiracy theories grew. The entire scene had been shot live by CNN. Yet a documentary film characterized glints of light from sunlight on broken glass and debris as evidence that FBI agents fired at the compound.

A local arson investigation established that the fire began with internal fires that had been set. In addition to the obvious evidence— billowing black clouds of smoke, signifying the use of an accelerant— the FBI had infrared aerial video photography that showed at least four fires, separated by more than one hundred feet, starting almost simultaneously in different parts of the compound.

Beyond the infrared photography, FBI snipers peering through the windows of the compound saw Davidians pouring what appeared to be a liquid seconds before the fires started. They also saw cultists cupping their hands as if lighting matches. Kerosene and gasoline were detected on the clothes of some of the survivors who had maintained that the FBI had started the fire.

After enhancing tapes of electronically bugged conversations, the FBI learned that as the flames started, the Davidians were telling each other to pour more fuel about the compound. Years later, the FBI released transcripts:

"Pablo, have you poured it yet?" one Davidian asked.

"You got to get the fuel ready," another said.

"I already poured it," a voice responded.

"Is there a way to spread fuel in there?" another asked.

"So we only light them as soon as they tell me last chance?"

"The fuel has to go all around to get started."

"Give me the match."

"Is it lit?"

"Let's keep that fire going."

The conversations had been picked up by electronic bugging devices provided by the CIA. Smaller than dimes, the devices were concealed by the FBI in the milk cartons and tapes sent in to Koresh. Like the infrared evidence, the FBI did not disclose this to the public because it was considered a sensitive technique.

Eighty Davidians, including twenty-five children, were identified as having been killed in the fire. Seven—including Koresh—had gunshot wounds in their heads, most likely self-inflicted. The autopsy reports showed that some of the children had been stabbed or bludgeoned to death. Another five bodies found in the rubble were those of people killed in the ATF's initial assault.

Devastated by the outcome, FBI agents who had risked their lives to try to rescue the Davidians faced a barrage of criticism from the media, Congress, the survivors, and the families. Why couldn't the FBI have waited? It was a good question. The negotiators wanted more time, while the HRT, headed by Richard M. Rogers, took a more aggressive approach.

"We had waited for two months," Rogers told me. "What is reasonable for a government agency? Four government agents were dead and sixteen wounded. They had weapons they had used on helicopters. What is the least amount of force that can be used? Tear gas. What would have been said if we had allowed it to go on and they died of disease? You want to end it on your terms."

"A lot of pressure is coming from Rogers," Deputy Assistant FBI Director Danny Coulson complained in a March 23 memo.

In retrospect, it was clear the FBI should have waited out the Davidians, as the bureau often does in hostage situations. Because the various FBI elements at the scene—the HRT, the negotiators, and the profilers—did not come under one commander, the HRT won.

■ ■ ■

Having already called for the removal of Sessions for abusing his position, the *New York Times* now called for his removal over Waco. At a news conference, a reporter asked Clinton if he would accept Janet Reno's resignation as well.

The frustration and anger were understandable. No one wanted to see innocent children die. But there was a difference between an avoidable mistake, such as sending in ATF agents when the ATF knew that Koresh was expecting them, and a reasonable tactical judgment that led to disaster.

Public opinion supported the FBI. An ABC poll found that 72 percent of Americans believed the FBI had done the right thing. The poll also found that 95 percent of the public believed Koresh, not the FBI, was responsible for the outcome. In ruling on a civil suit, U.S. District Court Judge Walter Smith came to the same conclusion.

Still, the raid had failed in its purpose—to get the Davidians out alive. The FBI had hoped that the CS gas would so disorient the Davidians that they would not be able to orchestrate a mass suicide. But because they had gas masks, because the wind was blowing strongly, and because the FBI had knocked large holes in the compound, the gas had little effect. While the bureau could have killed Koresh when he came within their sights through windows, the fact that he was not an immediate threat meant that killing him could have been considered murder.

"Looking back, if we had had a crystal ball, had we known they were going to immolate themselves and murder their children, we would obviously have taken a different tack," Rogers said.[162]

For many of the agents involved, the outcome was a personal tragedy. Dozens received trauma counseling and had flashbacks and sleepless nights after the raid. Jamar, the agent in charge, never quite recovered from the incident. "I think about it every day," he told me. "I feel horrible about it, and everybody connected with it feels horrible about it."[163]

"Jamar still blames himself for the death of the kids," Weldon Kennedy said. "He has never been the same."

■　■　■

Ironically, the standoff only prolonged Sessions's tenure. Early on, the consensus among Clinton's senior staff was that he would have to go, but, fixated on spin, they wanted to make it appear that Reno had made the decision. Clinton White House staffers were mindful of the legislative history behind the ten-year limit on the tenure of the FBI director. The idea was not only to prevent another FBI director from amassing the unbridled power of a J. Edgar Hoover but also to help insulate the director from political pressures.

Not realizing that the OPR report on Sessions had been prepared by career Justice Department officials and FBI agents under the direction of Michael Shaheen, whose integrity was unquestioned, Clinton's aides were deeply mistrustful of the motives of what they called the Barr Justice Department. They were impressed by Sessions's efforts to promote equality in the FBI and naively tended to credit his claim that he was the victim of unnamed bigoted agents out to get him. Instead of focusing on Sessions's abuses, they were more concerned with his loss of credibility and support within the bureau.

On the other hand, the standoff sealed Sessions's fate with Reno. Having worked with him closely on the issue, she was unimpressed. She found his manner of making pronouncements rather than discussing issues irritating. The fact that Sessions kept calling her "General," when she repeatedly asked him to call her "Janet" or "Miss Reno," only added to her disdain.

When Reno learned that Sessions planned to go to Waco to present a plaque to the mayor, she was appalled. Sessions's grandstanding was so obvious that it was embarrassing.

FBI agents became increasingly bitter and demoralized as they realized they had become pawns in a political battle. Every day, they investigated people who had abused their positions. Yet their own director engaged in similar misconduct. The White House was so unconcerned that it let the impasse drag on.

"It's like waiting for David Koresh to come out," said an agent in headquarters. "We know Sessions will be leaving. The question is when."

With Sessions under a cloud, the Clinton administration and members of Congress took to going around him, preferring to deal with Clarke, Sessions's deputy. Meanwhile, the investigative side of the FBI continued to thrive, symbolized by a case called ILLWIND that never would have been tackled under Hoover. The case began when a vice president of a company told the Naval Investigative Service that he had been offered information on a competitor's Defense Department bid. At one point, the bureau had three hundred agents working the case. They intercepted ten thousand telephone calls and conducted two thousand interviews. Altogether, the agents obtained 1.2 million documents.

The investigation resulted in the conviction of fifty-four Defense Department and private defense contracting officials on bribery, fraud, and other charges. Unisys Corporation paid a fine of $190 million, while United Technologies Corporation paid $6 million in penalties.

But the standoff over Sessions paralyzed every other facet of the bureau's operations—administration, personnel, legislative, and budget. With crime increasing and the federal budget tightening, the FBI needed to enhance its technological capabilities. For months, such proposals had been piling up on Sessions's desk.

Twice, Sessions met with Reno in a futile effort to refute the charges against him and try to shift the blame to others. Twice, Reno refused Sessions's requests to fly on a Justice Department plane to visit his son in San Antonio and to see his daughter in San Francisco. Each time, Sessions invented business reasons for the trips. Reno, like Bill Barr, had taken to groaning each time she heard Sessions's name.

"I knew I should have stayed in Miami," she remarked one time when she heard of Sessions's latest misuse of power, saying he had "brought this all on himself."

After Reno gave a speech in the courtyard of the Justice Department on April 6, 1993, Sessions began walking toward her, hoping to speak with her. Pointedly ignoring him, Reno walked in the other direction. Finally, Reno asked Sessions to meet with her at the Justice Department on Saturday morning, July 17, 1993. With White House Counsel Bernard Nussbaum present, Reno told Sessions that President Clinton would fire him if he did not resign by Monday.

After leaving the meeting with Reno, in full view of television and newspaper cameras, Sessions tripped on a curb outside the Justice Department and broke an elbow. After spending the evening in a hospital, Sessions appeared outside his home. Defiantly, he told reporters that as a "matter of principle" he would not resign. Beyond promoting his own self-interest, it was not clear what principle he was upholding. By ignoring Clinton's request that he resign gracefully, Sessions had plunged the FBI into turmoil as he pointlessly battled to keep his job.

On Monday, July 19, 1993, Clinton made the announcement he should have made six months earlier. In the White House briefing room, the president said he had telephoned Sessions to tell him he was removing him. In a blow to Sessions, Clinton then said he was naming Floyd Clarke acting director. Quietly, Sessions and his lawyers had been trying to negotiate the terms of his resignation, demanding, among other things, that he be allowed to remain in office until a successor was confirmed so that Clarke would not become acting director. Brainwashed by his wife, Sessions had come to believe that Clarke, among others, was behind all his troubles. Reno would have none of it. Appearing with Clinton at the White House, Reno said she had concluded that, as outlined by the facts contained in the OPR report, Sessions had exhibited "a serious deficiency in judgment."

In the end, it came down to the question of whether Sessions would leave FBI headquarters on his own or whether he would have to be dragged out. To make sure he got the message when Clinton called him at 3:50 P.M. to dismiss him, Philip Heymann, the deputy attorney general, met with Sessions in his office to warn him the call was coming. Heymann explained what the procedures would be once he got the call. Like any agent removed from the rolls, the director would have to turn in his FBI credentials and badge and remove from his office only personal effects. Meanwhile, Clinton faxed Sessions a letter informing him of his removal. But Sessions was still in his office at 3:59. Clinton called him a second time, this time telling him his firing was to take effect "immediately."

Finally, Sessions got the message. As instructed, he handed over his FBI credentials to Heymann. Now considered a visitor, Sessions had to be escorted through the halls by his security detail. He gave a final press conference at headquarters. Saying he had been subjected to "scurrilous attacks," Sessions vowed to continue to "speak in the strongest terms about protecting it [the FBI] from being manipulated and politicized both from the inside and out."

Sessions left the building at 6 P.M., receiving one last ride home from his security detail. It was the first time an FBI director had been fired.

Within the FBI, there was jubilation, tinged with sadness that events had taken such a tragic turn. Darlene Fitzsimmons, Sessions's secretary, began sobbing. "Sessions is a very nice man, but he was led around by Sarah Munford and his wife," she said. Other secretaries on mahogany row broke out a bottle of champagne.

BOOK THREE

25

BRICK AGENT

As it became clear that William Sessions's days as director were numbered, the usual debate erupted: Should an FBI director come from the inside or from the outside? As always, agents hoped one of their own would be chosen. The bureau is incredibly complex, and it takes two to five years for a director to learn it all. The last two directors had been judges, but many thought that trend need not continue. Judges generate trust, but they do not necessarily have experience managing a large agency. Even William Webster, himself a former judge, thought being a judge should not be a prerequisite.

"Surely we have demonstrated the trustworthiness of the FBI during all this time," Webster told me. Not since Hoover had there been a "single proven case of a violation of constitutional rights," he said. "You always have people claiming it. It costs $10 to file a lawsuit. But there hasn't been a single one. The organization is composed of individuals, and individuals will not always be perfect. But if the training is there, if the adherence to law is there, if the understanding of the law is there, the systems are there, and the leadership is there, it's not going to happen."

Just before President Clinton fired Sessions, Rudolph Giuliani mentioned to White House Counsel Bernard Nussbaum that Louis J. Freeh would make a fine FBI director. Nussbaum pushed the idea, and Clinton nominated him. At Freeh's swearing in, Clinton said he was "the best possible person to head the FBI as it faces new challenges and a new century."

In Freeh, Clinton got both an insider and an outsider, a former agent who was a U.S. District Court judge. Born in Jersey City, New Jersey, on January 6, 1950, Freeh was the second of three sons of a real estate broker. When he was growing up, one of Freeh's favorite TV shows was *The FBI*. His father, William Freeh, recalled his son saying that he would like to be an FBI agent or J. Edgar Hoover when he grew up. Freeh was an altar boy and Eagle Scout. While only five feet nine inches tall, he never backed down from a fight.

Freeh went on a scholarship to Rutgers College. He graduated Phi Beta Kappa in 1971. He attended Rutgers School of Law at night and obtained a J.D. degree in 1974. From 1974 to 1975, Freeh was on the staff of U.S. Senator Clifford P. Case, a Republican from New Jersey.

In 1975, Freeh became an FBI agent in New York, drafting memos on how the relatively new RICO law could be used to fight organized crime and drawing up applications to courts for wiretaps. Frank Storey, one of his supervisors, said Freeh was "totally dedicated, incredibly bright, and thorough."

In 1980, the FBI promoted Freeh to a supervisory job at headquarters in organized crime. There, he developed a hatred of the bureaucracy but met his future wife, twenty-two-year-old Marilyn Coyle, a bureau paralegal working on civil rights cases. The following year, Freeh left the FBI to became an assistant U.S. attorney in New York. In 1987, he became chief of the Organized Crime Unit under U.S. Attorney Giuliani. Freeh was the lead prosecutor of the Pizza Connection case. It was a landmark in the bureau's fight against organized crime, focusing on the Mafia's use of pizza parlors as fronts to sell heroin. For the case, the FBI developed evidence that the American Mafia worked with the Sicilian Mafia to smuggle $1.6 billion in heroin into the United States. When the jury announced its verdict in March 1987, a former chief of the Sicilian Mafia was among those convicted. Freeh meanwhile managed to attend New York University Law School and receive an LL.M degree in criminal law in 1984.

In 1990, Freeh was named a special federal prosecutor to oversee the prosecution of Walter Leroy Moody Jr., who eventually was convicted in the bombing death of federal Judge Robert Vance. Finally, in 1991, President George Bush appointed Freeh a federal judge in New York.

While Freeh had no experience running a large agency, his skill at dealing with people and coordinating the work of different agencies suggested that he would have no problem managing the FBI.

When he was sworn in as the ninth director of the FBI on September 1, 1993, the forty-three-year-old Freeh talked of the need to support the street agent, who does the "work of the bureau." He criticized the Inspection Division's fixation on minutiae, such as checking that oil in bureau cars was changed on time. Freeh questioned whether 8 percent of the FBI's agents should be assigned to headquarters when they were needed on the streets to fight crime. Finally, Freeh alluded to "the failings of our past." It was the first time since Clarence Kelley that a director had acknowledged publicly that the FBI was not perfect.

Within two weeks, Freeh began issuing orders firmly establishing himself as the boss. Adopting some of the recommendations of a committee Sessions appointed a year earlier, Freeh renamed the Intelligence Division the National Security Division, which reflected the fact that it conducted both foreign counterintelligence and foreign counterterrorism. He made the head of the Washington Metropolitan Field Office an assistant director, just as at the New York office. He abolished the position of associate deputy director, took away top officials' special assistants, and eliminated assistant section chiefs.

As promised at his swearing-in speech, Freeh immediately detailed 150 of the 806 agents at headquarters to positions in the Washington Metropolitan and Baltimore field offices. Over the following year, he planned to move 300 agents in headquarters and field offices from administrative jobs to investigative jobs. Another 150 headquarters personnel were reassigned to street-level jobs in the field. When all the changes had been made, the number of agents assigned to headquarters would be slashed by 37 percent.

Freeh cut the required number of signatures to apply for authority to wiretap in counterintelligence cases from about two dozen to four, and he moved to reduce the backlog of internal discipline cases by delegating to SACs the authority to suspend agents for minor infractions.

At the same time, Freeh issued a memo warning that in the future, agents who stepped over a "bright line" by lying, refusing to cooperate in an internal inquiry, cheating, or stealing would be fired. In the past, these infractions were not necessarily grounds for dismissal.

In visiting field offices, Freeh spent most of his time talking with field agents, often without the SAC present. In Miami, he went for a run on the beach at 6 A.M., then talked with agents on each squad for the rest of the day. In Chicago, Freeh spent just a half an hour with top officials, then devoted the day to talking with agents. In a visit to the laboratory, Freeh told agents they could call him directly if they had problems or suggestions. When one agent took him up on it, Freeh returned his call the same day. Agents were delighted. Freeh was not only one of their own, he was approachable.

While Freeh initially expressed misgivings about taking the FBI job because he did not want to spend time away from his family, he turned out to be a workhorse, arriving in his office at 7 A.M. and working until 6 P.M. In contrast to Sessions's compulsion to use the FBI plane for trips with his wife, Freeh usually flew commercial. After a visit to the Los Angeles Field Office, Freeh took a red-eye flight back to Washington and immediately went to work.

Freeh abolished the executive dining room. That saved money but soon posed problems. When taking officials from Scotland Yard, for instance, to lunch, bureau officials could not discuss business with them because other diners at the restaurant might overhear them. Freeh was sometimes seen diapering one of his sons—he and Marilyn eventually had six—in his seventh-floor office. Freeh carried a gun but dispensed with his security detail.

For lunch, Freeh often ate only a banana at his desk. His graying hair was shorn in a brush cut, and he looked so pallid he appeared to have an iron deficiency. An indifferent dresser, Freeh worked in shirtsleeves and often wore a blue suit with brown shoes. His narrow tie was usually askew, his belt worn, his shirt collar frayed, his shoes scuffed. The appearance of impropriety was more important, and when Weldon Kennedy gave him a baseball cap as a gift, Freeh returned it. Robert M. "Bear" Bryant, who was deputy FBI director under Freeh, recalled putting on Freeh's suit jacket by mistake. In a pocket was a worn Roman Catholic prayer book.

Unlike Sessions, who referred to himself as "your director," Freeh insisted on being called by his first name. But while Freeh bonded with street agents and dispensed with the perks that Sessions so loved, Freeh brought to the job his own idiosyncracies. In the end, they would turn out to be far more disastrous to the bureau than Sessions's abuses.

■　■　■

At his first meeting with assistant directors, Freeh said, "I want you to talk to me straight. If I'm full of shit, I want you to tell me." But soon Freeh made clear his distaste for countervailing opinions; in fact, there would be a penalty for expressing them.

At a second meeting of the executive conference a week after taking over, Freeh asked each assistant director to speak for ten minutes about the work of his division. G. Norman Christensen made a pitch for Total Quality Management, a program Sessions had promoted for focusing on the need to do things right the first time. Christensen took a trip to the West Coast, and when he returned, he had a message to see Weldon Kennedy, who headed the Administrative Services Division. Kennedy told Christensen that Steven L. Pomerantz had just informed him that he had been placed in charge of Christensen's division. Freeh abolished the Total Quality Management program. Apparently, Freeh did not agree with Christensen's support of the program.

Freeh offered Christensen an SAC job; he resigned instead. Ironically, just before he did, Freeh held a ceremony to award bonuses to FBI managers. Christensen received $2,000.[164] "I don't believe in bonuses," Freeh informed the honorees. "This is the last time I'll give out bonuses."

While everyone recognized that Freeh had the right to place his own people in charge, the way he abruptly removed Christensen after he gave his opinion suggested that those who expressed views that differed from Freeh's would suffer consequences. That became more apparent when Freeh held a meeting of the SAC Advisory Committee, which consists of senior SACs elected by their peers. The SACs found that Freeh not only ignored their ideas, but also expressed hostility when they offered them.

"His response to suggestions was to sit there and say nothing," said D. Caroll Toohey, a member of the board who was SAC in Atlanta and who previously had been assistant director over the Inspection Division. "He would listen and have this stern look on his face. He would say, 'Next issue.' He would show his disapproval by the look on his face. It meant, 'Don't bother me with this.' "[165]

"There was talk of disbanding the SAC Advisory Committee," another member of the board said. "When we brought up a subject that was controversial, Freeh got this icy, silent stare. After a while, we realized he didn't value what we had to offer. If you questioned him, you would not be on his team. Or he would say, 'That's the dumbest question I ever heard.' We became blacklisted."

Managing a major investigation requires immense experience, sophistication, and balance. Webster appointed to the top positions seasoned agents with the intellect to handle such cases. To a large extent, Sessions kept those same officials. They managed collegially, eliciting the opinions of their colleagues. Freeh's approach was quite the opposite, a fact that quickly spread throughout the bureau. Only the pluckiest agents dared disagree with him, and they often regretted it. Freeh either removed them or, like a child, would not speak to them for weeks.

After Freeh appointed Roger Nisley to head the HRT, Nisley decided that the way to deal with Freeh was to adopt the posture of a private addressing a senior officer in the military.

"Request permission to be candid, sir," Nisley said the first time he wanted to disagree with Freeh.

Grudgingly, Freeh said, "I guess I don't have a choice."

Under Webster, bureau officials were in trouble if they *didn't* offer him their honest advice. That was what they were being paid for. Now the head of one of the most important agencies in the U.S. government made it clear that he knew all the answers.

In April 1994, Freeh created a Critical Incident Response Group (CIRG) whose purpose was to coordinate the Hostage Rescue Team, negotiators, profilers, and other specialists assigned to hostage rescue situations, terrorist incidents, and other emergencies. Freeh appointed Nisley SAC in charge of the new unit. Important as this job was, Nisley continued to feel the need to preface his remarks to Freeh by asking if he could give his honest advice.

"Freeh killed the messenger. After a while, there were no more messengers," said an agent who worked with Freeh and later was promoted by him to SAC.

"Freeh said he wants everything straight. The first person who told it to him straight, he cut his head off," said Weldon Kennedy, whom Freeh promoted to deputy director.

"Freeh took away from the SACs the desire to make decisions because they feared repercussions," said Anthony E. Daniels, whom Freeh named assistant FBI director to head the Washington Field Office. "They were terrified of him. Freeh had contempt for management."

"If you can't accept contrary views, you shouldn't accept the job," said Herbert L. "Larry" Collins, a former special assistant to Deputy Director Floyd Clarke promoted by Freeh to be SAC in Chicago.

■ ■ ■

The job of an FBI director is to manage an agency with close to twenty-eight thousand employees—including eleven thousand agents—and an overt budget of $3.4 billion. A classified budget for counterintelligence brings the total to roughly $4 billion.

Freeh viewed his job as directing major cases, which would be like the chairman of GE designing a jet engine or sitting in for Tom Brokaw on NBC's *Nightly News*. From procurement of computers to the services the bureau provides law enforcement, Freeh ignored what goes on in the rest of the bureau. With only six years as an agent, Freeh had never supervised a case, yet he considered himself the bureau's premier case agent.

Freeh "had the perspective of a [brick agent]," said Charles J. Parsons, who was SAC under Freeh in Los Angeles. A brick or street agent investigates and has no supervisory duties.

"He was like a private who became a member of the Joint Chiefs of Staff," said a former assistant director promoted by Freeh. "He just focused on investigations to the exclusion of everything else that is important."

"Freeh wanted to be the case agent on the big cases. When that happens, you begin to second-guess everything you're doing," said James V. DeSarno Jr., who was promoted by Freeh to be assistant director in charge of the Los Angeles Field Office.

Freeh's concept of investigations was limited to what he had done as an agent ten years earlier—knocking on doors and interviewing people. He did not understand how essential technology had become to law enforcement. In fact, as soon as he took over, Freeh ordered the computer in his office removed. He did not use E-mail.

"He had no use for automation, and he made that clear," said an agent formerly assigned to the Office of Public and Congressional Affairs.

Peter T. Higgins, who was a deputy assistant director over a program to digitalize fingerprint records, offered to brief Freeh on the program, but Freeh never wanted to hear about it. The program was already incurring major delays and cost overruns that amounted eventually to $120 million. At a talk given by Attorney General Janet Reno at the Justice Department, Higgins—who was formerly at the CIA—spotted Jamie S. Gorelick, the deputy attorney general.

In contrast to Reno, who zeroed in on minute factual issues, Gorelick, a Harvard Law School graduate, kept her eye on the big picture. She kept the trains running on time, always looking for what she called "alternative sources of information" to guide her decisions. It might be a chat with an employee in an elevator or a subordinate's aside that others would overlook.

"I run this program, which spends 5 percent of the FBI's budget, and I've never briefed Louis Freeh," Higgins told her.

"You can come over and brief me," Gorelick said.[166]

Prompted by alerts from the Justice Department's Management Division, Gorelick and Reno frequently raised management issues with Freeh. Usually, when they raised concerns about the FBI's computers, the laboratory, or procurement problems, he would assure them that everything was fine. Gorelick was particularly concerned about the FBI's lack of analytic capabilities. She found that the bureau could not produce a quality report on possible threats at the 1996 Olympics in Atlanta.

"Freeh was not getting good information about management issues from within the bureau," she told me.[167]

"Louis never grasped that the FBI is about more than investigations. It is about law enforcement," Larry Collins, the former Chicago SAC, said.

In making key appointments, Freeh tended to choose candidates whom he had worked with or who were recommended by a few of his bureau friends, such as Bob C. Reutter, the SAC in Philadelphia. They became widely known as Friends of Louis (FOL). Freeh often bypassed the FBI's Career Board and forced relatively inexperienced agents to become SACs.

"After Hoover, we put a career system in place," said Bob A. Ricks, who was SAC in Oklahoma City and a member of the SAC Advisory Committee. "All of a sudden, that was pretty much thrown out the window. Freeh selected people he knew or friends of people he knew. Some may have been quality people, but when you jump people over the four or five positions that are traditionally served in first, it becomes very disheartening."

Brick agents, especially those from New York, tend to see management as the enemy. Freeh never lost that mentality. Even if he had been the one to promote a manager, Freeh viewed the official as a threat to his own authority and treated him or her with suspicion and hostility. It was as if Freeh were exacting retribution for every slight he had suffered as a street agent.

"Freeh seemed to be trying to get even with management," said I. C. Smith, whom Freeh promoted to be SAC in Little Rock. "He did not have the required intellect."

While Freeh's habit of meeting with field agents without their SAC present at first appeared to be refreshing, it turned out the reason he did so was that he valued their opinions more than those of their bosses. When he said field or brick agents "do the work of the bureau," he meant that managers are superfluous. When issues arose about discipline, Freeh tended to side with field agents over their SAC.

Freeh often made snap judgments based on fragmentary information. Back when he was an agent, an inspector might have checked the oil in bureau cars, as Freeh mentioned in his speech when he was sworn in. But the Inspection Division had long since dropped its fixation on such trivia. Instead, it evaluated how well field offices addressed crime. The General Accounting Office, the audit arm of Congress, had called the FBI's inspection system the best audit function in the government. Yet Freeh still despised the inspection staff, and he changed its emphasis so that it became primarily a popularity poll.

Larry Collins noted that Freeh's main interest was "whether the SAC was popular. The inspectors did not look at cases. That demonstrated his disdain for management and his desire to look good to the street agent."

"Under Freeh, they [inspections] became like climate surveys," said Barry Mawn, the head of the New York Field Office. "It became, to an extent, what do the agents and community leaders think of the management?"[168]

The quality control system that had performed so well over the years broke down.

■ ■ ■

Through friends, Freeh heard that Caroll Toohey, the SAC in Atlanta, had put up bail for Danny A. Scott, an agent who had killed a twenty-seven-year-old father while driving a bureau car drunk just after midnight on August 4, 1994. The reason Toohey had done so was that the agent was suicidal and did not have the funds to make bail.

Toohey had just become SAC and was not aware of Scott's drinking problem. Two years earlier, Scott had pleaded no contest to a charge of driving under the influence. At six o'clock on the morning of the accident, Toohey visited Scott in his cell at the Cobb County jail.

"They had Danny isolated because he had made some statements like, 'Why don't you go around and shoot me. I don't deserve to live,' " Toohey said. "I spent time with him trying to explain his life didn't have to be over. His career as an FBI agent in all likelihood was over, but he had to deal with it. Basically, I was trying to save the guy's life. I got him to agree to go into rehab. I got the bail for him—$2,500— from my account."[169]

An enraged Freeh called Toohey later that day. The director stubbornly refused to listen to Toohey's explanation. "His assumption was I had pulled strings in some inappropriate way to get him out," Toohey said. "All I had done was bail him out, as anybody could have. He wanted Danny fired. He wanted him off the rolls. I told him as a veteran, he had certain rights. You couldn't immediately fire a veteran. He was raising his voice. He would say, 'Do you understand?' I said, 'I do.' "

Soon after that, Toohey was notified he was being transferred back to Washington. Instead, he retired. Scott stopped drinking and retired before he could be fired.

As field agents began to recognize that Freeh had little respect for SACs, discipline throughout the bureau broke down. The players were running the football team.

"Freeh would meet with agents, they would bad-mouth the SAC, and he would remove the SAC. So the SACs hunkered down and stopped doing anything," Buck Revell, an SAC in Dallas under Freeh, said.

Appalled at Freeh's arrogance and hostility, many of the best and most seasoned managers either returned to the field or retired.

"We didn't have the same quality of SACs as under Webster and Sessions," an agent said. "You saw people who were more concerned about their next inspection report than operations and cases. Things were done with the thought, 'How will this look on my next review?' "

"Freeh is bright, but he destroyed the management system," Collins said. "Louis never felt SACs were worth a damn. No one became interested in serving in management. You had mediocre people staying in headquarters."

26

PELTIER

As his chief of staff, Freeh chose Robert B. Bucknam, Freeh's friend and closest confidant. It was the first time an FBI director had such an assistant. When Bucknam was an assistant U.S. attorney in New York, Freeh had worked with him on the prosecution of the Pizza Connection case. Bucknam became deputy chief of the Criminal Division and, when Giuliani ran for mayor of New York, he worked for his campaign. From 1991 to 1993, Bucknam was deputy assistant attorney general in the Justice Department's Criminal Division.

At Justice, Attorney General William Barr considered Bucknam, a political appointee, the sort of person who had gotten his job by "sucking up" to the right people.

"He [Bucknam] was obnoxious—arrogant even by Justice standards," said David P. Bobzien, who worked with Bucknam when Bobzien was in the Office of Professional Responsibility. "We thought, 'God, how will he go over at the FBI?' " where arrogance is tolerated even less. The fact that Bucknam, who acquired the nickname "Dough Boy," was obese did not help. "You don't put a guy who is grossly overweight in the FBI," Bobzien said.[170]

Bucknam's job was to tout Freeh, often to the detriment of the bureau. Early on, the FBI rejected two of Freeh's proposed assistants because they had in the past used heroin or cocaine. Bucknam told Weldon Kennedy, who headed administrative services, to hire them anyway. He suggested that they could be called Justice Department employees and therefore would not be subject to the same rules as FBI employees. Kennedy refused.

"He wanted some way to bring these guys on board regardless," Kennedy said. "I said, 'No, we're not doing it.' It wasn't marijuana that they had used; it was hard drugs."[171]

On February 3, 1994, Freeh tried to solve the problem by issuing a memo relaxing the rules for all employees. Previously, the FBI had accepted employees who had used marijuana "experimentally" when they were young. Now an applicant who had taken hard drugs could be accepted if the activity was "experimental" and if he or she had stopped using hard dugs more than ten years earlier and was not a law enforcement or court officer at the time. Even if the activity were more recent, an applicant could still be hired under Freeh's new policy if there were "compelling mitigating circumstances." As part of the change, Freeh required new employees to take a polygraph test on these and other issues.

In announcing the relaxation of the rules, Freeh made no mention of his desire to hire former aides with drug histories. Instead, he said that the FBI had been studying the question for some time. While that was true, when Freeh asked the SAC Advisory Committee for its opinion, the board told him SACs universally opposed the change. For one thing, defense attorneys could undermine testimony of agents who arrested suspects in drug cases by pointing out that they had used the same substances. The DEA, the other federal agency charged with combating drugs, continued to reject applicants who had ever used hard drugs.

"How will it look when it turns out an agent accusing a dealer of selling drugs himself committed a crime by taking drugs?" an SAC asked.

"The SACs were all universally opposed to changing the rules," Bob Ricks said. "That didn't matter much. If you were someone who didn't agree, you weren't going to be on the advisory board very long. Candid comments were not welcome. People stopped giving them. That's one reason I left the bureau."

Even more troubling was the appearance that Freeh was using his position to favor his former colleagues. Even after Freeh relaxed the rules, the former aides who had been rejected failed polygraph tests on their use of drugs and ultimately were not hired.[172]

■ ■ ■

To current and former agents, there is no more important cause than opposing efforts to pardon Leonard Peltier. Peltier was convicted of killing two FBI agents, Ronald A. Williams and Jack R. Coler, on the morning of June 26, 1975, on the Pine Ridge Indian Reservation near Wounded Knee in South Dakota. The two agents were looking for James "Jimmy" Eagle, who had been charged with robbery on an Indian reservation. The agents spotted him with several other individuals in a vehicle on the reservation. As they pursued the vehicle, the agents were fired upon. They called for reinforcements. During the subsequent shootout, the two agents were killed.

Although they did not see the actual shooting, witnesses described Peltier as the only person at the scene with a weapon capable of firing the .223-type bullets that killed the two agents. A shell casing found in the trunk of Coler's car matched Peltier's Wichita AR-15 weapon. Later recovered from a car owned by Peltier associates were Peltier's weapon and Coler's .308 rifle. Unknown to Coler and Williams, a warrant was outstanding for the arrest of Peltier for unlawful flight to avoid prosecution for the attempted murder of an off-duty police officer.

Peltier fled to an Indian reservation in Hinton, Alberta. In February 1976, Royal Canadian Mounted Police captured him. When asked if he knew why he was being arrested, Peltier said two FBI agents were shot when they came to a house to serve a warrant on him.

Peltier was sentenced to two consecutive life terms. On February 11, 1986, Federal Appeals Judge Gerald R. Heaney concluded, "When all is said and done . . . a few simple but very important facts remain. The casing introduced into evidence had in fact been extracted from the Wichita AR-15."

In March 1979, the U.S. Supreme Court refused to review the case. In an interview that aired on 60 Minutes on September 22, 1991, Peltier admitted firing at the two agents. Yet a procession of movie stars and other celebrities has claimed Peltier was unfairly convicted.

Among those calling for Peltier's release was M. Wesley Swearingen, a former FBI agent who has maintained that Peltier was "railroaded." Yet when asked why he believes Peltier is not guilty, Swearingen, who has testified against the FBI in twelve controversial cases, appeared to have no knowledge of the case.

"If you get in touch with the Peltier defense committee, they'll give you all the documents," he told me. Didn't Peltier confess on TV? "Somebody confessing on *60 Minutes* doesn't mean that he did it," Swearingen said.[173]

When Peltier was up for a pardon, Bucknam was supposed to prepare the bureau's position for the pardon attorney. Despite the importance of the issue to the FBI and its agents—a feeling shared by Freeh—Bucknam did nothing, according to an agent who was in the Office of Public and Congressional Affairs.

"Bucknam sat on it," the agent said. "Senator Arlen Specter heard about the delay and inquired about it. We asked Bucknam, and he said in effect it was none of our business." The agent quoted Bucknam as saying that the issue of Peltier's release was "not the director's problem."

Bucknam finally passed the job off to another Freeh appointee, who had only two days before the deadline to prepare and submit the bureau's written position opposing a pardon. That was not atypical. Bucknam often promised to supply members of Congress with information they had requested, then forgot about it.

"We would get a call from the Hill saying, 'Why haven't you sent this material?' " the agent from congressional affairs said. "We would say, 'We don't know anything about it.' They would say, 'Bob Bucknam said he would send it.' We would go to Bucknam, and he would act as if we were bothering him. Bucknam was only interested in promoting Louis."

When an agent told Bucknam about the cost overruns and procurement problems plaguing the new fingerprint identification system now known as CJIS, Bucknam dismissed the issue as not part of Freeh's agenda.

"He said that's not our problem," the agent said. "He said, 'That was started before Louis took over.' "

So important was the system that when it finally came on-line, fingerprints that once took six weeks to locate were retrieved in two hours.

As a result of quicker identification, vicious murderers and rapists who earlier would have gotten away were taken off the streets.

"Bob Bucknam didn't give a shit about the FBI. He cared about making Freeh look good. He was like a campaign manager for Freeh," former SAC Larry Collins said.[174]

Bucknam had his own ideas about where the FBI should open overseas legats. Thomas C. Knowles, who was over the legat program, would show him which areas of the world had the most leads to check out from FBI investigations. Bucknam would argue that the figures were irrelevant. What was important were "geopolitical considerations," as if the FBI were the State Department. When told the FBI had to justify each opening to Congress, Bucknam incorrectly said, "George Tenet doesn't have to justify where he opens CIA stations." When Knowles refused to present what he considered misleading justifications to Congress, Bucknam claimed that Knowles had been bad-mouthing Freeh, and Freeh removed him.

Bucknam tried to become involved in FBI operations or ordered agents to complete reports before they had all the facts, prompting complaints by SACs.

"I would hear Freeh's secretary tell Freeh, 'Another SAC called with a complaint about Bob,' " a high-ranking agent said. "Freeh would just laugh."

Bear Bryant, as deputy director, thought Bucknam was bright and admired his loyalty to Freeh, but he told Bucknam to stay out of operational matters. "Bucknam would tell Bear to do something, and Bear would say, 'You're full of shit.' He would laugh and walk out," an agent said.

"If Bob Bucknam's pants were on fire, no one at headquarters would have told him," said a high-ranking FBI official.

As part of his role of promoting Freeh, Bucknam talked to the press and was widely assumed to be a source of leaks. Key reporters who cover the FBI told me that while he did not leak operational details, Bucknam had regular not-for-attribution talks with them revealing sensitive information calculated to promote his boss. For example, one reporter said Bucknam gave him details of the memo Freeh wrote to Janet Reno taking issue with her opposition to the appointment of an independent counsel to investigate President Clinton and allegations of illicit fund-raising in the 1996 presidential campaign. The memo was considered so sensitive that Reno refused to turn it over to Congress even when Representative Dan Burton, an Indiana Republican, threatened to hold her in contempt of Congress. Reno told Burton's House Government Reform and Oversight Committee that making the memo public would endanger the investigation. Yet Bucknam, according to the reporter, freely discussed its contents with him.

Jamie Gorelick, the deputy attorney general, had a wide circle of friends in the media. On several occasions, they told her that Bucknam had been the anonymous source of stories about matters discussed in her confidential meetings. When she called Bucknam on it, he denied having been the source of the leaks.

Despite such evidence and the fact that everyone at the higher levels of the FBI was convinced that Bucknam's job description included leaking on Freeh's behalf, no one initiated an Office of Professional Responsibility investigation. Bucknam, after all, was a Friend of Louis.

My four attempts to obtain comment from Bucknam were unsuccessful. Each time, he said he was too busy to talk, or he promised to call back but never did.[175]

Bucknam's leak of Freeh's memo opposing Reno's position on appointing an independent counsel would prove crucial to Freeh's success in dealing with Congress. As in a game of musical chairs, the Democrats and Republicans suddenly switched positions. Traditionally considered soft on crime, the Democrats now supported law enforcement and the FBI, which they saw as an element of the Clinton administration. The Republicans, known as hard-liners when it came to security, now viewed federal law enforcement as a symbol of unrestrained government power under Clinton. By taking sides on the issue of a special counsel, Freeh endeared himself to the Republicans, immunizing himself from congressional scrutiny and criticism almost as much as Hoover immunized himself with his secret files.

Uncomfortable and stiff with people he did not know, Freeh could turn on the charm when he went to Capitol Hill. When FBI foul-ups occurred, members of Congress would posture before television cameras and demand that Freeh take action. But in closed sessions they would lavish praise on Freeh and ask how much more money he needed, just as they did with Hoover. Under Freeh, the bureau's annual budget increased 53 percent to $3.4 billion. A consummate politician, before the Republicans took over Congress in 1994, Freeh played to the Democrats, emphasizing liberal issues like hiring minorities.

"The Republicans were really starting to come down on Freeh," Buck Revell said. "All of a sudden this memo he wrote to Reno is leaked. It was a typical bureaucratic ploy. But it is not something that happened under Kelley, Webster, or Sessions."[176]

■　■　■

On March 22, 1993, David Willcox, a pro-Palestinian activist, was beaten as he demonstrated at the opening ceremonies of the U.S. Holocaust Museum. A year later, Willcox claimed to the press that he had immediately identified his three assailants in photographs the FBI showed him of the crowd. He asserted that the FBI ignored his identifications and said he was "horrified" when he learned that the FBI had dropped the case.

Willcox's claim had obvious political implications. Witnesses verified that he had been attacked. He said the three men who attacked him wore yarmulkes. A New York–based group calling itself the Jewish Defense Organization told news organizations it was responsible for the beating, which left Willcox with a head wound requiring twelve stitches. Was the FBI covering up for the Jews?

Absolutely not, said Frank Scafidi, the head of the FBI's press office. Neither Willcox nor his fiancée, who was also a witness, could identify his assailants from the photographs. "There was enough waffling going on there to open a pancake house," Scafidi told the *Washington Post*.[177]

On April 8, 1994, Freeh issued a teletype to all SACs and legats. Titled "Improper Comment to Press," the teletype, without naming him, criticized Scafidi's comment as "flippant." The FBI should "speak only from the witness stand," Freeh said in another memo.

The order was stunningly obtuse. It not only suggested that Freeh did not care enough about the bureau to allow it to respond to unfair charges, it also reversed the progress made by the FBI under Webster to earn the public's confidence through the media. Webster felt so strongly that the FBI could not properly function if it did not explain

itself to the public that he considered his press officer his "most important appointment."[178]

For all his faults, Hoover understood the importance of the press. It
could enhance the power of the FBI by creating an image of its agents,
albeit embellished, as supermen. If people believed in the bureau, they
were more likely to cooperate with agents. As part of their training,
SACs under Webster gave mock press conferences. Having been an
agent fewer than six years, Freeh never got near the FBI's press operations. He saw the bureau as an arm of prosecutors, who usually reserve
comment for press conferences, rather than as an American institution
accountable to the public.

When it fit his agenda, Freeh occasionally met with the press. Early
on, he took reporters on a trip to the Sicilian Mafia stronghold of Pa-
lermo to honor the slain Italian Mafia fighter Giovanni Falcone. Freeh's
Pizza Connection case overlapped with mass trials in Italy engineered
by Falcone, who was killed by a car bomb after 350 Mafia members
were sent to jail. But, while Freeh designated Bucknam to promote himself, Freeh hated dealing with the media. He soon cut off virtually any
contact with reporters beyond well-choreographed news conferences.

In the past, the FBI had allowed reporters to interview agents about
cases where convictions had been obtained. But Freeh decided that no
case should be discussed until all appeals were exhausted—a process
that often took decades. This meant that nearly all FBI cases were off-
limits. Because Freeh had press requests go through Bucknam, most of
them became lost on his desk, which was covered with papers several
feet high.

"Freeh practically closed down the FBI as far as the press is concerned," said Michael Isikoff, who covered the bureau for the *Washington Post* and later for *Newsweek*.

In his four-page, single-spaced teletype, Freeh said that when faced
with a question about a pending investigation, FBI agents were not even
to say "no comment" because that might be interpreted as confirming
that the FBI had an investigation going. Instead, agents were to refer
the inquiries to a media representative or to the U.S. attorney's office.
Freeh did not understand that by referring an inquiry to the U.S. attorney, FBI agents were confirming the existence of an investigation.

The media recognized that the FBI could not comment on ongoing

investigations and pending cases. But under Freeh, even favorable feature stories about the FBI's profiling program and other successes became off-limits. In the past, as with any beat, reporters and FBI media
representatives would manipulate each other. The media reps would
give reporters tidbits that did not jeopardize prosecutions but made their
stories more colorful. Reporters, in turn, might give the FBI a break
when a minor mistake occurred. Now, when mistakes occurred, reporters who had been ignored were less likely to be understanding and
more likely to emphasize the negative. Because Freeh would not allow
press officers to give the FBI's side, on the record or off, the negative
stories appeared without presenting the bureau's side. While Freeh did
not specifically ban press officers from appearing on TV, no one wanted
to take the chance that he or she might say something that would draw
Freeh's ire. If the KGB had wanted to befoul the FBI's reputation, this
was the way to do it.

"Freeh shut down the press operation," a former press officer said.
"When press officers were quoted, he chopped our heads off. He said,
'We'll speak from the witness stand.' "

Everyone in the FBI remembered what Freeh did to James M. Fox,
the assistant director over the New York office, when he defended the
FBI in a half-hour interview about his career on a local New York
television show. A lawyer who was the son of a Chicago bus driver,
Fox had one of the most distinguished careers in the FBI, rising to head
its largest office. He supervised SOLO, the critically important double-
agent operation involving Morris Childs, the principal deputy to the
head of the American Communist Party. As head of the New York
office for six years, Fox spearheaded the investigation of John Gotti,
who was found guilty of murder, racketeering, and other charges after
agents tape-recorded him at his headquarters in the Ravenite Social
Club in Little Italy.

A reporter asked Fox on the TV show about reports that the FBI knew
from Emad Ali Salem, an FBI informant, that the World Trade Center
was about to be bombed in 1993 and had done nothing about it. Since
February 26, 1993, when his beeper went off while he was eating sword-
fish and french fries at Harry's two blocks away from the World Trade
Center, Fox had not taken a weekend off. When he called the office, Fox
was told a transformer had exploded at the 110-story complex.

Fox suspected terrorists. He got in his FBI car, turned on the red light, and drove to the scene. Fire engines and ambulances had already surrounded the Twin Towers. Fox drove a few minutes to the New York Field Office at 26 Federal Plaza, where he opened its command center. The blast had killed six and injured more than one thousand.

In 1995, Sheik Omar Abdul-Rahman was convicted of setting off the bomb. In 1998, Ramzi Ahmed Yousef, the mastermind of the plot, was sentenced to 240 years in prison, with a recommendation from U.S. District Court Judge Kevin Thomas Duffy that he be kept in solitary confinement for the rest of his life.

When asked on the December 4 TV show about the informant's claim, Fox simply said, "He gave us nothing. No one gave us anything. If we had information, we would have prevented the bombing."

Freeh phoned Fox on December 10 to inform him he was putting him on leave with pay three weeks before Fox's planned retirement on January 2. Freeh told the FBI's press office to issue an announcement of the suspension, and it ran throughout the country.

While the judge on the case had imposed a gag order, the public had a right to know if the FBI had ignored a tip that the World Trade Center was about to be attacked. Balancing the two interests, Fox chose to defend the institution with the facts. In the same way, the CIA over the years had learned that, in a free society, adamantly refusing to comment when the agency was charged with reprehensible acts was shortsighted when the CIA needed the support of the public.

"On the surface, when faced with such an egregious allegation, it would be hard for anyone to let it go unchallenged," Webster told me.

Ironically, Freeh later promulgated a list of the FBI's "core values," which included "compassion." But if Freeh had compassion, it was reserved for field agents, not managers. Freeh could have reprimanded Fox, but he chose instead to embarrass him publicly. Fox died three years after he left the bureau.

"It hurt Jim a lot," said Richard F. "Rich" Green, a former New York agent who was assistant legal attaché in London and was a friend of Fox for twenty-five years. "He had done a great job throughout his career. He never really got over it."

27

RANDY WEAVER

At first, the shooting at Ruby Ridge was so obscure that it would be three years before the *Washington Post* reported criticism of the FBI's handling of the incident. Similarly, most Americans supported the FBI on its handling of Waco. But after Freeh took office, Ruby Ridge and Waco became synonymous with outrageous government conduct. Most Americans came to believe that the FBI had murdered innocent civilians in both incidents. In both cases, Freeh's policies were responsible for this misperception.

Like Waco, Ruby Ridge began with an abortive arrest by another agency. On August 21, 1992, U.S. marshals approached the property of Randall "Randy" Weaver, a self-proclaimed Christian white separatist who lived with his family in a remote mountain cabin near Ruby Ridge in northern Idaho. After his release on bond, Weaver failed to appear for a pretrial hearing on a charge of selling unregistered firearms—two sawed-off shotguns he bought for $450 from an ATF informant.

A neighbor of Weaver's quoted him as saying that if federal agents showed up on his property, "I'll take some with me."

In an effort to take Weaver peacefully, the marshals planned to buy a piece of property next to his. When Weaver came to visit his new neighbors, the marshals would arrest him. But as four marshals were checking out Weaver's property, his dog started barking and gave them away. A gunfight ensued, leaving marshal William F. Degan and Weaver's fourteen-year-old son Sammy dead.

When the marshals requested assistance from the FBI, an HRT team headed by Richard Rogers arrived the next day in two Air Force C-130s. The team made the same mistake it had made at Waco six months earlier by not waiting for suspects to leave the compound before arresting them. The HRT deployed eleven members to surround Weaver's cabin. Because a marshal had already been killed and Weaver was thought to be extremely dangerous, Larry A. Potts, the assistant director in charge of the Criminal Investigative Division, approved rules of engagement for the incident stating that agents "can and should" shoot any of the armed adults in Weaver's cabin.[179]

In firearms training at Quantico, every agent is taught the FBI's policy on use of deadly force: An agent may shoot to kill only when there is probable cause to believe that he or another person is in imminent danger of being killed or seriously injured by a suspect. Opening fire for any other reason amounts to "wartime rules [that] are patently unconstitutional for a police action," as an appeals court later said.

Occasionally, special rules of engagement were needed to modify that policy, but only to *limit* the use of deadly force. For example, when 121 Cuban inmates held nine hostages at the federal prison in Talladega, Alabama, in August 1991, Weldon Kennedy ordered the HRT not to shoot even if the inmates killed a hostage. If they did, the inmates might kill the remaining hostages. In the end, no one was killed.

The other policy the FBI drums into the heads of new agents is that sometimes the best thing to do is to do nothing. Over time, suspects will become tired and hungry and eventually give up peacefully. When dealing with what the FBI calls crisis management, agents are taught at Quantico to "isolate, contain, and negotiate."

At Ruby Ridge, both policies were violated. In fact, Rogers came up with an assault plan that called for dismantling the house with two armored personnel carriers if Weaver and his family did not come out within two days.

Danny Coulson, a deputy assistant director over violent crime who helped Potts with the rules of engagement, vetoed Rogers's plan, which had been faxed to him at headquarters. "What I had in my hand didn't resemble anything that the HRT or any law enforcement agency should do," he said. "We never, never set deadlines for hostage takers because that only escalates the crisis. Only bad guys set deadlines."[180]

HRT snipers began taking positions around the cabin at 5:07 P.M. It had started to sleet. At 5:58, an FBI helicopter took off for a reconnaissance run around the cabin. As the helicopter clattered overhead, Weaver, his sixteen-year-old daughter Sara, and his adopted son Kevin Harris came out of the cabin carrying rifles. Agent Lon Horiuchi thought one of the men looked as if he were about to shoot at the helicopter. Horiuchi fired at him. Because Horiuchi believed the man was preparing to shoot, his shot fell within the FBI's deadly force policy. The man he wounded was Randy Weaver.

As all three ran back toward the cabin, Horiuchi fired again at the same man. He figured the man would continue to threaten the helicopter from inside the house, where it would be difficult, with women and children around, for Horiuchi to get a clear shot. As it turned out, Horiuchi's second shot blasted through the cabin's wooden door and into the face of Vicki Weaver, Randy's wife, who had been standing behind the half-open door, beckoning the three to come back in. The round exited the other side of her head and struck Harris in the arm. Vicki Weaver died almost instantly. Not until bodies were recovered did Horiuchi realize he had killed her.

Since Horiuchi thought he was firing at a man he believed was endangering an FBI helicopter, the second shot fell within the deadly force policy as well. Ten days later, Randy Weaver surrendered.

A state prosecutor filed criminal charges against Horiuchi, but a federal judge agreed with him that because he had been acting in an official capacity, a federal court should hear the case, which was dismissed.

Weaver was charged with the murder of Degan. In July 1993, a federal jury, believing the marshals shot first, acquitted him. He was also acquitted of the weapons charge. Ultimately, the Justice Department agreed to pay Weaver $3.1 million to settle his wrongful death lawsuit.

During discovery proceedings over charges against Weaver, E. Michael Kahoe, the chief of the Violent Crimes and Major Offenders Section, destroyed an after-action critique that was critical of the FBI's actions. He also ordered Gale R. Evans, who worked for him, to get rid of his copies. Kahoe pled guilty to obstruction of justice charges and was sentenced to eighteen months in prison. Because Evans cooperated fully from the outset of the investigation without requesting immunity from prosecution, he was not charged.

While the FBI had made many missteps, Ruby Ridge came down to an accidental shooting. It appeared to have been related to the special rules of engagement, but was not. Anyone who has used firearms knows how easy it is to miss the target, particularly when under stress. Almost every day, police officers accidentally shoot suspects, and, unless it becomes a racial issue, there is little public outcry. A combination of factors made this case different. First, it involved the FBI, which is rightly held to a higher standard than local police and which is a symbol of the federal government and all its power. Second, as with Waco, right-wing antigovernment militia groups and fanatics turned the case into a cause célèbre and enlisted support of members of Congress. Third, Freeh appointed agents to conduct initial inquiries who were longtime friends of Potts or Coulson and who either exonerated them or minimized their involvement. An agent who worked on one of the investigations admitted to me that those connections "probably" ensured that Potts would not be implicated.

Potts, in turn, was a FOL who got to know Freeh when they both worked on the prosecution of Walter Moody for the murder of Judge Vance. When it came time to discipline him, Freeh gave Potts only a letter of censure.

In May 1995, Eugene Glenn, field commander at Ruby Ridge and the agent who received the stiffest punishment after the initial inquiries, complained to the Justice Department that he was made a scapegoat while Potts, who had devised the rules of engagement, got off the hook. A previous investigation specifically concluded that "neither Potts nor Coulson" approved of or was aware of the special rules of engagement saying agents "can and should" fire at armed adults.

Having read reports of the previous investigations into the case, Howard M. Shapiro, whom Freeh appointed general counsel of the FBI after they worked together on the Walter Moody case, responded to

Glenn's complaint by calling it "baseless." In a remark reminiscent of Hoover's "don't-embarrass-the-bureau" dictum, Shapiro added that bringing such charges was "absolutely irresponsible and destructive to the FBI."

"Shapiro's comment was exactly the opposite of the position a general counsel should take," Buck Revell said. "A general counsel should have an open mind and inquire into areas that could be problems for the organization or people in the organization."

Before taking the FBI job, Shapiro, a graduate of Yale Law School, had been an associate professor of criminal law at Cornell Law School. Prior to that, Shapiro was an assistant U.S. attorney in New York. Although Shapiro made some misjudgments, he was a sharp lawyer who, in contrast to Bucknam, genuinely seemed to care about the FBI. Because of that, agents liked him and confided in him. Shapiro had little use for Bucknam and tried to make it clear to everyone that he and Bucknam were different animals.

Freeh liked to tout Shapiro as someone who knew criminal law, suggesting that previous FBI counsels did not. "We never had anybody who knew what Brady obligations were, who knew what discovery allegations are in the course of giving information to a defendant in preparation for trial," Freeh told Congress in May 2001.

That, of course, was absurd. Any agent out of Quantico knew that Brady obligations referred to material that, under *Brady* v. *Maryland*, had to be turned over to the defense during discovery proceedings because it tended to help the accused. Shapiro was dismayed when he heard that Freeh was casting aspersions on capable, honorable lawyers like Joseph R. Davis, an agent who was the previous FBI counsel.

The final factor that turned Ruby Ridge and Waco into symbols of government treachery was that, in line with his policy of closing down the FBI to the press, Freeh refused to allow the FBI to respond to the increasingly wild charges. Rather than letting the FBI correct false claims and place both Ruby Ridge and Waco in context, Freeh, with great fanfare, called news conferences or issued statements to denounce what happened and announce disciplinary actions. In doing so, he made himself look good at the expense of the bureau. Because the initial inquiries that Freeh ordered had been so flawed by cronyism, a succession of new ones had to be undertaken. This gave critics more ammunition and kept the controversy blazing throughout Freeh's tenure of almost eight years.

"Freeh was out for himself," said a high-ranking FBI counterintelligence agent.

As charges against the FBI in the Midwest became increasingly virulent, Bob Ricks, one of the SACs in charge, pushed for a more open response to the allegations about Waco. Headquarters told him he could talk only locally about it, so Ricks gave a talk presenting the FBI's side at the Rotary Club in Tulsa. When the wire services picked up the story, Freeh saw the accounts and ordered an investigation of Ricks. When Ricks documented that headquarters had told him he could speak about the issue locally, he escaped disciplinary action. Freeh then banned agents from talking about Waco anywhere, so no one was allowed to put the events in perspective.

Freeh not only muzzled agents from talking to the press, he also opposed, in the early days, a routine postoperation critique of Waco. Such a critique would have cataloged the fact that the bureau fired pyrotechnic military tear gas rounds at an unoccupied concrete structure seventy-five feet from the Waco compound four hours before the fire started. It had nothing to do with the fire set by the Branch Davidians, but when the additional detail came out six years later, it looked as if there had been another cover-up.

"One of the SACs knew about the pyrotechnic rounds. The rest of us did not," Ricks said. "It was only because we had not done a postop analysis that no one knew about it. All the SACs asked for a critique. We were not allowed to do one. Louis Freeh decided he did not want Waco to touch him."

Republican members of Congress, some of whom viewed federal officers as black-booted thugs, adopted Waco and Ruby Ridge as symbols of the sins of federal law enforcement and assorted other outrages of the federal government. While Freeh barred the FBI from giving a more balanced account of Waco and Ruby Ridge, Freeh was perfectly free to talk about both fiascoes—and did so with gusto.

"I mentioned before Waco and Ruby Ridge," Freeh told a House appropriations subcommittee on May 16, 2001. "You know, we got it wrong in those two instances. And there's people in my agency who don't like to hear me say that," Freeh said.

By denouncing the FBI's actions, Freeh aligned himself with the Republicans who now controlled Congress. Instead of running against the Communists, as Hoover did, Freeh had discovered that by running against the bureau, he could look good in the press and obtain generous funding from Congress. To promote himself as the good guy, Freeh turned the FBI and its agents into the bad guys.

"I think the big issue is the way the bureau handled the aftermath of Waco and Ruby Ridge," Ricks said. "We needed to respond to these outlandish accusations and put out the facts quickly. Even when we were called murderers, we were supposed to sit there and smile," he said. "I had never seen the FBI in that position before. No one was willing to defend the FBI because these problems had not happened on Freeh's watch."[181]

■ ■ ■

After censuring Larry Potts for his actions in the Ruby Ridge case, Freeh promoted him in May 1995 to deputy director of the FBI. Once more, Freeh demonstrated that Friends of Louis were held to a different standard.

Gorelick, the deputy attorney general, questioned the promotion. Although she admired Potts, she pointed out that another investigation was pending, and it might produce more damaging information about his role at Ruby Ridge. Freeh claimed he "could not function" without Potts as his deputy, and Gorelick, having voiced her concerns, let the promotion proceed.

CENSURED BY THE FBI—AND THEN PROMOTED read the headline over Richard Cohen's column in the *Washington Post*.

Congress and the press criticized the promotion. Gorelick and Reno told Freeh "something has to be done." Ten weeks after promoting him, Freeh had to back down and remove Potts as deputy director. In August, after the results of another Justice Department investigation were in, Freeh suspended Potts and others who were in the chain of command at Ruby Ridge. He then left Potts and the others in limbo, paying them while they were on leave as criminal investigations dragged on for two years or more. Potts and Freeh never spoke again.

"I gave my life to the bureau," Potts commented. "I feel very hurt by all this."

When Freeh suspended Potts, he used the occasion to give a rare interview, which focused even more attention on the problems while distancing him from them. The allegations of the previously disclosed cover-ups over Ruby Ridge were "shocking," he told the *Washington Post.*

When Potts finally retired, bureau friends concocted a reason for the FBI to pay for their trip to Washington, setting up an "ethics forum" at Quantico. Only five attended the forum for ninety minutes, including lunch. Inspectors determined that some of the agents had engaged in voucher fraud and had not been candid about what happened, grounds for dismissal under Freeh's new rules. But the charges were reduced to "inattention to detail" and "inappropriate travel," resulting only in letters of censure for four agents.[182]

In August 2001, John E. Roberts, the lead agent looking into Ruby Ridge for the Justice Department's OPR, told the Senate Judiciary Committee that senior FBI officials harassed him and his associate, John Werner, because they were trying to conduct an honest investigation after Eugene Glenn charged that there had been a cover-up. FBI officials told him and Werner that being assigned to the investigation could "have an impact on our careers," Roberts said. Fourteen times, Roberts's request for a promotion was rejected. In addition, his wife, a support employee in Boston, was hounded from her job. Those charges prompted a new investigation, this one by the Justice Department's inspector general, bringing to nine the number of investigations of Ruby Ridge. That fact alone spoke volumes about the enormity of Freeh's mismanagement.

Roberts and Werner concluded that Freeh should be censured for not ordering impartial, complete inquiries in the first place. With some justification, the Justice Department rejected that idea. The job of FBI director is one of the most important and politically sensitive in the government. The FBI director should not be subject to discipline by the Justice Department, which is headed by an appointee who is traditionally politically tied to the president. Instead, if an FBI director fails to carry out his job properly or abuses his position, he should be fired.

But beyond failing to order impartial probes of Ruby Ridge, Freeh's calculated insistence on positioning himself as avenger of the FBI's sins at Waco and Ruby Ridge, feeding the often paranoid views of right-wing politicians, led to the perception that they were scandals of monstrous proportions.

After Waco, public opinion overwhelmingly supported the FBI. Most believed that Koresh was responsible for the outcome. Yet after Freeh took over, public opinion swung the other way. By 1999, a majority of the public believed that the FBI had murdered innocent people at Waco, where an honest miscalculation led to a tragedy, and Ruby Ridge, where an accidental shooting led to a death.

28

ROLL-UPS

Since 1991, the FBI and CIA had looked for a mole in their midst, as intelligence operations went awry and assets—agents working for the CIA—were "rolled up" and executed. In 1993, from an agent in place who was code-named AVENGER, the CIA learned enough details about a mole in the CIA to narrow the focus to Aldrich H. Ames. Then the question became: How could the CIA have ignored the warning signs so long?

A heavy-smoking, heavy-drinking intelligence officer, Ames began working for the CIA in 1962. While he was assigned to Mexico City twenty years later, Ames met Maria del Rosario Casas, a Colombian cultural attaché, and recruited her to work as an agent for the CIA. They began an affair, which led to Ames's divorce from his wife and his marriage to Rosario.

By 1983, Ames had been named chief of the counterintelligence branch in the Soviet/East European Division within the Directorate of Operations. In 1985, Ames began working with a joint FBI-CIA squad within the FBI. Called COURTSHIP, this squad recruited KGB officers to work for the United States. Later, Ames was assigned to the CIA's Counternarcotics Center, with responsibility for the Balkans.

Because Ames's job in counterintelligence required him to review files and ask questions not only at the CIA but also at the FBI and other sensitive agencies, he was in a better position to help the Russians than even the director of Central Intelligence. It was the agency's worst nightmare, the kind of wholesale treachery that James Angleton, the former CIA counterintelligence chief, had warned about but was too inept to find on his own. Haunted by the Angleton legacy, the agency was wary of appearing to besmirch its employees' reputations. Once officers joined the exclusive club that constitutes the CIA's Directorate of Operations, they believed themselves immune from accountability to the outside world.

The warning signs were all there. Ames made $69,843 a year, yet he drove to work in a Jaguar paid for with cash. He bought a home at 2512 North Randolph Street in Arlington, Virginia, for $540,000 in cash and spent another $99,000 on home improvements. His wife was a notorious spendthrift. From 1985 to 1994, their total credit card charges were $455,000. In his bank account, Ames would deposit just under $10,000 in cash so the deposits did not have to be reported under banking regulations.

Over the years, the FBI had observed Ames meeting with Soviets. He had not reported the contacts as required by CIA regulations. Whenever the FBI asked the CIA about this, the agency stonewalled. On top of it all, Ames had flunked routine polygraph tests. While the machines showed deception, the polygraph examiners ignored the results and accepted Ames's explanation that he was nervous, just as they had when Karl Koecher flunked the polygraph test.

Before the agent in place narrowed the field, the CIA listed Ames as a possible spy in part because he had access to most of the compromised information. But efforts to investigate Ames were amateurish. The agency checked Ames's credit card bills for a month and found they amounted to $3,000. That happened to have been a slow month for Ames and his wife. Normally, they charged $18,000 to $30,000 a month. His wife owned 500 pairs of shoes and 150 packages of panty hose that she had never opened. In one single year, they paid $18,000 in credit card finance charges.

The CIA examined real estate records to see how Ames paid for his home. When no mortgage was found, the CIA twice returned to the recorder of deeds' office to try to find a record of one. Anyone familiar with land records knows that a mortgage must be officially recorded. If it is not part of the official record, it is not a valid lien.

In trying to determine if Ames's wealth might have come from his wife's family in Colombia, the CIA station there asked a local source, who said her family was wealthy. A few weeks later, the agency fired the contact for giving incorrect information on another matter. No one thought this fact important enough to pass on to those who were investigating Ames. Meanwhile, no one yanked Ames's security clearance.

As it turned out, since 1985, Ames had received $2.5 million from the Russians. It was a measure of the value of his information. Never before in U.S. history had any known spy received anywhere near that sum. The closest figure was the $1 million received by John Walker, who collected the money over an eighteen-year period. Ames received more than twice as much in just over eight years.

In all, Ames betrayed more than a hundred CIA operations and wiped out the CIA's assets in Moscow. The Soviets executed ten and sent others to prison. Ames not only compromised current assets, he also impaired the ability of the agency to recruit new assets for years to come. Aware of how negligent the CIA had been in protecting its own agents, any potential recruit would have to think twice about cooperating with the agency.

In the middle of the FBI's investigation, my 1993 book *The FBI* reported that, based on a KGB defector's information, the bureau was investigating hundreds of Americans who spied for the Soviets over the years. On August 18, 1993, the *Washington Post* quoted the FBI as confirming that the bureau had opened "a number of cases related to the activities of the KGB and its successor agency."

At the time, the FBI had been conducting a trash cover on Ames— picking up and sifting through his garbage for incriminating evidence. Fearing that Ames would become more wary because of the book, the FBI stopped the trash cover. Robert B. Wade, an FBI agent detailed to the CIA, was brought into service to reassure Ames. Wade, who had been deputy chief of the FBI's Soviet Section, knew Ames from counterintelligence work they had done together. A former smoker, Wade agreed to resume his habit so he could shmooze with Ames during smoking breaks outside the CIA's gleaming white building at Langley.

Ames was aware of the book and brought up the subject with Wade. "What do you think of that Kessler book?" Ames asked him.

"It's bullshit," Wade said, puffing up a cloud of smoke. "Reporters make up so many stories."[183]

Ames looked visibly relieved. Wade reported Ames's comment to Paul Redmond in the CIA's counterintelligence center, and soon the trash cover resumed. It produced the first hard evidence of Ames's spying, including a printer ribbon used to produce letters to Ames's handlers.[184]

Just before Christmas, Wade was leaving CIA headquarters when he saw Ames.

"Have a good Christmas," Wade said, knowing that this would be his last outside a jail cell.

All the FBI agents who worked what was called the NIGHTMOVER case—Bear Bryant, Bob Wade, Raymond A. Mislock Jr., John Lewis, James P. Milburn, Jim Holt, Tim Caruso—were products of John Martin's lectures at Quantico or of his advice on other cases. They knew how important it was to consult with the prosecutors during the investigation. Leslie G. Wiser Jr., the FBI case agent, was a lawyer who had been a Navy judge advocate general officer. Martin conferred with Wiser and his agents about what they needed for an affidavit to go with arrest and search warrants, how to interview Ames and his wife, and how to try to get admissions from them.

On the morning of February 21, 1994, agents arranged to have a CIA counternarcotics official ask Ames to come to CIA headquarters. As Ames drove his Jaguar to Langley, Agent Michael Donner followed him and turned on his flashing red dashboard light. He turned on his siren. Ames stopped a few feet short of a SWAT truck that was driving in front of him. Gun in hand, Donner raced to the driver's side. Ames rolled down his window, and Donner held up his badge and pulled a Benson & Hedges cigarette from Ames's lips.

"FBI," he said. "You're under arrest."

Donner opened the door and yanked Ames into the street.

"For what?" Ames yelled. "For what?"

"For espionage," Donner said. "Put your hands on the roof of your car."

"What!" Ames cried. "This is unbelievable. Unbelievable!"[185]

In return for Ames's plea, Martin agreed to recommend a much lower sentence for his wife. Both defendants agreed to be debriefed by the government and undergo polygraph tests on the truthfulness of their statements. Unhappy in her marriage, Rosario soon refused to respond to Ames's letters. Asked about her husband by Diane Sawyer on ABC's *Primetime Live*, Rosario said, "I despise him."

On April 28, Ames and his wife pleaded guilty. After Ames cooperated, he got life without parole. He also lost his CIA pension and his other assets. Rosario was sentenced to five years and three months in jail.

It was a victory not only for the FBI but also for Martin, who had always fought the CIA's tendency to try to cover up its embarrassments by turning spies into double agents.

"That was the kind of foolish trade the CIA always wanted. It was part of the gobbledygook of 'interdicting' or 'neutralizing' spies," Martin said. "The fact is you can prosecute spies, then get your damage assessment after they're convicted and before they're sentenced. When you offer them immunity up front, as the old counterintelligence boys used to do it, you're giving everything away and getting very little in return. Moreover, if you find after granting immunity that the person has been lying to you, there's nothing you can do. On the other hand, if you get him to plead guilty as part of a plea agreement, you can require him to tell what he knows before sentencing. If he lies, you can tell the judge he's lying, and the sentence will be harsher. When you have them by the balls, their hearts and minds will follow."

■ ■ ■

In contrast to what happened in the Ames case, CIA polygraphers did not ignore the readings that showed Harold J. Nicholson, a former CIA station chief in Bucharest, gave deceptive answers when asked if he was hiding his involvement with a foreign intelligence service.

After the FBI began investigating, its surveillance cameras caught Nicholson copying documents under his desk with a special camera he had obtained from the CIA. The FBI also watched Nicholson on a trip to Singapore as he made contact with his handlers in the backseat of a Russian embassy car. In his bank accounts, the FBI found unexplained cash deposits.

Nicholson began spying for the Russians in 1994 as he was completing a tour of duty as deputy chief of the CIA station in Malaysia. Later that year, he was assigned to the CIA's training center at Camp Peary near Williamsburg, Virginia. Nicholson told the Russians the identities of every CIA case officer trained between 1994 and 1996. He also gave them a summary of debriefings of Ames after his guilty plea. Over a two-year period, Nicholson received $120,000 from the Russians. When FBI agents arrested him on November 16, 1996, as he boarded a flight to Switzerland, Nicholson was carrying rolls of film with images of top-secret CIA documents.

Nicholson was the highest-ranking CIA officer ever charged with espionage. He pleaded guilty and was sentenced to twenty-three years and seven months in prison.

■   ■   ■

A month after Nicholson's arrest, the FBI arrested another of its own. Earl E. Pitts began spying in July 1987 when he wrote a letter offering his services to a Soviet assigned to the Soviet Mission to the United Nations. At the time, Pitts was assigned to foreign counterintelligence investigations in New York. Later, he was assigned to the FBI Legal Counsel Division in Washington. For documents that included a list of FBI assets who were providing intelligence on Russia, Pitts received $224,000 from the Russians.

After Pitts came under suspicion, the bureau transferred him to the training academy at Quantico. By then, Pitts had become dormant. The KGB was not interested in the work he did in the Legal Division, which was to conduct research in civil cases filed against the bureau. As with the Richard Miller case, the FBI had to be extraordinarily careful not to tip off Pitts that he was under investigation. Every agent who worked the case was polygraphed.

With the Cold War over, the Soviet Union having disintegrated in 1991, the FBI obtained the cooperation of the person Pitts had originally written to at the Soviet Mission to the UN. As part of a false flag operation, the FBI arranged to have the former contact show up at Pitts's house at 13415 Fox Chase Lane in Spotsylvania, Virginia, in August 1995. At the Chancellorsville Battlefield Visitor Center, the man introduced Pitts to an FBI agent posing as an officer of the SVR, the

Russian Foreign Intelligence Service, which succeeded the KGB in December 1991.

Pitts fell for the ruse. While he confessed that he did not have the access he once had, Pitts told the bogus SVR officer, "I'll do what I can." The agent gave Pitts $15,000 in cash and instructions on leaving material at a dead drop.

Ironically, Pitts at one point told a class of new agents at Quantico, "Criminals usually get caught." Yet in the ensuing months, Pitts turned over secret FBI documents, the handset of the secure phone known as a Stu III, and an FBI cipher lock combination. He even agreed to help smuggle into the academy a bogus SVR technical expert.

After the man with the Russian accent showed up at their home, Mary Pitts, who had worked for the bureau as a secretary, became suspicious and searched her husband's briefcase. She found a cryptic note from one of his KGB contacts in New York. When she confronted Pitts, he gave unconvincing answers. She confided her suspicions to Tom Carter, a friend who was in the FBI's Fredericksburg, Virginia, resident agency.

"I probably . . . shouldn't have gone to the bureau, and it will probably be the end of my marriage either way it goes," she told a neighbor on the phone later that day. "If he is on the up and up and he finds out that I went behind his back, we're finished." Later, in a fit of rage, Mary Pitts told her husband what she had done. He told her the bureau knew all about the visitor, who was an asset from New York. Even after his wife confronted him, Pitts continued to accept money from the bogus SVR officer and give away bureau secrets.

Agents had a tense moment when Pitts found an FBI surveillance camera concealed in the ceiling above his desk at Quantico. John Martin watched the video of Pitts finding it. Pitts leaned back in his chair in his office, looked up, then looked down and up again. He stood on a chair and began removing a tile from the ceiling. Then, as he removed the camera, the video went blank.

Luckily, an FBI agent had placed a tag on the video camera saying it was for surveillance of employees who were late. Reassured, Pitts continued to give classified documents to the FBI agent posing as an SVR officer and to accept money in return.

During the surveillance of Pitts, agents found that he answered personal ads placed by men. One night they watched as he met a man in a motel room. After Pitts's arrest, Mary found a list of names and phone numbers of male and female prostitutes.

Pitts later said he began spying because he was unhappy that the FBI had assigned him to New York. He said he wanted to "pay them back." At the time, the bureau did not offer a pay differential to make up for higher living costs in New York. In the days before Giuliani, crime was out of control, and agents were being mugged on the way to work.

Agent Eileen J. Roemer was on a surveillance with another agent and two New York City detectives working an Asian organized crime case. Two neighborhood toughs, apparently unhappy that their turf was being invaded, began assaulting one of the detectives. The second detective scrambled out of a car to help. The first detective pulled out his gun and identified himself as being with the police.

"Shoot me, shoot me! I'll make you eat that fuckin' gun," one of the toughs said.

The detective replaced his gun in its holster, but one of the men grabbed it. At that point, Roemer, who had been watching from inside a surveillance van, rushed the two men.

"FBI! You're under arrest," she yelled, lunging at the man who had taken the detective's gun. She got him in a choke hold, and he dropped the gun. The two men then fled, but not before Roemer had taken down their license number, leading to their arrest.

One afternoon, New York agents were showing a series of photographs of possible suspects to a teller at a bank that had been held up the day before. Pointing to a photo, the teller said, "That's him." Then she pointed to a man standing in line. "And that's him right there, standing in line."

Edward J. Roach and other agents chased the robber as he fled the bank, apprehending him after a fight.

Because of high living costs, many New York agents lived in remote areas of New Jersey or New York State. To beat the rush hour, some tried to leave the office precisely on time. One agent got the bright idea of turning ahead the hands of the clocks by five or ten minutes. In response, the SAC had technicians snip off the control levers on the clocks so they could not be turned ahead. But when a power failure occurred, the clocks could not be readjusted. Nor had anyone thought about what would happen when daylight savings time came. It took months to fix the clocks so they told the correct time again. So it goes in New York.

"Any horror story coming out of any bureau office will end up happening in New York," Roach said.

In February 1997, Earl Pitts pleaded guilty. In contrast to what happened in the Richard Miller case, no one suggested firing Pitts before his arrest so the FBI could call him a former agent. Pitts's lawyer hired a psychiatrist who wrote a memo saying Pitts's anger pushed him "beyond his limits." Enraged, U.S. District Court Judge T. S. Ellis III in Alexandria, Virginia, gave Pitts twenty-seven years in prison, three more years than Martin had recommended.

"There are folks in every veterans' hospital and [on grave] markers from here to Europe to Asia that you have dishonored," the judge told Pitts as he handed down the sentence. "You did it in part out of simple greed."

Asked in a *60 Minutes* interview if there was anything he would have done differently, Pitts said, "I would not have gone to New York."

■　■　■

Important as the Nicholson and Pitts cases were, when it came to spotlighting the intricacies of the spy game, nothing in recent memory compared with the case of Robert Stephan Lipka.

In his 1994 book, *The First Directorate,* former KGB officer Oleg Kalugin mentioned a "young soldier" who worked at NSA and supplied the Soviets with "reams" of top-secret documents. "He handed us the NSA's daily and weekly top-secret reports to the White House, copies of communications on U.S. troop movements around the world, and communications among the NATO allies," Kalugin wrote.

While Kalugin did not name the individual, the FBI at that point was already investigating him. The case began in 1968 when a defector tipped the FBI to two KGB officers who were illegals living near Philadelphia. One afternoon, agents followed the two, Peter Fischer—originally Petrovich Blyablin—and his wife Ingeborg. Posing as West German citizens, they entered the United States from Canada in 1965, and Fischer took a job in a chewing gum factory. Agents followed the two from their home to Manhattan, where they saw them disappear into dense shrubs in Riverside Park near Grant's Tomb. That night, Artem Petrovich Shokin, a KGB officer who was a Russian interpreter at the United Nations, disappeared into the same shrubs, came out, and drove away.

After they returned from Grant's Tomb to their apartment in Upper Darby west of Philadelphia, the FBI's electronic bugs picked up the Fischers expressing joy over their rendezvous. "The Russians always have it secure. It makes a difference, doesn't it?" Ingeborg Fischer said.

"We drink to our success, sugar," her husband replied.

A few days later, the Fischers drove to Lancaster, Pennsylvania. The FBI did not follow them, but the microphones picked up the Fischers' conversations after the trip.

"It is over with," Peter Fischer said.

"We must be careful," she said.

The FBI then picked up the sounds of paper being torn.

"These go in the toilet, don't they?" Mrs. Fischer said.

"Okey-doke," he said as a toilet was flushed.

The FBI later searched their apartment. Agents found a piece of paper with the notation "30 and Harrisburg Pike," along with the word "Roeck" in quotation marks. Lancaster is at the intersection of Harrisburg Pike and Route 30. But what did Roeck mean?

The Fischers left the United States in August 1968. While they appeared to be spies, the FBI did not know what material they were compromising or where it originated. The case stalled. Then in 1993, new information focused the FBI's attention on Robert Lipka. The information came from Vasili Mitrokhin, the defector mentioned in my 1993 book *The FBI*.

For almost thirty years, Mitrokhin had worked in the KGB's foreign intelligence archives. Disgusted with the Soviet regime, he began taking notes in 1972 on the incredibly sensitive material he saw. He typed up his notes at his dacha and buried the material in the ground under the floor. In September 1992, he left Moscow on a train and defected with his notes to the British MI-6.[186] The material documented that Lipka had walked into the Soviet embassy in Washington and turned over secrets to Kalugin, who was then assigned to the embassy.

A native of Niagara Falls, New York, Lipka joined the Army at the age of eighteen. For almost four years, he was assigned to NSA as an intelligence analyst working in the Priority Materials Branch of NSA's Current Intelligence Division at Fort Meade, Maryland. His job was to deliver documents received by courier or teleprinter from the CIA, State Department, Defense Intelligence Agency, the Army, Navy, and Air Force, and other parts of NSA.

After FBI agents began focusing on Lipka, they interviewed Lipka's first wife, Patricia. She said that soon after they were married in 1966, her husband told her he had been selling secrets to the Russians. One day, she and Lipka drove to a Maryland restaurant where Lipka said he had to deliver a package for "Ivan." Lipka went into a men's room and later told her he left the package in a toilet tank.

Patricia identified wooded areas where Lipka placed packages. She said he would pick up packets of money in the woods. After they returned to their Baltimore apartment, they would count the money, usually $500 or $1,000. Lipka also showed his wife a camera similar to one the KGB routinely supplied for copying documents. He told her he would have face-to-face meetings with his contact over games of chess in a park. He said "Ivan" taught him to play well.

In 1967, Lipka left the Army and moved with his wife to an apartment at 403 Lancaster Avenue in Lancaster. He told her he took a stash of NSA documents to keep his "options open." Lipka opened a rare coin business and gambled on horses and cards. During this time, the Soviets had no contact with Lipka, apparently because he no longer had access to classified material. Then they decided he could be useful after all. They chose Shokin, another KGB officer, to coordinate plans for meeting with Fischer again in Lancaster. That was the purpose of notes left at Grant's Tomb in 1968, the ones the Fischers flushed down the toilet.

In 1974, Lipka resumed his meetings with the Russians. That same year, his wife divorced him. In 1991, Lipka, by then remarried, suffered a back injury and became unemployed.

With the help of agents who had worked the case almost three decades earlier, the FBI mounted a false flag operation. Dimitry Droujinsky, an agent often used for the purpose, called Lipka on the morning of May 12, 1993. Identifying himself as Sergey Nikitin, the agent said, "Ah, Mr. Robert Lipka? Hello, my name is Sergey Nikitin. I am from the Russian embassy in Washington, D.C."

"Yes," Lipka replied.

"And my superiors in Moscow have instructed me to meet with you and discuss something very important about your safety and security," he said. "I am here today in the Lancaster area, and I would like to meet. . . . Can you come to the Comfort Inn?"

Fifteen minutes later, Lipka drove into the motel's parking lot. "Nikitin" joined him in the front seat. He told Lipka he was from the GRU, which had taken over the case from the SVR. The GRU, according to Nikitin, wanted to learn "how you started and how things went, so that we can learn from you."

Lipka wasn't buying the story. He began discussing chess, then wrote the letter "R" on a sheet of paper and asked the agent to complete the code word.

"You know what it is," Lipka said.

Nikitin told him the files were in Moscow, and he did not have the code word. Lipka told him to obtain it by the following day or he would not meet with him again. From Patricia, his former wife, the FBI knew that Lipka was a chess player. In German, "Roeck" is pronounced "rook," the name of a chess piece. Nikitin decided "rook" was Lipka's code word. The next morning, when Lipka and Nikitin met again in the same parking lot, Nikitin said, "Does, ah, rook, ah, have any meaning to you?"

An FBI video camera trained on Lipka from outside his green Chevrolet van captured his expression. "Yes," he said, as he visibly relaxed. He shook Nikitin's hand as he placed his hand over his heart. Patricia later confirmed that Lipka's code word was "rook."

Lipka agreed to join Nikitin in his motel room at the Comfort Inn. In that meeting and another, Lipka said he had broken off his relationship with the Soviets because he was not satisfied with the payments.

That jibed with information supplied by Mitrokhin. "During the two years after he walked into the Soviet embassy, he [Lipka] received a total of $27,000 but regularly complained that he was not paid enough and threatened to break contact unless his remuneration was increased," according to Christopher Andrew and Vasili Mitrokhin's *KGB: The Sword and the Shield.*

Lipka filled in Nikitin on his spy activities. He said the Fischers had indeed contacted him, and he acknowledged giving NSA material to the Soviets once or twice a month. He said he smuggled NSA documents from the agency by hiding them under his hat or taping them to his leg. The Fischers and Shokin delivered the documents to Moscow.

Incredibly, Lipka demanded from Nikitin money for his past espionage work and for NSA documents still in his possession. The FBI gave Lipka $10,000 for the documents, but Lipka became suspicious again and refused to turn them over. In December 1993—their last meeting— Nikitin told Lipka that his security was in jeopardy; a former KGB officer might have betrayed him. The FBI wanted to see how Lipka would react.

"Do you have equipment that, ah, that I can use to sanction?" Lipka asked.

"To sanction?" Nikitin said. "What is this? You mean to kill him?"

"Yeah," Lipka replied. "I'm talking about Bandera style. You understand what I mean, the Bandera style?"

This was a reference to the KGB's 1959 assassination of Ukrainian nationalist Stefan Bandera, who was killed when an agent fired cyanide capsules at him.

"Well, not right now," Nikitin said.

At 8:30 A.M. on February 23, 1996, dozens of FBI agents surrounded Lipka's home and arrested the fifty-year-old man. John Martin met with Mitrokhin at a safe house in London and asked if he would testify against Lipka. While he said no initially, he later agreed to testify.

If the case had gone to trial, Martin would have had to reveal that the FBI's 1968 entry into the Fischers' apartment had been an illegal black bag job performed without a search warrant. Because the target of the entry was the Fischers, who were not defendants in the case, Lipka could not challenge the search under the Fourth Amendment. It was that kind of lawyering by Martin and his staff that led to so many prosecutive successes.

In May 1997, Lipka pleaded guilty. He was sentenced to eighteen years in prison. Patricia Lipka was given immunity from prosecution as part of an agreement to obtain her help.

In the criminal complaint against Lipka, Martin took the unusual step of citing Kalugin's reference in his book to an unnamed NSA employee spying for the Soviets. With the Cold War over, Martin later met Kalugin. Martin had helped Tom Clancy with background for some of his books. In *Executive Orders*, Clancy made him a character, Patrick Martin, a Justice Department lawyer. Clancy also picked Kalugin's brain. Clancy invited the two former adversaries to watch the Baltimore Orioles from the owner's box. They drank beer and ate hot dogs and barbecue.

Afterward, Martin offered Kalugin a ride back to Washington. They joked about Kalugin's unwitting help with the case, and Kalugin confirmed that the person referred to in his book was indeed Robert Lipka.[187]

29

JEWELL

On April 19, 1995, Bob Ricks, the SAC in Oklahoma City, was at a golf tournament with other law enforcement officials to raise funds for the Special Olympics. At 8:50 A.M. his pager went off. When he called his secretary, she told him a bomb had exploded at the Alfred P. Murrah Federal Building downtown.

Forty minutes later, police cars escorted Ricks's FBI car through roadblocks to the building. A truck bomb had blown out the entire front of the building. The blast had killed 168 people, 19 of them children.

Ricks agreed with the fire and police chiefs that rescue efforts would take precedence over gathering evidence. He established a command post at a Southwestern Bell facility a block and a half from the site.

"You know what day it is today?" one of Ricks's assistants asked.

Ricks realized the date was April 19, the second anniversary of the FBI's raid at Waco. Ricks believed it had a connection to Waco.

Normally, the local SAC would head the investigation, but Freeh placed Weldon Kennedy, the SAC in Phoenix, in charge of the case. This led to rumblings of discontent among SACs, who admired Kennedy but did not like having their power usurped. Ricks, for one, felt he knew his agents better and could deploy them more effectively. But Kennedy had proved to be a superb leader during the prison uprising in Talladega, Alabama, and Freeh felt more comfortable with him.

Within an hour of the explosion, Sergeant Melvin Sumpter of the Oklahoma County Sheriff's Office found the rear axle of the truck, which had come smashing down on the hood of a red Ford Fiesta as its owners were getting out of the car not far from the building. Jim Norman, who was designated the FBI case agent, located the identification number etched into the axle. The FBI called the National Insurance Crime Bureau, which identified the truck as a twenty-footer owned by Ryder Rental Inc. Ryder said a man named Robert Kling rented it two days earlier from Elliott's Body Shop in Junction City, Kansas.

By midafternoon, agents were interviewing Eldon Elliott, the owner of the body shop, along with his cashier and mechanic. They said Kling—which was a phony name—was in his twenties and had small, piercing eyes, a long, thin face, pale skin, and a military-style brush cut. Tom Kessinger, the mechanic, thought he saw Kling with a companion when he picked up the truck. At first, Elliott did not mention a companion, but later he agreed with Kessinger. In FBI lingo, the suspects became Unsub One and Unsub Two, for unidentified subject one and two.

Based on the descriptions, an FBI artist made sketches of both men. Agents distributed flyers with the sketches all over Junction City and Oklahoma City. In Oklahoma City, three people who had been near the Murrah building identified Unsub One as a man they saw near the building's front entrance between 8:40 and 8:55 A.M.

In Junction City, Lea McGown, the owner of the Dreamland Motel, saw one of the flyers and recognized Unsub One. She said the man had occupied Room 25 from April 14 to April 18. He registered under the name of Tim McVeigh of Decker, Michigan. He had been driving an old yellow Mercury Marquis with Arizona plates.

Agents in Michigan verified that Timothy James McVeigh, a former Army sergeant who received a Bronze Star during Operation Desert Storm, lived at the address he had given at the motel. The address turned out to be a farm owned by James D. Nichols and his brother Terry L. Nichols.

A relative confirmed that James Nichols was a friend of McVeigh's, a former Army buddy. Another person said that James had large quantities of fuel oil and fertilizer. In the past, he had built bombs.

Dave Williams, a lab bomb specialist who handled the World Trade

Center bombing in 1993, had already flown in. "We haven't examined the debris for traces yet, but it looks like we're dealing with fertilizer and fuel oil," Williams told Danny Coulson, who came in from Fort Worth.[188] Early on April 20, Williams said the bomb had consisted of four thousand pounds of ANFO—ammonium nitrate fertilizer and fuel oil.

When a friend of McVeigh's saw the sketch of Unsub One on television, he called the FBI office in Buffalo and informed agents that McVeigh had extreme right-wing views and was furious about the government's actions at Waco. McVeigh even made a pilgrimage to the Branch Davidian compound during the siege.

By the morning of April 21, the FBI had run McVeigh's name through the National Crime Information Center. It scored a hit. It turned out that shortly after the bombing, an Oklahoma state trooper, Charles Hanger, ran a check of McVeigh through NCIC. Mark Michalic, an ATF agent working out of the FBI's command center, tracked down the trooper, who said he arrested McVeigh at 10:22 A.M. for driving without license plates and for carrying a concealed weapon, a .45-caliber Glock semiautomatic pistol. The trooper said he made the arrest seventy miles from Oklahoma City; the bomb had gone off seventy-five minutes earlier.

Michalic found out that McVeigh was still in the Noble County jail in Perry. His bail hearing was coming up in an hour. Over the phone, as calmly as he could, Michalic told a deputy sheriff, "Spin that boy around and put him back in your hotel."

Agents took a helicopter to Perry, where they placed McVeigh under arrest on federal charges. They also arrested Terry Nichols.

Freeh had been micromanaging the cases, pestering SACs with constant frantic calls. James Nichols was charged as a material witness, but Freeh wanted him arrested and held in jail so he would not flee. Yet the evidence on him was skimpy. He had fertilizer, blasting caps, and fuel oil on his farm, but that was not a crime. All were commonly used on farms.

Joseph D. Martinolich Jr., the SAC in Detroit, told Freeh there was nothing linking James Nichols directly to the conspiracy. Freeh became furious and ordered him to charge him with conspiracy anyway.

"We don't have the evidence," said Martinolich, who had slept six hours in five days.

"We'll sort it out later," Freeh said.

When Martinolich again told Freeh there was no evidence, Freeh screamed, "If you don't do it, I'll find someone who will," meaning he would replace Martinolich as SAC.

A month later, U.S. District Court Judge Paul D. Borman in Detroit ordered James Nichols freed without bond. "I don't see a connection [to Oklahoma City], no evidence other than friendship," the judge said.

When the judge threw out the charge, the press cited the issue as an example of the FBI's overzealousness. Once again, Freeh had ignored the opinion of his own SAC. In doing so, Freeh undermined the credibility of the FBI without disclosing that he had been responsible. Martinolich, a rising star in the bureau, retired early because he lost confidence in Freeh.

During the investigation, the bureau conducted twenty-eight thousand interviews and gathered three and a half tons of evidence. The FBI eventually concluded that the two men at the body shop were mistaken when they said they thought another customer was with McVeigh, a point McVeigh confirmed. McVeigh and Terry Nichols were convicted. McVeigh was executed, and Nichols was sentenced to life in prison.

■　■　■

In 1978, a bomb exploded on a Chicago-area campus, injuring a security guard. The bomb was mailed and came in a carved wooden box. A second bomb the next year injured a Northwest University graduate. In 1980, a fourth explosion injured United Airlines President Percy Wood at his home.

A pattern emerged. The bombs used smokeless black powder and came in handcrafted wooden boxes. They were made from parts seemingly collected from a junkyard, with improvised switches and handmade screws. Usually, "FC" was stamped on a part.

Along with the bombs, the bomber sent cryptic notes or, in the case of Yale University victim David Gelertner, a subsequent letter. The bombs targeted universities, airlines, and other industries. Over eighteen years, the bombs killed three people and injured twenty-three.

In 1993, the FBI for the first time used the Internet to appeal for tips in the case, called UNABOMER. During the course of the investigation, the FBI checked out fifty-six thousand tips from people who were sure they knew who the bomber was. Agent Peter Smerick visited newspaper morgues in the Chicago area, trying to find letters to the editor that might match the Unabomer's style. The FBI distributed a profile. The Unabomer was said to be a white male in his thirties or forties who had a history of menial jobs and few friends. He was a neat dresser, meticulously organized, and probably an ideal neighbor. Nothing worked.

Finally, the Unabomer asked that newspapers publish his thirty-five-thousand-word manifesto, an irrational tirade against technology. If it were published, he promised to stop killing. Traditionally, the FBI does not cave in to threats. But in this case, the possible benefit of finding the killer outweighed other considerations. Freeh agreed with agents that the bureau should go along with the request in case someone recognized the writing or thoughts expressed. Both the *Washington Post* and *New York Times* agreed to publish the fifty-six-page document as a public service.

At his wife's urging, David Kaczynski, a Schenectady, New York, youth shelter social worker, read the manifesto. He recognized the delusional themes he had heard or read in letters over a lifetime. He approached FBI agents through an intermediary and expressed concerns that the Unabomer might be his fifty-five-year-old brother, Theodore, who had graduated from Harvard when he was barely twenty. Theodore Kaczynski became a brilliant tenured mathematics professor at the University of California at Berkeley but left abruptly in 1969.

On April 3, 1996, FBI agents arrested Ted Kaczynski at his cabin in Lincoln, Montana. While an FBI SWAT team hid in the woods, agents D. Max Noel, a supervisor on the case, and Tom McDaniel, the senior resident agent from Helena, Montana, approached the cabin with someone Kaczynski knew—Jerry Burns, a U.S. Forest Service police officer. Burns told Kaczynski that the two others were from a mining company planning to do exploratory work. Since the corner posts of Kaczynski's cabin were covered by snow, they wanted him to come out and show them his property lines so the mining company would not encroach on his property in the spring.

Kaczynski stepped out of the cabin, then hesitated. He said he needed to retrieve his coat. As he turned to reenter, Burns grabbed him. As Burns and McDaniel struggled with him, Noel stepped in front of Kaczynski, pointed his weapon at him, and displayed his credentials.

"He was shocked we were able to penetrate the sanctity of his area," Noel said. "He complimented me on the way we lured him out of his cabin. He almost seemed relieved."[189]

Inside the cabin, agents found components for making bombs and the original typewritten version of his manifesto. He had used carbon paper to make four copies that he mailed to newspapers. They also found a journal in which Kaczynski explained that his motive for the killings was "simply personal revenge."

Kaczynski pleaded guilty to first-degree murder. Citing his mental illness, the government agreed not to seek the death penalty.

"Lock him so far down that when he dies he will be closer to hell," Susan Mosser, widow of New Jersey victim Thomas Mosser, told the judge.

Kaczynski was sentenced to four life sentences in prison without possibility of parole.

David Kaczynski received a $1 million reward from the FBI. He said he would distribute much of it to the families of the victims. During the pretrial hearings in the Sacramento, California, federal court, David sat ten feet behind his brother. Theodore never looked at him or acknowledged his presence.

All along, media critics whipped the FBI for taking two decades to solve the case. When a family member turned Kaczynski in, they castigated the FBI for having solved it by luck. But when a careful and determined killer drops bombs in a mailbox, it is very difficult to trace him. The FBI's recognition that publishing the manifesto might lead to the killer was critical to solving the case.

■ ■ ■

The Pizza Connection case that Freeh prosecuted demonstrated the global nature of crime, a point that Freeh never forgot. As FBI director, Freeh began expanding the FBI's presence overseas. By the time Freeh left, the FBI had forty-four legats from Moscow to Panama City, Nairobi to Islamabad, compared with twenty when Freeh took over. It was

Freeh's most important contribution, one that he made despite opposition from some bureau officials who did not have the foresight to see the need for an expanding presence overseas. Sessions had opposed such an expansion.

To negotiate agreements to open new offices, Freeh would meet overseas with foreign leaders. It was not always necessary for Freeh to become personally involved, and often his appearances did nothing to sow goodwill. Typically, he would spend three or four hours in a country, embarrassing the State Department and local FBI representatives.

"He was saying, 'We're the FBI, and we're so important that we can only spend three hours in your country,'" an agent who went on the trips said. "Only the pope and the president can get away with doing that."

Despite his claim that he wanted to spend as much time as possible with his family, Freeh spent at least 20 percent of his time visiting field offices and eighty-eight countries, usually with an FBI entourage that filled entire floors of hotels. In the meantime, the bureau was so starved for funds that thirteen thousand of its personal computers were 386- and 486-chip pre-Pentium machines, incapable of using the current software, handling graphics, or even working with a mouse. Agents had to double up to use computers, and the FBI's internal E-mail was so slow that agents used their personal E-mail addresses instead. The FBI system did not allow E-mail outside the agency. Often because of funds from the Justice Department, local police were far more technologically advanced than the FBI.

More shocking, during the spring and summer of 2000, about half the bureau's cars sat idle in parking garages because the FBI did not have money for gasoline. Agents either doubled up, rented cars, took taxis or buses, or walked. Freeh's appointees had underestimated the cost of personnel, draining money from other areas.

For all his faults, Freeh did learn from mistakes. A range of FBI officials, including Deputy FBI Director William J. Esposito, along with the FBI Agents Association, which represents current agents, expressed concern to Freeh about the damage his press policy was doing to the FBI. He finally made minor adjustments to the policy in August 1997, allowing the press office to report to John E. Collingwood, the respected head of Public and Congressional Affairs, instead of to Bob Bucknam.[190] But Freeh's aversion to dealing with the press continued to color the FBI's relations with the media.

Similarly, when the antigovernment Freemen in Jordan, Montana, refused to come out, Freeh ordered CIRG, which he had created to coordinate such crises, to wait them out. He did not want another Waco. The sixteen members of the group refused to acknowledge the legitimacy of the federal government and waged a two-year campaign of intimidation against their neighbors in the plains of eastern Montana. After eighty-one days, the siege ended peacefully. On March 25, 1996, using a sting to lure them from their compound, the FBI arrested LeRoy Schweitzer and Daniel Petersen, the leaders of the Freemen, on federal bank and check fraud charges.

But after correcting a mistake, Freeh would make two more. On June 7, 1996, the White House admitted that during four months in 1993, it wrongly collected FBI files on more than three hundred people, including former secretary of State James A. Baker III. Ostensibly, the files were requested so the White House could update personnel clearances.

For once, an FBI gaffe was not directly Freeh's fault. Low-level FBI file clerks blindly complied with the requests, even though it was obvious the Republican leaders whose files were requested could not possibly be working for the Clinton White House. Anthony B. Marceca, a civilian investigator for the Army, testified he worked off the Secret Service's weekly list of personnel with passes to the White House. He reported to D. Craig Livingstone, the White House personnel security director, whose hiring became an issue when everyone disclaimed responsibility.

On July 15, 1996, Howard Shapiro, Freeh's hand-picked general counsel, warned the White House counsel's office that the FBI had discovered notes of a 1993 FBI interview of Livingstone in which he credited Hillary Clinton with hiring him. He also advised Republican congressional investigators of the new information. Still, Shapiro's heads-up to the White House was a step back to the Hoover years, when the FBI operated as a political arm of the White House.[191]

Shapiro also personally delivered to White House Counsel Jack Quinn a copy of the manuscript of FBI agent Gary Aldrich's exposé of the Clinton White House. As required of all agents, Aldrich had submitted the book to the FBI for confidential review.

In explaining both incidents, Shapiro said he was trying to be an "honest broker." But the actions called into question the FBI's independence and impartiality. A Justice investigation found that while Shapiro had not engaged in professional misconduct and had not been politically motivated, he had exercised "very poor judgment" and had created an appearance that the FBI was not "sufficiently independent of the White House."

What did not come out was that, at a meeting with Freeh present, Shapiro mentioned that he was going to give the White House the manuscript. Freeh did not object. When the ensuing publicity hit, Freeh let Shapiro take the blame.

Freeh assigned Shapiro to investigate how the FBI came to give the White House the files on Republicans. Because of the short deadline Freeh imposed, Shapiro for several nights slept one hour a night on his office couch. The report was hard-hitting and widely praised. But the June 14, 1996, press release quoted Freeh as saying of the files matter, "Unfortunately, the FBI and I were victimized."

Jamie Gorelick, the deputy attorney general, immediately tried to find Freeh. He was often on the road, and she frequently had difficulty reaching him. She tracked him down at Quantico and told him that she considered the comment "outrageous." There was no indication in the report that the White House had corruptly obtained the files to seek political advantage or had tried to take advantage of the bureau. In fact, there was no evidence that the problem amounted to anything more than a mistake by low-level employees.

"How could you say this?" Gorelick asked Freeh.

Freeh said his aides had written the quote. He had never seen it. Freeh agreed to issue a revised statement, which turned out to be grotesquely tortured. "The FBI and I fell victim to my lack of vigilance," it said.

Bucknam had written the original quote, but he told Freeh that Shapiro had approved it. That was not the case. The net effect of the FBI's dealings with the White House was to tarnish the bureau's image as a nonpolitical agency that investigates professionally and impartially.

Despite such actions and despite Janet Reno's refusal to appoint an independent counsel, the FBI investigated Clinton's campaign fund-raising practices as dispassionately as—aside from Pat Gray's actions—it investigated Watergate.

"We should have had an independent counsel," said James V. DeSarno Jr., the agent who headed the investigation. "At times, Janet Reno focused on detail rather than looking at the patterns and whether the act applied. But that did not affect our work. Once a week we briefed Reno. She would say each time, 'Make sure you turn over every rock.' In the end," DeSarno said, "there wasn't the kind of evidence that would be needed to support a prosecution."

Nor is an independent counsel a guarantee of success. Ironically, according to I. C. Smith, who headed the FBI's Little Rock Field Office, independent counsel Kenneth Starr actually impeded the bureau's investigation of Clinton's dealings in the Whitewater land development. Starr insisted on having "inexperienced" prosecutors ask questions instead of FBI agents.

"There might have been" more indictments if Smith's agents had had free reign, Smith said.

■   ■   ■

When a pipe bomb exploded at Centennial Olympic Park on July 27, 1996, the FBI became interested in Richard Jewell, a security guard at the A&T light and sound tower who had alerted police to a suspicious green backpack at 12:57 A.M. The blast occurred twenty-three minutes later. Afterward, Jewell appeared on TV to describe how he tried to help evacuate the area after the bombing, which killed two and injured 111.

Three days later, the *Atlanta Journal-Constitution*, citing unnamed sources, published a story saying Jewell was a suspect in the FBI investigation. The story pointed out that sometimes those who claim to be heroes at crime scenes are the perpetrators.

Because of the story, the FBI decided to speed up its timetable for interviewing Jewell. That afternoon, agents Don Johnson and Diader Rosario drove to Jewell's apartment and asked him if he would come into the field office. If Jewell could clear up questions to the agents' satisfaction, they planned to drop their interest in him. When Jewell hesitated, Johnson said that with his permission, they would be video-taping the interview and would use it for training purposes.

"You'll be a superstar," Johnson said.

Johnson got the training video idea from a cameraman who was to videotape the interview for profilers who were flying in to town. Jan Garvin, the cameraman, suggested that the tape could be used for train-ing because it would contain "sound bites" from a "first responder."

Jewell agreed and followed the agents to the field office in his car. An hour and fifteen minutes into the interview, the agents were still going over Jewell's background with him when Freeh called David W. "Woody" Johnson Jr., the SAC in Atlanta. Johnson was in his office down the hall from the room where Jewell was being questioned. With him were other SACs and Kent B. Alexander, the U.S. attorney. Before the bombing, Woody Johnson had been working eighteen-hour days. Since the bombing, he had slept an hour a night.

Freeh was on the speaker phone as they discussed the case. Freeh had visualized that Jewell would be questioned at his home. When he learned that, because of the crush of reporters around his apartment, he was being interviewed at the field office, Freeh said the agents should read Jewell his rights.

Any agent out of Quantico knows that, under a long line of court rulings, a suspect must be read his Miranda rights if he is in custody or is about to be arrested. In Jewell's case, neither was true. Nor does the location of the interview have any relevance. Johnson pointed this out to Freeh, as did Barry Mawn, who said, "It's as consensual as you can get." The FBI director was adamant.

U.S. Attorney Alexander told Freeh he agreed with Johnson and with Mawn. "I said there's no legal requirement to read him his rights," Alexander recalled. "Jewell wasn't in custody. Under those circum-stances, there was no need to read him his rights."[192]

Bear Bryant, who was over the Criminal Investigative Division, was with Freeh when Freeh made the call. A lawyer, Bryant made the same point Alexander and the SACs had made. Afraid that hearings would be held in Congress about why Jewell had not been read his rights, Freeh wouldn't listen.

After they hung up, Freeh called Johnson back. This time, they were not on the speaker phone. Again, Freeh told Johnson to have the agents read Jewell his rights. Johnson objected, and Freeh said, "Listen, this is an order."[193]

Woody Johnson walked down the hallway to the conference room and pulled the two agents out to pass along the instruction. Rosario objected, but the two agents went back to the conference room and read Jewell his rights. Don Johnson told Jewell that the Miranda warning was "customary in pretty much all cases of this magnitude." According to a report by the Justice Department's Office of Professional Responsibility, the agent said, referring to the training video, "We're gonna use it for the purposes I told you before, but in order to do so, I want to go through it just like it's [a] real interview, okay?"

Although OPR said the training video ruse was legally permissible, many SACs, when they learned about it, said it went too far. Woody Johnson had not been told about it. Certainly mentioning the training video in connection with the Miranda warning improperly diminished the impact of the warning. But the agents also gave Jewell the standard "advice of rights" form to read and sign. Clearly, Jewell understood he was being given his rights. He said he would like to call G. Watson Bryant, an attorney, and that ended the interview.

Later that day, Freeh called U.S. Attorney Alexander and argued his position. "I said to Freeh I did not have a problem with reading someone his rights," Alexander said. "It was an investigative decision."

While prosecutors always prefer to have rights read, the fact was that the Miranda warning was not required. The result of Freeh's order was that, instead of clearing Jewell of suspicion, the FBI was obligated to continue its investigation of him.

"If we could have continued with Jewell, we could have confirmed what he told us and cleared him more quickly," Woody Johnson told me.

Another SAC who worked on the case said Freeh applied so much pressure on this and other cases that it led to misjudgments by everyone. "He would panic," the SAC said. "He would say, 'We have to do something!' You couldn't get your job done."

That evening, Freeh called to berate Woody Johnson and the other SACs over the speaker phone about the leak to the Atlanta paper. Freeh was oblivious to the fact that five hundred law enforcement officers from nine agencies were aware that Jewell was one of dozens of suspects. "Freeh seemed to assume that it had come from the FBI," Johnson said. "He said, 'Whoever did it will suffer the consequences.' "

As the publicity about Jewell mounted, Freeh gave orders to agents on a cell phone as they searched the apartment where Jewell lived with his mother.

"They took Richard's guns," Jewell's mother said on *60 Minutes*. "Then they took all my Tupperware. I mean, every piece of Tupperware. They took twenty-two of my Walt Disney tapes."

Jewell's attorney went on the attack, saying Jewell's rights had been violated. As he had on Waco and Ruby Ridge, Freeh ordered Woody Johnson not to respond.

"I said to Louis, 'We have to defend ourselves,' " Woody Johnson said. "Louis would not allow it. Jewell's attorney realized he could say anything, and we wouldn't react, so we looked guilty of everything. Hoover would have defended us."

"It was inappropriate for Louis to run that operation," said Caroll Toohey, the former SAC in Atlanta. "He did that on major incidents. You can't do that because you don't have all the information you need. If you have a senior SAC on site with twenty or thirty years of experience in the bureau, that is the person most qualified to make decisions."

"The FBI has always held the SAC on site accountable," said James D. McKenzie, an assistant director over the Training Division under Webster. "The more decisions are made in Washington from the SIOC, the less informed and more political they become."[194]

Freeh suspended Agent Don Johnson for five days without pay for not reading Jewell his rights in a straightforward manner. Because he was in charge, Woody Johnson received a letter of censure.

Not until seven months after the incident did Freeh acknowledge in congressional testimony his own role in the fiasco. Pointing out that he had been a federal judge, Freeh said, "It is a matter of legal speculation whether a court would have ruled that Miranda warnings were required in Mr. Jewell's case." Freeh said he decided to order the warning "in an excess of caution" when he learned that the interview was "being conducted in a law enforcement structure [the FBI office]." By May 2001, Freeh was telling Congress that he insisted on giving Jewell his rights because "my view of the situation was that he was in custody."[195]

In his testimony, Freeh did not mention the SACs and deputy FBI director who told him he was wrong. Instead, he said that Alexander "concurred with me."[196] In fact, while Alexander had no problem with rights being read, he had disagreed with Freeh that the Miranda warning was required.

"Reading Jewell his rights in the middle of the interview would have sent a clear signal that something had changed," Alexander said. "There was no requirement to do it, and with his law enforcement background, Jewell would have been expected to end the interview. If I had been asked initially, especially if I had been told about the ruse, I would have said to read him his rights at the beginning of the interview."

Referring to Freeh's order to read Jewell his rights in the middle of the interview, John Martin, who successfully prosecuted seventy-five spies as head of the Justice Department's internal security section, said, "You just don't do that. It's bad law and bad psychology. Reading him his rights in the middle of the interview means, in effect, you are ending the interview. Freeh acted like a young, inexperienced agent."

The proper role of an FBI director, Martin said, is to "select the right people, ask the right questions, and let them do their job. You didn't see Schwarzkopf driving a tank in the Persian Gulf War."

Three months after the interview of Jewell, the FBI cleared him, as it could have done immediately if Freeh had not intervened. Eventually, Eric Robert Rudolph, a fugitive, was charged with the bombing, along with the 1998 bombing of a Birmingham, Alabama, clinic that performed abortions and the 1997 bombings of a nightclub and a women's clinic in the Atlanta area. Rudolph has not been caught.

"For eighty days, I lived a nightmare," Jewell said in tears at a press conference he called after being cleared.

It was another embarrassment traceable to Freeh.

30

LOS ALAMOS

As Weldon Kennedy was directing the Oklahoma City bombing case, Freeh named him deputy director of the FBI. Kennedy was smart and seasoned. Unlike Freeh, he understood the importance of the press. While he was no pushover, Kennedy had a soft, charming manner. He found that if no one else was present, he could disagree with Freeh and not suffer any consequences. Whether Freeh would listen was another question.

Early on, when Freeh began slashing headquarters personnel and sending them to the field, Kennedy warned Freeh that the bureau needed to keep experienced people on hand to supervise cases. Moreover, because Quantico and the FBI lab were considered part of headquarters, the cuts diminished the number of agents available to perform laboratory examination or devise profiles. When profiling was cut back, law enforcement officers complained that they could not solve serial murder and rape cases because they were not getting the FBI's help.

"Quantico was decimated," said Tony Daniels, who headed the Training Division under Sessions. "It was the crown jewel of the FBI."

John Hicks, the assistant director over the lab, also forcefully warned Freeh about the personnel cuts, saying the quality of work would suffer and backlogs would grow if he proceeded with his plan to transfer to the street half of the 130 agents who were lab examiners. It was foolish to turn experts who had decades of experience in ballistics or explosives into street agents. Freeh's animus toward headquarters would not be appeased. When Freeh ignored him, Hicks resigned from the bureau.

"There was a guy who had been in the lab for twenty years," Weldon Kennedy said. "He was a world-renowned expert on shoe prints and tire prints. But the decision was made he has to go to Jacksonville and be a street agent. That was crazy. Freeh took a meat-ax to headquarters."

Soon, the backlog of cases in the lab grew from six months to a year. Frederic Whitehurst, an FBI chemist and supervisor in the lab, alleged to the press that not only was the lab doing shoddy work, its examiners had committed perjury and fabricated evidence. After an investigation, Michael R. Bromwich, the Justice Department's inspector general, determined that the more serious charges had no basis in fact. But as many as fifty cases over the years might have been mishandled.[197] With six hundred thousand examinations being conducted for all law enforcement each year, that was not a large number. Yet procedures clearly needed tightening. Like the rest of the FBI, the lab had always resisted outside scrutiny. There was a need to bring the lab into line with procedures used by other forensic laboratories and to improve record keeping and evidence handling.

Without mentioning how he had contributed to the problems by slashing experienced examiners, Freeh announced that the lab would seek outside accreditation, that he had transferred four senior staff members, and that he would appoint a world-class scientist to head the lab. This was a break with the bureau's parochial tradition of appointing agents to head technical areas like computers and finance.

Despite claims that thousands of cases would be affected, no case was ever overturned as a result of the problems found at the lab.[198] Yet the damage had been done. Since Hoover's days, the credibility of the lab had always been beyond question. Now that reputation was tarnished.

■　■　■

Because Freeh's policy of transferring headquarters agents to the street gave preference to agents who had seniority and because they were allowed to choose their field office, the most experienced agents elected to return to the field. Yet those were the agents the bureau most needed to supervise sensitive investigations. Because such experienced supervisors in Chinese counterintelligence had been sent to the field or encouraged to retire, no one was in a position to direct the investigation of Wen Ho Lee, a Taiwanese-born scientist at Los Alamos who had a history of trouble.

In 1982, the FBI was investigating another Taiwanese-American scientist suspected of spying for the Chinese at the government's Lawrence Livermore Laboratory in California. A wiretap of the scientist picked up Lee offering to help find out who had "squealed" on him.

When confronted, Lee claimed he did not know the scientist and had not tried to contact him. When presented with evidence of the call, Lee said he was merely consulting with the other scientist because he was concerned that he himself had given Taiwanese officials unclassified information.[199]

The son of uneducated farmers, Lee studied mechanical engineering at Cheng Kung University and came to the United States in 1964. In 1970, he earned a doctorate in mechanical engineering from Texas A & M. In 1978, Lee joined Los Alamos nuclear laboratory in New Mexico. Two years later, he joined the X Division, the unit that designs nuclear bombs.

For trying to expose someone who was assisting an espionage investigation and lying about it, Lee should have been fired. Instead, he was allowed to make about a dozen trips to Beijing, where he met with Chinese scientists working on nuclear weapons. Unlike the Russians, who seek classified information by cultivating Americans and paying them, the Chinese tend to focus on Chinese Americans, appealing to a perceived obligation to help their homeland. Instead of using dead drops, Chinese intelligence officers meet with prospects in a social, academic, or professional setting. Most of the information is passed orally, and the contacts continue on a personal basis.

Normally, Chinese-American scientists who visited China reported that the Chinese tried to acquire information from them in this way. But Lee never reported such advances. In fact, Lee often did not inform his supervisors about the trips, as security regulations required.

On September 25, 1992, China detonated a small, sophisticated nuclear bomb. Its design represented a breakthrough in China's quest to match American technology. That raised a question: Did the Chinese come up with the design, or did they steal secrets from the United States?

On February 23, 1994, Los Alamos hosted a delegation of Chinese weapons officials, including Hu Side, the head of China's bomb-making unit. Lee was not on the guest list but showed up and was greeted warmly by Dr. Hu, who had designed China's new bomb, called a two-point bomb. A translator overheard Hu quietly thanking Lee for providing computer software and calculations that helped China. Why Hu would even acknowledge that he knew Lee if he were obtaining classified information from him remains a mystery. In any case, Los Alamos informed the FBI, which opened an investigation of Lee—something it should have done after the bureau's first encounter with him.

When pursuing an espionage suspect, the FBI normally thoroughly investigates the individual—including electronically eavesdropping on his conversations, searching his computers, and conducting surveillance. As a last resort, the bureau may devise a plan to trap him, usually by having an agent pose as an intelligence officer from the suspect's country in a false flag operation. If that falls through, the FBI has a fallback position—perhaps another sting. In addition, the bureau consults with the person in charge of espionage prosecutions at the Justice Department. At the time it was John Martin.

In the Lee case, the FBI took none of these steps. David Lieberman, an Albuquerque agent with no counterintelligence experience, got the case, which he pursued between bank robberies and Indian reservation crimes. Neither Martin nor John J. Dion, Martin's deputy who replaced him after he retired, learned of the Lee case until the *Wall Street Journal*, without naming Lee, ran a story about an espionage investigation at Los Alamos. Nor did the FBI have a plan for catching Lee. In fact, the bureau did not search his computer—a logical first step—because the Justice Department incorrectly told the FBI it did not have authority to do so. In fact, any employer has the right to search the equipment it owns. Moreover, a waiver Lee signed in April 1995 explicitly stated that "activities on these systems are monitored or recorded and subject to audit."

■ ■ ■

In June 1995, a walk-in delivered to a Taiwanese official a document purporting to show that seven years earlier, the Chinese had obtained portions of the design of America's most advanced nuclear bomb, the W-88. The official gave it to the CIA. Notra Trulock, the new counterintelligence director of the Energy Department, which includes Los Alamos, assembled nearly twenty intelligence and weapons experts to analyze the document and sift through the evidence. He concluded that the Chinese had obtained American secrets as suspected when China detonated its new nuclear weapon in 1992. Trulock drew up a list of people at Los Alamos who had access to the information, who had traveled to China in the mid-1980s, or who had security problems. Lee popped up in all three categories.

In August 1997, after the FBI assigned a new agent to the Lee case, the FBI requested permission to wiretap him. In spy or terrorism cases, the Foreign Intelligence Surveillance Act of 1978 established a court that hears requests in secret for wiretaps. Located in a sixth-floor room of the Justice Department, the court normally consists only of a clerk. Every two weeks, a judge from one of seven rotating federal district courts sits for as many hours as are required in the room, which is shielded to prevent electronic bugging of conversations. Here, the judge signs off on requests submitted by the Justice Department's counsel for Intelligence Policy and Review to eavesdrop electronically.

For years, Mary C. Lawton, a diminutive, highly respected attorney, served as counsel. While Lawton turned down some requests, the court approved every request she recommended. After Lawton died in 1993, Janet Reno appointed Richard Scruggs, whom she knew from Miami, to the position heading the Office of Intelligence Policy and Review (OIPR).

When advising agents, Martin made the point that while watching KGB officers who have diplomatic immunity as part of a routine counterintelligence investigation, they might very well develop information that implicates a government employee passing secrets to the Russians. FISA specifically recognized that this routinely happens and that therefore a counterintelligence investigation and an espionage investigation were often indivisible. Under court rulings, so long as the "primary purpose" of the initial investigation was to gather intelligence, the evidence collected could be used to support a prosecution without any problem. To preserve that option, Martin needed to consult with agents as soon as they suspected they might have an espionage case. But Scruggs said that to demonstrate that the primary purpose of an investigation was originally counterintelligence and not a prosecution, those who worked on the case initially should have absolutely no contact with prosecutors.

Suddenly, the cooperation between the FBI and Justice that had allowed Martin to prosecute seventy-six spies without any allegation of improper conduct or illegality evaporated. Scruggs pursued his separation doctrine with religious fervor, and FBI agents and Justice Department prosecutors considered crossing the line he imposed to be a "career stopper." It was exactly the opposite of what was needed to pursue successful investigations and prosecutions.

Even after Scruggs left, fear of cooperation continued to govern relations between the FBI and Justice Department internal security prosecutors. Scruggs denigrated Mary Lawton's work and used the issue he had manufactured to enhance his importance with Reno, who increased the size of his staff.

"There was no basis for Scruggs's interpretation of the law," Martin said. "Janet Reno knew little about the subject and fell for Scruggs's construction hook, line, and sinker. The sinker was the Wen Ho Lee case because the FBI never told us about it. If it had, we could have put it back on track."

Besides ruining the relationship that had worked so well in the past, Scruggs and OIPR often opposed FBI surveillance requests that should have been approved. Such was the case with the FBI's application to eavesdrop electronically on Lee's telephone calls.

Asked why he made an issue of contact between the FBI and Justice Department prosecutors in view of the record of success in espionage prosecutions, Scruggs told me a court had held that Justice acted "improperly" in the prosecution of Ronald Humphrey, an employee of the U.S. Information Agency, and David Truong, who turned over top-secret State Department documents from Humphrey to the North Vietnamese. But that case, brought in early 1978, was before the enactment of FISA. It was therefore irrelevant. Moreover, an appeals court found no impropriety and upheld the convictions. Asked about that, Scruggs said he "thought" the case occurred after FISA was passed.[200]

■　■　■

As the bureau and the Justice Department's OIPR dropped the ball in the Lee case, political pressure was building to focus on the Chinese. When allegations surfaced that the Chinese were funneling money to the Democrats, the Republicans created a House select committee, headed by Christopher Cox, a California Republican, to investigate whether the Chinese were obtaining secrets from the United States. Trulock testified about problems with the Lee investigation. Still, the FBI did nothing. In fact, in May 1998, Lee left the country; the FBI knew nothing about it.

In August, the FBI set up a false flag operation. An FBI agent who spoke Chinese posed as a Chinese intelligence officer and tried to lure Lee into a meeting. Yet because the Chinese rely on personal relationships, Lee never could have been expected to fall for the trap. To make matters worse, the phony intelligence officer spoke the Cantonese dialect; Lee spoke Mandarin. Lee rejected the advance.

"The sting should have been the last resort," said Edward J. Curran, a former head of the FBI's Russian Section who had been detailed to the Energy Department. "There was no backup plan if it fell through. He should have been watched twenty-four hours a day after that."

When Freeh became director, he had no experience with—or interest in—foreign counterintelligence. Typically, the more aggressive agents who enjoyed tracking the Mafia or other violent criminals did not take to counterintelligence, which was more cerebral. Early in Freeh's tenure, when he was over counterintelligence, Bear Bryant, an agent with the intellect and judgment to handle the sensitive job, coached Freeh on the subject and tried to interest him in it. Until later in his tenure, Freeh let foreign counterintelligence take a backseat to other FBI pursuits.

To head counterintelligence, Freeh placed Neil J. Gallagher in charge of the National Security Division. Like Reno, Gallagher tended to focus on minute details without looking at the big picture. While Gallagher had a solid reputation in counterterrorism, he, like Freeh, had little interest in counterintelligence, despite having been a counterintelligence supervisor in New York. He holed up in his office and rarely met the agents under his command.

"I talked to Gallagher about the problems with the investigation," Curran said. "Nothing was happening. He had no comprehension of counterintelligence. He had very little background in the subject. He only knew counterterrorism."

While the best agents sought Martin's advice, bureau officials like Gallagher had a competitive attitude and took the position that Justice should prosecute his cases once he was ready to present them. Scruggs's insistence on artificially separating counterintelligence from espionage only encouraged that attitude.

In October 1998, David V. Kitchen, who had become head of the Albuquerque office only two months earlier, learned of the case when he was told that headquarters was unhappy about the progress of the Wen Ho Lee case.

"What Wen Ho Lee case?" he asked.

Curran, the agent detailed to the Energy Department from the FBI, told the bureau that agents should polygraph Lee and investigate more aggressively. Nothing happened for six months. By December, investigators knew that Lee was going to Taiwan for three weeks. No one followed him.

Based on Curran's recommendation, Bill Richardson, the new energy secretary, decided that having Lee in X Division was "unacceptable," and he reassigned him to a less sensitive area. On December 23, when Lee returned from Taiwan, Curran had Wackenhut Inc. give Lee a polygraph test. The polygraph examiner asked nonspecific questions like, "Did you commit espionage?"

"An FBI polygraph examiner would never ask that question," said Richard W. Keifer, a top former FBI polygrapher now in private practice. "It violates all the rules of question construction. It allows the person in the chair to decide what is or is not espionage. If he is working for a foreign power, he may not consider what he's doing to be espionage."[201]

The Wackenhut examiner told Lee he had passed. However, Lee

admitted during the polygraph test that during his 1988 trip to Beijing, a Chinese scientist whom he knew called him in his hotel room and asked to meet with him alone. Lee agreed, and the scientist showed up with Hu Side, who asked Lee about techniques for making smaller hydrogen bombs. Lee said he did not tell him anything. Lee did not report the contact, as was required.

The FBI did not ask Lee about this latest admission until three weeks later. Even then, agents did not press him for details. The local police would have done a better job. Believing that Lee had passed the polygraph test, Kitchen proposed closing the case. By then, FBI polygraph examiners in Washington had examined the charts of Lee's test. They said that on crucial questions, the results were inconclusive and that Lee probably had failed.

On February 10, FBI polygraphers examined Lee in a hotel room in Los Alamos. For the first time, the FBI asked Lee, "Have you ever provided W-88 information to any unauthorized person?"

"No," Lee said.

When asked if he gave nuclear weapons codes to any unauthorized person, Lee said no again. He showed deception on both questions.

The *New York Times* was preparing a story on the investigation, and the FBI asked the paper to hold the story for several weeks while the investigation continued. The paper agreed to hold the story a day. It would consider a further delay if Freeh called. When he did not, the story ran on March 6, 1999.

For the first time in the on-again, off-again investigation, the FBI asked Lee's consent to search his office. When he agreed, agents found a record showing that over seventy days, Lee had downloaded sensitive files equal to 430,000 pages of information from the laboratory's classified computer system. He transferred them to his unsecure desktop computer and portable tapes. Nine of the fifteen tapes were missing. Lee later said on *60 Minutes* that he had copied the information as a backup for his work.

The FBI found that after failing the polygraph, Lee started deleting files he had downloaded. He also continued to sneak into the bomb design area after his access had been canceled.

The day the *Times* story ran, agent Carol Covert, after being given a crash course in "hostile interrogation," interviewed Lee. Normally, John Martin insisted on weeks of preparation and consultation before agents confronted a suspect in an espionage investigation. Covert had had two days to prepare, and her painfully amateurish questioning showed it. A good interrogator makes the suspect think the bureau already knows what he has done. Repeatedly, Covert said Lee "must" have engaged in illegal activities. As if it would prove her case, Covert thrust the *Times* story in front of Lee. "Basically, that is indicating that there is a person at the laboratory that's committed espionage, and that points to you," she said. It was like telling a murder suspect he should confess because he was named in a newspaper story.

"But do they have any proof, evidence?" Dr. Lee asked.

"The Rosenbergs are the only people that never cooperated with the federal government in an espionage case," she told Lee. "You know what happened to them? They electrocuted them, Wen Ho Lee."

Lee denied that he had done anything wrong. Always polite, he thanked the FBI agent as she left. "I hope you have good health," he said.

On March 8, 1999, the day after the interview, Bill Richardson announced Lee's dismissal for failing to report contacts with people from a "sensitive country" and for mishandling classified documents found on his desk.

Representative Cox accused the Clinton administration of dragging its feet. Freeh, who had generally been kept in the dark about the problems with the case, saw an opportunity to score points with Congress. Suddenly, after languidly pursuing the investigation for four and a half years, the FBI decided Lee was a great danger to the country.

Now that Freeh had become interested in the investigation, Curran decided to try to get in to see him and tell him of the problems with the case. He purposely chose a day in March when Gallagher, the chief of the National Security Division, was off.[202] Curran was never able to get in to see him again, but Freeh listened. Suddenly, with Freeh calling the shots, the bureau conducted a thousand interviews. Agents conducted surveillance of Lee around the clock. They uncovered nothing.

Lacking evidence of espionage, Freeh approved an indictment on

December 10 requiring prosecutors to prove that Lee acted with intent to "injure the United States or . . . to secure an advantage to any foreign nation." The maximum penalty was life in prison.

By now, John Martin, who had always rejected FBI efforts to indict suspects when there was insufficient evidence, had retired. No one had the guts to stand up to Freeh and declare that the evidence was not there. Those bureau managers who had disagreed with Freeh in the past had lived to regret it. Or, as happened with Joe Martinolich, the SAC in Detroit who stood up to Freeh over the unjustified indictment of James Nichols, Freeh would simply tell them he would replace them if they did not follow his orders.

"Because Freeh did not have the evidence for a classic espionage case, he painted this as a devastating case and tried to cover up the lack of evidence by bringing a fifty-nine-count indictment citing vague and unsupportable charges," Martin told me.

At Lee's bail hearing in December, the government convinced a judge that Lee was so dangerous he had to be jailed without bail. To show how deceitful Lee was, Robert Messemer, a new agent on the case, said Lee told a colleague he wanted to borrow his computer so he could download a "résumé." In fact, Messemer testified, Lee borrowed the computer to download more files.

Lee spent nine months in restrictive conditions. A small light burned constantly in his cell so he could be watched. During his daily hour of exercise, Lee was required to wear leg shackles.

During discovery proceedings, the defense found that Messemer had testified falsely: Lee's colleague never told the FBI that Lee had said he wanted to download a résumé. Lee had told the colleague the truth— that he needed the computer to download files.

At a second bail hearing on August 17, 2000, Messemer claimed he had made an honest mistake. The admission was devastating. The fact that an agent could give false testimony in such an important case showed how far the bureau had fallen since the days of William Webster. In 1985 alone, the FBI under Webster arrested eleven major spies without a single claim that rights had been violated or that the FBI had acted improperly. Nor would Webster or Martin have approved such an obviously flawed indictment.

Outraged that he had been "led astray . . . by the executive branch of our government," Judge James A. Parker freed the sixty-one-year-old Lee on September 13. The judge said his jailing "embarrassed our entire nation and each of us who is a citizen of it." Sobs could be heard coming from Lee's friends and family.

Lee pleaded guilty to a single felony count of illegally gathering and retaining national security data. He agreed to a sentence of time served and to undergo sixty hours of debriefing under oath. He acknowledged making copies of the tapes and mishandling national security information.

It seemed that the agency that Hoover so lovingly created was self-destructing. Once again, the debacle was traceable to Freeh, who had wiped out the experienced Chinese counterintelligence section and had approved the indictment of Lee. By imposing his will in areas he knew little about, Freeh disrupted the normal deliberative processes within the FBI. His emphasis was on making himself look good in the short run. In the long term, that approach damaged the credibility and reputation of the FBI.

For Martin, the case was a personal tragedy. He had spent more than twenty-five years creating an espionage prosecutions program that had never resulted in an embarrassment. Of the seventy-six cases he brought, all but one resulted in a conviction or a guilty plea. No judge had ever said the government had misled the court, used improper techniques, or abused its power. When Martin approved an indictment, everyone knew the defendant was going to jail. Now, in a case he had never been told about, all that hard work had been undercut.

"Don't fuck it up," Martin would tell agents jokingly after advising them on how to proceed on an espionage case. Under Martin's tutelage, they rarely did. But Freeh, who presided over the Wen Ho Lee disaster, was sure he knew all the answers. He never sought Martin's advice.

In the end, the CIA raised questions about the veracity of information showing China had stolen the secrets to the W-88 in the first place, and Freeh admitted he failed to pass these questions along to agents working the case. As for Lee, because the FBI had so bungled the investigation, no one knew if he was a spy or—as his defenders claimed—naive and quirky. "He's clueless," said his twenty-six-year-old daughter Alberta.

Asian-American groups claimed Lee was a victim of racial profiling. Scientific and civil liberties groups joined in. The problem was not racial profiling: China enlisted only Chinese Americans for its espionage efforts. The problem was the FBI's sheer ineptitude. China undoubtedly was trying to obtain secrets, and the investigation should have been broadened to include other possible suspects.

Randy I. Bellows, a federal prosecutor, exhaustively investigated the FBI's actions. "This investigation was a paradigm of how not to manage and work an important counterintelligence case," he concluded. Bellows reserved special criticism for Scruggs and OIPR, which was "needlessly restrictive" in its interpretation of the law and imposed a "roadblock" to cooperation between the FBI and John Martin.

Prodded by Weldon Kennedy, Freeh eventually realized that his childish resentment of managers was harming the bureau. The FBI did need experienced supervisors after all. Freeh began restoring headquarters positions he had abolished. But by then, it was too late. From the laboratory to the National Security Division, the seasoned experts who had successfully handled so many cases in the past had either retired or become street agents in sunny places like Florida. They did not want to return to headquarters, and the damage to cases had been done.

Each move to the field had cost the FBI $60,000. Yet the money, totaling tens of millions of dollars, was all wasted. By the time Freeh left, headquarters had more personnel than when he took over.

31

FRAMED

Joseph Salvati, eighteen, and Marie Moschella, sixteen, met on Revere Beach outside of Boston. It was her white bathing suit with the red lobster that got his attention. They disagree on whether it was a one-piece or a two-piece.

Three years later, they married. Joe drove a truck for a meat-packing company. Marie took care of their four children. On Sundays, she made big family dinners of ravioli and meatballs in their home in the North End, Boston's Italian section.

On October 25, 1967, Marie was walking to pick up her kids at a parochial school when neighbors told her that her husband had been arrested for murder.

"I could not believe it," Marie recalled. "My legs turned to jelly."

Marie was thirty-two when her husband went to prison. He did not come home for thirty years. Joe missed his children's birthday parties, their communions, their high school graduations.

"There was always a void, always an emptiness," Marie said. "I want to tell you, when that verdict comes in, you go into a state of shock," she said. "I told the kids that Daddy had nothing to do with this. I told them that we needed to go see him and support him. I told them that the truth would come out."

The truth came out, but only after special U.S. Attorney John Durham, backed by U.S. District Court Judge Mark L. Wolf, conducted a vigorous investigation into corrupt relationships between agents of the

FBI's Boston office and mob informants. For forty years, the FBI concealed documents that showed the FBI knew exactly who killed Edward "Teddy" Deegan, a small-time hoodlum from nearby Chelsea, on March 12, 1965. Chief among the murderers was Mob hit man Joseph "The Animal" Barboza. It was Barboza who framed Joseph Salvati and three others by testifying against them. A second innocent man, Peter J. Limone, served thirty-two years in prison. The other two innocent men died in prison.

Salvati had made the mistake of borrowing money from Barboza, a loan shark. He was repaying the $400 with interest. But Barboza demanded the entire balance. When he didn't get it, he decided to blame him and the three others for the murder of Deegan.

The FBI documents showed that two days before the murder, an FBI informant told Special Agent H. Paul Rico, who was on the organized crime squad, that Vincent J. "Jimmy the Bear" Flemmi was planning to kill Deegan. It seems that Deegan was "an arrogant, nasty sneak, and he should be killed." The informant said the murder had the blessing of New England Mafia boss Raymond Patriarca.

"Informant advised that he had just heard from Jimmy Flemmi, and Flemmi told the informant that Raymond Patriarca has put out the word that Edward 'Teddy' Deegan is to be 'hit,' and that a dry run has already been made and that a close associate of Deegan's has agreed to set him up," Agent Rico wrote on March 10, 1965.

A day after the murder, the same informant told Rico in detail how the murder was carried out by three mobsters as Barboza and Flemmi watched, facts that Rico recounted in one of the suppressed reports. Within hours of the murder, Chelsea police obtained the same information about the murderers. However, Barboza, himself an FBI informant, named the four innocent men. The FBI agents suppressed the truth and allowed the innocent men to spend the best part of their lives in jail.

Copies of the documents were sent to Hoover and other headquarters officials at the time. Given Hoover's practices, there can be no question that he read them. Even if he did not, in Hoover's FBI, FBI officials who received them would have made sure they obtained Hoover's approval before making any decisions on the case.

In a June 4, 1965, memo evaluating Flemmi's fitness as an FBI informant, the SAC in Boston wrote that the agent handling him "believes that Flemmi murdered Deegan" and "from all indications, he is going to continue to commit murder." As far as Rico and another agent, Dennis Condon, were concerned, those were great credentials. After writing the memo, Rico and Condon made Jimmy Flemmi an FBI informant.

Now that it was fashionable to go after the Mafia, Hoover was more interested in scoring political points by developing Mafia informants than in the question of whether innocent people went to jail. That was the opinion of current agents assigned to investigate the Boston cover-up for the special U.S. attorney.

Over the years, Hoover had engaged in a range of practices that could have sent him to jail, from illegal wiretapping to use of government funds to refurbish and maintain his house. A Jekyll and Hyde, he built a superb organization but also presided over monumental abuses. Whether he was ignoring organized crime, hiding incriminating information from judges with his "Do Not File" procedure, blackmailing members of Congress, or spying on political adversaries of presidents, preserving his own job came first. Eight years after the Appalachin meeting, Hoover saw developing Mafia informants as expedient.

The cover-up began to unravel after Jimmy Flemmi claimed in 1998 that the government had promised him immunity from prosecution. Judge Wolf began holding hearings on Flemmi's informant status, and a special Justice Department task force began investigating the Boston office. After finding the suppressed documents at FBI headquarters, the task force released them on December 19, 2000. A small number of reports were released later because, according to the FBI, they were misfiled at headquarters. Meanwhile, Jimmy Flemmi died.

"[The] FBI is an organization that we the people are supposed to be protected by," said Victor Garo, the attorney who represented Salvati free of charge for twenty-five years. "And they are breaking the law whenever they want. This cover-up started in 1965, and it continues into the year 2000."

Nor was this the only outrage. The investigation determined that another Boston agent, John J. Connolly Jr., warned Flemmi's brother, Stephen "The Rifleman" Flemmi, and James "Whitey" Bulger in 1995

In 1974, the FBI moved to the J. Edgar Hoover Building at 935 Pennsylvania Avenue. *FBI*

Mary Ann Krauss, a firearms instructor and supervisor in the FBI's program for helping police target serial murderers and rapists, briefed Jodie Foster on the life of a female agent for her role in *The Silence of the Lambs*. *Kurt Crawford, FBI*

Karl Koecher became a mole in the CIA and spied for the KGB with the help of his wife, Hana, who regularly attended sex orgies with him to obtain information. In 1986, they returned to Prague, where this photo was taken. *Ronald Kessler*

BELOW LEFT: Howard D. Teten is the father of FBI profiling. *Gentry Photography*

BELOW RIGHT: John A. Walker Jr. gave the Soviets codes to Navy communications. *FBI*

RIGHT: As director, William H. Webster restored the FBI's credibility with Congress and the media. *FBI*

LEFT: As chief of the Justice Department's internal security section, John L. Martin, a former FBI agent, prosecuted seventy-six spies. Only one was acquitted. *Ronald Kessler*

RIGHT: William S. Sessions was fired by Bill Clinton in July 1993 after he abused his position as director. *FBI*

Under Louis J. Freeh, the FBI lurched from one debacle to another. *FBI*

Deputy Director Weldon L. Kennedy told Louis Freeh his reduction in headquarters supervisors would harm investigations. *FBI*

FBI agent Robert P. Hanssen was the most damaging spy in American history. *FBI*

Joseph Salvati, wearing glasses, left Superior Court in Cambridge, Massachusetts, after a judge vacated his murder sentence in January 2001. Knowing Salvati had been framed, Hoover and agents in the FBI's Boston office let him go to jail in 1967. *AP/Wide World Photo*

Agent William L. Flemming, *left,* and analyst Ben Herren brought to justice Thomas E. Blanton Jr. for the 1963 bombing of the 16th Street Church in Birmingham. *FBI*

In the Rose Garden at the White House, President Bush announced that he was nominating Robert S. Mueller III as FBI director on July 5, 2001. Mueller reorganized the FBI to place more emphasis on technology and analysis.
Reuters NewMedia Inc./Corbis

Smoke billowed from the North Tower of the World Trade Center as the South Tower plunged to the ground after attacks by al-Qaeda on September 11, 2001. *AP/Wide World Photo*

Barry Mawn, assistant director in charge of the New York Field Office, was almost killed in the attacks on the World Trade Center. *AP/Wide World Photo*

ABOVE: As assistant director in charge of the Washington Field Office, Van A. Harp directed the investigations into the anthrax mailings and the attack on the Pentagon. *FBI*

LEFT: Gregory Jones, an SAC in New York, headed the anthrax investigation there. *FBI*

that they were about to be indicted. Connolly grew up in South Boston with Bulger and his brother Billy, the former president of the Massachusetts Senate. Stephen Flemmi and Whitey Bulger ran the Winter Hill Gang in Boston's Irish enclave of South Boston. Both were FBI informants.

After the warning, Bulger disappeared, and the FBI offered a $1 million reward for his capture. Stephen Flemmi was sentenced to ten years in prison for extortion, money laundering, and obstructing justice. In addition, Bulger and Flemmi were charged with killing nearly two dozen people while working as FBI informants.

Essentially, the FBI ran a protection racket for the Winter Hill Gang in return for their information on the New England Mafia and the ego gratification of recruiting informants. Besides giving them tips on pending investigations, the FBI agents protected them from the Massachusetts State Police, local police, and district attorneys while the agents lied and stonewalled to protect themselves. While Connolly and John M. Morris, who headed the organized crime squad, were supposed to be controlling Bulger and Stephen Flemmi, the two gangsters were manipulating the two agents.

The agents accepted expensive Christmas gifts from the gangsters and, in the case of Morris, $7,000 in bribes, which he admitted taking. On an FBI salary of $60,000 a year, Connolly managed to acquire a $400,000 house and a $300,000 summer home in Cape Cod. Connolly, who retired in 1990, has denied all charges and is awaiting trial. Rico and Condon are under investigation.

"We're embarrassed," said Barry Mawn, who became SAC in Boston in 1997. "The system obviously broke down, and it's overshadowed a lot of great work done out of this office."

Amid mounting evidence that Salvati did not murder Deegan, Governor William Weld commuted his sentence in 1997. Limone was released in 2001. Ultimately, both convictions were overturned. Barboza, who had set them up, was murdered by a Mafia hit man in San Francisco.

As the new SAC, Mawn moved aggressively to turn over every document. But in December 2001, President George W. Bush ensured that the cover-up would continue by invoking executive privilege to prevent the House Government Reform Committee, headed by Representative Dan Burton, from seeing some of the material. The decision was part of a broader effort by the Bush Justice Department to shield prosecutive decisions from review by the Hill so that attorneys making them could feel freer to express their opinions. But the Boston case, which was both historical and entailed abuses by the bureau, should have been considered as a separate category.

When Marie Salvati visited her husband in prison, she was not permitted to touch him. Guards searched her each time, running their hands under her bra and panties. Every week, Joe sent her a card. "I'll love you forever" or "I miss you so much," he would write.

After he was freed, Joe told the *Boston Globe* he regretted that his parents did not live to see him cleared. As for his wife, "They broke the mold when they made [Marie]. . . . Who would stay with you for thirty years in prison and raise the children and do what she's done?"[203]

At ages sixty-eight and sixty-six, Joe and Marie took a vacation in Aruba, their first trip out of state since 1967, when they went to Maine. It was, Marie said, their second honeymoon.

32

BIRMINGHAM

After a jury convicted former Ku Klux Klan member Thomas E. Blanton Jr., sixty-two, of participating in bombing the 16th Street Baptist Church in Birmingham on September 15, 1963, Freeh called the case "a disgrace to the FBI." According to Freeh, "That case should have been prosecuted in 1964. It could have been prosecuted in 1964. The evidence was there."

Freeh's comment at a congressional hearing followed a May 3, 2001, *New York Times* op-ed by Bill Baxley, a former Alabama attorney general, who accused the FBI of "stonewalling" by withholding from him tapes that might have led to convictions when the state investigated the case back in 1977. In that year, Baxley successfully prosecuted one of the four main suspects, Robert "Dynamite Bob" Chambliss, the alleged ringleader. Chambliss died in prison eight years later.

The agents who had worked the Blanton case could not believe that Freeh would make such a statement. Once again, Freeh did not have his facts straight. That day in 1963, Denise McNair, eleven, and Carole Robertson, Cynthia Wesley, and Addie Mae Collins, all fourteen, were dressed in white party dresses and patent leather shoes for a youth service. Nineteen bundled sticks of dynamite concealed under a stairwell exploded inches from them. All four died, and another girl, Sarah Collins, was blinded in one eye. Immortalized by a Bob Dylan song, the bombing shocked the country and contributed to passage of the 1964 Civil Rights Act.

No one was prosecuted. Then, in 1993, G. Robert "Rob" Langford became SAC in Birmingham. Originally from Tuscaloosa, an hour to the west, Langford wanted to avoid the kind of problems he had had with black leaders when he was SAC in Buffalo. There, the FBI had arrested a black politician and some black police officers, leading to charges that the bureau was targeting blacks. In Birmingham, Langford decided to try to open a dialogue with black leaders.

At first, many would not return his calls. But after several months, Langford met at the field office with thirty black pastors and other leaders of the black community. Even then, Reverend Abraham Woods, pastor of St. Joseph Baptist Church, did not want to try the cookies, coffee, and punch that Langford was offering.

"I thought they might be poisoning us," Woods, the head of the local chapter of the Southern Christian Leadership Conference, said. "Finally, I tasted of what they had—but just a little bit."

"We've made mistakes in the past. But we need to work together and communicate," Langford told the community leaders. "If you have issues, we can work on them."[204]

Why didn't the FBI investigate the bombing back in 1964? Woods asked the SAC.

"I can't imagine the bureau did not investigate," Langford said. "I know we were active by then against the Klan." He promised to look into it.

In a large room where the field office kept closed files, Langford had support employees locate ninety volumes of material from the original investigation. Each file contained hundreds of documents compiled by the FBI on the bombing.

Langford began attending services at black churches. When he and his wife, Martha, went to Woods' church, they were the only whites. Spotting them in the congregation, Woods said, "We have agent Langford here. Welcome." Thinking he would discourage Langford from staying, he said, "This will be a long service. We're having a baptism. You're welcome to leave if you want to leave." Langford stayed for the entire four hours.

Langford became friends with Christopher Hamlin, the current pastor of the 16th Street Baptist Church, and the SAC took him into his confidence. "Chris, I think I'm going to open the bombing case," Langford said. "What do you think?"

"Rob, that would be tremendous," he said. "But be prepared. Some will say you're just doing it for political reasons or, 'Let's not open up old wounds.' But I think it would be great."

In 1994, Langford met again with black leaders. He told them the FBI did investigate the bombing but the files indicated that the FBI did not turn over the results to the Birmingham police or state troopers because the Klan had infiltrated those organizations. The Alabama Department of Public Safety actively tried to throw roadblocks in the way of FBI agents investigating the bombing.

In a memo in the files, Hoover said he opposed prosecution because the likelihood of obtaining a conviction was "remote." But he directed the Birmingham office to ensure that the investigation "receive continuous aggressive action and that all investigative avenues be pursued in an effort to obtain sufficient evidence so that successful prosecution can be secured." In February 1967, Hoover renewed that order. However, by 1968, any federal prosecution was precluded by a five-year statute of limitations. Still, the investigation continued until 1971.

Without telling headquarters, Langford assigned William L. Flemming, who had been an agent for twenty-five years, to the case. The Birmingham police assigned Ben Herren, a detective with twenty years of experience, to work with Flemming. Herren eventually became an FBI analyst. They were to see what potential witnesses were still living. A total of 140 witnesses and other key individuals had died or were mentally incompetent. But by 1995, Langford decided the case had enough potential to turn it into an active civil rights investigation. On contract, the FBI hired Bob Eddy, an investigator who had worked on the previous state case, to assist with the investigation.

In the state case, because the FBI did not have an active investigation going at the time, the bureau let Eddy set up an office in the FBI field office. He would ask for specific items but did not see the entire ten thousand documents. He never saw a reference to tapes or transcripts. Langford saw memos referring to microphones, but "I just assumed that the tapes had all been destroyed," he said.

In 1996, when Langford retired, Joseph R. Louis, the new SAC, continued to support the investigation.

"After fourteen months, we decided the main suspects were still the main suspects," Flemming told me. "We didn't have a lot of hope. It had been thirty-three years. Memories had faded, witnesses had died. But we thought some might want to clear their consciences. We talked to ex-wives and widows. They were still fearful. A lot of their husbands physically abused them. Many of the men had extramarital affairs."

Besides Blanton and Chambliss, the FBI, in the initial investigation, identified two other suspects: Herman Frank Cash, who died a free man in 1994, and Bobby Frank Cherry. In 1997, Herren and Eddy spent four hours with Cherry, interviewing him at the sheriff's office in Athens, Texas. Cherry denied his involvement. Several days later, Cherry called a press conference to denounce the FBI. The media coverage of the press conference led close family members to step forward. Teresa Stacy, twenty-four, Cherry's granddaughter, said Cherry bragged about the bombing. She said she was thankful the FBI was investigating, and she was willing to testify.

"This is just something that had to be done," she said. "Four little girls died for nothing."

Cherry's ex-wife, Willadean Brogdon, also volunteered to help. She recalled driving past the church with Cherry in 1970. "He said that was the place he had bombed," she said. "He used to tell me if I ever talked, the same thing would happen to me."

In the files, Flemming saw transcripts and noticed, in a 1981 evidence inventory, an oblique reference to the tapes themselves. Under Hoover's system, because microphone surveillance entailed break-ins, tapes of such surveillance were kept separately from the cases. Because the surveillance involved illegal entry, the material was to help generate leads and not to be used as evidence in court. Agents essentially had to know that a surveillance had been conducted before they could find the records.

At first, support employees told Flemming they could not find the inventoried tapes where they were supposed to be. Eventually, Flemming and Herren found them in a different area, where current tapes were kept. The tapes were of Blanton and his wife, Jean, talking in their kitchen, where the FBI, using a mike that penetrated a wall to an adjoining apartment, had placed a bug under the sink.

The recordings were virtually inaudible. Even after the tapes were enhanced, using methods that had not existed thirty years earlier, they were difficult to understand. The investigators could hear Blanton's wife asking whether, when he broke a date with her on the Friday night before the bombing, he had taken out another girl. No, Blanton said, he had been down at a meeting of local Klansmen under a bridge over the Cahaba River "planning the bombing." It was the Friday before the Sunday morning bombing of the church.

Stored with those tapes, Flemming and Herren found other tapes of incriminating conversations between Blanton and Mitchell Burns, a gravelly voiced Klan member. To make the recordings, the FBI had installed a bulky reel-to-reel tape recorder underneath the spare tire in the trunk of Burns's 1956 Chevrolet. Because the quality was so poor, these tapes also had to be enhanced. In 1965, Burns agreed to cooperate after agent Brooke Blake gave him a ride and showed him autopsy photos of the four victims, their bodies burned and mangled. The photos, he said later, made him sick to his stomach.

At Blanton's trial, prosecutors played the tape of the twenty-five-year-old Blanton bragging to Burns about the bombing.

"They ain't gonna catch me when I bomb my next church," Blanton said. "The boys done a good job on this one. There are a few Negroes now who won't grow up to bother us."

Although the tapes were convincing, they never caught Blanton admitting outright to the bombing. He is believed to have driven the bombers to the church that day.

The trial was held in state court but prosecuted by U.S. Attorney G. Douglas Jones, who was appointed special prosecutor by the state. Jones, along with Assistant U.S. Attorney Robert O. Posey and Assistant District Attorney Jeff Wallace, argued that the tapes could be introduced as evidence because the laws governing electronic interceptions had changed and the bugging was done for reasons of national security. The judge bought the argument.

On May 1, 2001, the jury of eight whites and four blacks deliberated for two hours before finding Blanton guilty of first-degree murder. He was sentenced to four life terms. Cherry was also charged, but the judge decided that because he suffered from dementia, he was not competent to stand trial. After further evaluation of Cherry, the judge reversed himself in January 2002 and decided he is competent to stand trial.

Thus, instead of being a disgrace, as Freeh had claimed, the case was an FBI success story. Because of the laws at the time and witnesses' fear, it was highly unlikely—as Hoover had said—that the FBI could have brought a prosecution in 1964. The tapes of the kitchen bugging could not have been introduced, and the three witnesses who testified at the trial either were not known to the FBI at the time or—in the case of Burns—would not have testified. Instead of withholding evidence from Alabama Attorney General Baxley in 1977, as Baxley claimed, the FBI did not realize it had the material.

Because of the tenacity of Langford, Flemming, Herren, and the others involved, the FBI brought to justice a man who had blown up four girls because of the color of their skin. After the charges were brought, Hamlin's message to his congregation included the words of the eighth-century B.C. prophet Amos: "But let justice roll down like waters and righteousness like an ever-growing stream."

After Baxley's piece appeared in the *Times*, Charlene B. Thornton, who became SAC in Birmingham at the end of 1999, wrote a letter to the editor giving the FBI's side. The same letter appeared on the FBI's Birmingham Field Office Web site. To write the letter, Thornton had to obtain permission from the FBI's Office of Public and Congressional Affairs.

If Freeh had read the letter on the Web site or in the paper, he might have realized that his comments were off base. But Freeh was not known for checking his facts. Once again, he had gotten good press by denouncing the FBI.

Freeh's comments came as a shock to the FBI's Birmingham office and to the retired agents who had investigated the case. They had worked hard to see that justice was done. While Baxley's piece could have been dismissed, the FBI director himself had said that, once again, the bureau had screwed up. Freeh's remarks turned what should have been seen as a triumph into something shameful and another black eye for the FBI.

"Back in 1963, we could not have used the tapes," Flemming said. "Witnesses would not have testified. Jurors would not have convicted. Freeh's comment showed ignorance of the case."[205]

33

AVENGER

Since the mid-1980s, Robert Wade, assistant chief of the Soviet Section, had been trying to find a mole in the U.S. intelligence community. As one asset after another was rolled up, Wade and his boss, Donald E. Stukey, became convinced that the KGB had a high-ranking source whose information was leading to the executions of American agents. While the arrest of CIA officer Aldrich Ames in 1994 explained many of the roll-ups, some remained unexplained. Yet another mystery was why the Russians did not push Earl Pitts, the FBI agent arrested in 1995, to reveal more FBI secrets.

When a CIA source said an FBI agent in the New York office could be working for the Soviets, Wade rented an apartment in New York and began checking on nearly a dozen agents' backgrounds and credit records. He came up with nothing.

In November 2000, the FBI received the original file of an American double agent working for the SVR, the successor to the KGB's foreign intelligence component. AVENGER, the code name of the defector who fingered Ames and who had since left Russia, helped the CIA recruit the defector who gave up the file, for which he was paid more than $1 million.

The material provided by the defector included a black plastic trash bag in which the American left classified documents for the Russians at a dead drop. It also included a tape recording of the individual making arrangements with KGB officer Aleksander Fefelov.

So crafty was the American that he never let the Russians know his name or even what agency he worked for. At various times, he called himself B, Ramon Garcia, G. Robertson, or Jim Baker. But when FBI agents listened to the tape, they immediately recognized the voice of Robert Philip Hanssen, an FBI agent who worked down the hall from Wade and had access to the most sensitive secrets in the government. On the plastic bag, the agents found Hanssen's fingerprints.

The discoveries sent a shudder through the FBI. Earl Pitts and Richard Miller, the two FBI agents previously caught spying, were minnows compared to Hanssen. Hanssen's clearances not only allowed him access to secrets at the CIA, NSA, the White House, and Defense Department, they allowed him to check an FBI database that would show if the FBI was investigating him.

Most spies lead curious lives. Growing up in Illinois, for example, Glenn Michael Souther, a Navy photographic specialist who gave the Soviets American nuclear war plans, identified with the Confederacy and wore Confederate uniforms. As a teenager, he masturbated so compulsively that he developed lesions on his penis. In college, as a prank, he bit women on the neck. An ideological spy, he finally defected to the Soviet Union, where he committed suicide. He got his wish to be buried in a KGB uniform.[206]

Yet no spy was as bizarre as Hanssen. When Hanssen was six or seven, his father, a Chicago policeman, wrapped his son in towels and twirled him around until he threw up, according to David A. Vise's *The Bureau and the Mole*. Out of sheer meanness, when Hanssen took his driving test to obtain a license, his father bribed the examiner to fail him. Hanssen found out about it.

At Knox College in Galesburg, Illinois, Hanssen majored in chemistry and took Russian. He would later say he became fascinated by the spy game after he read Kim Philby's memoirs at the age of fourteen (the book actually came out when he was twenty-four). In 1973, after obtaining an M.B.A. from Northwestern University, Hanssen became a certified public accountant.

After a stint as a Chicago police officer assigned to a unit investigating corrupt cops, Hanssen, at the age of thirty-two, joined the FBI in 1976. He was assigned to counterintelligence in New York. Because of his sallow complexion, dark hair, black suits, and humorless stare, Hanssen acquired the nickname "The Mortician" or "Dr. Death." Like Earl Pitts, he resented the FBI and the way New York's high living costs devoured his salary.

A computer whiz, Hanssen helped create a database where agents entered personal data about Soviet intelligence officers, including their addresses, appearance, and likes and dislikes. He worked with the technicians who installed bugs and video surveillance systems on the Soviets.

In 1979, Hanssen began spying, selling the GRU classified documents for $20,000. He compromised Dmitri F. Polyakov, a Soviet general in the GRU who was code-named TOPHAT. A double agent for the FBI since 1961, Polyakov considered himself a Russian patriot, dedicated to the cause of overthrowing the Communist regime. He would accept no more than $3,000 a year, provided mostly in the form of Black & Decker power tools, fishing gear, and shotguns.

The GRU, apparently covering up for one of their own, did nothing. Only when Aldrich Ames told the KGB about Polyakov did the Soviets execute him in 1988.

In 1980, Hanssen's wife, Bonnie, walked in on him in the basement of their Scarsdale home when Hanssen was writing a note to the GRU. When Hanssen tried to conceal the note from her, she suspected he had a girlfriend. To allay her fears, he admitted that he had been giving the Soviets information in return for thousands in cash. He said the information was of no value, and he promised to break off the relationship, consult a priest, and give the money to charities of Mother Teresa. He continued to spy but stopped in 1981, when he was transferred as a supervisory agent to headquarters.

After returning to New York in 1985, Hanssen resumed his spying. This time, he chose to deal with the KGB, which was more prestigious and powerful than the GRU. Hanssen knew that the FBI did not monitor mail sent to KGB officers' homes, so on October 4, 1985, he sent a letter to the home address of a KGB officer in Washington. Inside the envelope was a second envelope marked "Do Not Open. Take this envelope unopened to Viktor I. Cherkashin." Cherkashin was over the KGB's Line KR or foreign counterintelligence at the Soviet embassy. Inside the second envelope was an offer to turn over highly classified papers in exchange for $100,000. Hanssen identified himself only as "B."

As a sign of his bona fides, Hanssen listed the names of three KGB officers the United States had recruited—Valeriy Martynov, Sergey Motorin, and Boris Yuzhin. Shortly, they were recalled to Moscow. Yuzhin was jailed for fifteen years, and the other two were executed. Like Polyakov, Ames also had fingered them.

By 1989, Hanssen was back in headquarters. He told the Soviets that the French had uncovered the fact that Felix Bloch was spying for the KGB. A longtime State Department employee, Bloch was deputy chief of mission in Vienna until 1987. In Paris, French counterintelligence officers conducting surveillance of Reino Gikman, a KGB officer, photographed Gikman having a drink with Bloch in the bar of the Hotel Meurice on the Rue de Rivoli on May 14, 1989. After downing whiskeys, Bloch and Gikman had dinner together in the hotel's dark-paneled restaurant. At the end of their meal, Gikman walked off with a black carry-on bag, which Bloch had left under their table. They met again in Brussels on May 28.

Hanssen let the KGB know that American intelligence was aware of the meeting. "Bloch was such a schnook," he wrote to the KGB. "I almost hated protecting him."

On June 22, a man phoned Bloch and said he was calling on behalf of Pierre, the code name Gikman used with Bloch. In the intercepted conversation, the man cryptically told Bloch that Pierre could not see him in the near future because he was sick. "A contagious disease is suspected," he said. "I am worried about you. You have to take care of yourself."

John McWethy, an ABC-TV correspondent, received an anonymous call about the investigation. Checking with his State Department sources, he was able to confirm the tip. ABC's *World News Tonight* aired the story on July 21, 1989.

An FBI investigation established that, while at the embassy in Vienna, Bloch had been paying exorbitant sums to a prostitute who whipped him and led him around with a dog chain. Bloch loved to be demeaned and scolded.

John Martin met with FBI agents who planned to try to interview Bloch. He went over with the agents how to establish the elements of the crime of espionage, a conspiracy to commit espionage, or an attempt to commit espionage. The interviews with Bloch took place in the State Department on June 22 and 23, 1989, after officials there informed Bloch that he was being put on leave with pay. While there was not enough evidence to arrest him, there was enough evidence to indicate he should not have access to classified information. Simply meeting with a foreign intelligence officer without reporting it is a violation of security regulations.

Bloch began talking to the agents. He seemed on the verge of making an admission about money he had received from the Soviets. At that point, the agents stopped the interview and read Bloch his Miranda rights.

"If I have the right to remain silent, I will remain silent," Bloch said.

Martin was furious. It was the same mistake Freeh had made when he ordered agents to read Richard Jewell his rights in the middle of an interview.

"I specifically advised the agents that they were under no obligation to give Bloch his rights," Martin said. "I expected that if they gave him his rights, they would do so when they started the interview. Only if the agents had enough evidence to arrest him going into the interview and intended to arrest him, or if Bloch already was in custody, did they need to warn him of his rights. Giving him his rights in the middle of an interview was inconceivable. To this day, I don't know what they were thinking. Clearly, they had their own ideas."

While Bloch was never charged, the FBI kept him under surveillance for the next six months. As in a parade of circus clowns, while FBI agents followed Bloch, television networks and newspaper reporters followed the agents.

An article in the *New York Times Magazine* by David Wise quoted Bloch as saying the bag he left for Gikman in Paris contained stamps for Gikman's collection. Bloch, a stamp collector, said he knew Gikman as Pierre Bart, a fellow collector. He said he never asked the man's business and did not know he was a spy.

While confirming to Wise that Gikman called him a month after their meeting in Paris, Bloch gave a more benign version of Gikman's message. He claimed Gikman told him he wasn't feeling well, and he hoped Bloch did not catch "the same thing."

"The government, the leaks, assert that I'm guilty," Bloch told Wise. "Apparently, they can't prove it. . . . There's a presumption of innocence in this country. Someone should not be put in the position of saying, 'I'm innocent.' "

While that may be true, the standard of proof imposed by criminal law does not apply to the government's personnel policies. In November 1990, Secretary of State James A. Baker III announced that, in the interests of national security, Bloch had been dismissed. Not only was the fifty-five-year-old Foreign Service officer out of his $81,400-a-year job, after thirty-two years with the State Department, he lost his pension.

With his wife, Bloch moved to the Chapel Hill, North Carolina area, where he worked two jobs, driving a city bus and bagging groceries. In January 1993, Bloch was charged with stealing about $100 in groceries from the Harris-Teeter Supermarket. Employees said they saw Bloch putting the bags of groceries into the trunk of his 1980 Mercedes. Bloch paid a $60 fine and performed community service.

Unlike the other roll-ups, the compromise of the investigation of Bloch could not be attributed to Ames. Clearly, there was another high-level mole in the intelligence community. Bear Bryant, who headed the National Security Division and assigned Wade to the mole hunt, thought the culprit worked for the CIA. He assigned sixty-five agents in the Washington Field Office to look for a mole.

"We knew, after Ames, there was another significant spy," Bryant told me. "We didn't know where he or she was. Cases had been compromised. Felix Bloch could not be tied to the others. When we found Pitts, the issues still were not resolved."[207]

In 1997, Bryant assigned Thomas J. Kimmel to conduct a damage assessment of the Pitts case. Kimmel wrote a memo concluding that there likely was another mole in the bureau, not the CIA. In February 1999, he reported his findings to Freeh, who was "very attentive," Kimmel recalled. But both Gallagher, who was over the National Security Division, and Bryant, who had become deputy FBI director, thought Kimmel had failed to provide any useful new information.[208]

Hanssen continued to spy sporadically until December 1991. At one point, he told Ray Mislock, who headed the Russian Section, that a new FBI computer system was not secure. Mislock was skeptical, so

Hanssen broke into his computer and handed him a secret document he had downloaded from the startled official's computer.

Concerned about the mounting investigations and defectors who turned on the KGB after the collapse of the Soviet Union, Hanssen anxiously began running his name, address, and keywords, like the name of the park where he left documents for his KGB handlers, through the FBI's automated database, which included listings of all investigations. Only when he found he was not a target did he get back in touch with his former handlers, now the SVR. Hanssen was facing retirement and wanted to renovate his kitchen. In October 1999, the SVR wrote, "Dear Friend: Welcome! It's good to know you are here."

Of his own motives, Hanssen wrote dramatically in March 2000, "One might propose that I am either insanely brave or quite insane. I'd answer neither. I'd say, insanely loyal."

If Hanssen was not insane, he certainly was kinky. On the surface, he seemed a devoted family man, with a wife and six kids who lived in a four-bedroom split-level house on a cul-de-sac on Talisman Drive in Vienna, Virginia. Almost every day, he attended Mass at St. Catherine of Siena Church in Great Falls, Virginia. Coincidentally, it was the same church Freeh attended. Hanssen belonged to the church's conservative Opus Dei society, which was fiercely anticommunist.

Yet there were many compartments concealed behind Hanssen's perpetual smirk. Besides spying for the Soviets, Hanssen befriended Priscilla Sue Galey, a well-proportioned woman Hanssen met at a Washington strip club where she worked. Hanssen bought her a used Mercedes-Benz and jewelry and paid for her trip to Hong Kong, where he went to inspect the FBI legal attaché office or legat. He also gave her a personal tour of Quantico and tried to lure her to his church so she could see Hanssen with his family and gain a greater appreciation of religion. She drove to the church separately and saw Hanssen and his family enter. She could not bring herself to go in.

Hanssen gave her an American Express card for car-related expenses, but when a statement listed charges for cigarettes and Easter dresses for her nieces, he became livid. He flew to Columbus, Ohio, where Galey was visiting her mother for Christmas in 1991. He retrieved the card and ended their relationship.

Galey said that despite her offers, they never had sex. While a friend of Hanssen's claimed that Hanssen told him he had sex with her once and found it unsatisfying, the FBI found the friend to be unreliable.

Eventually, Galey became a crack addict and pawned everything Hanssen had given her. To support herself, she worked the streets as a prostitute. After an arrest for drug dealing in 1993, she served a year in jail.

When Hanssen's high school friend Jack Hoschouer came to visit, Hanssen would rig a closed-circuit video camera so his friend could stand on a deck outside the Hanssens' bedroom and watch him and his wife have sex. He also posted erotic stories about Bonnie on the Internet, using his full name and E-mail address, along with his wife's name.

Hanssen looked down on everyone, especially women at the FBI. He told colleagues women never should have been accepted as agents. At one point, he became involved in a dispute with a female intelligence analyst. He pushed her, and she fell. In 1995, Bryant transferred him to work at the State Department's Office of Foreign Missions, where he had less access to secrets.

"Eventually I would appreciate an escape plan. (Nothing lasts forever)," Hanssen wrote to his handlers back in November 1985. Indeed, on January 13, 2001, the FBI reassigned Hanssen to headquarters to a manufactured position so he could be watched. A little after 8 P.M. on February 18, ten FBI agents shivered in the cold as they observed Hansen walk to a dead drop, a spot under a bridge in Foxstone Park in Vienna, Virginia. As the fifty-six-year-old Hanssen emerged from the bridge, the agents, guns drawn, surrounded their fellow agent and placed handcuffs on him. Another team of agents found $50,000 in $100 bills left for Hanssen at a second drop site.

Charged with spying for the Russians, Hanssen pleaded guilty to selling the Soviet Union and later the Russians six thousand pages of documents and twenty-seven computer disks cataloging secret and top-secret programs over twenty-one years. He left more than two dozen packages in dead drops for his handlers in parks in New York and Washington. Besides compromising nine agents working for the United States, Hanssen gave the Russians the Continuity of Government Plan, a program to ensure the survival of the U.S. government in the event of a nuclear attack; the National Intelligence Program, which revealed everything the U.S. intelligence community planned for the coming year; and the FBI's Double Agent Program, which evaluated double agent operations worldwide. Hanssen informed the Russians that the United States had the capability of reading certain Soviet communications, gave them the methods NSA used to eavesdrop on communications of foreign countries, let them see the results of debriefings of KGB defector Vitaly Yurchenko, and provided them with a range of documents from the CIA and National Security Council.[209]

Perhaps most intriguing, Hanssen let the Soviets know that the United States had built a secret tunnel under the Soviets' new diplomatic compound at Mount Alto along Wisconsin Avenue in Washington. The second highest point in Washington, Mount Alto would give the Soviets a tremendous advantage in intercepting microwave communications. As part of the agreement, the United States would build a new embassy in Moscow.

In 1982, the State Department noticed that some of the steel in the new building in Moscow was not configured according to the plans. The CIA proposed examining the building with neutron-bombarding x-rays. After six months of wrangling over the health effects and the Soviet reaction, U.S. Ambassador Arthur A. Hartman approved the plan. There were literally thousands of electronic bugs in the building.

Meanwhile in Washington, the Americans drilled a tunnel under the Mount Alto embassy using new technology NSA developed for drilling silently. NSA also began developing highly advanced bugging devices that the FBI hoped a double agent might be able to place inside the embassy. The cost of the tunnel, which ran from a townhouse the FBI bought, was nearly $1 billion, including development of new technology.

As envisioned, the equipment inside the tunnel would pick up the signals from the bugs. However, because so many agents were being compromised by Ames, the FBI never got a chance to place the bugs in the embassy. The Soviets found less technologically advanced bugs in the residence portion of the embassy. They displayed them at a press conference in 1985.

While Ames's spying had led directly to more deaths, Hanssen gave up far more critically important information. On February 2, 2001,

John D. Ashcroft, a former Missouri senator, became attorney general under George W. Bush. He pushed for the death penalty for Hanssen. Plato Cacheris, Hanssen's lawyer, told the Justice Department that if the death penalty were imposed, Hanssen would not cooperate with FBI and CIA officers who wanted to know more about what he gave up. Instead, Hanssen would go to trial, and Cacheris—considered one of the finest criminal lawyers in the country—would demand that the government produce for trial and reveal the identity of the defector who gave him up.[210]

George J. Tenet, the CIA director, said the agency needed Hanssen's cooperation. In the future, the CIA wanted to be able to go back to Hanssen and ask him questions as other spies were uncovered. Ashcroft backed down, and Cacheris negotiated a plea agreement.

Dressed in a green jumpsuit, Hanssen, looking gaunt, pleaded guilty on July 6, 2001. He began twice-weekly debriefings. Hanssen would get life in prison without the possibility of parole.

Back in the 1940s and 1950s, ideological spies like the Rosenbergs spied because they believed in the Communist cause. In more recent years, every spy except Glenn Souther was in it for the money. But while Hanssen received $600,000 in cash and three diamonds and had been promised $800,000 in a foreign bank account, he made it clear to the Russians that money was not his primary interest. More than a $100,000 payment, he told the KGB at one point, would only create "difficulty" since he could not "spend it, store it, or invest it easily without triping [sic] 'drug money' warning bells." As for the money in a foreign bank account, "we do both know" that the money is not really put away "except in some vague accounting sense," Hanssen wrote. "Never patronize at this level." After his arrest, none of the money from the Russians could be recovered. In fact, Hanssen's home was heavily mortgaged.

More than the money, Hanssen seemed to enjoy getting back at the FBI and outwitting the intelligence community. He hated uncertainty, he told the KGB. Spying gave him power and control over both the FBI and the KGB. He loved dispensing advice to the KGB, telling his handlers at one point that they should "rein in" the GRU. "The U.S.," he said, "can be likened to a powerfully built but retarded child, potentially dangerous but young, immature, and easily manipulated. But don't be fooled by the appearance. It is also one which can turn ingenius [*sic*] quickly, like an idiot savant, once convinced of a goal."

Hanssen's father had taught him to mistrust and resent authority. Spying for the Russians was the ultimate revenge as well as an ego trip that demonstrated his superiority. Yet his letters to the Russians betrayed loneliness and a need for friendship and acceptance.

Richard Ault, an FBI profiler who interviewed convicted spies for a study called Project Slammer, concluded that treason often conceals an urge to commit suicide. "What you see in these people is a way to alleviate psychological pain and discomfort," Ault said. "Betraying your country is often the end game of years of suppressed anger."

While Hanssen betrayed her as well, Bonnie Hanssen remained loyal to her husband, visiting him regularly in jail. It was not that she still loved him, she explained to her family. It was that as a good Catholic, she would never divorce him and wanted to save his soul. Under a 1996 law, because she cooperated with the investigation, Bonnie received $40,000 a year, or 55 percent of his pension.

After Hanssen's arrest, according to David A. Vise, Mark Wauck, a Chicago FBI agent who is Bonnie Hanssen's brother, told the bureau that in 1990 he reported to his superiors that Hanssen was spending beyond his means and that he had thousands of dollars in cash in his home. "He told bureau officials that he suspected his brother-in-law was spying for the Russians," Vise, a *Washington Post* reporter, wrote in his book, *The Bureau and the Mole*.

The account by Vise—who later became embroiled in controversy because he bought between 16,000 and 18,000 copies of his own book from barnesandnoble.com and then returned most of them—was untrue. After Hanssen's arrest, Wauck told the FBI that he had told a counterintelligence supervisor in 1990 that Bonnie Hanssen had found several thousand dollars in unexplained cash in a dresser drawer. Wauck did not claim to have made any allegation to the FBI about spying.

The supervisor, a highly regarded counterintelligence agent later detailed to the CIA, disputed even Wauck's recollection that he mentioned anything about money. After Hanssen's arrest, the supervisor told the

FBI that Wauck, while sitting on the edge of his desk, mentioned to him in the squad room that Hanssen was having marital problems. He said Wauck made no allegations of any kind about Hanssen. The supervisor therefore did not pass anything along even within the Chicago Field Office, let alone to headquarters.

According to Vise, after Hanssen's arrest, Wauck told family members that he reported Hanssen to the bureau in 1990. He said he was surprised that nothing happened. But Janine Brookner, who represents Bonnie Hanssen, said, "That's not true. According to Bonnie and the family, Wauck said nothing to them about reporting Hanssen to the bureau years earlier."[211]

Considerable confusion occurred because after Hanssen's arrest, "Wauck's wife thought she remembered that Bonnie had found a thousand or two thousand dollars at their home in 1990," Brookner said. "But Bonnie said she must have misremembered because she did not find any unusual sums. Wauck said he heard the money story only from his wife, who told him that Bonnie was upset about finding the money and went running to tell Bonnie's sister. But neither Bonnie nor the sister remember any such thing."

In sum, there was nothing to the claim that Wauck told the FBI about Hanssen back in 1990. A former high-ranking bureau official familiar with the case said he thinks Wauck, who is highly regarded, wished in retrospect that he had been more suspicious of Hanssen and became confused by his wife's even more muddled recollections. After his conversation with the supervisor, Wauck continued to E-mail his brother-in-law in friendly fashion. Nor did he pursue any allegation with the bureau. One misrecollection had been piled upon another.

"There was no corroboration for his claim," the former FBI official said. "The bureau was tarnished over an allegation that is just not true."

Still, when the *Washington Post* asked for comment on the allegation, John Collingwood, the FBI's assistant director for public and congressional affairs, did not specifically deny the claim. A lawyer from Ohio who studied Cantonese early in his FBI career, Collingwood became a special assistant to John Otto when Otto was acting FBI director. In 1989, Collingwood took over the FBI's congressional affairs function. In 1992, he became head of public affairs as well.

Collingwood knew more about the FBI than anyone else. Besides having been at the highest levels of the bureau longer than anyone, he sat in on key strategy meetings and was asked for his counsel beyond his areas of congressional and public affairs. When bureau officials would complain to him about negative stories, Collingwood would respond by saying the story would not have run if they had not screwed up in the first place. Because he was trusted, everyone seemed to confide in him.

Collingwood had kept his job so long because, besides being smart, he was honest and cautious. No one in the press or Congress ever found that he lied to them or misled them. Collingwood never forgot that, back when the press first reported on the FBI's investigation into CISPES, a left-wing group that raised money in America for humanitarian aid to El Salvador, William Sessions defended the investigation. A congressional investigation later documented that the FBI had improperly targeted the group.

As a fact-finding agency, the FBI must be especially careful about issuing a statement that could be successfully challenged later, Collingwood felt. While a comment based on what was known at the time might make the bureau look better in the short term, in the long term the bureau's reputation would suffer if new facts later showed that the comment was wrong. Collingwood, who worked fourteen-hour days, would even check 302s—agents' reports of interviews—himself to make sure he knew the facts about a particular issue.

Thus, because the Justice Department's inspector general had launched an investigation into Mark Wauck's claim, Collingwood chose to respond by saying only that the FBI "evaluated" the "episode" at the time. "It did not result in the discovery of Hanssen's activities," he said.[212]

■   ■   ■

When Freeh announced Hanssen's arrest at a press conference, he made the point that while Hanssen's spying was a disaster, the FBI's impressive investigation was a success story. A reporter asked the director how much responsibility he accepted for the fact that Hanssen had evaded detection by the FBI for fifteen years.

"Well, the buck stops with me," Freeh declared. "I'm accountable, I'm responsible."

Freeh's comment was artful public relations, but it masked the fact that after Ames's arrest in 1994, Bear Bryant, as head of the National Security Division, urged Freeh to approve regular polygraph tests for all counterintelligence agents. After encountering opposition from many SACs and from the FBI Agents Association, Freeh shelved the proposal. James Geer had made a similar proposal to Webster, who also rejected it. But by 1994, after the extent of Ames's treachery became known, the need to take stronger measures to uncover spies had become far more apparent.

Debates about polygraph tests are as intricate as religious dissertations, but the fact is that polygraphs work, both as a deterrent and as an aid in detecting deception. Ames failed a polygraph test at the CIA, but the operators chose to accept Ames's explanations for why he had failed. FBI polygraphers who looked at the charts said he clearly showed deception. CIA officer Harold Nicholson was caught when he failed a polygraph test.

Although it's true that polygraphs sometimes falsely show that a person is lying, if properly handled, these cases can be investigated so that the subject is cleared without ruining his or her career. Of course no investigative technique is foolproof, but polygraphs are a more effective tool for detecting spying than anything else available.

Ironically, the FBI urged other agencies like the Energy Department to screen employees with polygraphs. The bureau gave polygraph tests to agents working highly sensitive investigations and to criminal suspects who agreed to take them. But when it came to a blanket screening of its own, many agents, mesmerized by their own image of incorruptibility, became experts at advancing countless arguments against it.

For all his quirks, Hanssen was a master spy, one who knew just how far he could go. On the one hand, he knew a defector could compromise him, so he was careful not to reveal to the Russians his own identity. Nor would Hanssen meet with his handlers, as they had suggested. "I am much safer if you know little about me," he wrote.

On the other hand, Hanssen felt confident that the FBI would not catch him—not even if he broke into an FBI official's computer, which drew no discipline, or assaulted an FBI analyst, which resulted only in a five-day suspension. He could post erotic stories on the Internet using his real name and heavily mortgage his house without raising any suspicion. So complacent was the FBI that, when a computer repair technician found hacker software on Hanssen's computer, no one asked him about it. Nor were five-year background checks done on a regular basis, as is required for agents with Hanssen's level of clearances.

Most agents did not believe that one of their own in such a sensitive, high-level position could ever be a spy. They were sickened when they learned of Hanssen's treachery.

Complacent as he knew the FBI to be, when Hanssen thought the mole hunts were intensifying, or when he heard about Vasili Mitrokhin defecting with notes on KGB files, he would stop spying. Given that pattern, there can be no question that, if Freeh had approved Bryant's proposal in 1994, Hanssen never would have resumed his relationship with the Russians. It was another debacle traceable in part to Freeh.

After the arrest of Hanssen, Freeh appointed former FBI director William Webster to head a blue-ribbon commission to look into FBI security and come up with proposals to improve it. Belatedly, Freeh ordered polygraph tests of all counterintelligence agents and top officials, five hundred in all. Only twenty-five failed.

When asked at a congressional hearing whether he would take one himself, Freeh said a test was already scheduled. He left the FBI without ever taking it.

34

MISSING DOCUMENTS

In his final months in office, Freeh seemed distracted. He came in late and sometimes did not come in at all. On May 1, 2001, Freeh announced that he planned to resign in June. He made it known that he did not want to leave when Clinton was in office because he did not want the president the FBI had investigated to choose a new director. All along, Freeh had dropped hints about the difficulties of bringing up six kids on his FBI salary of $145,100 a year.

Freeh claimed he would explore job options, but former agents already working for MBNA in Wilmington, a major credit card company, said Freeh would join the firm, which had three former FBI officials working for it. In July, Charles M. Cawley, MBNA's chairman and CEO, named Freeh senior vice chairman for—ironically—administration.

Nine days after Freeh's announcement, the FBI told Timothy McVeigh's attorneys that it had failed to turn over to them about three thousand pages of documents relating to the Oklahoma City bombing investigation. Normally, law enforcement agencies turn over to the defense only material that has evidentiary value or that could exculpate the defendant. In an effort to put down conspiracy theories, the Justice Department had approved a unique deal that called for giving McVeigh's lawyers every scrap of paper mentioning him.

Even with the best computer systems, the promise was virtually impossible to carry out. Almost every field office had participated in the case, generating dozens of duplicate reports about leads that were checked out and abandoned. Because the FBI could not come up with a credible plan to replace its computers, Congress for the previous three years had withheld $20 million a year for upgrades and new systems. From the day the existing computer system was installed, it proved to be unreliable. It therefore was a foregone conclusion that all the documents would not be turned over. While Freeh had issued requests to SACs for the documents, only the last few asked for everything, and many assumed he wanted the kind of pertinent documents they had always produced during discovery—not everything the FBI had. Even if they realized what was wanted, the FBI's computers could not locate all the documents.

When the FBI began archiving the material, analysts realized that not all the material had been sent to McVeigh's lawyers. Not until four months later did anyone tell Freeh, known to punish the messenger.

The disclosure caused an uproar. Ashcroft delayed McVeigh's execution to give his attorneys time to review the documents, which eventually totaled 4,034 items. There was talk of a new trial. Families of the victims of the Oklahoma City bombing were devastated. McVeigh's death would bring some degree of closure. Now the FBI, not the defense, had created uncertainty about the outcome.

"The ball is now back in McVeigh's court, and it should never be there," said Kathleen Treanor, who lost her four-year-old daughter in the blast.

Freeh, as usual, claimed responsibility but blamed everyone else. "As director, I have taken responsibility," Freeh solemnly told a House appropriations subcommittee. "I'm accountable for the failure." He then outlined all the requests he had made to field offices for documents relating to McVeigh. "As we now know, there were still many offices that had failed to comply," Freeh said.

Self-righteous and sanctimonious, Freeh never admitted a personal mistake. He never pointed out his own role in the McVeigh debacle. While he did not approve the sweeping discovery agreement, he ignored the need to revamp the FBI's computers. For years, David G. Binney, a former deputy FBI director under Freeh who became chief of security for IBM, had been warning Freeh about the deplorable state of the FBI's computers. In an age when even eighty-five-year-old grandmothers used E-mail, Freeh still refused to use it or to employ a computer himself. That same retrogressive attitude colored his perception of the FBI's computer needs.

In his final months in office, Freeh finally listened to Binney and others and appointed Bob E. Dies to overhaul the FBI's computer systems. After being with IBM for thirty years, Dies had retired at the age of fifty-two and was doing local volunteer work. His son Jason happened to be the FBI's IBM account representative. When an opening for a computer executive at the bureau came up, Jason was only half joking when he told his father that the bureau's computers were so "messed up" that he would be doing a public service by applying.

Dies, who is six feet seven inches tall, began in July 2000. Never in his career had he seen or heard of an organization with such antiquated technology. The FBI had something called an Automated Case Support System, which was developed in the mid-1990s and used 1980s technology. It could not connect to the Internet and did not use a mouse. The system was so slow and useless that for investigations alone, the bureau had developed forty-two additional, separate systems to get around it. Each of the additional systems had to be checked to make sure all references to an individual were obtained. It was the Automated Case Support System that had contributed to the problem of the missing McVeigh documents.

The bureau needed at least one computer for each of its nearly twenty-eight thousand employees. Dies could not determine how many computers the bureau had, but it was far fewer than one per employee. A total of thirteen thousand computers were four to eight years old. Many of them did not work, and of those that did, few could run standard software or connect to the Internet because they had no browsers. Nor did they have CD-ROM drives.

Instead of using the Internet, FBI personal computers communicated with each other in smaller offices over telephone lines shared with twenty or thirty other computers. Data moved so slowly that agents gave up. Because few of the computers could handle graphics, agents had to have photos of suspects E-mailed from local police departments to their home computers.

"They had stuff I had never heard of," Dies told me. "No wonder they couldn't maintain the stuff. They had only recently gotten E-mail. It was amazing. The FBI was running on technology that in many cases was a decade out of date. The FBI was asking its agents and support personnel to do their jobs without the tools other companies use or that you may use at home."[213]

Anyone with a computer understood what it meant to use one more than four years old. Even if donated, charities would not accept such machines. Yet, at the same time, Freeh continued to find the money to open new legats at a cost of $1 million to $2 million each per year.

"Somebody didn't care," Dies told me.

It was a devastating indictment of Freeh, one that would reach scandalous proportions when the FBI began investigating the attacks of September 11. As with Freeh's decision to slash headquarters staff, by the time Freeh listened to recommendations he had been given over the course of his term in office, the damage had been done.

■ ■ ■

The fiasco involving the McVeigh documents was the final catastrophe in a series of disasters that had plagued the FBI ever since Freeh took over. Whenever the media mentioned the FBI, they now added a litany of calamities. Representative David R. Obey, a Wisconsin Democrat, called it a "failed agency." The bureau became the butt of jokes on late-night comedy shows and in cartoons in *The New Yorker*, a sad contrast to the proud image the FBI had before Freeh came in.

A Gallup poll found that Americans had twice as much confidence in their local police as in the FBI. Not since the Church Committee hearings back in 1975 had morale at the bureau plummeted to such depths. The bureau appeared to be a bunch of incompetents.

Still, as in the Hoover days, many members of Congress frantically sought to shift the blame away from Freeh. Senator Charles E. Grassley, an Iowa Republican who rarely had a good word to say about the FBI, commented, "Because of one embarrassment after another, the public has been losing confidence in the FBI, and that is very bad for the country. Freeh tried to some extent, but he was not able to change the cowboy culture inside the FBI."

Freeh happily chimed in, saying that when he was an agent back in 1975, the agency's culture had been defective. The implication was that he had rectified the problem. For many agents who had continued to defend Freeh, that statement was a turning point. The truth was that despite the shortcomings of some of its directors, the FBI was a remarkably efficient agency that was both law-abiding and responsive to the director.

"Agents want you to succeed," Webster said. "If you succeed, they succeed."

Through all the problems during Freeh's nearly eight years, FBI agents continued to investigate more than one hundred thousand cases a year, bringing to justice Mafia leaders, fraudulent health care providers, kidnappers, terrorists, spies, computer hackers, and corrupt politicians and police officers. With few exceptions, the cases held up in court. As in the Hoover days, the agents were smart and dedicated. Anyone whose child was kidnapped would want FBI agents on his or her side. Even the bureau's secretaries were a breed apart: In her sixty-two years with the FBI, Millie Parsons, still secretary to the head of the Washington Field Office, never took a day of sick leave.[214]

If there was a cultural problem, it related to the FBI's self-protectiveness. When Randy Weaver went to trial on murder charges in 1993, the bureau resisted producing records that would reveal internal criticism of its rules of engagement at Ruby Ridge. In a posttrial decree, Judge Edward J. Lodge of the U.S. District Court in Boise, Idaho, angrily fined the FBI $1,920, saying its "behavior served to obstruct the administration of justice."

Similarly, former senator John C. Danforth complained that during his investigation of Waco, the FBI was so uncooperative about turning over documents that he had to threaten Freeh with a search warrant before he got what he wanted.[215]

While most agents thought Sessions was an embarrassment, and about half thought Freeh was a disaster, many resented the outside criticism. An attack on the director was an attack on the bureau and therefore on them. Even though none of the current agents served under Hoover, they absorbed by osmosis his instruction about not embarrassing the bureau.

Larry W. Langberg, a former president of the FBI Agents Association, even told me that L. Patrick Gray, who destroyed evidence during Watergate and impeded the FBI's investigation, was "a good man" who "had the potential to be a very good FBI director." Langberg said Gray was new to the job and in an acting capacity when given a "direct order" by the president's counsel, John Dean. Yet when asked if he would find similar excuses for an FBI agent doing the same thing, Langberg said, "An agent would not have destroyed evidence."

Explaining why he did not want to be interviewed for this book, W. Raymond Wannall Jr., an assistant director under Hoover, told me, "You are responsible for the firing of Sessions, and you've been critical of Freeh." Similarly, some of the officials under Sessions who should have reported his abuses to the Justice Department in the first place have a "sour taste," as one of them put it, about my book *The FBI* because it led to Sessions's firing. While these agents are proud of the FBI's reputation for pursuing impartial investigations of others, they view their own director and agency through a different prism. That kind of attitude inevitably leads to cover-ups of the kind that occurred at Ruby Ridge, errors in judgment, and the sort of complacency that allowed Robert Hanssen to spy for so many years without being caught.

Nowhere is that self-protective attitude better reflected than in the E-mail messages distributed by the Xgboys, which consists of fifteen hundred of the eight thousand members of the Society of Former Agents of the FBI. Since 1995, the Xgboys—which includes some current agents—has received and forwarded as many as twenty to sixty E-mails a day from its members. On what is known as a LISTSERV, they discuss which journalists or television anchors are friends or foes, and they suggest letters to the editor or to members of Congress for other members to copy. When they appear on television or are quoted in the press, they critique each other, proudly recounting how they defended the bureau and whoever happened to be the director at the time.

As criticism of Freeh mounted, the Xgboys began exchanging messages angrily denouncing the critics, who included former FBI official Buck Revell.

"I find unbelievable these public, nonspecific and sniping personal criticisms of Freeh from a former bureau agent, no matter what his former position in the bureau," a retired agent wrote of Revell's comments about Freeh. "Such pontifications serve absolutely no positive purpose at this point and smack of some personal animosity. Put a muzzle on them."

"Eureka! I think I've got it; Senator Grassley is an old Soviet mole still trying to impede the efficiency of the FBI," another Xgboy wrote about the FBI's congressional critic.

While even Hoover's staunchest defenders concede he stayed too long, many Xgboys still worship him. When Richard Cohen wrote a column in the *Washington Post* urging removal of Hoover's name from FBI headquarters, an Xgboy sent him a nasty letter and posted it. "You suggested that Martin Luther King Jr.'s name replace Hoover's name," the former agent wrote. Referring to the fact King had been jailed for leading a civil rights demonstration in the South, the former agent said, "That is just what we need—a convict's name on the FBI Building."

"You can't judge Hoover by today's standards," Larry Langberg said. Why not? Although it is important to place historical figures in the context of their times, to excuse the excesses of the past is to create the possibility that they will be repeated. To be sure, Hoover built the FBI into a great organization. But he is seen by the public as the man who outrageously violated the rights of Martin Luther King and many other Americans. Their insistence on wearing blinders when looking at Hoover undermines the credibility of former agents and therefore of the institution.

After I called him, a former agent confided to the Xgboys that he declined to be interviewed and warned that I might be calling them. "Kessler has done nothing to particularly enhance the bureau's image," the former agent groused to his fellow Xgboys. He equated me with Anthony Summers, whose book claimed that Hoover was a crossdresser.

According to another message to Xgboys from Tom McGorray, the retired agent who runs it, the topics discussed on the Xgboys include "bureau critics, such as *60 Minutes*, Senators Grassley and Leahy, and Ron Kessler," along with "prostate cancer, colon cancer, and heart attacks."

After a conversation with me, Lane Bonner, a former FBI public affairs official, told his fellow Xgboys that my book was going to be highly critical of Freeh and would cite FBI memos showing that Hoover knew that Joseph Salvati, who was falsely imprisoned in Boston, was innocent.

The FBI had released the documents showing that Hoover was informed of Salvati's innocence. In public statements, the FBI characterized the allegations as "appalling." But Bonner, refusing to believe it, said the claim that Hoover knew was "nonsense." As for Freeh, Bonner told the Xgboys that he informed me all he knows about the former director is that he had "impeccable integrity."

Bonner warned that my book would do "irreparable harm" to the FBI, thanks in part to "those few crybabies in our midst (and others) who have collaborated with" me. Bonner said he used to think of FBI agents as understanding the need for integrity and loyalty. Instead, he said, it seems that "some in our midst are either naive or are of the Robert Hanssen mold."

As in any large group, present and former agents have multiple attitudes and opinions. The Xgboys represents only a small portion of former agents. The more sophisticated agents and those who rose in the bureau laugh at the Xgboys. They look at Hoover with balance, recognize that an FBI director should be held at least to the same standards as everyone else, and believe Sessions's abuses and Freeh's mismanagement needed to be exposed.

Bill Baker, the former head of the FBI's Criminal Investigative Division who was once Lane Bonner's boss, said much of the chatter on the Xgboys is "unprofessional." It was Baker, a prominent member of the Society of Former FBI Agents, who recommended to Sessions the bureau's unprecedented cooperation with me for my previous FBI book so that I could "test" what FBI officials were telling me. Bucky Walters, the assistant FBI director under Hoover who is the longtime membership chairman of the Society of Former FBI Agents, said of the Xgboys, "I would get angry if I sat reading that crap. People have sent it to me. A lot of it is unfactual."[216] Courtland Jones, a former chairman of the society's Washington chapter, said, "It's a gossip group of people who seem to be two-year agents who are sure they know everything. Buck Revell is ten times smarter than they are. I happen to have been familiar with the details of what they talk about, and they don't know what they're talking about. They act as if they are spokesmen for the bureau. Most of us laugh at it and ignore it."[217]

As those who worked with Freeh began relating horror stories they had long kept to themselves, sentiment even among the Xgboys began to shift. Once Freeh was out of power, members of Congress woke from their slumber as well, just as they did after Hoover died. Patrick J. Leahy, a Vermont Democrat who was chairman of the Senate Judiciary Committee, said, "There are some very, very serious management problems at the FBI." Richard J. Durbin, a Democrat from Illinois, said, "It's hard to believe the situation has deteriorated and disintegrated the way it has. How did this great agency fall so far so fast? The FBI has been starved for leadership." The real question was: Where had these members been for the past nearly eight years?

As Freeh was leaving, he put out the word that the Bush administration had asked him to stay on until a successor was found. In fact, the White House did not ask Freeh to remain in his job. So skillful was Freeh at manipulating public opinion that he had an "associate" tell the *Washington Post* that when his sixth son was born in 1998, Freeh responded to rumors that he might resign by saying he had a mission to make the bureau "more efficient, more professional, more tech-savvy and, along the way, to rebuild confidence in the nation's largest law enforcement organization." To the unwary, it sounded as if the FBI was in trouble before Freeh took over, rather than the other way around. The comment was in line with Freeh's and Bucknam's strategy of having Freeh distance himself from the problems of the bureau—even if he had caused them—so that he could pose as a reformer.

"He's been rushing and rushing around trying to plug holes in the dike, but it has become impossible to keep all the water out," echoed Senator Arlen Specter, the Pennsylvania Republican. Orrin G. Hatch, the Utah Republican who headed the Senate Judiciary Committee, called Freeh "one of the best FBI directors to serve the American people." Four years earlier, Hatch said there were serious problems at the FBI, "but I would be remiss if I did not mention the positive leadership of Director Louis Freeh." Senator Leahy, who would soon take over as chairman, praised Freeh by saying his legacy was "an updated attitude appropriate to twenty-first-century law enforcement." No matter how bad things got, Freeh could do no wrong.

While for the most part the bureau's problems were obvious, the agency was also good at concealing the extent of its problems and covering up for the director. Over the years, SACs gave the press favorable quotes about Freeh while privately calling him "Hoover with children." That referred to his arbitrariness and to his disciplinary rules, including no drinking on the job. In some respects, the comparison was unfair to Hoover, who knew how to manage and, while he promoted himself, also promoted the bureau and was loyal to it.

Only a few press accounts saw through the haze. In one of them, *Newsweek* noted, "In scandal after scandal, Director Louis Freeh would dutifully take responsibility. Yet with his priestly aura, he would at the same time leave the impression that he had been let down or victimized by his subordinates. Congressional Republicans were always ready to forgive Freeh because he seemed so morally censorious of the Clinton White House."

In two opinion pieces in the *Washington Post*, I called attention to the problems caused by Freeh's management style and said agents had lost faith in him. After "a promising start, Freeh has settled into a controlling, self-protective, image-conscious style that suppresses internal debate while promoting a double standard of conduct: one for favored aides and one for the rest of the bureau," I wrote on April 13, 1997. The second piece, "Fire Freeh," appeared two months before Freeh announced his departure.[218]

In his last year in office, Freeh gave interviews to Elsa Walsh of *The New Yorker* portraying his starring role in the FBI's investigation of the Khobar Towers bombing and his meetings with Saudi officials to obtain their cooperation. After the bombing of the dormitory for U.S. military personnel in Dharan, Saudi Arabia, on June 25, 1996, Freeh became obsessed by it. The explosion killed nineteen American military personnel. As soon as it occurred, Freeh boarded an Air Force jet to go to the crime scene.

Until he left the FBI five years later, Freeh would act as the case agent, flying back and forth and meeting with Saudi leaders in Washington and Saudi Arabia. While Freeh was genuinely concerned about

the victims' families—he met with them for three days at Quantico—
the role of an FBI director is to manage the agency, not to be a highly
paid case agent. Normally, high-level meetings with foreign officials are
conducted by the FBI's deputy associate directors, but Freeh, in his quest
to stamp out bureaucracy, had eliminated those positions.

"Freeh was interested in prosecutions, the Khobar Towers bombing,
New York, Congress, his family, and his religion," said a high-ranking
official who worked closely with him.

Titled "Louis Freeh's Last Case," the *New Yorker* piece hinted that
Iran was behind the bombings. Finally, just as he was leaving, Freeh
got his wish to look like a great case agent. The amount of time he
devoted to telling the story to Walsh—eight interviews in the course of
a year—suggested his priorities. Freeh, who had no time to update the
FBI's computers or to defend the bureau from outlandish charges about
Waco and Ruby Ridge, had seemingly limitless time to promote himself.
Yet even that article included a disclosure that agents found devastating:
Because a prosecution of the case involved national security issues,
Freeh felt he had to present a list of proposed indictments to the president before he proceeded. The Clinton administration did not want a
military confrontation with Iran, which was becoming more moderate,
and Freeh did not trust Clinton to move forward with prosecutions
because they might require a military response. Freeh therefore held off
on presenting the list until the new administration came in.[219]

If an agent had made such a politically motivated decision, he would
have been fired. Similarly, an agent widely suspected of leaking, as Bob
Bucknam was, would have been investigated and polygraphed. "In the
interest of this great institution, swift and decisive action will be taken
to redress any unauthorized disclosure of information," Freeh told all
employees in an April 1994 memo. But Freeh saw himself and his aides
as being governed by different rules. If Friends of Louis received favored
treatment, certainly Louis himself should. Many naively overlooked the
double standard because of the air of piety Freeh projected. Like Hoover, Freeh wore his integrity on his sleeve. But in law enforcement,
protecting friends is hardly a sign of integrity.

"Power corrupts, and the longer he was in office, the more corrupted
Freeh became," said an agent who worked closely with him.

Freeh did not respond to my letter seeking comment.

Despite the tilt toward Freeh by Republicans in Congress, John Ashcroft had nothing good to say about Freeh. In the light of the latest gaffe involving the McVeigh documents, the attorney general announced three investigations into what had gone wrong at the FBI. He also removed restrictions on the Justice Department's inspector general, allowing him to investigate the FBI without prior approval by the attorney general or his deputy. The FBI had long resisted such a move, but now, with its credibility shattered, the bureau was powerless to prevent inroads on its turf.

Everyone had a solution—more oversight, a restructuring, a reduction in size or jurisdiction, even splitting up the agency. When a publicly held company like Lucent or Enron self-destructs, everyone recognizes that the CEO was responsible and must be replaced. Similarly, when General Electric did well, everyone understood that CEO Jack Welch was responsible.

In the case of the FBI, one man was responsible. His last day on the job was Friday, June 22, 2001, timed to coincide with indictments of thirteen Saudis and a Lebanese man in the Khobar Towers bombing. Because they were in foreign countries, it was not clear whether the alleged terrorists would ever be brought to trial.

Freeh had gotten his men—sort of. But he left the FBI in a shambles. In a farewell to employees in the FBI's courtyard, Freeh, wearing a rumpled suit, airily dismissed the fiascoes and embarrassments of his administration as "bumps in the road."

35

SEPTEMBER 11

In describing the qualities he sought in an FBI director, President George W. Bush pointedly mentioned, "somebody who is a good manager." With the bureau in disarray, it was a foregone conclusion that, while the FBI Agents Association was pushing former FBI Assistant Director Bill Baker to replace Louis Freeh, the next director would come from the outside.

The Bush administration seriously considered two candidates: George J. Terwilliger III, a former deputy attorney general who represented Bush in the Florida election dispute, and Robert S. Mueller III, a former head of the Justice Department's Criminal Division who was U.S. attorney in San Francisco. When John Ashcroft became attorney general, Mueller, a Republican, was already acting deputy attorney general. Having worked with him, Ashcroft pushed Mueller.

"I saw first hand his strong ability to manage," Ashcroft said.

Bush announced Mueller's nomination in a Rose Garden press conference on July 5, 2001. Mueller, fifty-six, with a craggy face, slightly graying black hair, and ramrod straight posture, spoke for forty-eight seconds, thanking Bush several times.

Mueller (pronounced MULL-er) was a no-nonsense former Marine with a long record as a seasoned prosecutor and manager. Born in New York City on August 7, 1944, Mueller grew up in Philadelphia. His father was a DuPont executive. Mueller graduated from St. Paul's School in Concord, New Hampshire, which is affiliated with the Episcopal church but accepts students of all faiths. He received a B.S. degree from Princeton University and an M.A. in international studies from New York University.

A first lieutenant in the Marines, Mueller served in the Vietnam War and was awarded the Bronze Star and the Purple Heart. He married his high school sweetheart, Anne Standish, who was the beneficiary of family trusts valued at more than $4 million. Mueller was worth at least $1.7 million.[220] They have two daughters, twenty-nine and thirty-two.

Thinking he would become an FBI agent, Mueller obtained a J.D. degree from the University of Virginia Law School in 1973 but then accepted an offer from a law firm in San Francisco. He decided becoming a prosecutor would allow him to pursue both investigations and trial work. Mueller applied to the U.S. attorney's office there but was not hired. He finally was accepted in 1976. Until 1988, Mueller was a prosecutor and supervised cases, first in the U.S. attorney's office in San Francisco and then in Boston, where he became head of the Criminal Division and was named U.S. attorney after William Weld, who had recruited him, left office. For a year, Mueller was an assistant to Attorney General Richard L. Thornburgh, then became assistant attorney general in charge of the Criminal Division of the Justice Department. In that position, he supervised prosecutions of John Gotti, the Libyan suspects indicted in the bombing of Pan Am 103, and Panamanian leader Manuel Noriega.

In 1993, Mueller left the Justice Department to become a partner in the prestigious Boston law firm of Hale and Dorr. "When he came over to us," said Bill Lee, the chief of the firm's litigation department, "he was one of those guys who gets in at 6 A.M., reads the paper, and gets ready so that when the younger guys arrive, he's ready to rock and roll with them."

But Mueller hated private practice. One day, Mueller called Eric H. Holder Jr., the U.S. attorney in Washington. When Mueller headed the Criminal Division, Holder reported to him. Now Mueller called to apply for a job. "He called up out of the blue and said he wanted to try murder cases," Holder said. "I was like, 'What?' Here's this guy who was the former assistant attorney general, the head of the Criminal Division, and he came to the U.S. attorney's office and tried cases as a line guy."

Having tossed aside his $400,000-a-year partnership for a government salary in May 1995, Mueller began working on knifings, batterings, and shootings. He answered the phone, "Mueller, Homicide." Tough and businesslike in court, he worked from color-coded files with plastic labels. A colleague called him a "well-organized pit bull."

Eli Gottesdiener, a public defender who had a first-degree murder case before him, said that after reviewing the evidence against Gottesdiener's client, Mueller dropped the charges. "It was a drug shooting," Gottesdiener said. "There were a lot of scummy witnesses who had their own motives and said my client did it. There was no forensic evidence. A lot of prosecutors would have let the guy sit there in jail because he was an indigent African American. With Mueller, there was no B.S. He said he didn't think there was sufficient evidence, and he dropped the charges. The wrong prosecutors with these low-life witnesses, this guy could have been put away on a murder charge and have been innocent," he said. "He's judgment without ego."[221]

In 1996, Mueller became chief of the Homicide Section. He poked his head into every corner of the criminal justice system, including the morgue. "He was consummately interested in figuring things out," said Dr. Jonathan L. Arden, the district's medical examiner. "He was literally and figuratively sleeves-rolled-up and in the trenches."

Mueller went on to become U.S. attorney in San Francisco, first on an interim basis in August 1998. President Clinton nominated him for the position, and he was confirmed in October 1999. After President Bush took office, Mueller continued as acting deputy attorney general until May 2001.

Those who worked with him found Mueller to be fair, organized, disciplined, and prepared. Having supervised 865 employees in the Justice Department's Criminal Division, Mueller was an experienced manager. When he took over in San Francisco, the U.S. attorney's office was in poor shape. Prosecutions had declined to a record low, some of the best lawyers were leaving, and even the defense bar was demanding change. Mueller rotated the supervisors to different positions. He doubled the number of prosecutions and expanded efforts against financial fraud and cybercrime in Silicon Valley. He also increased the number of women in supervisory positions by half again and increased the number of minorities.

In San Francisco, Mueller did what some called "bed checks," looking at 5:30 or 5:45 P.M. to see who was still on the job. About every six months, he issued what some called "the chess memo," shuffling people to new slots.

"Bob really doesn't like people to get too comfortable," said Laura Gonzales, an attorney who worked in the office. "He was always moving people, and if it wasn't perfect—and it never is—he moved them again. He's always trying new things."

"It was a troubled office, and he shook things up," Senator Barbara Boxer, a California Democrat, said. "The U.S. attorney's office had an ingrained culture that was hard to change, but he was able to change it very rapidly."

Joseph Russoniello, a former FBI agent who was U.S. attorney in San Francisco during the Reagan and Bush administrations, said Mueller's style was to set up a formal chain of command, with extensive reporting by each line of supervisors, a system that "probably rankled some in the office who were used to more flexibility, but it got the job done."

Mueller's weak spot was dealing with the press, according to Russoniello. A story from Boston followed Mueller around. It seems a cat was hanging around the snack bar in the federal building there. Some employees complained that it was not sanitary. When reporters asked Mueller for comment, he wouldn't talk about it. Other prosecutors nudged him to say something, so he called a press conference. Mueller uttered a single sentence: "The cat is fine."

Mueller associated talking to the press with calling attention to himself and to boasting. In three years on the job in San Francisco, he gave two press conferences. He told aides that when he had something to say, he would say it. His interest was in looking forward, not backward. Reputations are based on what people do, not what they say. Because of that posture, some basic details of his personal life—like the fact that he became a lawyer to become an agent—have not come out until now.

After he had been director almost six months, Mueller gave me the first interview since his nomination.[222] As one FBI wag put it, the bureau had just "scared" the public again, warning of a possible al-Qaeda attack on U.S. interests in Yemen. Mueller, in shirtsleeves, greeted me in his reception room, its walls lined with photos of the thirty-three FBI agents killed in the line of duty.

"No doubt this looks familiar," he said as we walked into the FBI's conference room.

"Yes," I said. "This is where Sessions bawled me out for going into his personal abuses."

Mueller asked about my background, particularly my newspaper experience in Boston. He clearly preferred to be the one conducting the interview. I asked why he wanted to be an FBI agent. "To serve my country, because it seemed an exciting thing to do, and because I loved investigations," he said. "I love finding what the truth is, or at least the closest approximation of the truth there is."

In the same vein, Mueller did not like to talk about what led to his decorations from the Vietnam War. He would say only that he "got into some firefights." He added, "You never get the medals for that which you probably deserve them. You always get the medals for that which you don't even think about doing."

Because he always kept a low profile, some in the Bush administration had wondered if Mueller had enough star power. But White House counsel Al Gonzalez quoted Bush as saying, "Mueller's my man."

"Bob has a quirky kind of charisma. You end up wanting to make the guy happy, a little out of fear and a little out of respect," said Rory Little, a San Francisco law professor who was a leading candidate for the U.S. attorney's job in San Francisco in 1998.

"He's just very professional in what he does," said Marilyn Hall Patel, chief judge of the U.S. District Court in San Francisco. "I trust him. That's very important."[223]

"He's kind of one of these Jimmy Stewart characters, with old-fashioned American values," said Michael Burt, a San Francisco deputy public defender who worked on a case prosecuted by Mueller.

"He comes off as your central-casting ex-Marine—tough, no-nonsense, and not suffering fools gladly," said Michael R. Bromwich, the former Justice Department inspector general.

Aside from work, Mueller enjoys running and lifting weights. In San Francisco, he ran the 7.1-mile Dipsea race. "Other people fantasize about going to Paris or Hawaii. Bob Mueller doesn't care about any of that," said Dennis Saylor, his deputy when Mueller headed the Criminal Division. "He's an athlete, he loves his exercise, he loves his family, but he's a prosecutor at heart."

At office parties at his home, Mueller signaled that the festivities were over by flicking the lights on and off. "Mueller is tough as nails, but once you get to know him, he has a soft heart," said David Margolis, an associate deputy attorney general who was one of his deputies when Mueller headed the Criminal Division.[224]

Two weeks before his confirmation hearing, Mueller had lunch with William Webster at the Metropolitan Club in Washington. Webster, who wears Brooks Brothers suits similar to Mueller's, counseled him about the press, suggesting he meet informally on a regular basis with reporters. Webster talked about the delicate balancing act an FBI director must perform. On the one hand, he works for the president and needs his support on FBI issues. On the other hand, he must maintain a distance from politics and remain independent of the president, who could wind up as a target of FBI investigations.

"Mueller is a good listener," Webster observed.[225]

At his confirmation hearing on July 30, 2001, Mueller made it clear that he understands that the FBI must be accountable to the public. He rejected the self-protective culture that some in the bureau continued to promote. "All institutions—even great ones like the FBI—make mistakes," he said. "The measure of an institution is in how it responds to its mistakes. I believe the FBI can—and must—do a better job of dealing with mistakes. We must tell the truth and let the facts speak for themselves."

Acknowledging that the FBI had serious problems, including a perception that it was arrogant, Mueller told the senators, "If I have the honor of being confirmed by the Senate, I will make it my highest priority to restore the public's confidence in the FBI—to re-earn the faith and trust of the American people."

In contrast to Freeh, who said he would take a polygraph test but never actually did, Mueller, when asked if he would take one, said, "This may be my training from the Marine Corps, but you don't ask people to do that which you're unwilling to do yourself. I have already taken the polygraph."

"How did you do?" Senator Orrin Hatch asked.

"I'm sitting here; that's all I've got to say," Mueller answered, and the senators laughed.

Mueller had support from California's two Democratic senators, Boxer and Dianne Feinstein. Boxer said Mueller was "not political" and "doesn't polarize." Senator Charles E. Schumer, a New York Democrat, called him "just what the doctor ordered." The one person who opposed Mueller's nomination was Freeh, who, when asked by Bush administration officials about each candidate, bad-mouthed them all.

Because of the need to restore confidence in the FBI quickly, the Senate confirmed Mueller in record time, on August 2, 2001. On that day, Mueller had an operation in San Francisco to remove his cancerous prostate gland. His urologist and surgeon, Dr. Peter R. Caroll, said Mueller had a "very high likelihood of cancer cure." Four days after the operation, Mueller was back at his desk at the U.S. attorney's office.

Ashcroft swore him in on September 4 in the attorney general's office. Mueller planned to have a formal swearing-in ceremony with the president a month or two later. Because of the events of September 11, that would not happen.

The day before he was sworn in, Mueller moved into his office and got acquainted with his computer. Unlike Freeh, Mueller used E-mail and was a proponent of new technology. In 1989, he bought a Gateway computer for his home so he could tally items for taxes more easily with a Quicken program. When he was U.S. attorney in San Francisco, he tasked a talented computer programmer to create new software for tracking cases. The program—called Alcatraz—has been adopted by U.S. attorney offices throughout the country.

Several weeks before taking over, Mueller met with Bob Dies, the FBI's new computer guru. Mueller listed standard software such as Microsoft Office that he wanted on his computer. Dies told him he could have it installed, but none of it would work with anything else in the bureau. Mueller was flabbergasted.

On Friday, September 7, Mueller paid his first visit as director to the FBI Academy at Quantico. Because of court decisions, the FBI no longer gave preference to minorities and females, and classes were not as diverse as in Webster's day. Of the bureau's 11,275 agents, 48 were native Americans, 327 were Asian Americans, 631 were blacks, and 830 were Hispanics. Of the total agents, 1,996 were women.

In training, academy officials openly referred to the public perception that the FBI is an agency of bumblers. It was just one more challenge they would face as agents. "If you don't have credibility, you are not going to be effective," Joseph Billy Jr., the acting assistant FBI director for training, told classes.

Mueller toured the grounds and saw the new FBI laboratory building, to be completed in September 2002. He inspected the Hostage Rescue Team building, which includes the cabin of a wide-body jet, where agents can train to seize hijackers. While Ashcroft shot the Glock semiautomatic pistol after he was sworn in, Mueller did not shoot that day.

■ ■ ■

Mueller scheduled a regular 7 A.M. meeting with FBI officials who oversaw all the FBI's divisions, including those that deal with information resources, criminal justice information, training, and the laboratory. He also held regular working lunches to address specific issues or chart future direction. Freeh had met daily only with the heads of the FBI's investigative divisions and finance, administration, and public and congressional affairs, reflecting his narrow view of his job.

Mueller asked everyone to call him "Bob" instead of "Director." It didn't fly. When he realized people still used the honorific, he gave up.

Bureau officials who dealt with Mueller said he is direct and encourages them to express their opinions. Once he makes up his mind, he sticks to his position but gives his reasons.

"If you make a good argument, he accepts it," an SAC said. "If he doesn't, he does not ignore you. He explains his reasoning. But he is demanding. He follows up to make sure you've done what he wanted. He's a little intimidating, but maybe that's what we need right now."

"He's engaged and follows up, but he is not micromanaging, and people are not afraid to tell him things because he might chop their heads off," said another agent who works closely with Mueller.

"He listens to what people say, whereas Freeh would not listen to anyone," another SAC said.

Heeding Webster's advice about meeting with the press, Mueller was

planning a brown bag lunch with reporters when his secretary told him
to turn on the TV at 8:45 A.M. on Tuesday, September 11, 2001. The
first plane had hit the North Tower. At 9:05, the second plane hit the
South Tower. Mueller rushed down the stark white corridors of FBI
headquarters from his fifth-floor office to the SIOC. With his eye on the
Republican Congress, Freeh had named it the George H. W. Bush Strategic Information Operations Center.

Under Freeh, each deputy director of the FBI lasted an average of
thirteen months, which was barely enough time to learn the job. Thomas J. Pickard, the seventh in a long line of deputy directors under
Freeh, was in his office briefing Gregory Jones, who was about to go
to New York as an SAC under Barry Mawn. After the first plane went
in, John Collingwood, the FBI's assistant director for public and congressional affairs, went to Pickard's office to find out the latest news.
After the second plane hit, they both went to the SIOC and met Mueller
there.

Opened in 1998, the SIOC consists of 40,000 square feet of offices
and command centers on the fifth floor of FBI headquarters. The FBI
building itself is a skewed tetrahedron, not quite a square. To conform
with local restrictions, the building is seven stories along Pennsylvania
Avenue but, to the rear, rises eleven stories. From the side, the grotesque
overhang at the rear gives the impression that the building is poised to
topple on pedestrians below, no doubt the image Hoover wanted to
create when he designed the building.

In the only tour of SIOC given to a journalist since the September
11 attacks, I saw a succession of rooms, each looking like the newsroom
at CNN Center in Atlanta, only with low ceilings, plush green seats,
and video monitors displaying selectively the latest items of interest—a
critical piece of evidence, a photograph of a suspect, or a log of incidents
and leads arranged chronologically. The previous operations center
could have fit into the lobby of the new one. Here, in Operations Room
H, is where agents staring at computers or talking on the phone monitor
the terrorism investigation. It is one of four such 3,000-square-foot
rooms designed to handle as many major incidents simultaneously.

Other rooms in the center look like amphitheaters, where briefings
on the latest events can be given to those with access to top-secret,

compartmentalized information. One room contains the FBI's switch-board, with four or five operators taking calls to the FBI's main number. If the number of calls waiting in line becomes excessive, agents from nearby rooms are called in to handle them. Still another room receives tips over the internet—130,000 since September 11. The entire center is shielded to prevent electronic signals from entering or leaving.

When the second plane hit the World Trade Center, Dale L. Watson, the chief of counterterrorism, was already in the command center, con-ducting a briefing. Michael Chertoff, the assistant attorney general in charge of the Justice Department's Criminal Division, converged on the center.[226] Ashcroft turned back from a trip and arrived later that after-noon. Eventually, five hundred people from thirty-two agencies were stationed in the center. Ashcroft and Mueller took temporary offices there.

"The question was, 'Is there someone else out there?' " Chertoff said.

Reports that there had been an explosion or fire at the State De-partment and that another plane was heading for Washington turned out to be false.

Mueller placed Deputy Director Tom Pickard in charge of the in-vestigation, with Dale Watson under him. Figuring FBI headquarters would be next, nonessential employees began leaving. The backup to leave the FBI's underground garage was half an hour. Police blocked off Ninth and Tenth streets alongside headquarters. Bomb-sniffing dogs and the FBI police armed with submachine guns patrolled the perimeter. The FBI public tour was canceled indefinitely.

Because flight attendants on the doomed planes had called in the seat numbers of some of the hijackers, agents began matching seat as-signments to the hijackers' names on flight manifests. Agents ran out leads from credit card and telephone records. Anyone who shared a residence or a hotel room with a hijacker was placed on a growing watch list.

"You had conference calls with SACs from fifty-six field offices," said the head of one of the offices. "We were trying to pronounce and spell Middle Eastern names."

Because the FBI's Automated Case Support System was so primitive, agents had designed a system called Rapid Start. It kept track of investigative reports at the scene of a crime, but it was never intended to manage a big case. Because of Freeh's disdain for technology, that was all the bureau had. As reports and leads poured in about the attacks, Rapid Start became so overloaded that documents could not be retrieved. This led to delays in pursuing information that required investigation.

Even worse, because Rapid Start did not connect to field offices, reports had to be downloaded and transmitted to the Automated Case Support System in each field office. Aside from the time involved, the process was unreliable, so agents at the SIOC would often call and fax leads to the field.

"Sometimes, three teams of agents were dispatched to one house when only one team should have been sent, because we had three duplicative leads being sent out," Dies said. "Meanwhile, we needed those extra agents to work other leads."

In some cases, because the downloaded material never showed up and no follow-up calls were made or faxes sent, leads were not covered for days. Instead of relying on the antiquated computers, agents in field offices faxed reports to headquarters, inundating the SIOC with paper.

There was "a degree of pandemonium," admitted one of the FBI officials in the SIOC.

It quickly became apparent that four commercial jets had been hijacked in a coordinated attack on America. American Airlines Flight 11, with eighty-one passengers and eleven crew members from Boston to Los Angeles, slammed into the North Tower of the 1,350-foot-high World Trade Center at 8:45 A.M. United Airlines Flight 175 from Boston to Los Angeles, with fifty-six passengers and nine crew members on board, crashed into the South Tower at 9:05. American Airlines Flight 77 took off from Washington's Dulles Airport en route to Los Angeles carrying fifty-eight passengers and six crew members. It crashed into the Pentagon at 9:40 and killed 189 people. After passengers tried to storm the hijackers, United Flight 93, en route from Newark to San Francisco, crashed at 10:10 near Shanksville, Pennsylvania. It had thirty-eight passengers and seven crew members aboard.

Normally, as many as fifty thousand people worked in the Twin Towers. Because the planes hit early, most people had not yet come to work. The observation deck did not open until 9:30, so few tourists were in the buildings. An estimated eighteen thousand people vacated the towers before the South Tower collapsed at 9:50 and the North Tower collapsed at 10:20. The total of 3,024 killed at the Trade Center, Pentagon, and in Pennsylvania compared with 2,388 who perished at Pearl Harbor. It was the most devastating attack ever on America.

The towers were built to withstand hurricane-force winds and the impact of a Boeing 747. But when jet fuel from the planes bound for the West Coast ignited, it softened steel and caused the top portion of the buildings to collapse on the rest. The impact of the debris from above caused the buildings to pancake to the ground.

As the world now knows, firefighters and police heroically tried to save people trapped in the burning World Trade Center. In the end, nearly everyone on or above the floors struck by the jetliners was killed, while almost everyone below survived. People trapped above the strike in the North Tower were still calling 911 operators an hour and twenty-four minutes after the hit. They had no way of escape.

Bridges and tunnels to Manhattan were closed. The FAA ordered all air traffic shut down. Financial markets closed. Inbound transatlantic flights were diverted to Canada. The White House and Capitol were evacuated. The United States shut border crossings to Canada and Mexico. Air Force planes were deployed to defend the skies over American cities.

President Bush was reading to schoolchildren in Florida when Andy Card, his chief of staff, leaned over him and whispered, "A second plane has hit the World Trade Center. America is under attack." Card had previously informed Bush of the first hit.

By the time the president boarded *Air Force One,* he had made the fundamental decision about how to proceed. "We're at war," he told his aides. "That's what we're paid for, boys."[227]

Bush flew to Barksdale Air Force Base near Shreveport, Louisiana. At 1:04 P.M., he told the country, "Make no mistake. The United States will hunt down and punish those responsible for these cowardly acts." That night, in a televised address to the nation, Bush said, "We will make no distinction between the terrorists who committed these acts and those who harbor them."

■   ■   ■

Van A. Harp, the fifty-six-year-old assistant director in charge of the Washington Field Office, had taken over the office in July. Previously, he was SAC in the Cleveland Field Office, the eighteenth largest but, he liked to point out, the first in arrests. In Cleveland, Harp directed probes of official corruption leading to cases against judges, sheriffs, and police officers.

A soft-spoken, intense man with blue eyes and white hair, Harp had not taken a vacation in three years. He had just rented a beach house in Hilton Head, South Carolina, for a week with his family, who still lived in Cleveland. Donna Cummings, his secretary, paged him at 8:45 A.M. After he called her back and learned what had happened, Harp turned on the TV in the beach house. When the second plane hit, he knew he had to return to Washington. Cummings called again. The Pentagon had been hit. For the first time in American history, all airplanes except Air Force jets were grounded.

"I wanted to get back, but there were no planes," Harp told me.[228]

At first, the Beaufort resident agency arranged to have state troopers from three states ferry Harp back to Washington. Then the FBI arranged with the FAA for a special exception to allow the FBI's plane to pick him up at Hilton Head Airport and fly him to Manassas, Virginia, where the FBI has its own small air force.

Harp drove to an FBI command post at Dulles Airport and arrived in the afternoon at the Washington Field Office at 601 Fourth Street NW. He stayed at the field office until 2:20 A.M., went to his apartment for an hour's sleep, and returned at 5 A.M.

■   ■   ■

Just before noon, Barry Mawn returned to the New York Field Office from the World Trade Center a few blocks away and began deploying agents to check out leads. The day after the attacks, agents had set up a command center in the FBI's block-long garage, where vehicles were parked and repaired. Agents and detectives assigned to the Joint Terrorism Task Force huddled shoulder to shoulder in space that reeked of motor oil. Handmade signs were taped to wires suspended from the ceiling: FBI, NTSB, NYPD. Three hundred new phone lines were installed.

"We're making progress," Mawn announced over a speaker system. "Thanks for the hard work."

Back in 1980, when Mawn was a New York agent, he became the first supervisor under Kenneth L. Walton of the city's Joint Terrorism Task Force, which brought FBI agents and New York City police together to coordinate terrorism investigations. Known as the "Prince of Darkness," Walton wore white shirts with wide cuffs made by his wife. A chain smoker, he drew cigarettes from a gold case and wore a gold Rolex watch.

"In the 80s," Mawn said, "we had Omega 7, an anti-Castro group that ordered the murder of a Cuban diplomat at the United Nations, the Croatians bombing Yugoslavian missions, the Puerto Ricans who wanted independence, the Jewish Defense League, the Weather Underground. We were bumping into each other on terrorism cases. It was counterproductive. Ken said, 'You're going to make this work.' That was the prototype for task forces on organized crime, violent crime, and terrorism."

Mawn was born to be an agent. Sharp, witty, and direct, Mawn immediately inspired trust and enlisted followers. Born in Woburn, Massachusetts, Mawn graduated from Boston College. He taught fifth grade for a year in Bourne, Massachusetts, before enlisting in the Army, where he became a second lieutenant. He tried to apply to the Secret Service but was told he wouldn't be accepted because he was near-sighted and needed glasses. The recruiter said he thought the FBI would take him.

Mawn applied to the bureau and meanwhile enrolled at the University of Massachusetts to obtain an M.B.A. After he had taken courses for a semester and a half, the FBI called to say it had an opening. Mawn became an agent in 1972. After a year in Detroit, he was transferred to New York, where he worked bank robberies on a squad headed by Thomas L. Sheer, who later headed the New York office. Sheer admired Mawn as a "leader who is totally honest."

After leaving New York in 1982, Mawn went on to become SAC in Knoxville, Newark, and then Boston before returning to New York as assistant director in April 2000.

Beginning with the first attack on the World Trade Center in 1993, the New York office had been in charge of investigating each incident tied to al-Qaeda. John P. O'Neill, forty-nine, who was over counter-terrorism and counterintelligence in the field office, was the FBI's lead-ing expert on that amorphous terrorist organization. He was in charge of the investigations into the attack on the USS *Cole* on October 12, 2000, which killed seventeen sailors, and the bombings of American embassies in Kenya and Tanzania on August 7, 1998, which killed 224 people. Over the years, O'Neill had warned that al-Qaeda would strike again.

If O'Neill had remained in the FBI, he would have been Mawn's principal deputy in charge of the investigation of the September 11 at-tacks. But two weeks before the attacks, O'Neill left to take a $300,000-a-year job as chief of security for the World Trade Center.

On Monday, September 10, O'Neill had drinks at Windows on the World with his friend Robert Tucker, a former Queens district attorney. They moved to Elaine's, then on to China Club.[229] The next morning at 9:17 A.M., O'Neill called Valerie James, his girlfriend of eleven years. By then, both towers had been hit.

"Honey, I want you to know I'm okay," he said. "My God, Val. It's terrible. There are body parts everywhere."[230]

O'Neill also spoke to his twenty-nine-year-old son, John, who was going to visit him on the morning of the attacks at his new job. "He said he was okay. He was on his way out to assess the damage," John recalled.

O'Neill's body was found a week later. Besides O'Neill, Special Agent Leonard W. Hatton was killed at the Twin Towers.

"That was the supreme irony," said Mawn, who gave the eulogy for O'Neill in Atlantic City, as an Army helicopter patrolled overhead. "The second day on the job, he was a victim of bin Laden. He was in the North Tower, helping people evacuate. His office was in the North Tower up around 82nd floor. He was seen by a number of our guys. He was in the lobby, working with the fire department to get people out. One of our supervisors helped carry out Father Mychal Judge, the fire department chaplain who was killed after administering last rites to a dying firefighter. The supervisor saw John just before that."

Like Mawn, everyone in the SIOC believed that Osama bin Laden was responsible for the attacks. Born in 1955 in Jeddah, Saudi Arabia, bin Laden was one of fifty-three children of Mohamed bin Laden, an illiterate bricklayer from Yemen. Bin Laden's mother was Syrian, one of Mohamed's four wives. According to family legend, Mohamed bin Laden was laying brick for one of King Abdul-Azziz's royal palaces when he suggested a way for the king—also known as Ibn Saud—to get around more easily in his wheelchair. The king, who proclaimed Saudi Arabia an Islamic monarchy in 1932, helped Mohamed get started in the construction business and steered contracts his way.

Paul Swenssen, a former FBI agent who represented financier Clint Murchison in Saudi Arabia and dealt with the bin Laden family, recalled that they considered Osama a "black sheep."

"He was a religious zealot, and they shunned him," Swenssen said. "They laughed about him. They would say, 'That's our brother,' like he was wacky."

After fighting against the Soviets in Afghanistan in 1979, bin Laden formed al-Qaeda, meaning "the base," in 1988. It was a loose-knit group of terrorist organizations and cells. In 1991, bin Laden relocated to the Sudan. Algeria, Saudi Arabia, and Yemen accused bin Laden of supporting subversive groups. In 1994, the Saudis stripped him of his citizenship. In May 1996, under Saudi and U.S. pressure, the Sudan expelled him, and he returned to Afghanistan. A few months later, the Taliban, a conservative Islamic group, gained control of some areas of the country and offered bin Laden protection.

After his father died, bin Laden inherited an estimated $30 million. However, most of the money to fund al-Qaeda came from wealthy Muslims who believed in his cause.

Just as Adolf Hitler blamed the Jews for the economic problems of Germany after World War I, bin Laden blamed the United States for sins against Muslims, including sending thousands of troops to Saudi Arabia after the Persian Gulf War in 1991. Because it did not follow his corrupted version of Islam, the United States was the infidel.

In 1996, bin Laden called for holy war against "Americans occupying the land of the two holy places"—the Muslim shrines at Mecca and Medina. In August 1998, bin Laden issued a fatwa, or ruling on Islamic law, telling Muslims it was their duty to kill Americans and their "allies, civilians and military . . . in any country in which it is possible to do it." In return, he promised his followers an honored place in paradise.

The Americans, bin Laden told ABC News in 1998, "rip us of our wealth and resources and of our oil. Our religion is under attack. They kill and murder our brothers. They compromise our honor and our dignity, and dare we utter a single word of protest against injustice, we are called terrorists."

■ ■ ■

Two days after the attacks on the World Trade Center and the Pentagon, Bush called bin Laden a "prime suspect." He vowed to conduct a military campaign to demolish terrorist networks and topple the governments that harbor them.

On TV, Mueller said that seven thousand FBI agents were working the case. The truth was that almost every one of the FBI's eleven thousand agents was working it. In the first week alone, eighty-six thousand tips poured in, more than half on the Internet. Nearly all were useless.

"We're running ourselves silly with tips," an agent assigned to the SIOC said. "People are coming out of the woodwork. One said, 'My next door neighbor has washed his car only twice in fifteen years, and he's washing it now.'"

Mueller came in at 6 A.M. and left at 10:30 P.M. Three times a day, Mueller and Pickard conducted conference calls with field offices. That leveled off to two a day, at 7 A.M. and 4 P.M.

Spouses of agents supplied snacks and fruit to the agents and support personnel in the SIOC. A church group contributed fried chicken. Agents had to scout the entire building to find Coke machines because machines near the SIOC were sold out.

The bureau gave the case the code name PENTTBOM, the extra "T" standing for the Trade Center. Pickard, an accountant who joined the FBI in 1975, divided the investigation into three segments: the nineteen hijackers who had spent time in al-Qaeda training camps; the support who helped with the logistics of renting apartments, securing driver's licenses, and distributing cash to the teams that would take the four planes; and the financing behind it all.

The investigation took agents from Vero Beach, Florida, to Portland,

Maine, from Laurel, Maryland, to San Antonio, Texas. A total of four thousand subpoenas were served, and 921 people were detained on immigration violations. Thirty-five prosecutors from the Justice Department's Terrorism Section, plus David Kelley, who almost was killed with Barry Mawn at the World Trade Center, worked the case in Washington. Freeh's newly opened legats helped. It was the most massive investigation in FBI history.

Mohamed Atta quickly emerged as the ringleader of the plot. His luggage, which did not make it onto Flight 11 from Boston, contained a five-page handwritten document in Arabic urging the hijackers to crave death and "be optimistic."

By the end of September, the United States had amassed twenty-eight thousand sailors and troops and more than three hundred warplanes and two dozen warships in the Indian Ocean and Red Sea for an attack on the Taliban who harbored bin Laden and al-Qaeda. On October 7, the bombing, aided by the British, began on Kabul, the capital and the largest city in Afghanistan. Bombers, fighter planes, and Tomahawk cruise missiles pounded the airfields and other strongholds.

A defiant bin Laden responded by videotape that "America will not live in peace." By December 7, it was almost all over. The Taliban had abandoned Kandahar, their last stronghold.

On December 13, the Bush administration released a videotape of bin Laden chatting with followers. It showed he had prior knowledge of the attacks. Gloating over the deaths, he said, "We calculated in advance the number of casualties" that would result when two airliners crashed into the World Trade Center. "I was the most optimistic of all" in predicting who would be killed, he said. On the morning of the attacks, bin Laden turned on a shortwave radio to hear the news. His followers, he said, were "overjoyed when the first plane hit the World Trade Center, so I said to them, 'Be patient.' " Chuckling, he said that most of the hijackers recruited for the "martyrdom operation" were not aware until the last minute that they were going to their deaths.

■ ■ ■

Six days a week, Mueller briefed President Bush at 8 A.M. Bush wanted to know the status of each threat. He made it clear he did not want another attack and would hold Mueller accountable if one occurred. It stoked Mueller's sense of urgency. He would ask an SAC to carry out an order and, two hours later, call to see if it had been done. "Prevention" became the watchword.

Of course, going back to the bureau's earliest days, the FBI had been in the business of prevention, as when the bureau rolled up the Nazi saboteurs in 1942. The bureau called it being proactive. That meant infiltrating groups and wiretapping their calls to uncover plots before they were carried out. If an attack were about to occur, the bureau would roll it up before it happened.

Between 1993 and 1999, the FBI did, in fact, prevent forty terrorist acts that would have killed tens of thousands of people. One was an al-Qaeda plot to blow up the Holland and Lincoln tunnels, the United Nations, and the FBI's New York Field Office. Sometimes, pure luck or a hunch did the trick. That happened on December 14, 1999, when an alert U.S. Customs officer noticed Ahmed Ressam acting nervously as he tried to enter the United States from Canada in Port Angeles, Washington. In the trunk of his car, he had the makings of an Oklahoma City-type bomb he planned to detonate at Los Angeles International Airport just before the millennium celebrations. Ressam turned out to be an al-Qaeda operative. After his capture, he cooperated with the FBI.

After the attacks on the World Trade Center, the New York Field Office would normally be called the office of origin, meaning it would direct the investigation into the hijackings. The case was, in fact, assigned a number that began 265-A-NY, referring to the number of the criminal violation. But Mueller wanted headquarters to direct the investigation.

"An investigation of this size involving so many different locations needs to be coordinated from the center," Mueller told me.

Mawn agreed that initially, centralization of the terrorist investigation made sense. But as weeks dragged on, he argued that New York should take over. New York had the expertise in investigating bin Laden. Moreover, headquarters was not set up to follow and distribute leads. That was done by the field.

In one example of that, the Washington Field Office forwarded to the SIOC for investigation names and addresses of people and businesses called by the hijackers. The SIOC, overloaded, did not distribute the leads to field offices for a day or two. Dale Watson, the chief of the Counterterrorism Division at headquarters, was supposed to look at the big picture, not act as a case agent.

To turn headquarters into an investigative center, Mueller had twelve New York agents who would normally work the case come to Washington to oversee it. Pasquale J. "Pat" D'Amuro, who replaced John O'Neill, was one of them. In Washington, Mueller felt, they would have immediate access to the CIA and other national security agencies. In addition, Michael Chertoff, the head of the Justice Department's Criminal Division, and other Justice Department prosecutors could more easily supervise the prosecutorial end.

Many bureau officials saw this as a Justice Department takeover. Mueller, a creature of the Justice Department, was closely tied to Ashcroft, who had pushed his nomination. Now Justice, which was seen as political, was running the investigation.

As in the choice of directors, what was important was not so much whether prosecutors or FBI agents, judges or nonjudges, were running the FBI, but what kind of people they were, what their agenda was, and whether they knew what they were doing. A man like Michael Chertoff, the senior Justice Department official over the case, brought a lot to the table. A Harvard Law School graduate and former clerk to Justice William Brennan Jr., Chertoff, forty-seven, had been a prosecutor in New York and then U.S. attorney in New Jersey. The son of a rabbi, Chertoff prosecuted the bosses of the five New York Mafia families, known as the Commission. When a police sergeant told Fat Tony Salerno, one of the convicted defendants, that Chertoff's career was now thriving, Salerno responded, "Well, you give him a little message from Fat Tony. You tell that son of a bitch he owes me a thank-you note."

Chertoff likened his relationship to the bureau to the one he had with the local SAC when he was U.S. attorney in Newark. To bring a successful prosecution, the FBI and prosecutors had to work together.

"I think we work as a team," Chertoff told me. "If Bob Mueller wants to suggest how we should handle something in a prosecution, he doesn't hesitate, and I don't hesitate to listen and take his advice. If I want to suggest something investigative, I'm not bashful about doing that."[231]

An example of what happens when the FBI and Justice don't work as a team, Chertoff said, was the damage that occurred because agents and prosecutors could not talk to each other about cases when applications for electronic intercepts had to be submitted under the Foreign Intelligence Surveillance Act. The division that existed was "mind-boggling," he said.

Centralization of investigations allowed for more cooperation. "The traditional model of the bureau was very decentralized. The SACs would do their thing, and headquarters would not do anything operational. But terrorism and national security or espionage cases are really national. What goes on in Miami and San Francisco may be linked," Chertoff said. "The old method of having an office of origin in a particular city doesn't make sense in terrorism and national security. There is no real center of gravity, and they need to be part of the national security components."

36

THE MARINE

At 2:20 A.M. on October 2, 2001, Robert Stevens, a sixty-three-year-old photo editor at tabloid publisher American Media, was admitted to JFK Medical Center in Atlantis, Florida. Vomiting and confused, he had a 102° fever. The next day, doctors determined that Stevens had contracted anthrax by inhaling spores. On October 4, doctors called a press conference to announce the confirmation of anthrax. They believed Stevens to be an isolated case. Perhaps he had contracted it in the woods.

A day before Stevens was admitted, Erin M. O'Connor, a thirty-eight-year-old assistant to Tom Brokaw, went to the doctor with a low-grade fever and a bad rash. The doctor suspected anthrax and prescribed Cipro. That same day, Ernesto Blanco, seventy-three, an American Media mail room employee, was hospitalized with pneumonia. By October 5, Stevens had died, the first known anthrax fatality in the United States since 1976.

The U.S. Centers for Disease Control and Prevention found anthrax spores on Stevens's computer keyboard and in Blanco's nasal passages. The agency decided that the American Media building should be sealed.

Soon, there were more anthrax cases, from Washington to New York. At first, it seemed to be another attack by bin Laden. Unlike the September 11 cases, Mueller allowed the Washington Field Office to direct the anthrax investigation. The case did not appear to have the global dimensions of the terrorist attacks. Agents headed by Bradley

Garrett, who had been working on the disappearance of Chandra Levy and a possible obstruction of justice charge against Representative Gary Condit, were pulled off the celebrated case.

The FBI traced the new anthrax cases to letters addressed to Brokaw, to Senate Majority Leader Thomas A. Daschle, to Senator Patrick Leahy, and to other news outlets. The letters went through mail-processing facilities in Hamilton Township, New Jersey, and the Washington sorting center on Brentwood Road. Through cross contamination, traces of anthrax turned up at mail rooms used by the White House, the State Department, the CIA, Walter Reed Army Medical Center, the U.S. Supreme Court, and the Hart and Dirksen Senate office buildings. More traces were found at the Morgan Station postal facility in Manhattan and at other sorting centers in New York. Spores turned up at ABC and CBS as well.

At one point, the House suspended work, and three Senate office buildings were closed. In all, eighteen people contracted anthrax, either though skin contact or inhalation. Five died.

■ ■ ■

On September 25, more than a week before any anthrax cases had been detected, NBC security called the New York Field Office about a letter addressed to Brokaw containing white powder. The letter was mailed on September 20 in St. Petersburg, Florida. O'Connor, Brokaw's assistant, opened it. It turned out that this letter, unlike the second one she opened, was a hoax. It contained talcum powder.

Still, Mayor Giuliani criticized the FBI for being slow to react. The two agents who showed up at NBC normally were assigned to investigate drugs. They had no idea anthrax might be involved and treated the case like an illicit drug case. Without explanation, they were told that O'Connor was not available to be interviewed. The agents put the letter in an evidence vault instead of having the powder tested. They waited until they could interview O'Connor.

Subsequently, O'Connor developed anthrax from the second letter. On October 6, one of her doctors notified the city health department, which notified the FBI. Only then did Barry Mawn became aware of the delay in investigating the first, bogus letter. He made sure the powder was tested immediately. Since that letter turned out to be a hoax, the delay did not make any difference.

The call from NBC about the first letter was "one of maybe about eight thousand leads we had received," said Mawn, who was working eighteen-hour days, seven days a week. "The letter should have been sent to headquarters for immediate testing. The agents who normally pursue drug cases handled it like a drug case," he said.

At the Washington Field Office, Van Harp pursued three theories: that the anthrax letters came from al-Qaeda, from a domestic right-wing terrorist group, or from a lone suspect like the Unabomer. After a month, the bureau had developed enough investigative information to suggest that this last possibility was the right one. As the investigation into the airplane attacks began to wind down, Harp had practically the entire office of 659 agents working the anthrax case.

In the middle of it, Al Kamen of the *Washington Post* noted that an FBI advisory warned citizens to look for indications that a letter or package might be suspicious and might contain anthrax or a bomb. The indications might include excessive tape or string, protruding wires, no return address, or a strange odor. Recipients should also be on the lookout for misspelled words, the poster said. In addition, the FBI advised recipients to check to see if it's "*Possiblly* [*sic*] mailed from a foreign country."

"Yikes!" Kamen commented. "They've taken over the FBI!"

■ ■ ■

In the months leading up to the September 11 attacks, the CIA, whose job it is to spy overseas, and NSA, which intercepts communications, had been picking up fragmentary intelligence that al-Qaeda might be planning another attack on U.S. interests. An intercept picked up Osama bin Laden telling one of his four wives to return to Afghanistan immediately. "There is a big thing coming," an al-Qaeda operative said.

"There was general intelligence that al-Qaeda was up to something," Mawn said. "We heard the drums beating. There were specific threats about Yemen. We thought there might be an attack overseas."[232]

That the attacks came as a surprise was widely called an "intelligence failure." The term implies that the CIA and FBI have a foolproof way of detecting attacks and crimes before they happen. To be sure, some developments should be detected and, when they are not, can legitimately be characterized as failures. For example, the CIA failed to detect movements indicating that India and Pakistan were about to detonate nuclear test weapons in 1998. With satellite coverage, there was no excuse for not warning of such a development. But no one would suggest that when a bank has been robbed or the federal building in Oklahoma City blown up, the FBI "failed" to detect the plot.

Penetrating an organization like bin Laden's was extremely difficult. While twenty-year-old American John Philip Walker Lindh joined the Taliban and met bin Laden several times, he learned few secrets. For his inner circle, bin Laden was careful to recruit fanatics whom he or his people had known for years. The fact that even after the U.S. government offered rewards that began at $5 million and eventually zoomed to $25 million, no one turned him in demonstrates how loyal his organization was.

In the year before the attacks, George Tenet, director of Central Intelligence, told the Senate Select Committee on Intelligence that bin Laden posed the "most serious and immediate threat" to the United States. But an assessment from the CIA director was hardly needed. Anyone who read the newspapers or watched television knew of al-Qaeda's previous attacks and threats.

Sheik Omar Abdel Rahman, the radical Islamic leader who was convicted of plotting to bomb the United Nations, the FBI's New York Field Office, and the Holland and Lincoln tunnels, urged followers to "break and destroy the morale of the enemies of Allah" by attacking their "high world buildings . . . and the buildings in which they gather their leaders." Ramzi Yousef, the mastermind of the 1993 plot on the World Trade Center, told FBI agents as they flew in a helicopter over Manhattan that the World Trade Center would not "still be standing if I had enough money." In 1995, a terrorist based in the Philippines threatened to fly a plane loaded with chemical weapons into the CIA at Langley and to blow up twelve U.S. airliners. All these plots were linked to bin Laden, and all were made public.

In retrospect, no one took the threats seriously enough. The Clinton administration's response to the bombings that bin Laden masterminded of the two American embassies in East Africa only demonstrated America's weakness and lack of resolve. In response to the attacks, the United States launched two strikes, one on training camps where bin Laden was supposedly hiding and one on a pharmaceutical plant where the CIA believed chemical weapons could be made for bin Laden.

Certainly American arrogance played a role. How could people with unpronounceable names living in caves threaten American might and technology? But al-Qaeda had a sophisticated appreciation of America's vulnerabilities. The FAA allowed knives up to four inches long to be taken on airplanes. Without any difficulty, the hijackers could pack knives and box cutters that they would use to threaten passengers and crew. Thanks to lax regulation and the airlines' shortsighted fixation on cost cutting, airline security had long been a joke.

Hijacking airplanes and plunging to one's death is not exactly high tech. But the FBI soon learned that the dead hijackers had been as sophisticated as KGB officers at concealing their activities. They used phony names and public libraries for communicating on the Internet. They used couriers and codes embedded in graphics to convey their messages, a system called steganography. They listed Mail Boxes outlets as home addresses and transferred money through an ancient secret system called *hawala,* which relies on trust to move sums around the world.

"To me, they acted like normal human beings, nothing abnormal," said Henry George, a flight instructor who taught Atta and another hijacker to fly. "They were polite, maybe even shy."

To finance the plot, the hijackers used at least $500,000 funneled by Mustafa Ahmed al-Hawsawi, a fugitive believed to be al-Qaeda's finance chief. At least $325,000 of the money was disbursed through ATMs, money orders, and credit cards, the rest in cash. Al-Qaeda operatives hatched the plot in Germany with connections in France, Britain, Spain, the Netherlands, Italy, Bosnia, and the Czech Republic.

Most important, to avoid detection, each group or cell targeting a plane kept itself totally separate from the others. As specified in an al-Qaeda training manual, the hijackers themselves did not go to mosques or see other Muslims. Some of them even drank alcohol, which was forbidden by Islam.

"There was no information about them before the attacks," Mawn said. "I'm still shocked and amazed it happened here. These people didn't necessarily bring attention to themselves. All but one was here legitimately. They were not involved in criminal activities. They were separate and unaware of each other until the end."

■ ■ ■

Looking back, the one hope of foiling the plot might have been determining what Zacarias Moussaoui was up to when he was taking lessons at the Pan Am Flight Academy in Eagan, Minnesota. On August 15, 2001, an official of the school called the FBI and reported that Moussaoui, a thirty-three-year-old French national of Moroccan descent, wanted to concentrate on navigation and midair turns, not landings or takeoffs. He lacked flight skills and was belligerent and evasive about his background. He paid $6,800 of the $8,300 fee in cash. The biggest plane he had ever flown was a single-engine Cessna, and then only with an instructor. Yet he wanted to learn to fly "one of these Big Bird," as he put it in an E-mail to the flight school—a Boeing 747-400 or Airbus A-300.

Minneapolis was not exactly a hotbed of terrorists. To Dave Rapp, the Minneapolis counterterrorism agent who got the case, this was like Watergate to Bob Woodward and Carl Bernstein. The agent pursued it as if it were the threat it turned out to be.

During an interview at FBI headquarters, I saw the agent's original classified report sitting on the desk of an FBI official. It was a foot high and included a four-inch stack of printouts of the contents of Moussaoui's computer obtained after the attacks.

While Moussaoui's actions were suspicious, there was nothing to tie him to a foreign power or foreign political faction, a requirement to obtain a FISA warrant to wiretap his calls or search his computer. French intelligence officials said only that he had connections to radical Islamic extremists. When the FBI finally was able to look at his hard drive after the events of September 11 provided more evidence linking him to the hijackers, it found information about airplanes, crop dusting, and wind currents. That in itself would not add to the evidence needed to obtain approval to conduct electronic surveillance of him under FISA.

Because of the lack of evidence, FBI lawyers at headquarters told the

Minneapolis agent they could not support either a FISA or criminal warrant. Lacking that, the FBI decided to turn him over to the INS. He was incarcerated on August 16 because his visa had expired.

Chertoff, for one, thought that if the wall between the FBI and Justice Department on FISA applications had not existed, agents working with prosecutors and Justice Department legal advisers might have devised a way for the FBI to develop the information needed to obtain authorization to intercept Moussaoui's communications.

As part of new antiterrorism legislation, Chertoff inserted language that would make it even clearer that a counterintelligence or counterterrorism investigation could morph seamlessly into a criminal case without posing any legal problems. Now information learned from FISA wiretaps and bugs could be used for prosecutions if "a significant purpose" rather than "the primary purpose" of the original application was to obtain intelligence. It was a semantic change that demonstrated that FISA as originally enacted never prohibited prosecutors and FBI agents from consulting with each other when FISA applications were considered. Yet the harmful attitudes spawned by Richard Scruggs, the Justice Department's counsel for the Office of Intelligence Policy and Review who first claimed that such a demarcation was required, lived on. Even after the change in the law, agents and prosecutors were still wary of consulting with each other. When I told him that nothing had, in fact, changed, Chertoff said, "I think there has been a change in thinking, but I think we have more work to do."

"It's about turf and control, not about what's right for the country," said former spy prosecutor John Martin.

Besides the FISA problem, civil libertarians, privacy advocates, extreme conservatives, and tech industry lobbyists had succeeded over the years in imposing restrictions that made no sense on FBI investigative operations. To be sure, Americans should always be wary of the FBI's power. The bureau is a paramilitary organization that responds to its leader. Should a politically motivated director take over, it is possible he or she could order illegal activities that might initially be concealed.

Of the bureau's ten directors, three—William J. Burns, J. Edgar Hoover, and William S. Sessions—abused their position. A fourth, Louis J. Freeh, almost destroyed the bureau through colossal mismanagement born of sheer donkeylike stubbornness and arrogance. As with presidents, FBI directors wield tremendous power and are constantly courted, and this can lead to a sense of entitlement.

"The life of the White House is the life of a court," George E. Reedy wrote in *The Twilight of the Presidency*. The president "is treated with all the reverence due a monarch."

To a lesser extent, FBI directors are treated the same way. "The power and the privileges go to their heads," said former FBI deputy director Weldon Kennedy. "They start to believe what they read about themselves and react to the deferential way people respond to them."

But agents themselves have a clear appreciation of the need to remain within the law. They joined the FBI to do good, to risk their lives if necessary to make sure others are safe. Nearly all FBI agents would turn in their badges before committing an illegal act. The bureau's record speaks for itself. Not since the days of Hoover and L. Patrick Gray has the FBI as an organization engaged in illegal conduct.

Since that time, innovations in communications have made it far more difficult for the FBI to conduct electronic surveillance. Instead of using one phone, criminals use cell phones and pay phones, not to mention E-mail and the Internet, often with the help of sophisticated encryption software.

Yet even after September 11, privacy advocates continued to oppose any change that would allow the bureau to keep up with the bad guys. Thus, the bureau could obtain authorization to wiretap specific phone numbers or to intercept E-mail from specific addresses but could not target the communications of an individual regardless of which phones or E-mail addresses he or she used. To keep up with a suspect who switched from a disposable cell phone to a pay phone to a fax, the bureau would have to obtain new court authorization every time. It was easier to obtain wiretap authorization against organized crime figures than against terrorists. Even when the FBI had probable cause and court authorization, it could not easily intercept and read coded electronic messages. That was because, during the Clinton administration, Congress would not pass legislation requiring software manufacturers to include in their products ports that would allow the FBI to unscramble the coded communications. The software industry maintained that allowing law enforcement to defeat encryption detracted from the value of its products. The same kind of opposition prevented the FBI from unscrambling coded digital phone calls. Terrorists could buy encryption programs at any CompUSA and assure themselves that the FBI would not be able to unscramble their messages. What was the point of allowing court-ordered interception if it could not be carried out?

Despite the fact that no court had found that FISA as implemented by the Justice Department posed any legal problem, the American Civil Liberties Union even questioned legislative changes allowing the FBI to consult early on with prosecutors in intelligence investigations, as it once had. The ACLU's opposition to national ID cards illustrated its fuzzy thinking. The organization had no problem with driver's licenses or national Social Security cards, which could easily be counterfeited. When it came to similar cards that were reliable and would allow more intelligent screening of passengers at airports, the ACLU raised the flag of civil liberties concerns, saying the cards would centralize private information in a data bank. The fact is that anyone with $35 can obtain the same information on-line. Rather than allow positive identification of passengers, the ACLU was willing to have them subjected to intrusive and time-consuming body and luggage searches.

In a typical statement of the case against the FBI's proposals, Earl C. Ravenal of the Cato Institute wrote in a *Washington Post* op-ed, "The debate about encryption is nothing less than the Armageddon of government police power versus the heart and soul of the U.S. Constitution."

Civil libertarians complained that the number of FBI wiretaps had increased to record numbers. That was like complaining that the number of arrests had increased. The number of wiretaps rose because crime was increasing and the FBI was doing a better job of going after it. What was important was whether the wiretaps were legal and whether the FBI was abusing its authority. Each wiretap had to be approved by a judge, so it was not a question of infringing on rights. It was a question of making it at least as easy for the FBI to do its job as it was for criminals to do theirs.

The critics seemed to think that FBI agents relish wiretapping. In fact, because of the paperwork involved, it is the least appealing part of an agent's job. Because of lack of resources, the FBI literally cannot transcribe and translate all the wiretapped material it receives.

If the FBI cannnot be trusted to wiretap within the framework of the law, why trust agents to make arrests or carry weapons? What is the point of having an FBI if it is so hobbled that it cannot perform its mission? Whose rights were violated more, those whose phones are tapped by court order or those who died in the September 11 attacks?

If the FBI ever does abuse its authority, the appropriate response would be to prosecute those responsible and institute more oversight, not to diminish the number of wiretaps or make it more difficult to wiretap so that criminals can get away and terrorists can attack again.

Because of the relentless criticism and congressional restrictions, the FBI became so gun-shy that even though terrorists were known to hatch their plots there, the FBI was averse to following suspects into mosques. Because he was a cleric, FBI and Justice Department lawyers debated for months whether to open an investigation of Sheik Omar Abdel Rahman.

"I remember discussions when we said, unfortunately, it will take a tragedy before the issue of the tools we need is recognized for what it is," said Larry Collins, the former SAC in Chicago. "Maybe a congressman's daughter has to be kidnapped, and we can't track her. Congress tied our hands."[233]

"A crime practically had to be committed before you could investigate," Weldon Kennedy, the former FBI deputy director, said. "If you didn't have that, you couldn't open an investigation."

After September 11, Ashcroft pushed through the legislation that the FBI had been requesting for years, along with some additional measures. Now grand jury information can be shared with the CIA. Judges can approve roving wiretaps that follow a suspect to each phone he used.

In December 2001, Moussaoui was indicted. According to the indictment, the September 11 plot began in early June 2000, when Mohamed Atta and Marwan al-Shehhi, who would pilot the planes that crashed into the World Trade Center, arrived in the States. Soon, money for the operation started coming in. Because another hijacker, Ramzi bin al-Shibh, could not obtain a visa to enter the United States from Germany, Moussaoui, an understudy who was to replace other hijackers if needed, was to take his place as the twentieth hijacker. All the planes except the one that crashed in Pennsylvania had five hijackers. The Pennsylvania plane had four.

The indictment, which named bin Laden as an unindicted coconspirator, said Moussaoui was trained by al-Qaeda and received $14,000 from one of the terrorists in Germany. He allegedly bought knives and flight training materials and received wire transfers of money from abroad at about the same time as the other hijackers.

If Moussaoui was to be the twentieth hijacker, the FBI had placed him out of commission. Unfortunately, even if the FBI had been able to find out what Moussaoui was up to, it would not necessarily have been able to uncover the plots against the other planes.

■ ■ ■

In retrospect, despite the wiliness of the hijackers and the difficulty of penetrating al-Qaeda, the FBI, with the right focus and commitment, could have done far more. Under Freeh, Congress increased the FBI's budget to combat both domestic and foreign counterterrorism from $118 million to $423 million a year. The number of agents assigned to counterterrorism increased to 2,650. After September 11, that seemed a ridiculously low number.

Robert M. Blitzer, who was over terrorism prior to the attacks, said the bureau simply did not have the resources to deal with the problem. Bureau officials like Buck Revell and Bill Baker, who early on recognized terrorism as a problem, had long gone. Many who remained did not have the intellect to devise new strategies for dealing with the threat or, if they did, found that Freeh would not listen.

"I don't think Freeh ever trusted any of us," Blitzer said.

Under Freeh, the infrastructure for combating terrorism—computers, analysis, and translators—disintegrated. Blitzer recalled being inundated by threats and leads coming in from the CIA, State Department, NSA, and DIA. The FBI could not analyze it all, much less follow each lead to its logical conclusion.

"The FBI, because of lack of resources, was not able to analyze and exploit all of the intelligence on bin Laden," Blitzer said. "I would have reams of stuff on my desk. It was frantic. I came in on weekends. There was an ocean of work. We got thousands of threats every year. I would ask myself, 'What should we do with this? Is it real or not? Where should I send it?' We were trying to make sense of it. I don't think we ever came to grips with it."

The FBI should have been recruiting Arab-American agents to develop informants, Blitzer said. "We had no infrastructure. We had no analysts. Agents had to share computers. I am good on computers and couldn't figure out the FBI's computers, which were 386s. If an agent could find a computer, he typed up his reports himself. We couldn't afford to pay stenographers. We were paying agents $80,000 to $90,000 a year to type up reports."[234]

While the terrorists communicated by code on the Internet, agents had computers that lacked CD-ROM drives. Because of the lack of analysts and computers, "We didn't know what we had," Bob Bryant, the former deputy director, said. "We didn't know what we knew."

Even with more resources, fewer restrictions, and more focus, "I'm not sure we could have detected the plot," Mawn said. But, since September 11, "probably the entire government response has made a difference. We have people on the run. We're making it hard for them to communicate. We've disrupted their activities. We've frozen millions of dollars of individuals and organizations that allegedly fund terrorism. Now the guards at the tunnels are checking cars. Before, they stood around in the corner having coffee."

While passengers likely will never again allow a hijacker to get away with crashing a plane into a building, FBI officials believed that until all baggage was x-rayed or tested for bombs, the airlines would not be totally safe.

For the most part, FBI agents had no problem with the aggressive steps instituted by Ashcroft and Chertoff to prevent more attacks. Prosecutors always had discretion about whether to jail noncitizens who had violated immigration laws. If there was a possibility any of them might be al-Qaeda members, jailing them would remove the threat and still fall within the law. Unlike the Japanese detained during World War II, those jailed had violated criminal laws and were not American citizens. As it turned out, of those jailed, only Moussaoui was believed to have a possible connection to the plot.

Within the FBI, the Immigration and Naturalization Service was considered a joke, totally ineffective at doing its job. Putting violators in jail amounted to carrying out the job the INS should have been doing all along.

"Our job is to protect American lives, but we don't believe that is inconsistent with honoring the American Constitution," Ashcroft said.

Similarly, FBI officials had no problem with military tribunals. Citing the use of a military tribunal to try the eight Nazi saboteurs who landed in June 1942, former Attorney General Bill Barr suggested the idea to Ashcroft. To bureau officials, it made no difference how suspects were tried. The FBI investigates; it does not prosecute. The issue is one of philosophy, not of the law.

On the other hand, agents saw several of Ashcroft's other ideas as being clearly off base. In particular, agents viewed as pointless Ashcroft's directive that U.S. attorneys write five thousand noncitizens from Middle Eastern countries to ask that they come in for interviews by local police. With more than eleven thousand agents, the FBI could have conducted the interviews quickly, quietly, and far more effectively than local police. In some cities like Los Angeles, that is exactly what happened. The initiative produced exactly no useful information, while needlessly raising concerns of Arab Americans who already feared that they might be targeted unfairly.

"Ashcroft wants to show he is doing something," said a Washington Field Office agent.

Ashcroft's practice of acting as the spokesman for the FBI also troubled agents, who thought the attorney general came across as if he were the FBI director while Mueller was his deputy. Four months after the attacks, Webster mentioned to Mueller and to Larry Thompson, the deputy attorney general, that Ashcroft should give Mueller more space. It was important that the FBI "have a certain level of independence," Webster said, both because the bureau might have to investigate administration officials and because of the need to have "clarity of responsibility."

"The troops wonder who is the boss," Webster said to me. "It's better to let the director be the director."[235]

Mueller thought that initially, Ashcroft should take the lead. It would reassure Americans that the FBI and Justice Department were no longer fighting with each other and would also show that the problem-plagued FBI was under control. All along, his idea was that he would eventually assume a higher profile. In any case, on a tour of the Middle East and Asia, Mueller suddenly began giving press conferences by himself; Ashcroft was nowhere to be seen.

When the FBI and later Homeland Security Director Tom Ridge began to sound alerts based on fragmentary intelligence warnings of new attacks, pundits asked, "What should people be alert for?" Most Americans had no experience with security issues and threats. But they learned quickly. On December 22, 2001, an observant flight attendant on American Airlines Flight 63 from Paris to Miami noticed Richard C. Reid trying to light plastic explosives packed into the hollowed-out heels of his black suede high-tops. Reid turned out to have al-Qaeda connections. Passengers restrained him, saving the plane from destruction. That is what it meant to be on the alert.

As the FBI began distributing information about the hijackers, Baltimore Police Commissioner Edward T. Norris said he received from the FBI a list of people to watch for but no photographs, dates of birth, or physical descriptions. He implied that the FBI was withholding the information from the police. But the FBI did not provide the information because it did not have it. Even determining the hijackers' real names had been a challenge.

While SACs and local police chiefs in a few cities may not have gotten along, the fact is that for decades the FBI closely cooperated with local and state police through joint terrorism task forces. As in the New York task force, police assigned to these units worked side by side with FBI agents in field offices. They were given security clearances and saw the same information FBI agents saw. Of the fifty-six field offices, thirty-five had such task forces. Similarly, FBI agents worked at the CIA's Counterterrorism Task Force, and CIA officers were assigned to the FBI's Counterterrorism Division.

"Lack of cooperation is much ado about nothing," Mawn said. "There are apt to be cases where people don't get along. In one of my assignments, I didn't trust the guy. But if there's a public safety issue, we're going to get the information out."

■ ■ ■

After four months in the job, Mueller restructured the bureau and began elevating the people he had come to trust. While Mueller would not criticize his predecessor, the changes—emphasizing technology and analysis—made it clear what Mueller thought of Freeh and some of his policies. Most of his changes corrected Freeh's misjudgments.

While Freeh ignored the FBI's hopelessly outdated computers until his last months in office, Mueller appointed Bob Dies chief technology officer reporting directly to him. Instead of snubbing the SAC Advisory Committee, as Freeh had, Mueller placed it at the top of the organizational chart reporting to him. While Freeh ignored planning, Mueller created an Office of Strategic Planning reporting to him. A new Security Division was established to try to prevent another Robert Hanssen case. An Office of Analysis was created for counterterrorism and counterintelligence.

Instead of acting defensively to criticism about lack of cooperation with local law enforcement, Mueller added an Office of Law Enforcement Coordination to improve liaison with state and local police and public safety agencies. Mueller's top aide, Dan Levin, who was Mueller's aide in San Francisco, stayed in the background, as Webster's aides had. In contrast, Freeh's aide Bob Bucknam tried to involve himself in operational matters.

At Quantico, Mueller ordered a training program for analysts and more training in data mining and leadership. Asked what leadership means, Mueller got a gleam in his eye as he referred to his Marine Corps training. "There are certain things you are taught in the Marine Corps that stay with you forever," he said as he sat at the head of his conference room table. "You don't ask people to do things you are not willing to do yourself. You work harder than those you would lead. You praise in public and criticize in private. You delegate." The foundation of leadership is integrity, Mueller said. "With that goes speaking your mind, not dissembling, being blunt. It's not easy to criticize people, it's not easy to move people. Those are all difficult things that are all part of leadership."

In the past, directors met once a year with all SACs. In the space of four months, Mueller held two SAC meetings. Each lasted two days and included a visit to the White House for a pep talk from Bush and talks by Secretary of State Colin Powell and CIA Director George Tenet. SACs gasped when Mueller used a laptop computer and a PowerPoint program to illustrate the points he was making. Mueller kept their cell phone numbers in his Palm handheld computer. Even the FBI tour, once it reopened, was to reflect the new direction, including new exhibits on cybercrime.

As Mueller saw it, instead of responding to changes in threats as they arose, the FBI had to anticipate and plan for them. "Five years from now, is it going to be al-Qaeda or some other terrorist group we need to focus on?" he asked. "If it is some other terrorist group, we ought to start thinking now about the language skills we'll need, the cultural understandings, and the types of analysts we'll need to address the challenge down the road."

Stories by Jim McGee of the *Washington Post* gave the impression that Mueller planned to turn the FBI into an agency that focused largely on counterterrorism, prevention, and intelligence gathering, as in Hoover's day, without undertaking long-term investigations. That was untrue. In his meetings with SACs, Mueller talked about the need to make incremental changes in the FBI's mission. Compared with the handful of federal laws the FBI enforced when the agency was created in 1908, it now had five hundred laws to enforce. In most cases, Congress gave the FBI additional jurisdiction without providing additional agents.

Tracking delinquent dads was on everyone's list of violations that the FBI should not be involved in. Most drug cases could be handled by the DEA. Local police in most areas could handle bank robberies and carjackings. Just as Clarence Kelley got the FBI out of the business of investigating individual car thefts, Mueller was setting priorities. The beauty of Hoover's creation was that agents received broad training and could be shifted from one criminal program to another as the need arose.

"I think it's a mistake to think the FBI is just going to do terrorism, and everybody can go rob banks," Chertoff said. "I do think there will be a shift in focus, with the bureau deploying more of its strength to areas where it adds unique value—terrorism, national security, complex organized crime, and white-collar crime cases. Carjackings, federal program fraud cases, delinquent dads can be done by others. This forces us to be smarter about not having duplication of effort. It's probably something we should have done a long time ago so that everyone sticks to his knitting and does what they do best."

Nor was the bureau about to end long-term investigations. Quite the opposite. To be sure, more attention would be given to shutting down plots immediately using any law available—immigration violations, material witness warrants, lying to the FBI. "We don't necessarily need to convict people of a grand conspiracy if we can convict them of something straightforward and get them off the street right away," Chertoff said.[236] When the U.S. military in January 2002 found videotapes of five apparent al-Qaeda members discussing a suicide attack, the FBI released the tapes to see if anyone could identify or find them. In the past, the FBI would have conducted a quiet investigation.

But everyone in the bureau and Justice Department recognized that the only way to make a real difference in fighting terrorism was to penetrate organizations with informants and electronic intercepts, in investigations that could take years. No one talked about returning to the unfocused and often illegal intelligence gathering of the Hoover days. Nor did anyone consider using torture, another creation of a few in the press.

In reorganizing the bureau, Mueller appointed four executive assistant directors to oversee eleven divisions. It was more or less the structure every director except Webster and Freeh had used, one that Mueller discussed with Webster at their lunch at the Metropolitan Club. It took pressure off the deputy director and provided a line of FBI officials who could make policy and meet with leaders of foreign law enforcement and intelligence organizations.

Mueller removed key officials who did not measure up to his standards. He removed Sheila Horan as acting director of the Counterintelligence Division because, after he found she was generally not on top of the subject, he felt she did not appropriately brief him on a Chinese counterintelligence case, failing to warn him of problems with it. Perhaps more than anything else, that defined the difference between Mueller and Freeh: Freeh banished people for telling him the facts, whereas Mueller banished those who did *not* give him the facts.

Mueller was determined not to have another Wen Ho Lee fiasco on his watch. But because Freeh had driven away so many talented FBI officials, Mueller had a depleted lineup to choose from when replacing bureau executives.

After six months on the job, Mueller had chosen his own people for nearly all the top slots in the bureau, including a black woman to be assistant director over training. Bright and articulate, forty-four-year-old Cassandra M. Chandler, a lawyer who was once a television news anchor in Baton Rouge, most recently headed the FBI's criminal and domestic terrorism analysis.

As executive assistant director over counterterrorism and counterintelligence, Mueller elevated Dale Watson, who had been in charge of counterterrorism alone. In that job, Watson had been trying to make the bureau more proactive. Having previously been detailed to the CIA as deputy operations director, Watson, who looks like a college professor, was superbly qualified to lead the bureau's efforts in the national security area.

"Before, we were going from one crime to another," he told me. "We are now working on how to prevent attacks five years from now."

When Pickard, who had been acting director when Freeh left, retired in November 2001, Mueller decided to do without a deputy so he could force the changes he wanted. He wanted to learn the bureau so he could feel comfortable that the right decisions were being made. He thought the job of deputy director probably entailed too broad a range of responsibilities in any case.

Rather than micromanaging, Mueller saw himself as supervising. "I like to be included on the important decisions," he said. "I'm responsible for everything that happens. That being the case, I want a certain comfort level that this is being done the way I would like it to be done even though I have not been an FBI agent. I have a tremendous amount to learn. I need advice from those who have been there and done things that I have not."

Mueller said it was important for bureau officials to make their own decisions. "We're all going to make mistakes," he said. "I've made any number of mistakes. So long as they're made in good faith and you are doing the best you can, I just want to know about them, and we'll move on."

When Bob Dies told him it would take three years to bring the FBI's computer systems up to the level of most homes and offices, Mueller said he wanted it done sooner. "The work of the FBI is information," Mueller told me. "We don't do as good a job as we should in gathering the information in digital form, being able to analyze it using the software tools out there, and disseminating it digitally either within the FBI or to the CIA, Customs, DEA, INS, or state and local police. We have to drive the bureau into the twenty-first century. The bureau should be the most technologically proficient investigative agency in the world." With an extra $100 million on top of the $300 million already required, Dies said he could do the planned computer overhaul in fourteen months.

Even before September 11, Dies found that, when Congress learned how disastrous the problem was, it was completely willing to fund new computers. When Freeh was in charge, Congress did not believe the FBI was capable of knowing what it needed, much less how to obtain it. Dies insisted on allowing only brand-name companies to bid. Soon, thousands of new Dell machines began arriving at FBI offices throughout the world. Dies began putting in high-speed networks so field offices could communicate with each other more quickly, and he made dozens of other immediate changes. To avoid any conflicts of interest, Dies's son Jason, who had urged his father to apply for the job at the FBI in the first place, was no longer its IBM account representative.

But some clung to the old ways. Despite Mueller's position that the bureau must do a better job of admitting its mistakes and letting the facts speak for themselves, Kathleen L. McChesney, whom Mueller promoted to executive assistant director over law enforcement services, said that she would rather I not go on a tour of Quantico that had been set up for me. In a similar apparent attempt to distance herself from any possible criticism of the bureau, McChesney wrote in August 1993 on FBI stationery to my then publisher's legal counsel to ask for removal of her name in the acknowledgments to the paperback edition of my previous book on the FBI. She said that on at least two occasions, I contacted her but she said she was "not interested in providing information to him for his book."[237] When the legal counsel reminded her that, with her permission, my interview with her had been tape-recorded, McChesney lapsed into silence, and her name remained in new printings of the book.

McChesney's more recent objection to my visit to Quantico resulted in its cancellation. However, John Collingwood intervened, and I spent most of a day at the training facility—shooting the Glock semiautomatic; responding to simulated shooting scenarios; sitting in on a class on use of deadly force; revisiting the Hostage Rescue Team facility and Hogan's Alley, where agents are trained in making arrests; and interviewing the acting assistant director over training. The episode was a reminder that, thirty years after Hoover's death, the dictum about not embarrassing the bureau was alive and well, even at the highest levels of the FBI.

Still, under Mueller, the bureau appeared to be in good hands, its mission once again redefined by war. By January 2002, the bureau had narrowed the focus of the anthrax investigation to employees of military laboratories capable of making the form of anthrax that killed victims in Florida, Connecticut, New York, and Washington. They included the U.S. Army Medical Research Institute of Infectious Disease at Fort Detrick, Maryland, and the U.S. Army's Dugway Proving Ground in Utah. The FBI concluded that the physical properties of the finely powdered anthrax sent to Capitol Hill were consistent with secret U.S. processes for producing it. From knowing virtually nothing about anthrax, bureau officials like Van Harp had learned so much that they thought they qualified for degrees in microbiology.

The strength of the FBI was demonstrated by the fact that, in the middle of pursuing terrorists and anthrax suspects, the New York Field Office took down seventy-three leaders and associates of the Genovese Mafia family.

In the wake of the September 11 attacks, the FBI had at least 150 ongoing investigations into possible al-Qaeda activities in the United States, compared with virtually none before the attacks. While very few of those investigations was likely to lead to anything, it was the kind of effort necessary to root out the problem.

"Every single lead is being followed now," a bureau official said.

Some of the leads arose from interviews by ten FBI agents Mueller sent to interview al-Qaeda and Taliban prisoners in Afghanistan before they were shipped to a detention center at Guantánamo Bay Naval Base, Cuba. "We asked them, 'Where is bin Laden now? Sipping tea on a yacht somewhere? And where are you now?' " an agent familiar with the investigation said. "That often worked. These are not hardened criminals such as you find in the United States."

While Mueller became involved in key decisions like whether to conduct a surveillance, he respected the opinions of bureau officials, sought their advice, and listened carefully before making up his mind. Three times in his first four months in office, he found the time to meet informally over doughnuts, cookies, and coffee with thirty-five reporters who regularly cover the bureau.

With his aversion to hearing bad news or countervailing views, Freeh had corrupted the normally open deliberative processes of the FBI. Going back to the Hoover days, the most appealing feature of FBI agents was their honesty. It will take time to undo the damage.

"I think we all breathed a sigh of relief that Freeh was not here on September 11," said a longtime bureau supervisor.

But no one likes change. Within the bureau, Mueller's forcefulness, restructuring, centralization of the terrorism investigation, and closeness to the Justice Department evoked the kind of low-grade grumbling that could be heard even under William Webster, the most successful FBI director. Mueller, like Hoover, may not be warm and fuzzy, but he got the job done.

"I want people to tell me they are unhappy and that this change is wrong for these reasons," Mueller said. "I don't want people to come in and say we should do it this way because we have always done it this way. That argument doesn't go very far."

"No matter who sits there, Jesus Christ himself could come back and have the misfortune to be made director, and they would forget everything that happened during Christianity," John Otto, the former acting FBI director, said.

After September 11, the FBI performed flawlessly, helping to restore confidence in the agency. The FBI has always been a symbol of America. Whether hunting down John Dillinger or handing a kidnap victim back to a parent, the FBI has succeeded far more often than it has failed. Once again, Americans could feel proud of their G-men. They are true heroes, willing to give their lives to preserve America's freedom. Yet in the end, "I don't know how you stop people who are willing to kill themselves," said an FBI agent assigned to the SIOC. "It's like assassins who want to kill the president. The Secret Service will tell you there's no way to stop them, if they want to die."

Barry Mawn still thinks about the woman's leg on the street after the World Trade Center attack. Late in the afternoon of December 31, as he prepared to lead FBI agents deployed to Times Square for New Year's Eve, Mawn said, "I'm praying nothing happens." On the first day of the New Year, he said, "Praying worked."

Acknowledgments

After my book on Palm Beach, my agent, Robert Gottlieb, chairman of Trident Media Group, thought it was time to return to more serious subjects. His guidance, for which I am grateful, led me back to one of my favorite topics.

Like a hound on a fox hunt, an author with the right subject needs only space and encouragement. Matthew Shear, vice president and publisher of St. Martin's Press, and Charles E. Spicer, executive editor, gave me both. To an author, nothing is more important. Charlie's superb editing and inquisitive mind enhanced the book.

My wife, Pamela Kessler, is my secret weapon. Also an author and former *Washington Post* reporter, she conducted research in archives, pre-edited the manuscript, and came up with the title. She is my best friend, and her wise judgment informs everything I do.

As always, my children, Greg and Rachel Kessler, were sources of support and love. My stepson, Mike Whitehead, cheered me on as well.

I was lucky to have John L. Martin on my side. A longtime friend and former agent who prosecuted seventy-six spies as head of the Justice Department's Internal Security Section, John shared his unique experiences and provided counsel and encouragement at every step.

It would take another book to describe how I obtained the cooperation I did. Essentially, years of developing trust paid off. John E. Collingwood, assistant FBI director for Public and Congressional Affairs, and Ernest J. Porter of the Office of Public Affairs were critically important in providing that help. John has a sophisticated understanding of the FBI's role in society. An agent, he represents all the best in the FBI. I am grateful as well to Robert S. Mueller III for giving me the first interview since his nomination as director. Back when he was assistant director over the Criminal Investigative Division, William M. Baker made it all possible by giving me unprecedented access to the FBI for my previous book on the subject.

I was fortunate to have friends who read the manuscript to help catch errors. They are former Justice Department official John L. Martin and former FBI officials William M. Baker, Herbert L. "Larry" Collins, Weldon L. Kennedy, and Robert B. Wade. My daughter Rachel Kessler, son Greg Kessler, and John Martin's wife Carol also read the manuscript and offered helpful suggestions.

Those who were interviewed or helped otherwise include:

James B. Adams, Kent Alexander, Jack Anderson, Richard H. Ash, William M. Baker, William P. Barr, Donald A. Bassett, Benton Becker, Griffin B. Bell, Joseph Billy Jr., Robert M. Blitzer, David P. Bobzien, Lane Bonner, Kier T. Boyd, Clarence W. Brittain, Janine Brookner, Michael Brooks, Dr. Bertram S. Brown, Robert M. "Bear" Bryant.

Plato Cacheris, Edward A. Carpenter, Joseph J. Casper, James F. Cassidy Jr., Michael Chertoff, G. Norman Christensen, Floyd I. Clarke, Jay Cochran Jr., John E. Collingwood, Herbert L. Collins, Linda Colton, Danny O. Coulson, Wayne P. Comer, Ivan W. Conrad, Marie Cooke, Cameron H. Craig.

Kurt Crawford, John Crewdson, Ed Curran, Craig D. Dahle, John J. Danahy, Anthony E. Daniels, Joseph R. Davis, Dr. Roger L. Depue, John Devine, James V. DeSarno Jr., Bob E. Dies, Joseph E. diGenova, John M. Dowd, P. J. Doyle, E. Peter Earnest, John T. Elliff, Peggy Engel, David E. Faulkner.

Joan Felt, W. Mark Felt, Ron Ferguson, Fred F. Fielding, Darlene Fitzsimmons, Sidney Frank, Neil J. Gallagher, Richard T. Garcia, William A. Gavin, James H. Geer, Kenneth A. Giel, Michael Giglia, Robert L. Gleason, Jamie Gorelick, Eli Gottesdiener, R. Jean Gray, Richard F. Green, James W. Greenleaf.

Michael D. Grogan, Howard Gutman, Terrence Hake, Morton Halperin, Horace R. Hampton, Van A. Harp, William A. Harwood, William T. Hassler, Bell P. Herndon, Ben Herren, Philip B. Heymann, John W. Hicks, Peter T. Higgins, William L. Hinshaw II, James P. Hosty, William G. Hundley, James O. Ingram, Michael Isikoff.

Jeffrey Jamar, I. C. Lou Jenkins, David W. Johnson Jr., Don Johnson, Emanuel Johnson Jr., David Johnston, Alfred T. Jones, Courtland J. Jones, Gregory Jones, Edward H. Joyce, James K. Kallstrom, Nicholas deB. Katzenbach, Weldon L. Kennedy, Richard W. Keifer.

David N. Kelley, Thomas J. Kimmel, Ed Klein, Herman Klurfeld, Kris J. Kolesnik, Mike Kortan, Mary Ann Krauss, the late Robert J. Lamphere, Larry W. Langberg, G. Robert Langford, John C. Lawn, Joseph R. Lewis, Harold Light, Susan E. Lloyd, Dr. James L. Luke, Andrew J. Maloney, Gordon E. Malmfeldt.

James M. Margolin, David Margolis, Carol Martin, John L. Martin, Barry Mawn, Ken Maxwell, John C. McDermott, Nancy D. McGregor, James D. McKenzie, Edward S. Miller, Darrell W. Mills, Gwen Moore-Holliday, Robert Morgenthau, Robert S. Mueller III, James Murphy, Jack Nelson, C. Edward Nicholson, Ken Nimmich, Roger Nisley.

D. Max Noel, James E. Nolan Jr., Ron Ostrow, John E. Otto, Charlie J. Parsons, Mildred C. Parsons, Stanley Penn, Gary Penrith, Michael J. Perry, Steven L. Pomerantz, Ernest J. Porter, E. Barrett Prettyman Jr., Joseph D. Purvis, J. Stephen Ramey, Robert K. Ressler, Oliver B. Revell, Bob A. Ricks.

Harvey Rishikoff, Edward J. Roach, Fred G. Robinette III, Everett A. Robinson III, Richard M. Rogers, Stephen H. Sachs, George E. Saunders, Lenny Savino, Frank G. Scafidi, M. Dennis Sculimbrene, John Douglas Seward, Michael E. Shaheen Jr., Robert A. Shaheen.

Howard M. Shapiro, Thomas L. Sheer, Brian Sierra, Peter A. Smerick, I. C. Smith, Julian Stackhaus, Joseph M. Stehr, Carl Stern, Frank J. Storey, Walter B. Stowe Jr., Joseph Sullivan, Paul L. Swensen, M. Wesley Swearingen, John E. Taylor, Ralph Taylor, Len Tepper, Howard D. Teten.

Pierre Thomas, Colin Thompson, Fletcher D. Thompson, H. Edward Tickel, Michael E. Tigar, Victoria Toensing, D. Caroll Toohey, Rex Tomb, Duane L. Traynor, Walter J. Trohan, David M. Tubbs, Joe Valiquette, Robert B. Wade.

John C. Wagner, Michael J. Waguespack, Walter R. Walsh, Leonard M. Walters, Dale Watson, William H. Webster, Neil J. Welch, John L. Werner, Ron Wilcox, Chester J. Willett, Pete Williams, Representative Frank Wolf, R. James Woolsey, Charles B. Youmans Jr., Norman A. Zigrossi, and Steve Zimmerman.

Notes

1. Barry Mawn, December 27 and 31, 2001.
2. David N. Kelley, January 3, 2002.
3. Helen Gandy file, FBI.
4. David Fisher, *Hard Evidence*, p. 17.
5. Robert J. Lamphere and Tom Shactman, *The FBI-KGB War*, p. 13.
6. Hoover to attorney general, May 12, 1925, National Archives.
7. Pamela Kessler, *Undercover Washington*, p. 39.
8. Pretty Boy Floyd and Kansas City Massacre file, FBI.
9. George "Machine Gun" Kelly file, FBI.
10. John Herbert Dillinger file, FBI.
11. Richard Gid Powers, *Secrecy and Power*, p. 225.
12. J. Edgar Hoover, March 6, 1934, FBI.
13. Clyde A. Tolson file, FBI.
14. *The New York Times*, May 12, 1954.
15. Herman Klurfeld, July 29, 2001.
16. Barker-Karpis Gang file, FBI.
17. Neal Gabler, *Walter Winchell*, p. 275.
18. Curt Gentry, *J. Edgar Hoover*, citing Hoover memos to SACs on September 2 and December 6, 1939, and to Ed Tamm on November 9, 1939.
19. Letter of June 13, 1938, from Dr. Herbert von Dirksen to Ernst von Weizsäcker, state secretary, Documents on German Foreign Policy, 1918–1945, Part I, U.S. Government Printing Office, 1951, p. 713.
20. Athan Theoharis, *From the Secret Files of J. Edgar Hoover*, p. 7.
21. Walter Trohan, June 2, 2001.
22. Walter Trohan, June 3, 2001.
23. *Chicago Tribune*, October 10, 1954, p. 1.
24. Duane L. Traynor, January 12, 2002, *Washington Post Magazine*, January 13, 2002, p. 15.
25. Theoharis, *From the Secret Files of J. Edgar Hoover*, p. 203.

26. Gentry, *J. Edgar Hoover*, p. 324.
27. Kier T. Boyd, September 12, 2001.
28. James E. Nolan Jr., June 27, 2001.
29. Lamphere, *The FBI-KGB War*, p. 41.
30. John J. Danahy, November 6, 2001.
31. Robert J. Lamphere, June 15, 2001.
32. Walter R. Walsh, September 22, 2001.
33. Leonard M. Walters, August 17, 2001.
34. C. Edward Nicholson, *Never the Likes Again*, p. 21.
35. Allen Weinstein and Alexander Vassiliev, *The Haunted Wood*, p. xvii; *Introductory History of VENONA*, National Security Agency; Hayden B. Peake, *"The VENONA Progeny," Naval War College Review*, summer 2000.
36. John Earl Haynes and E. Harvey Klehr, *Venona,* p. 331.
37. *Washington Post*, March 16, 1977, p. A1.
38. Rudolf Abel file, FBI.
39. John J. Danahy, November 6, 2001.
40. Ibid.
41. Walter Trohan, June 2, 2001. Edwards died in December 1990.
42. *Chicago Tribune*, February 8, 2000.
43. Robert J. Lamphere, June 15, 2001.
44. Gentry, *J. Edgar Hoover*, p. 356.
45. Personal and confidential letter from SAC New York E. E. Conroy to FBI director, January 21, 1944, Lou Nichols file, FBI.
46. Don Whitehead, *The FBI Story*, p. 110.
47. Don MacLean, *Pictorial History of the Mafia*, p. 69.
48. Theoharis, *The FBI*, p. 51.
49. Gentry, *J. Edgar Hoover*, p. 588.
50. Neil J. Welch, July 27, 2001.
51. William G. Hundley, July 24, 2001.
52. Wayne P. Comer, October 20, 2001.
53. James V. DeSarno Jr., January 3, 1992.
54. Anthony Summers, *Official and Confidential*, p. 254.
55. *Richmond Times-Dispatch*, March 27, 1993, p. A14.
56. William G. Hundley, July 24, 2001, Robert Morgenthau, January 2, 2002.
57. Susan L. Rosenstiel, December 23, 2001.
58. *Esquire*, May 1993, p. 57.
59. FBI Airtel from SAC, New Orleans, to Director, FBI, April 27, 1967; *Los Angeles Times*, January 19, 1997, p. A4; *San Antonio Express-News*, January 23, 2000, p. A1.
60. Pete Hamill, November 21, 2001.
61. Anthony Summers, December 24, 2001, and January 2, 2002, and E-mail of January 4, 2002.
62. Joseph D. Purvis, August 5, 2001.
63. Fred G. Robinette III, September 27, 2001.
64. Bertram S. Brown, M.D., November 7, 2001.
65. Lawrence J. Heim, December 18, 1991.
66. Cartha D. DeLoach, *Hoover's FBI*, p. 31.
67. Roy L. Elson, September 28, 1995, and June 15, 2001.

68. U.S. House Select Committee on Intelligence, November 18, 1975, part 3, p. 1067.
69. Walter J. Trohan, June 2, 2001.
70. Theoharis, *From the Secret Files of J. Edgar Hoover*, p. 67.
71. John J. McDermott, August 30, 2001.
72. Stephen H. Sachs, September 26, 2001.
73. Ronald T. McCoy, (Arvad's son), Nigel Hamilton papers, Massachusetts Historical Society.
74. Pat Munroe, December 2, 1993.
75. Ronald Kessler, *The Sins of the Father*, p. 264.
76. Phillip M. King, October 26, 1991.
77. John L. Martin, August 15, 2001.
78. William C. Sullivan with Bill Brown, *The Bureau*, pp. 104, 112.
79. Fred G. Robinette III, September 27, 2001.
80. James P. Hosty, November 19, 2001.
81. FBI reports to the director, January 20, 1964, and February 24, 1976.
82. *The Warren Commission Report*, p. 18.
83. Ibid., p. 813; Bell Herndon, May 6, 2003.
84. James H. Gale to Clyde Tolson, September 30, 1964, FBI.
85. Powers, *Secrecy and Power*, p. 411.
86. John L. Martin, August 4, 1997.
87. John Barron, *Operation Solo*, p. 4, *Washington Post*, June 12, 2001, p. B6.
88. *Abridged History of the FBI*, Research Unit, FBI.
89. Sullivan and Brown, *The Bureau*, p. 135.
90. FBI Supervisor J. F. Bland to FBI Assistant Director William Sullivan, October 4, 1963, FBI.
91. C. D. Brennan to William C. Sullivan, June 23, 1969, FBI.
92. Nicholas deB. Katzenbach, November 5, 2001.
93. Joseph D. Purvis, August 21, 2001.
94. Assistant Director William Sullivan to Assistant Director Alan Belmont, January 27, 1964, FBI.
95. Jay Cochran, September 1, 2001.
96. Clarence W. Brittain, September 14, 2001.
97. Letter to the editor from W. Raymond Wannall (who headed the FBI's Intelligence Division after Hoover fired Sullivan and who conducted an investigation into the matter), *Washington Times*, February 10, 1995, p. A22.
98. Ronald Kessler, *Inside the White House*, pp. 1, 35.
99. DeLoach, *Hoover's FBI*, p. 12.
100. Courtland Jones, July 28, 2001.
101. Joseph D. Purvis, August 5, 2001.
102. FBI director to attorney general, June 20, 1974, FBI.
103. Hoover to SAC Memphis James Startzell, December 16, 1970, FBI.
104. *"My FBI File: (Censored),"* *Nieman Reports*, winter 1980, p. 4.
105. James K. Davis, and Clarence M. Kelley, *Kelley*, pp. 36–37.
106. Oliver G. Revell, November 22, 1991.
107. W. Mark Felt, *The FBI Pyramid*, p. 199.
108. Barrett E. Prettyman, Jr., June 15, 2001.
109. William Beecher, October 29, 2001.

110. Felt, *The FBI Pyramid*, p. 77.
111. Sullivan and Brown, *The Bureau*, p. 265.
112. Dr. James L. Luke, July 30, 2001.
113. FBI Supervisor Milton Jones to Assistant Director Thomas Bishop, November 4, 1972, FBI.
114. *Washington Post*, January 19, 1975, p. 1.
115. Interviews by FBI inspectors with Helen Gandy, June 9, 23, and 27, 1975, FBI.
116. Leonard M. Walters, August 17, 2001. Gray did not respond to a telephone message of November 9, 2001, requesting comment for this book.
117. Edward S. Miller, September 7, 2001.
118. Angelo J. Lano, December 27, 1991.
119. Teletype, June 17, 1972, FBI.
120. Angelo J. Lano, December 27, 1991; teletype, June 17, 1972, FBI; Barry Sussman, *The Great Coverup*, pp. 3–39; *Washington Post*, June 14, 1992, p. A1; Carl Bernstein, and Bob Woodward, *All the President's Men*, pp. 13–26.
121. Edward R. Leary, January 9, 1992.
122. Associated Press, June 15, 1992.
123. Leonard M. Walters, August 17, 2001.
124. Davis and Kelley, *Kelley*, pp. 298–303; and Wilbur K. DeBruler, April 16, 1992.
125. *New York Times*, April 25, 1982, p. A1.
126. H. N. Bassett to James B. Adams, January 28, 1975, FBI.
127. Cartha D. DeLoach to Clarence M. Kelley, January 17, 1975, FBI.
128. *New York Times*, February 28, 1975, p. 1.
129. James B. Adams, June 15, 2001.
130. John M. Dowd, July 31, 2001.
131. U.S. Recording Company report, Justice Department, November 11, 1976, p. 102. A condensed version of the report was issued by the Justice Department in January 1978.
132. Department of Justice, *Report on the Relationship Between U.S. Recording Co. and the FBI and Certain Other Matters Pertaining to the FBI*, January 1978, pp. 13–14. In referring to similar practices by former Hoover aides who were then living, the report states that such practices arguably violated federal criminal statutes barring conversion of government property to personal use and misuse of federal property.
133. Cartha D. DeLoach, December 30, 1991.
134. Oliver B. Revell, November 22, 1991.
135. Michael E. Shaheen Jr., August 13, 2001.
136. W. Mark Felt, August 26, 2001.
137. John T. Elliff, *The Reform of FBI Intelligence Operations*, p. 6.
138. William A. Gavin, February 18, 1992.
139. *The FBI and CISPES*, report of the U.S. Senate Select Committee on Intelligence, July 1989, p. 72.
140. W. Raymond Wannall Jr., November 25, 1986.
141. Griffin B. Bell, November 16, 2001.
142. John L. Martin, August 5, 1997.
143. James Murphy, September 4, 2001.

144. *People*, January 20, 1992, p. 76; *New York Times*, October 28, 1991; Neil Gallagher, January 17, 1992.
145. *Times of London*, June 20, 1993.
146. *History of the Intelligence Division: Brief Historical Outline*, FBI, p. 3.
147. Jury verdict in *U.S.* v. *Tickel*, Case No. CR 82-269-A, U.S. District Court, Eastern District of Virginia; Case No. CT87-1287, Prince George's County Circuit Court, State of Maryland; *Washington Post*, June 19, 1987, p. C3; interview with John Hume, October 4, 1991.
148. *Washington Post*, January 5, 1987, p. A4; *Miami Herald*, January 5, 1987, p. B1.
149. Michael Brooks, January 18, 2002.
150. Jack Lawn, March 3, 1992.
151. John E. Otto, August 30, 2001.
152. William S. Sessions, January 28, 1992.
153. Alice Sessions, May 20 and June 22, 1992.
154. John L. McKay Jr., June 1, 1992.
155. Stephen L. Boyd, May 21, 1992.
156. William S. Sessions, August 7, 1992.
157. John Werner, September 4, 2001.
158. William Barr memo of January 15, 1993, to William Sessions, p. 3. Sessions did not respond to a telephone message of November 20, 2001, requesting comment for this book.
159. *Washingtonian*, March 1993, p. 97.
160. Carl Stern, September 7, 2001.
161. Peter A. Smerick and Mark C. Young, March 5 and 8, 1993, FBI.
162. Richard Rogers, August 27, 2001.
163. Jeffrey Jamar, June 18, 2001.
164. G. Norman Christensen, August 18, 2001; Weldon Kennedy, August 19, 2001; Steven L. Pomerantz, July 25, 2001.
165. D. Caroll Toohey, June 24, 2001.
166. Peter T. Higgins, June 22, 2001.
167. Jamie S. Gorelick, January 24, 2002.
168. Barry Mawn, December 27, 2001.
169. D. Caroll Toohey, June 24, 2001.
170. David P. Bobzien, August 1, 2001.
171. Weldon Kennedy, May 26, 2001.
172. For the epilogue of the paperback edition of my previous book, I asked Freeh for comment on his attempt to hire former aides who had drug problems and his decision then to relax the rules on prior drug usage. He declined to comment and, when the paperback edition came out, he called the president of Simon & Schuster to complain that when I had said he tried to hire former aides with drug problems, then relaxed the rules on prior drug usage so they could be hired, I said they were hired when they were not. What Freeh did not say was that the reason some of them ultimately were not hired by the time the paperback edition came out was that they failed polygraph tests on their prior use of hard drugs despite the relaxed rules.
173. M. Wesley Swearingen, July 25, 2001.
174. Herbert L. Collins, August 20, 2001.

175. The last attempt to obtain comment from Bucknam by phone was on January 11, 2002. In addition, a letter requesting comment was sent to him on January 14, 2002.
176. Oliver B. Revell, May 26, 2001.
177. *Washington Post*, February 28, 1994, p. D2.
178. William H. Webster, November 28, 2001.
179. *Washington Post*, August 12, 1995, p. A1.
180. Danny O. Coulson and Elaine Shannon, *No Heroes*, p. 407.
181. Bob A. Ricks, June 14, 2001.
182. *Washington Post*, August 7, 2001, p. A6.
183. Robert B. Wade, January 9, 2002.
184. Criminal Complaint, *U.S.* v. *Aldrich Hazen Ames*, February 21, 1994, p. 15.
185. Peter Maas, *Killer Spy*, p. 210.
186. Christopher Andrew and Vasili Mitrokhin, *The Sword and the Shield*, p. 13.
187. John L. Martin, January 14, 2002.
188. Coulson and Shannon, *No Heroes*, p. 15.
189. D. Max Noel, May 17, 2001.
190. William J. Esposito to Louis J. Freeh, August 14, 1997, FBI.
191. Report of the House Committee on Government Report and Oversight, September 28, 1996.
192. Kent B. Alexander, August 30, 2001.
193. David W. Johnson, Jr., August 27, 2001.
194. James D. McKenzie, December 14, 2001.
195. House Committee on Appropriations, Subcommittee on Commerce, Justice, State and Judiciary, May 16, 2001.
196. *Atlanta Constitution*, June 6, 1997, p. 2D.
197. *Washington Post*, February 14, 1997, p. A1.
198. *Los Angeles Times*, August 17, 2000, p. A1.
199. *New York Times*, February 4, 2001, p. A1; *Los Angeles Times*, September 13, 2000, p. A1; *Wall Street Journal*, December 8, 2000, p. A1; *Vanity Fair*, December 2000, p. 142.
200. Richard Scruggs, January 3, 2002.
201. Richard W. Keifer, January 3, 2002.
202. Edward J. Curran, September 13, 2001.
203. *Boston Globe*, April 4, 2001, p. C1, December 21, 2000, p. B1; *Boston Herald*, August 22, 2001, p. 1; *Hartford Courant*, December 21, 2000, p. A1; Dick Lehr and Gerard O'Neill, *Black Mass*.
204. G. Robert Langford, June 5, 2001.
205. William L. Flemming, and Ben Herren, September 27, 2001.
206. Ronald Kessler, *The Spy in the Russian Club*.
207. Robert M. Bryant, December 20, 2001.
208. Thomas J. Kimmel, November 19, 2001; *New York Times*, April 22, 2001, p. A1.
209. Affidavit in support of search warrant, FBI.
210. Plato Cacheris, December 19, 2001.
211. Janine Brookner, January 6, 2002.
212. John E. Collingwood, January 10, 2002; *Washington Post*, December 16, 2001, p. A2. The story quoted an "FBI official familiar with the investigation" and did not name him as Collingwood.

213. Bob E. Dies, January 31, 2002.
214. Mildred C. Parsons, August 1, 2001.
215. *Washington Post*, June 1, 2001, p. A12.
216. Leonard Walters, August 17, 2001.
217. Courtland J. Jones, July 28, 2001.
218. *Washington Post*, April 13, 1997, p. C1, February 27, 2001, p. A23.
219. *The New Yorker*, May 14, 2001, p. 79.
220. Public Financial Disclosure Report, Office of Government Ethics, August 29, 2001.
221. Eli Gottesdiener, January 16, 2002.
222. Robert S. Mueller III, February 12, 2002. For a *Washington Post* series that began on January 27, 2002, and was called "Ten Days in September," Bob Woodward went over with Mueller on a not-for-attribution basis issues relating to the government's initial response to the attacks of September 11.
223. *The Recorder*, July 6, 2001.
224. David Margolis, January 22, 2002.
225. William Webster, November 28, 2001.
226. Dale Watson, February 27, 2002.
227. *Newsweek*, December 3, 2001, p. 24.
228. Van A. Harp, December 3, 2001.
229. *New York Magazine*, December 17, 2001.
230. *The New Yorker*, January 14, 2002, p. 61.
231. Michael Chertoff, January 7, 2002.
232. Barry Mawn, December 27, 2001.
233. Herbert L. Collins, Jr., September 23, 2001.
234. Robert M. Blitzer, September 30, 2001.
235. William H. Webster, January 24, 2002.
236. *The New Yorker*, November 5, 2001, p. 61.
237. McChesney's letter, dated August 24, 1993, was to Pocket Books/Simon & Schuster. She was then assistant special agent in charge of the Detroit Field Office. She did not respond to my January 28, 2002, letter seeking comment.

Bibliography

Andrew, Christopher, and Vasili Mitrokhin. *KGB: The Sword and the Shield.* New York: Basic Books, 1999.

Bamford, James. *Body of Secrets: Anatomy of the Ultra-Secret National Security Agency.* New York: Doubleday, 2001.

Barron, John. *Operation SOLO: The FBI's Man in the Kremlin.* Washington, DC: Regnery, 1996.

Bernstein, Carl, and Bob Woodward. *All the President's Men.* New York: Simon & Schuster, 1975.

Coulson, Danny O., and Elaine Shannon. *No Heroes: Inside the FBI's Secret Counterterror Force.* New York: Pocket Books, 1999.

Davis, James K., and Clarence M. Kelley. *Kelley: The Story of an FBI Director.* Kansas City, MO: Andrews McMeel, 1987.

DeLoach, Cartha D. *Hoover's FBI: The Inside Story of Hoover's Trusted Lieutenant.* Washington, DC: Regnery, 1995.

DeToledano, Ralph. *J. Edgar Hoover: The Man in His Time.* Bayside, NY: Arlington House, 1973.

Demaris, Ovid. *The Director: An Oral Biography of J. Edgar Hoover.* New York: Harper's Magazine Press, 1975.

Elliff, John T. *The Reform of FBI Intelligence Operations.* Princeton: Princeton University Press, 1979.

Felt, W. Mark. *The FBI Pyramid: From the Inside.* New York: G. P. Putnam's Sons, 1979.

Fisher, David. *Hard Evidence: How Detectives Inside the FBI's Sci-Crime Lab Have Helped Solve America's Toughest Cases.* New York: Simon & Schuster, 1995.

Fox, Stephen. *Blood and Power: Organized Crime in Twentieth Century America.* New York: William Morrow, 1989.

Gabler, Neal. *Walter Winchell: Gossip, Power, and the Culture of Celebrity.* London: Papermac, 1994.

Garrow, David J. *The FBI and Martin Luther King Jr.: From "Solo" to Memphis*, New York: Norton, 1981.

Gentry, Curt. *J. Edgar Hoover: The Man and the Secrets*. New York: Norton, 1991.

Haynes, James Earl, and E. Harvey Klehr. *Venona: Decoding Soviet Espionage in America*. New Haven: Yale University Press, 2000.

Jeffers, H. Paul. *Who Killed Precious?* New York: Pharos Books, 1991.

Kalugin, Oleg, and Fen Montaigne. *The First Directorate: My 32 Years in Intelligence and Espionage Against the West*. New York: St. Martin's Press, 1994.

Kessler, Pamela. *Undercover Washington: Touring the Sites Where Famous Spies Lived, Worked, and Loved*. Delaplane, VA: EPM Publications, 1992.

Kessler, Ronald. *Escape from the CIA: How the CIA Won and Lost the Most Important KGB Spy Ever to Defect to the U.S.* New York: Pocket Books, 1991.

———. *The FBI: Inside the World's Most Powerful Law Enforcement Agency—By the Award-Winning Journalist Whose Investigation Brought Down FBI Director William S. Sessions*. New York: Pocket Books, 1993.

———. *Inside the CIA: Revealing the Secrets of the World's Most Powerful Spy Agency*. New York: Pocket Books, 1992.

———. *Inside the White House: The Hidden Lives of the Modern Presidents and the Secrets of the World's Most Powerful Institution*. New York: Pocket Books, 1995.

———. *Moscow Station: How the KGB Penetrated the American Embassy*. New York: Scribner, 1989.

———. *The Sins of the Father: Joseph P. Kennedy and the Dynasty He Founded*. New York: Warner Books, 1996.

———. *The Spy in the Russian Club: How Glenn Souther Stole America's Nuclear War Plans and Escaped to Moscow*. New York: Scribner, 1990.

———. *Spy vs. Spy: Stalking Soviet Spies in America*. New York: Scribner, 1988.

Lamphere, Robert J., and Tom Shactman. *The FBI-KGB War*. Macon, GA: Mercer University Press, 1995.

Lehr, Dick, and Gerard O'Neill. *Black Mass: The Irish Mob, the FBI, and a Devil's Deal*. New York: Public Affairs, 2000.

Maas, Peter. *Killer Spy: the Inside Story of the FBI's Pursuit and Capture of Aldrich Ames, America's Deadliest Spy*. New York: Warner Books, 1995.

MacLean, Don. *Pictorial History of the Mafia*. New York: Pyramid, 1974.

Newton, Michael. *Hunting Humans: An Encyclopedia of Modern Serial Killers*. Port Townsend, WA: Loompanics Unlimited, 1990.

Nicholson, C. Edward. *Never the Likes Again*. Self-published, printed by Darien Printing and Graphics, Darien, Georgia, 1996.

Pistone, Joseph D. *Donnie Brasco: My Undercover Life in the Mafia*. New York: Signet, 1987.

Powers, Richard Gid. *Not Without Honor: The History of American Anticommunism*. New Haven: Yale University Press, 1998.

———. *Secrecy and Power: The Life of J. Edgar Hoover*. New York: Free Press, 1987.

Purvis, Joseph D. *The Era of J. Edgar*. Self-published, 1997.

Ressler, Robert, Ann W. Burgess, and John E. Douglas, *Sexual Homicide: Patterns and Motives*. Lanham, MD: Lexington Books, 1988.

Ressler, Robert K., with Tom Shactman, *Whoever Fights Monsters*. New York: St. Martin's Press, 1991.

Revell, Oliver, and Dwight Williams. *A G-Man's Journal: A Legendary Career Inside the FBI*. New York: Pocket Books, 1998.

Roberts, Sam. *The Brother: The Untold Story of Atomic Spy David Greenglass and How He Sent His Sister Ethel Rosenberg to the Electric Chair*. New York: Random House, 2001.

Robins, Natalie. *Alien Ink: The FBI's War on Freedom of Expression*. New York: Morrow, 1992.

Shannon, Elaine, and Ann Blackman. *The Spy Next Door: The Extraordinary Secret Life of Robert Philip Hanssen*. Boston: Little, Brown, 2002.

Sullivan, William C., with Bill Brown, *The Bureau: My Thirty Years in Hoover's FBI*. New York: Norton, 1979.

Summers, Anthony. *Official and Confidential: The Secret Life of J. Edgar Hoover*. New York: G. P. Putnam's Sons, 1993.

Sussman, Barry. *The Great Coverup: Nixon and the Scandal of Watergate*. New York: Crowell, 1974.

Theoharis, Athan. *From the Secret Files of J. Edgar Hoover*. Chicago: Ivan R. Dee, 1991.

Theoharis, Athan, et al., eds. *The FBI: A Comprehensive Reference Guide*. New York: Checkmark Books, 2000.

Turner, William W. *Hoover's FBI: The Men and the Myth*. Sherbourne Press, 1970.

Ungar, Sanford J. *FBI: An Uncensored Look Behind the Walls*. Boston: Atlantic-Little, Brown, 1975.

Vise, David A. *The Bureau and the Mole: The Unmasking of Robert Philip Hanssen, the Most Dangerous Double Agent in F.B.I. History*. New York: Atlantic Monthly Press, 2002.

Wannall, Ray. *The Real J. Edgar Hoover: For the Record*. Turner Publishing, 2000.

The Warren Commission Report: Report of President's Commission on the Assassination of President John F. Kennedy. New York: St. Martin's Press, 1992.

Weinstein, Allen, and Alexander Vassiliev. *The Haunted Wood: Soviet Espionage in America*. New York: Modern Library, 2000.

Welch, Neil J., and David W. Marston. *Inside Hoover's FBI: The Top Field Chief Reports*. New York: Doubleday, 1984.

Whitcomb, Christopher. *Cold Zero: Inside the FBI Hostage Rescue Team*. Boston: Little, Brown, 2001.

Whitehead, Don. *The FBI Story*. New York: Random House, 1956.

Index